THE BIG CHIP

By W. R. Philbrick

Illustrated by Bruce Jensen

Lettered by Kurt Hathaway

A Byron Preiss Visual Publications, Inc. Book

PUBLISHED BY
Microsoft Press
A Division of Microsoft Corporation
One Microsoft Way
Redmond, Washington 98052-6399

Library of Congress Cataloging-in-Publication Data
Philbrick, W.R. (W. Rodman)
   The big chip / W.R. Philbrick
       p.   cm.
    ISBN 1-55615-245-0 : $7.95
    I. Title.
PN6727.P47B54   1990
741.5'973--dc20   89-29683
                                CIP

Printed and bound in the United States of America.

1 2 3 4 5 6 7 8 9   HCHC   3 2 1 0 9

Distributed to the book trade in Canada by General Publishing Company, Ltd.

Distributed to the book trade outside the United States and Canada by Penguin Books Ltd.

Penguin Books Ltd., Harmondsworth, Middlesex, England
Penguin Books Australia Ltd., Ringwood, Victoria, Australia
Penguin Books N.Z. Ltd., 182–190 Wairau Road, Auckland 10, New Zealand

British Cataloging in Publication Data available

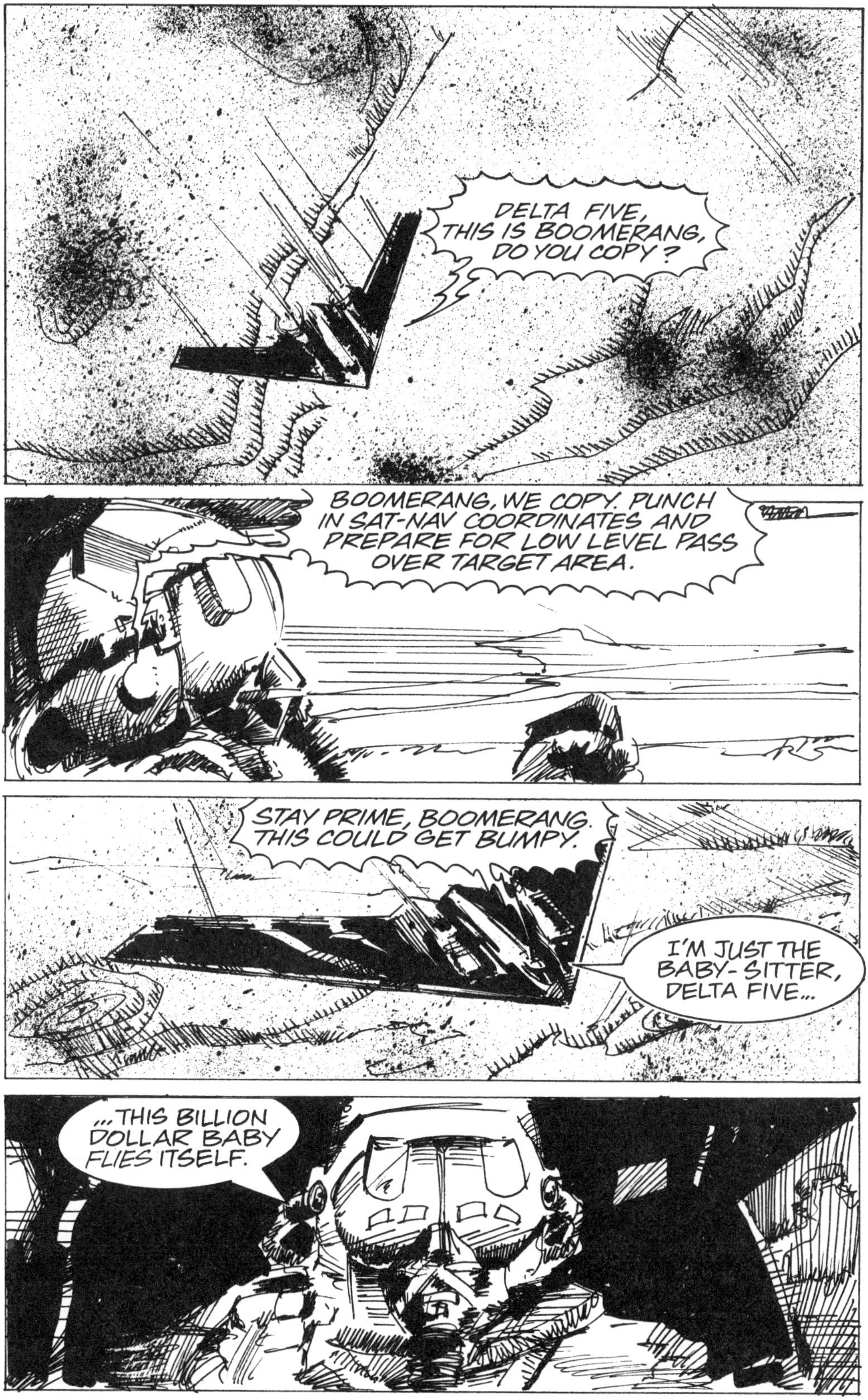
DELTA FIVE, THIS IS BOOMERANG, DO YOU COPY ?
BOOMERANG, WE COPY. PUNCH IN SAT-NAV COORDINATES AND PREPARE FOR LOW LEVEL PASS OVER TARGET AREA.
STAY PRIME, BOOMERANG. THIS COULD GET BUMPY.
I'M JUST THE BABY-SITTER, DELTA FIVE...
...THIS BILLION DOLLAR BABY FLIES ITSELF.

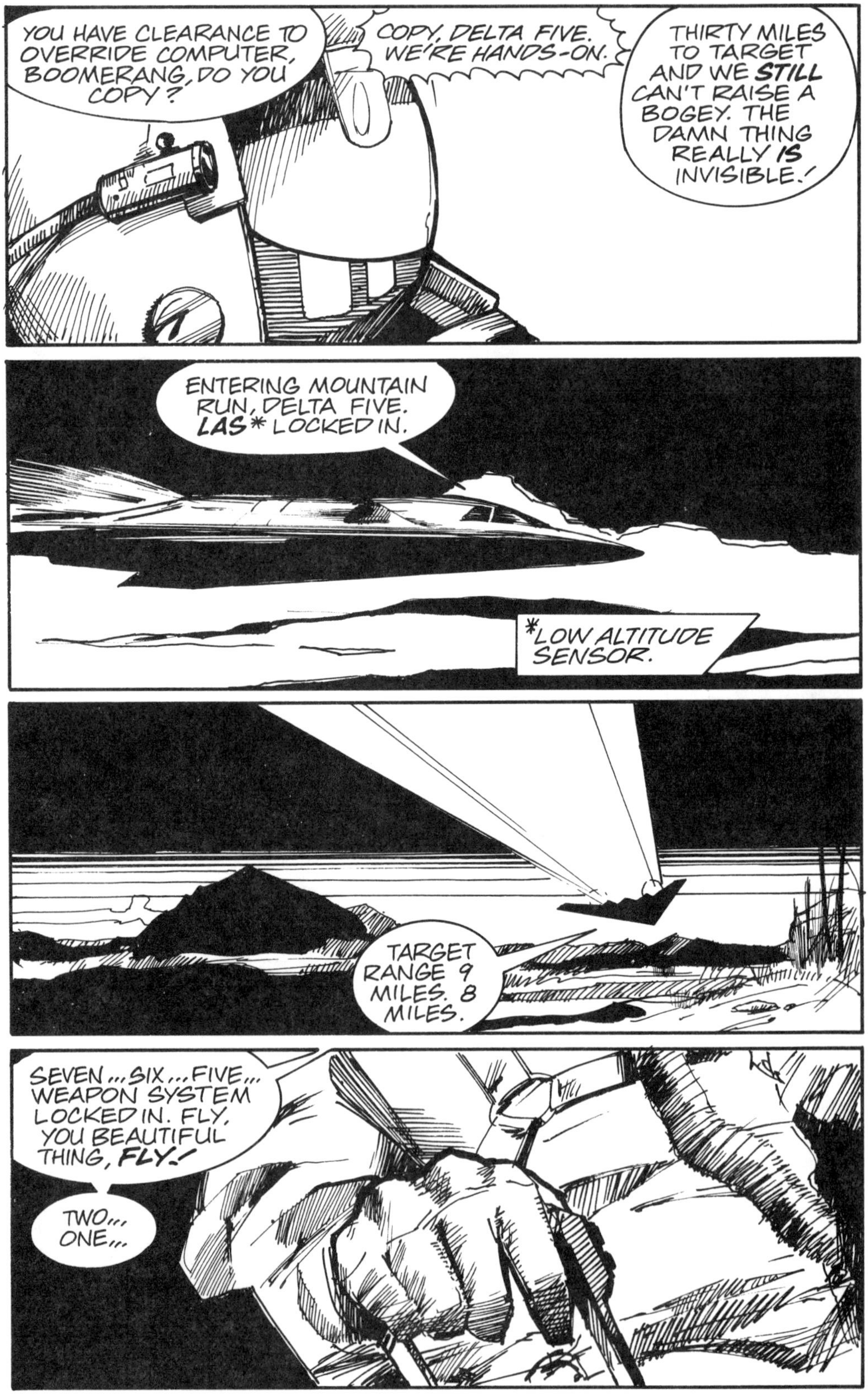
YOU HAVE CLEARANCE TO OVERRIDE COMPUTER, BOOMERANG, DO YOU COPY?
COPY, DELTA FIVE. WE'RE HANDS-ON.
THIRTY MILES TO TARGET AND WE **STILL** CAN'T RAISE A BOGEY. THE DAMN THING REALLY **IS** INVISIBLE!
ENTERING MOUNTAIN RUN, DELTA FIVE. **LAS*** LOCKED IN.
*LOW ALTITUDE SENSOR.
TARGET RANGE 9 MILES. 8 MILES.
SEVEN... SIX... FIVE... WEAPON SYSTEM LOCKED IN. FLY, YOU BEAUTIFUL THING, **FLY!**
TWO... ONE...

BOOMERANG, DO YOU COP—

KER-BLAM!!

RICHARDS? CAPTAIN RICHARDS?

GIVE ME A HAND HERE, HE'S TRANCED OUT.

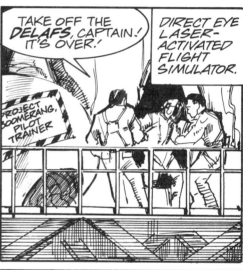

TAKE OFF THE *DELAFS*, CAPTAIN! IT'S OVER.'

DIRECT EYE LASER-ACTIVATED FLIGHT SIMULATOR.

PROJECT BOOMERANG, PILOT TRAINER

WHAT HAPPENED?

YOU SPLASHED IT ON PEAK 9.

RICHARDS

ANOTHER GLITCH IN THE NAVIGATION CHIP.

I THOUGHT THE DAMN THING WAS FIXED.'

SO DID WE.... AND THAT 'BEAUTIFUL FLYING MACHINE' WILL NEVER GET OFF THE GROUND UNTIL WE FIND OUT WHY.

Seattle in the rain. The way it made the streets glow as if lit from underground. The mist in the air that smelled of salt and seaweed. Maybe that's why I came back to the city after flaming out as a whiz kid at Vandox Instruments.

Or maybe I was running away from life with the fast Layne, my ex. Following her to that new job in Palo Alto was never in the program somehow. So it was home again, home again, back to where the sun never shines – not so you can trust it. Time to boot up another career – and this time I was going solo.

I wanted a new start.

Never again would I have to punch another time card, polish Apples, or report to a boss I didn't trust.

Never again.

Two little words but more than enough to choke on, if you're dumb enough to sign on with a man named Zenith Reck. . .

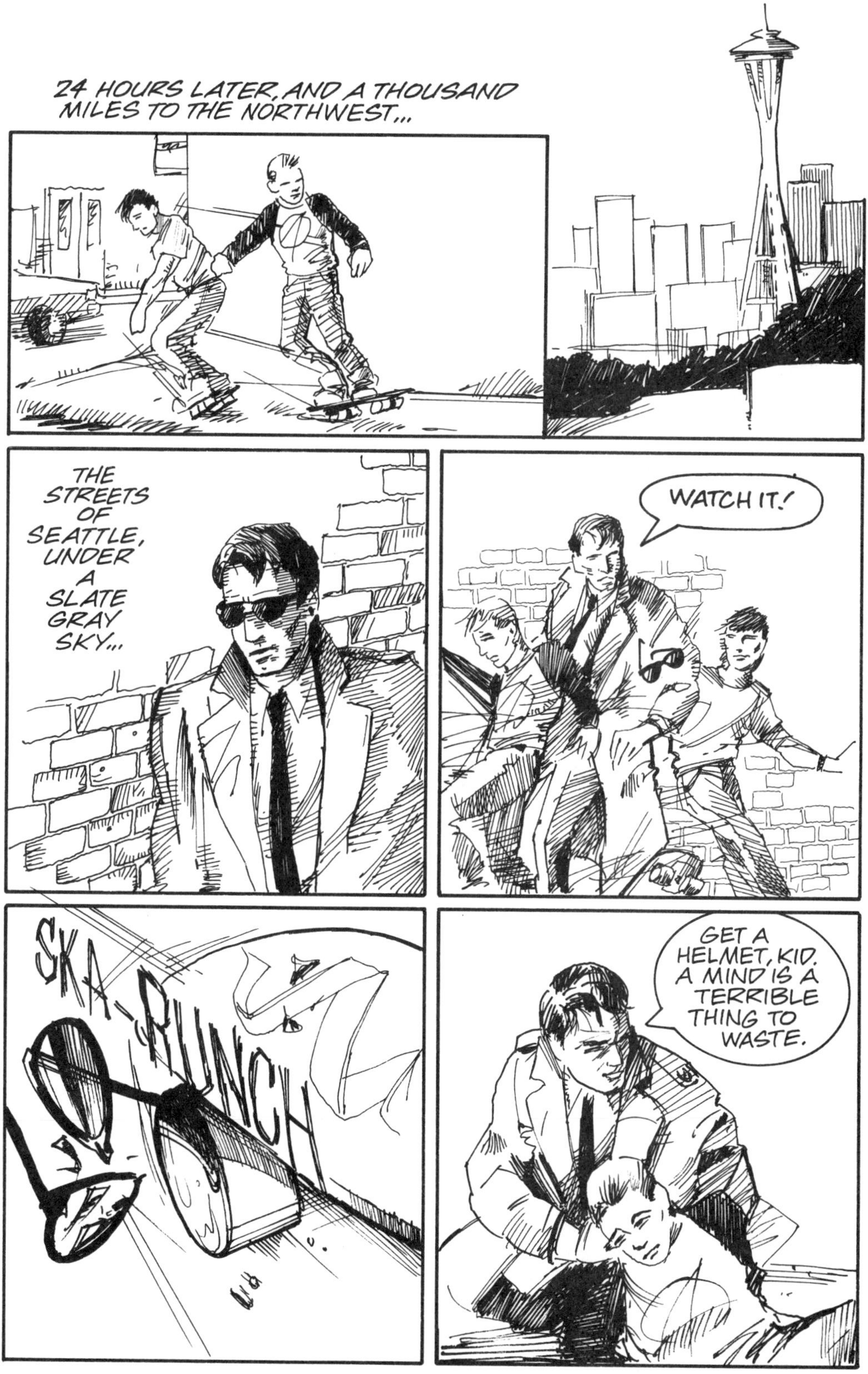
24 HOURS LATER, AND A THOUSAND MILES TO THE NORTHWEST...
THE STREETS OF SEATTLE, UNDER A SLATE GRAY SKY...
WATCH IT!
SKA-RUNCH
GET A HELMET, KID. A MIND IS A TERRIBLE THING TO WASTE.

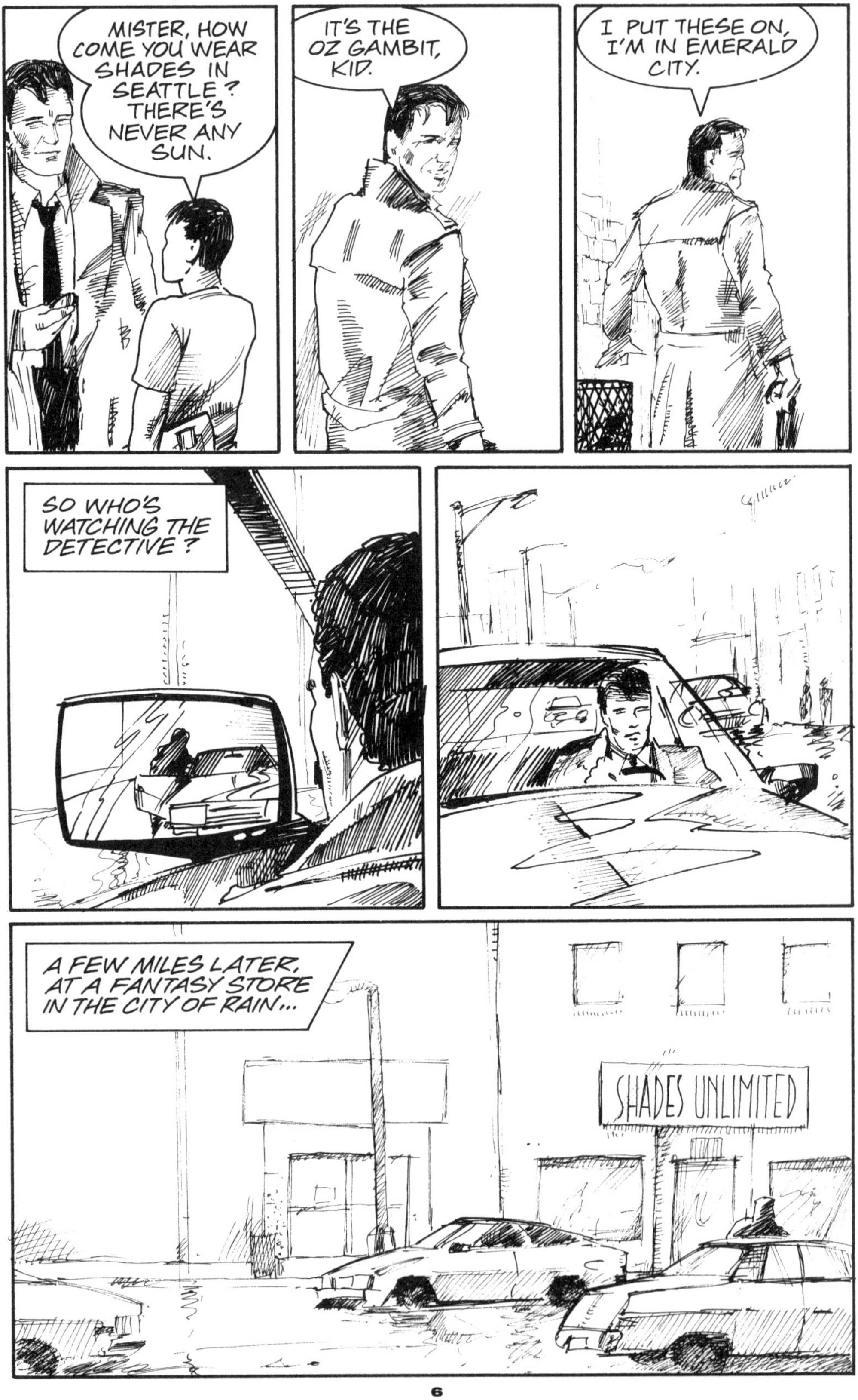
MISTER, HOW COME YOU WEAR SHADES IN SEATTLE? THERE'S NEVER ANY SUN.
IT'S THE OZ GAMBIT, KID.
I PUT THESE ON, I'M IN EMERALD CITY.
SO WHO'S WATCHING THE DETECTIVE?
A FEW MILES LATER, AT A FANTASY STORE IN THE CITY OF RAIN...
SHADES UNLIMITED

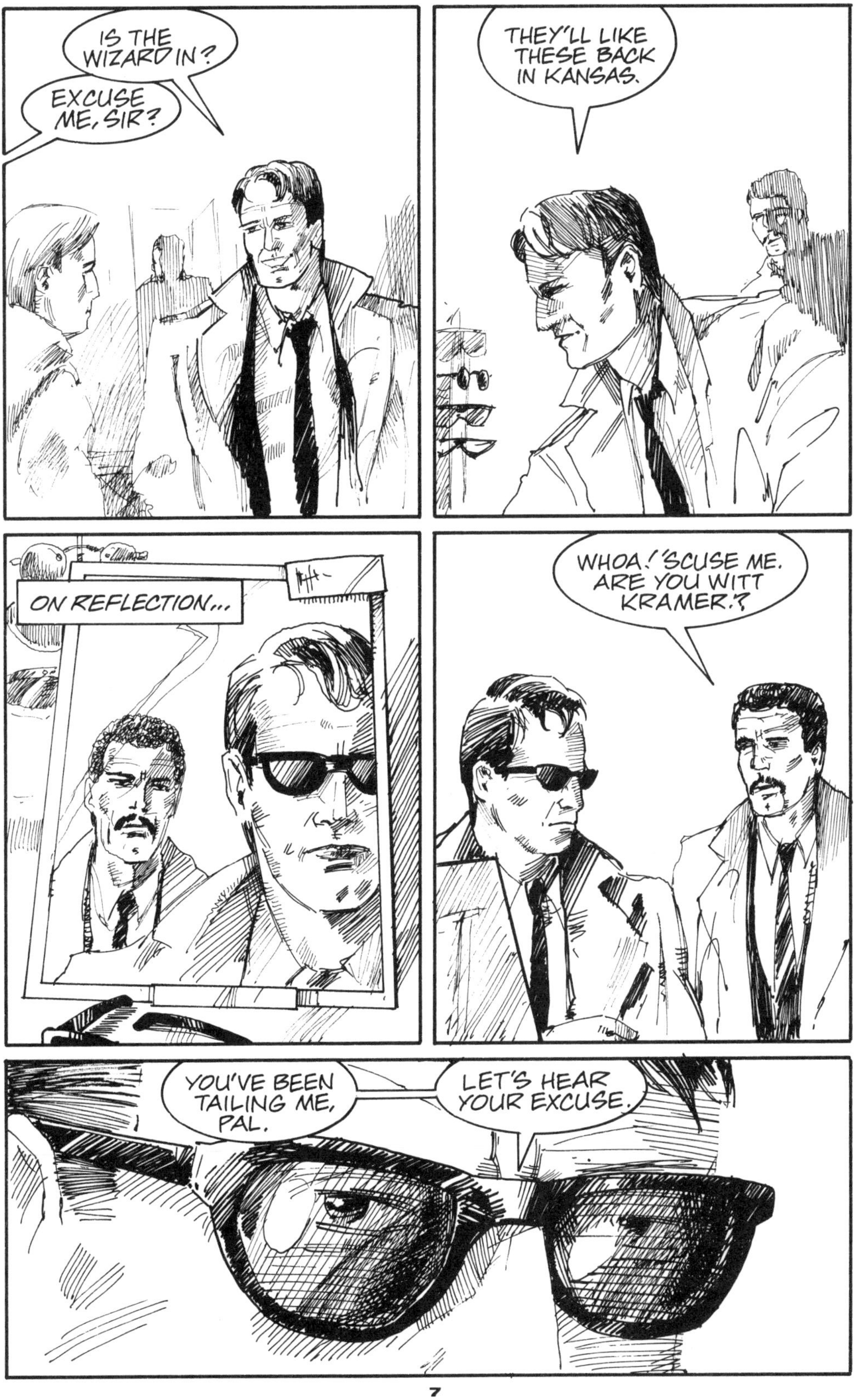
EXCUSE ME, SIR?
IS THE WIZARD IN?
THEY'LL LIKE THESE BACK IN KANSAS.
ON REFLECTION...
WHOA! 'SCUSE ME. ARE YOU WITT KRAMER?
YOU'VE BEEN TAILING ME, PAL.
LET'S HEAR YOUR EXCUSE.

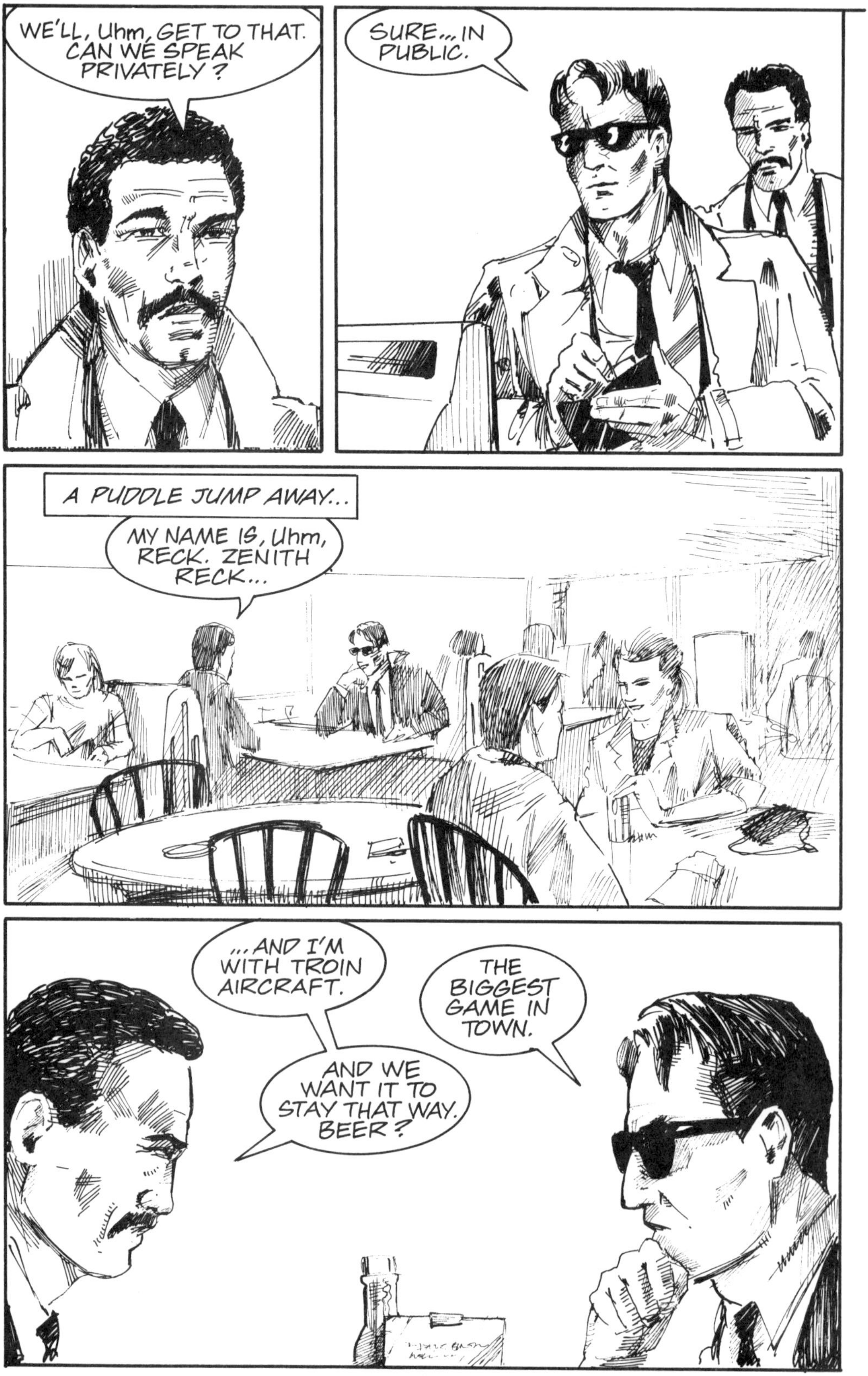
WE'LL, Uhm, GET TO THAT. CAN WE SPEAK PRIVATELY?
SURE... IN PUBLIC.
A PUDDLE JUMP AWAY...
MY NAME IS, Uhm, RECK. ZENITH RECK...
...AND I'M WITH TROIN AIRCRAFT.
AND WE WANT IT TO STAY THAT WAY. BEER?
THE BIGGEST GAME IN TOWN.

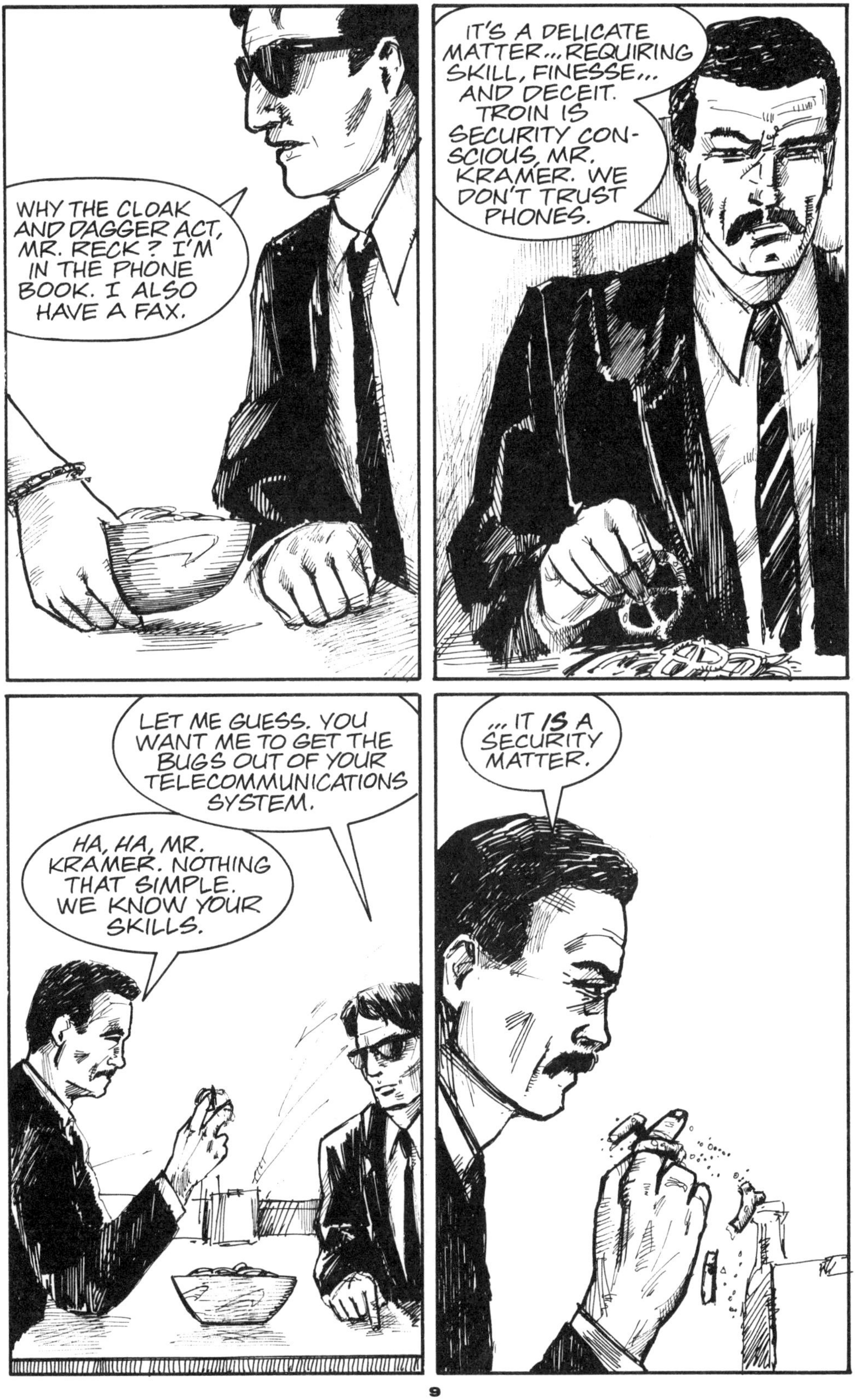
WHY THE CLOAK AND DAGGER ACT, MR. RECK ? I'M IN THE PHONE BOOK. I ALSO HAVE A FAX.
IT'S A DELICATE MATTER... REQUIRING SKILL, FINESSE... AND DECEIT. TROIN IS SECURITY CON-SCIOUS, MR. KRAMER. WE DON'T TRUST PHONES.
LET ME GUESS. YOU WANT ME TO GET THE BUGS OUT OF YOUR TELECOMMUNICATIONS SYSTEM.
HA, HA, MR. KRAMER. NOTHING THAT SIMPLE. WE KNOW YOUR SKILLS.
... IT IS A SECURITY MATTER.

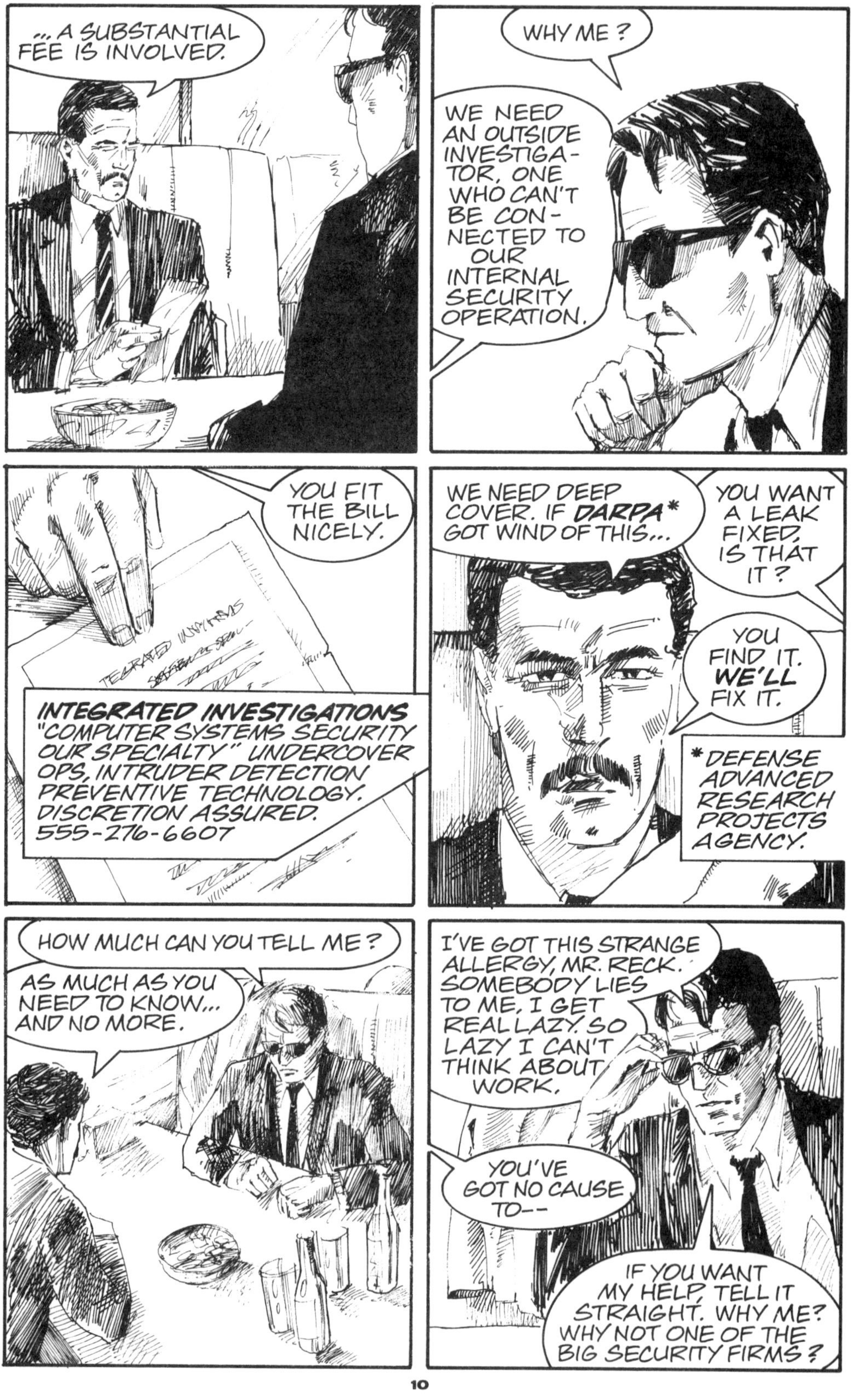
...A SUBSTANTIAL FEE IS INVOLVED.
WHY ME?
WE NEED AN OUTSIDE INVESTIGA-TOR, ONE WHO CAN'T BE CON-NECTED TO OUR INTERNAL SECURITY OPERATION.
YOU FIT THE BILL NICELY.
INTEGRATED INVESTIGATIONS "COMPUTER SYSTEMS SECURITY OUR SPECIALTY" UNDERCOVER OPS, INTRUDER DETECTION PREVENTIVE TECHNOLOGY. DISCRETION ASSURED. 555-276-6607
WE NEED DEEP COVER. IF DARPA* GOT WIND OF THIS...
YOU WANT A LEAK FIXED, IS THAT IT?
YOU FIND IT. WE'LL FIX IT.
*DEFENSE ADVANCED RESEARCH PROJECTS AGENCY.
HOW MUCH CAN YOU TELL ME?
AS MUCH AS YOU NEED TO KNOW... AND NO MORE.
I'VE GOT THIS STRANGE ALLERGY, MR. RECK. SOMEBODY LIES TO ME, I GET REAL LAZY. SO LAZY I CAN'T THINK ABOUT WORK.
YOU'VE GOT NO CAUSE TO--
IF YOU WANT MY HELP, TELL IT STRAIGHT. WHY ME? WHY NOT ONE OF THE BIG SECURITY FIRMS?

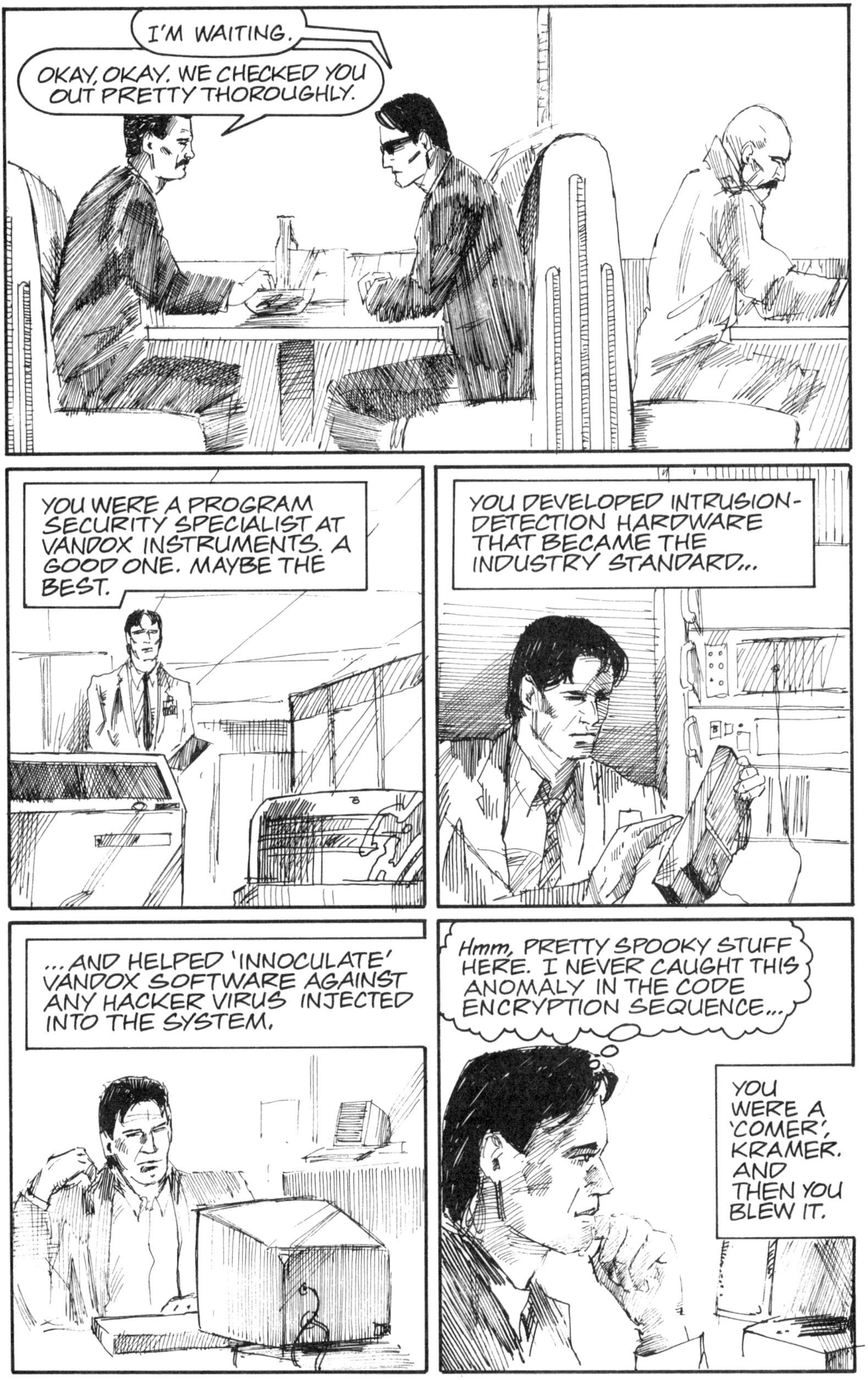
I'M WAITING.
OKAY, OKAY. WE CHECKED YOU OUT PRETTY THOROUGHLY.
YOU WERE A PROGRAM SECURITY SPECIALIST AT VANDOX INSTRUMENTS. A GOOD ONE. MAYBE THE BEST.
YOU DEVELOPED INTRUSION-DETECTION HARDWARE THAT BECAME THE INDUSTRY STANDARD...
...AND HELPED 'INNOCULATE' VANDOX SOFTWARE AGAINST ANY HACKER VIRUS INJECTED INTO THE SYSTEM.
Hmm, PRETTY SPOOKY STUFF HERE. I NEVER CAUGHT THIS ANOMALY IN THE CODE ENCRYPTION SEQUENCE...
YOU WERE A 'COMER', KRAMER. AND THEN YOU BLEW IT.

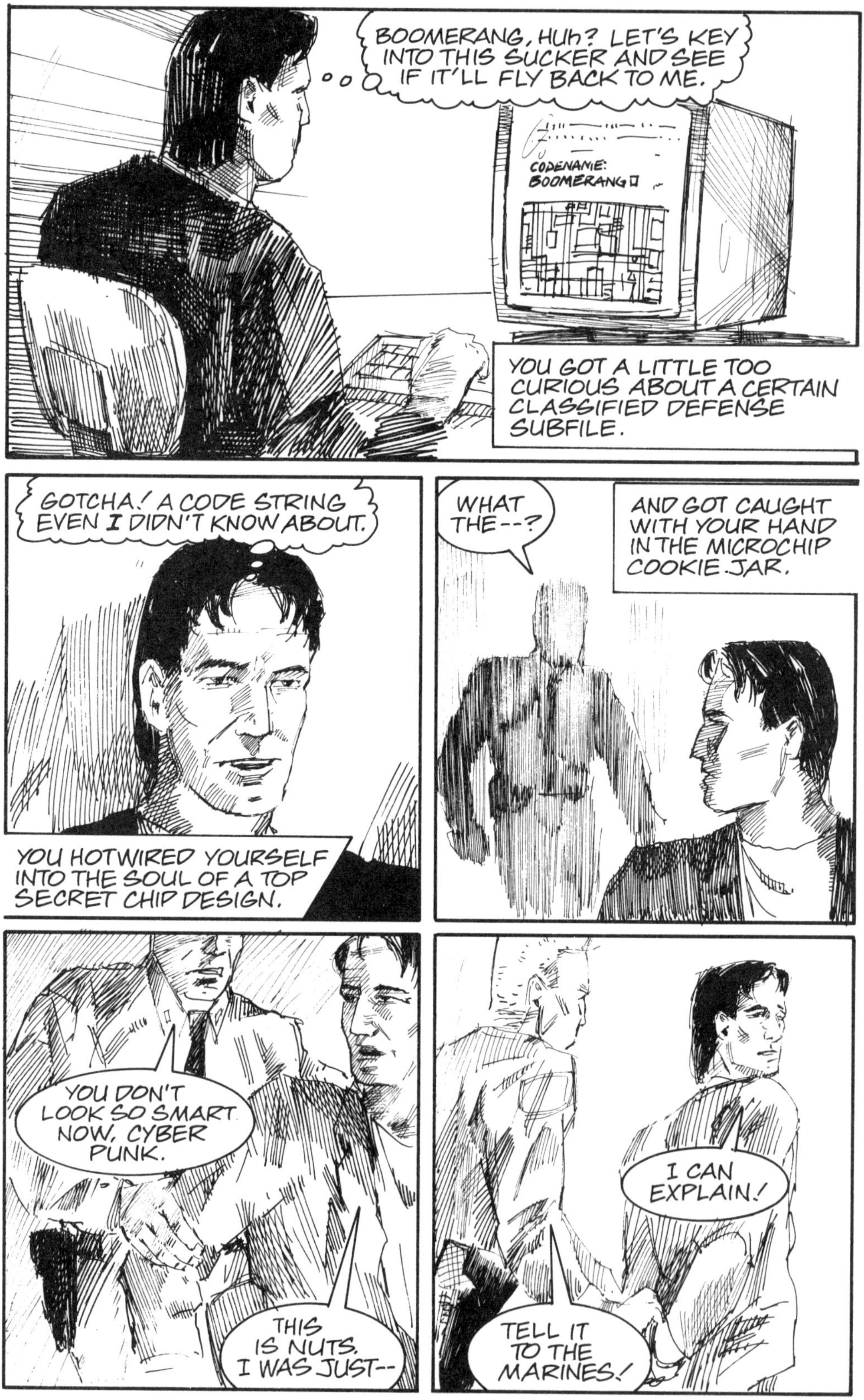
BOOMERANG, HUH? LET'S KEY INTO THIS SUCKER AND SEE IF IT'LL FLY BACK TO ME.
CODENAME: BOOMERANG
YOU GOT A LITTLE TOO CURIOUS ABOUT A CERTAIN CLASSIFIED DEFENSE SUBFILE.
GOTCHA! A CODE STRING EVEN I DIDN'T KNOW ABOUT.
YOU HOTWIRED YOURSELF INTO THE SOUL OF A TOP SECRET CHIP DESIGN.
WHAT THE--?
AND GOT CAUGHT WITH YOUR HAND IN THE MICROCHIP COOKIE JAR.
YOU DON'T LOOK SO SMART NOW, CYBER PUNK.
THIS IS NUTS. I WAS JUST--
I CAN EXPLAIN!
TELL IT TO THE MARINES!

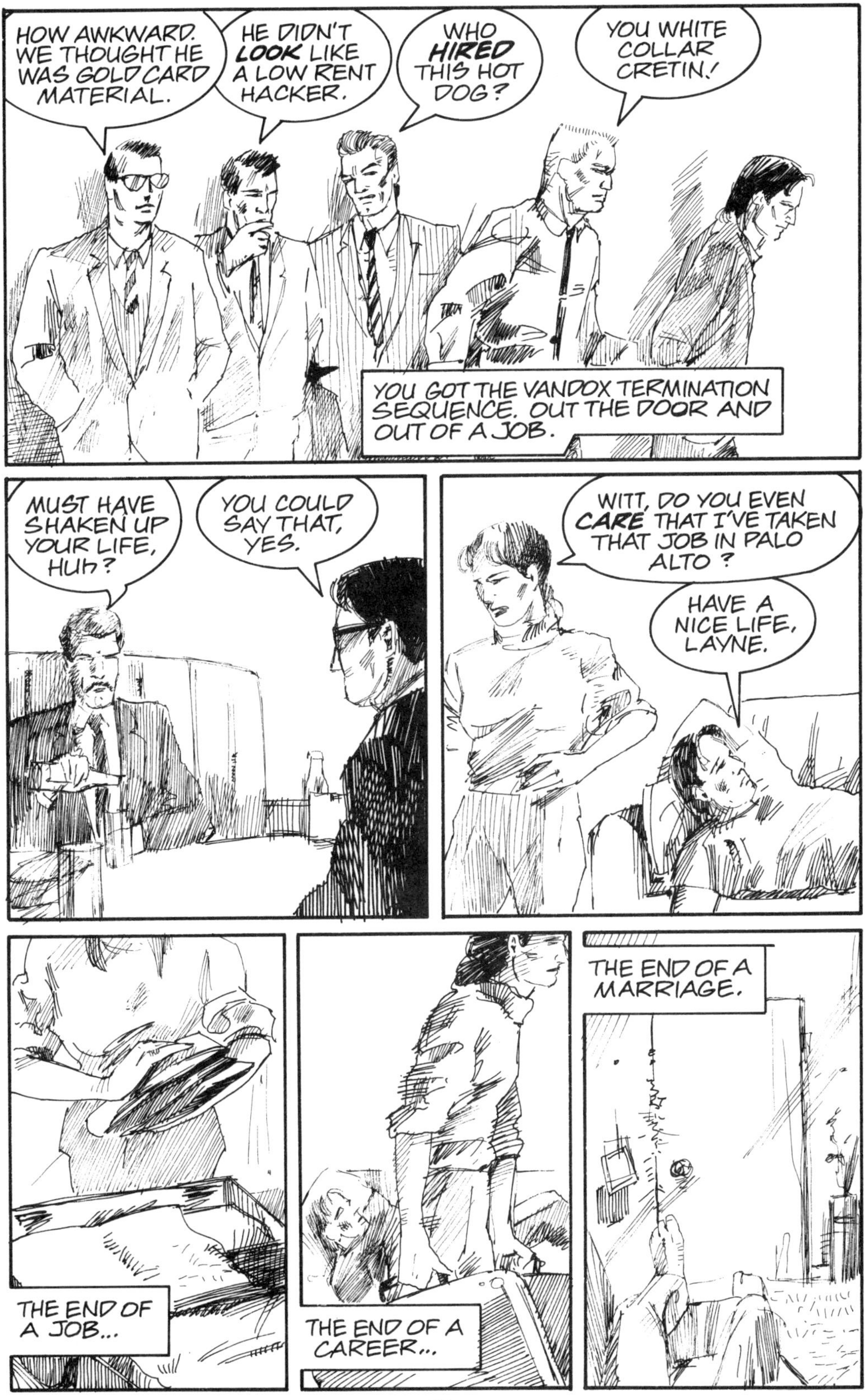
HOW AWKWARD. WE THOUGHT HE WAS GOLD CARD MATERIAL.
HE DIDN'T LOOK LIKE A LOW RENT HACKER.
WHO HIRED THIS HOT DOG?
YOU WHITE COLLAR CRETIN!
YOU GOT THE VANDOX TERMINATION SEQUENCE. OUT THE DOOR AND OUT OF A JOB.
MUST HAVE SHAKEN UP YOUR LIFE, HUH?
YOU COULD SAY THAT, YES.
WITT, DO YOU EVEN CARE THAT I'VE TAKEN THAT JOB IN PALO ALTO?
HAVE A NICE LIFE, LAYNE.
THE END OF A JOB...
THE END OF A CAREER...
THE END OF A MARRIAGE.

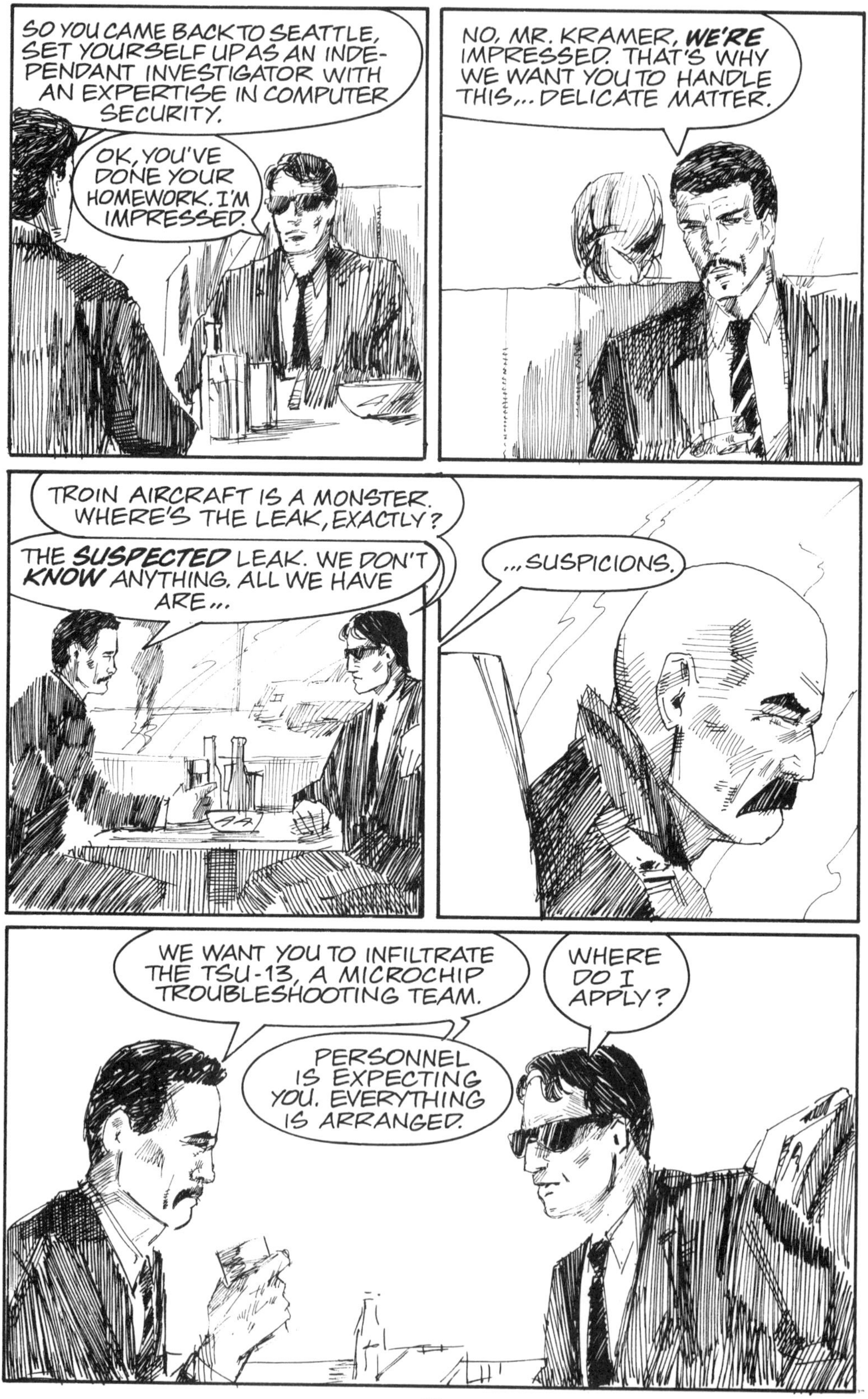
SO YOU CAME BACK TO SEATTLE, SET YOURSELF UP AS AN INDEPENDANT INVESTIGATOR WITH AN EXPERTISE IN COMPUTER SECURITY.
OK, YOU'VE DONE YOUR HOMEWORK. I'M IMPRESSED.
NO, MR. KRAMER, **WE'RE** IMPRESSED. THAT'S WHY WE WANT YOU TO HANDLE THIS,.. DELICATE MATTER.
TROIN AIRCRAFT IS A MONSTER. WHERE'S THE LEAK, EXACTLY?
THE **SUSPECTED** LEAK. WE DON'T **KNOW** ANYTHING. ALL WE HAVE ARE...
...SUSPICIONS.
WE WANT YOU TO INFILTRATE THE TSU-13, A MICROCHIP TROUBLESHOOTING TEAM.
PERSONNEL IS EXPECTING YOU. EVERYTHING IS ARRANGED.
WHERE DO I APPLY?

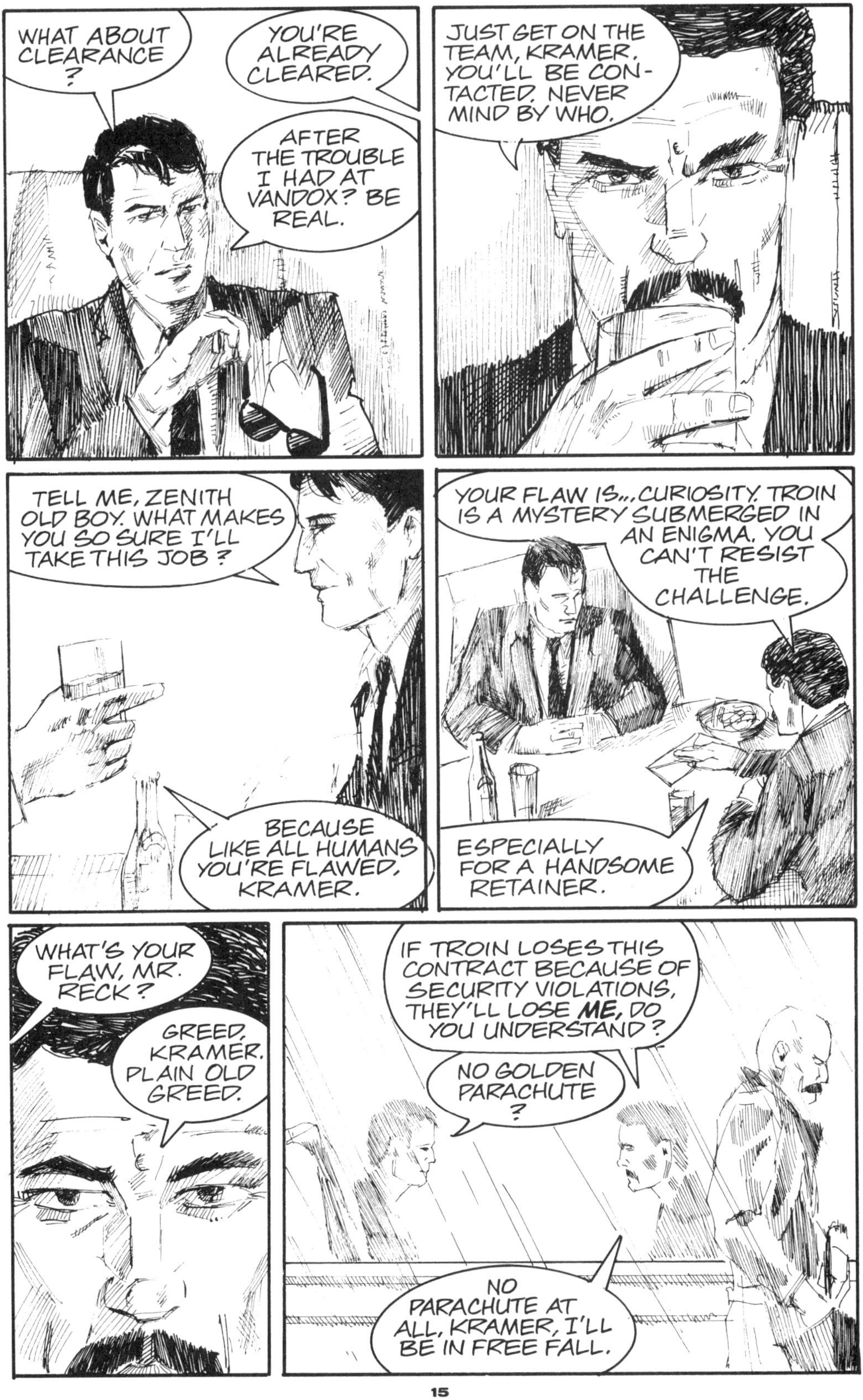
WHAT ABOUT CLEARANCE ?
YOU'RE ALREADY CLEARED.
AFTER THE TROUBLE I HAD AT VANDOX? BE REAL.
JUST GET ON THE TEAM, KRAMER. YOU'LL BE CON-TACTED. NEVER MIND BY WHO.
TELL ME, ZENITH OLD BOY. WHAT MAKES YOU SO SURE I'LL TAKE THIS JOB ?
BECAUSE LIKE ALL HUMANS YOU'RE FLAWED, KRAMER.
YOUR FLAW IS... CURIOSITY. TROIN IS A MYSTERY SUBMERGED IN AN ENIGMA. YOU CAN'T RESIST THE CHALLENGE.
ESPECIALLY FOR A HANDSOME RETAINER.
WHAT'S YOUR FLAW, MR. RECK ?
GREED, KRAMER. PLAIN OLD GREED.
IF TROIN LOSES THIS CONTRACT BECAUSE OF SECURITY VIOLATIONS, THEY'LL LOSE **ME**, DO YOU UNDERSTAND ?
NO GOLDEN PARACHUTE ?
NO PARACHUTE AT ALL, KRAMER, I'LL BE IN FREE FALL.

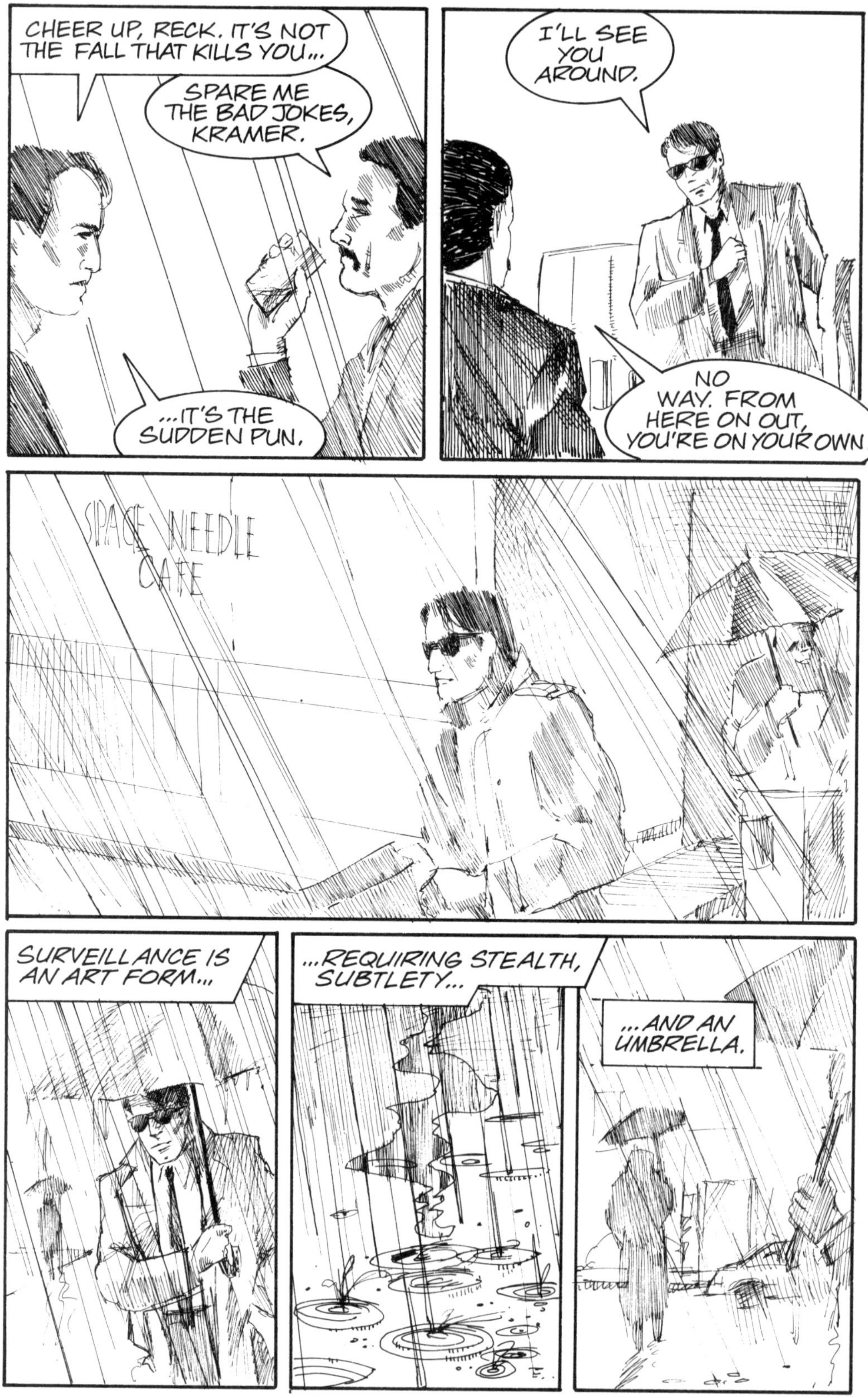
CHEER UP, RECK. IT'S NOT THE FALL THAT KILLS YOU...
SPARE ME THE BAD JOKES, KRAMER.
...IT'S THE SUDDEN PUN.
I'LL SEE YOU AROUND.
NO WAY. FROM HERE ON OUT, YOU'RE ON YOUR OWN.
SPACE NEEDLE CAFE
SURVEILLANCE IS AN ART FORM...
...REQUIRING STEALTH, SUBTLETY...
...AND AN UMBRELLA.

IF YOU'RE GOING TO STAND THERE DRIPPING, YOU MIGHT AS WELL DRIP ON THE GERANIUMS.

TERMINATE THE GERANIUMS.

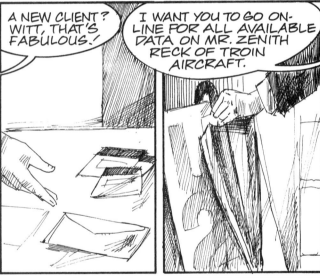

A NEW CLIENT? WITT, THAT'S FABULOUS.!

I WANT YOU TO GO ON-LINE FOR ALL AVAILABLE DATA ON MR. ZENITH RECK OF TROIN AIRCRAFT.

THE NEW CLIENT IS TROIN AIRCRAFT?

THAT'S WHAT I WANT TO FIND OUT WHILE I...

...GO HOME WITH A BEVY OF BEAUTIFUL FLOPPY DISKS.

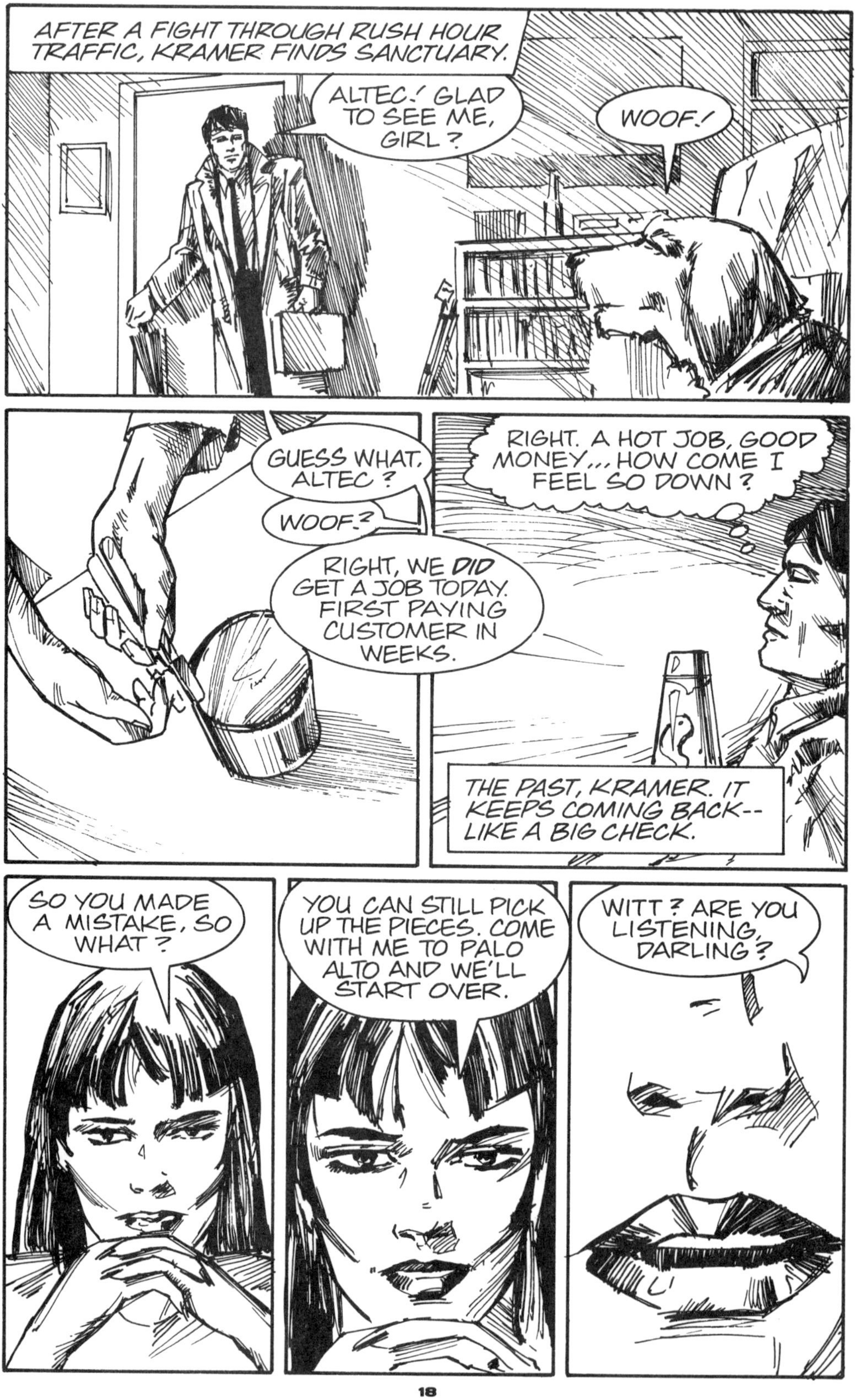
AFTER A FIGHT THROUGH RUSH HOUR TRAFFIC, KRAMER FINDS SANCTUARY.
ALTEC! GLAD TO SEE ME, GIRL?
WOOF!
GUESS WHAT, ALTEC?
WOOF?
RIGHT, WE DID GET A JOB TODAY. FIRST PAYING CUSTOMER IN WEEKS.
RIGHT. A HOT JOB, GOOD MONEY... HOW COME I FEEL SO DOWN?
THE PAST, KRAMER. IT KEEPS COMING BACK-- LIKE A BIG CHECK.
SO YOU MADE A MISTAKE, SO WHAT?
YOU CAN STILL PICK UP THE PIECES. COME WITH ME TO PALO ALTO AND WE'LL START OVER.
WITT? ARE YOU LISTENING, DARLING?

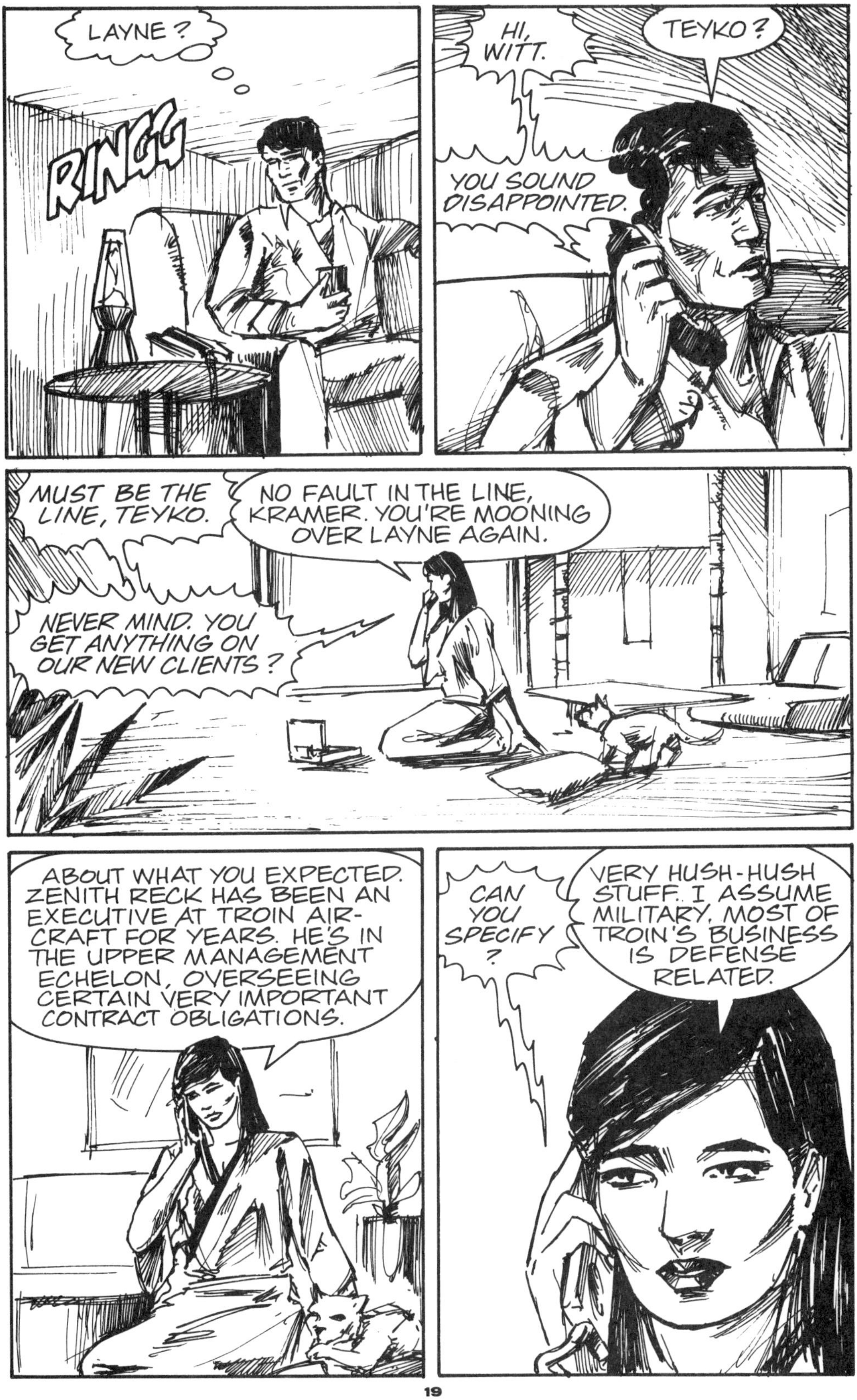
LAYNE?
RINGG
HI, WITT.
TEYKO?
YOU SOUND DISAPPOINTED.
MUST BE THE LINE, TEYKO.
NO FAULT IN THE LINE, KRAMER. YOU'RE MOONING OVER LAYNE AGAIN.
NEVER MIND. YOU GET ANYTHING ON OUR NEW CLIENTS?
ABOUT WHAT YOU EXPECTED. ZENITH RECK HAS BEEN AN EXECUTIVE AT TROIN AIR-CRAFT FOR YEARS. HE'S IN THE UPPER MANAGEMENT ECHELON, OVERSEEING CERTAIN VERY IMPORTANT CONTRACT OBLIGATIONS.
CAN YOU SPECIFY?
VERY HUSH-HUSH STUFF. I ASSUME MILITARY. MOST OF TROIN'S BUSINESS IS DEFENSE RELATED.

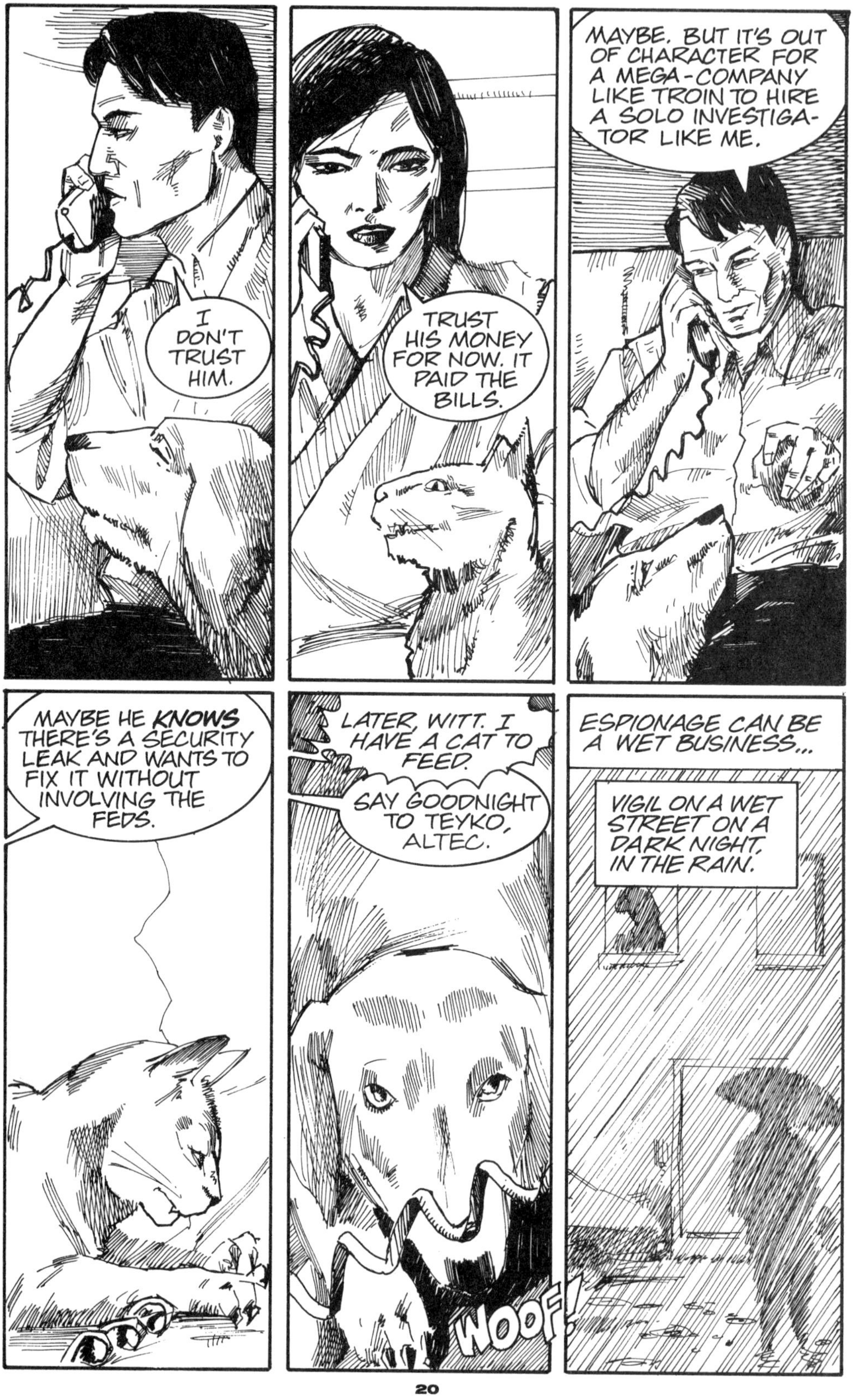
I DON'T TRUST HIM.
TRUST HIS MONEY FOR NOW. IT PAID THE BILLS.
MAYBE. BUT IT'S OUT OF CHARACTER FOR A MEGA-COMPANY LIKE TROIN TO HIRE A SOLO INVESTIGATOR LIKE ME.
MAYBE HE KNOWS THERE'S A SECURITY LEAK AND WANTS TO FIX IT WITHOUT INVOLVING THE FEDS.
LATER, WITT. I HAVE A CAT TO FEED.
SAY GOODNIGHT TO TEYKO, ALTEC.
WOOF!
ESPIONAGE CAN BE A WET BUSINESS...
VIGIL ON A WET STREET ON A DARK NIGHT, IN THE RAIN.

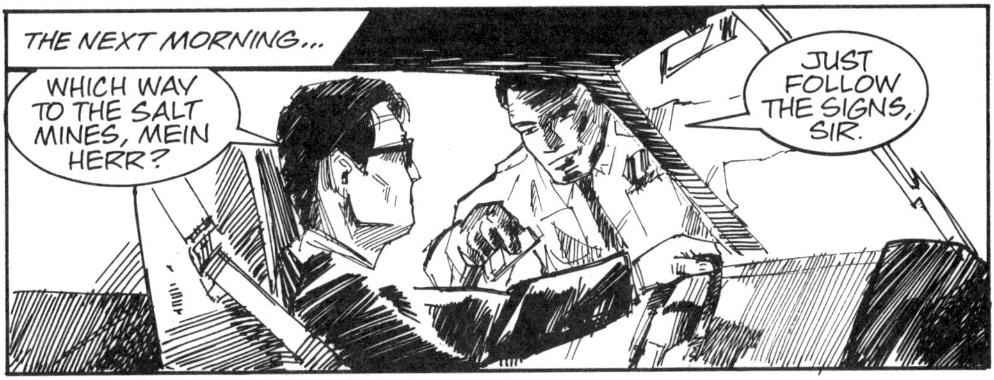
THE NEXT MORNING...
WHICH WAY TO THE SALT MINES, MEIN HERR?
JUST FOLLOW THE SIGNS, SIR.

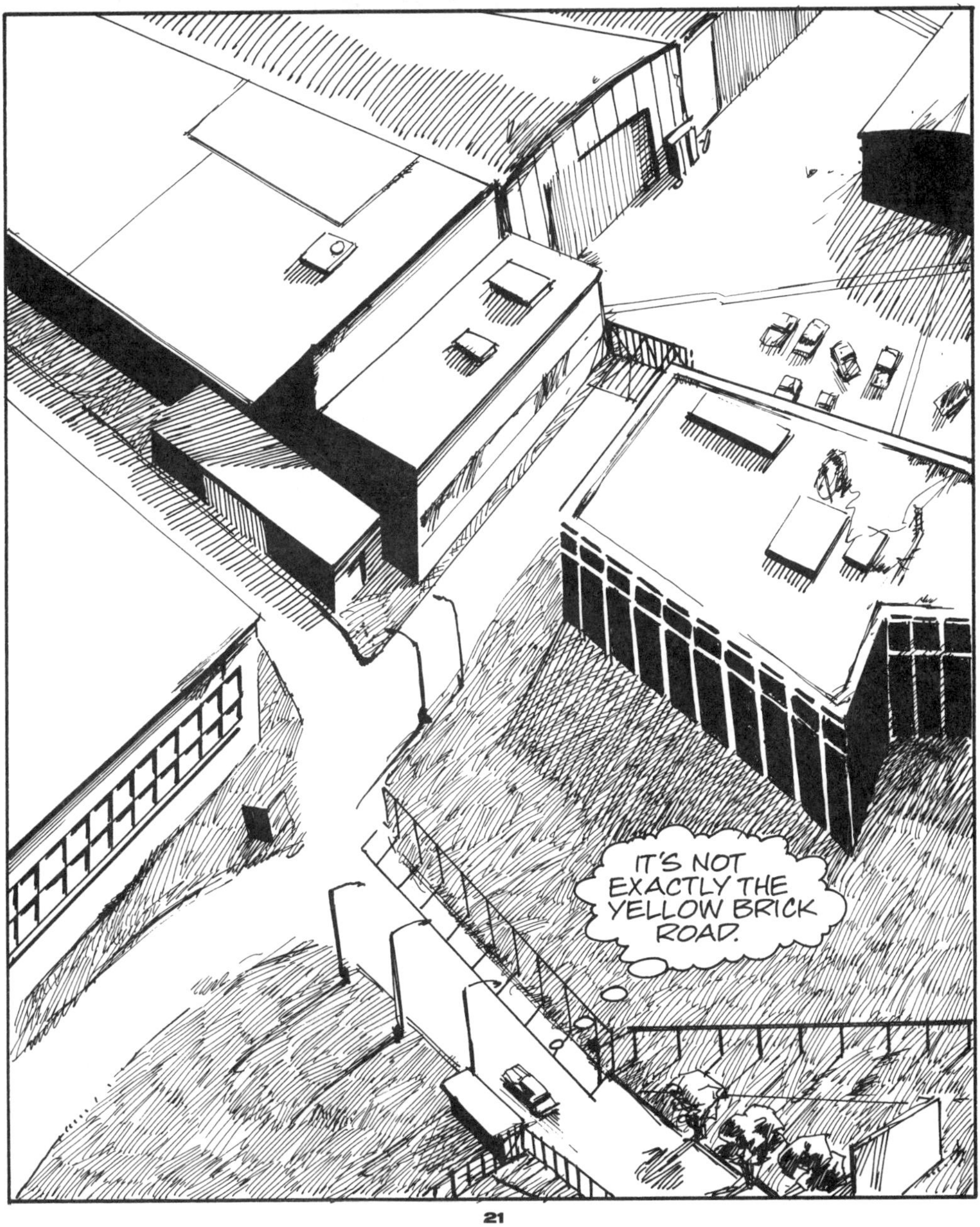
IT'S NOT EXACTLY THE YELLOW BRICK ROAD.

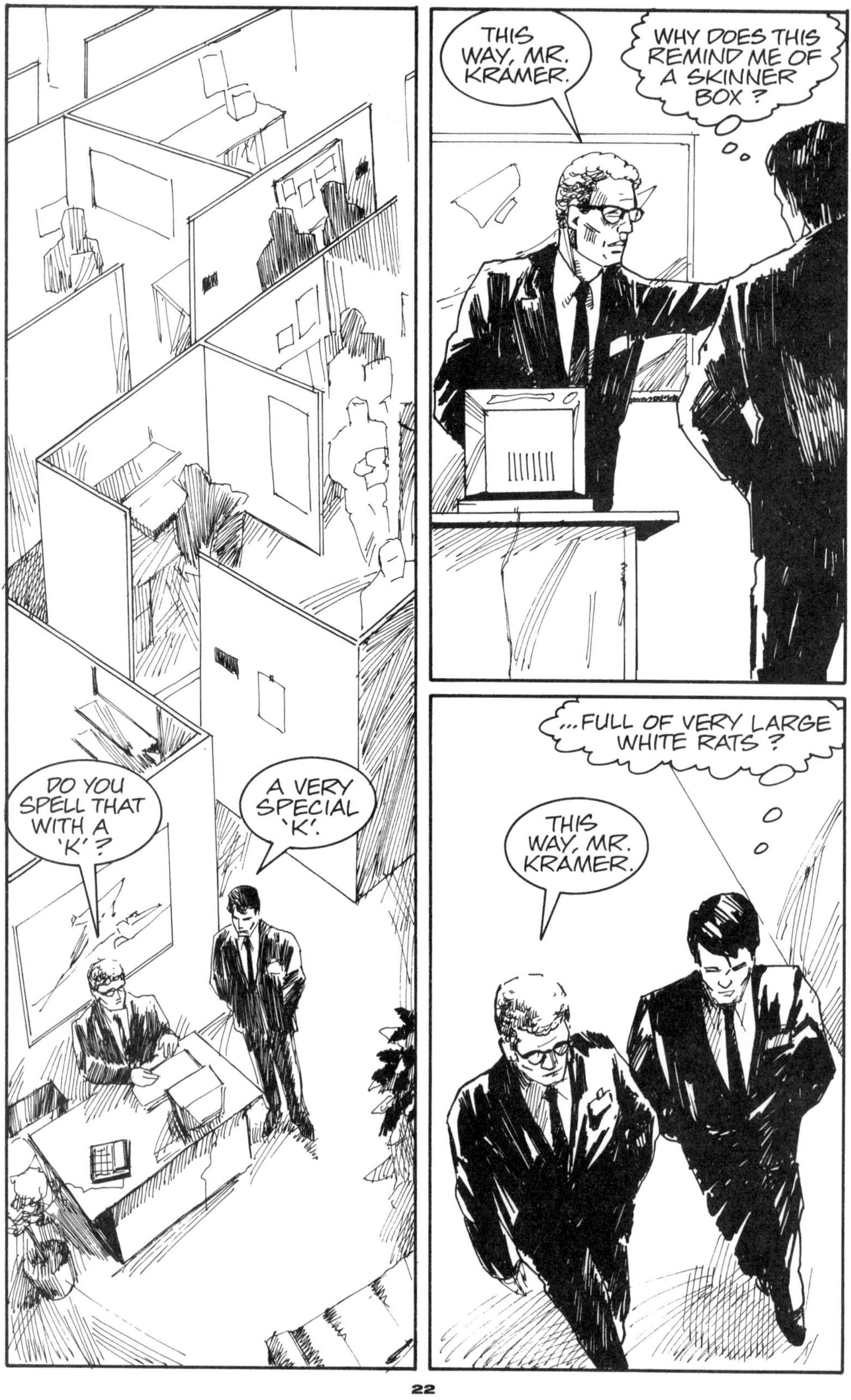
DO YOU SPELL THAT WITH A 'K'?
A VERY SPECIAL 'K'.
THIS WAY, MR. KRAMER.
WHY DOES THIS REMIND ME OF A SKINNER BOX?
...FULL OF VERY LARGE WHITE RATS?
THIS WAY, MR. KRAMER.

HAVE A SEAT, MR. KRAMER. I'M DOWN-LOADING YOUR FILE RIGHT NOW.

MY FILE? DOWNLOADING IT FROM WHERE?

DON'T ASK, PLEASE. I'M AFRAID THAT'S CLASSIFIED.

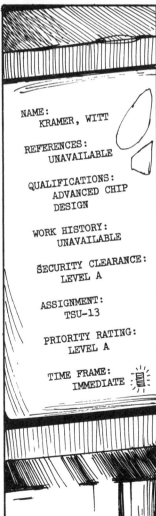

NAME:
    KRAMER, WITT

REFERENCES:
    UNAVAILABLE

QUALIFICATIONS:
    ADVANCED CHIP
    DESIGN

WORK HISTORY:
    UNAVAILABLE

SECURITY CLEARANCE:
    LEVEL A

ASSIGNMENT:
    TSU-13

PRIORITY RATING:
    LEVEL A

TIME FRAME:
    IMMEDIATE

GEE, THEY MISSED MY FAVORITE COLOR. IT'S GREEN, BY THE WAY.

ADVANCED CHIP DESIGN. THAT'S INTERESTING.

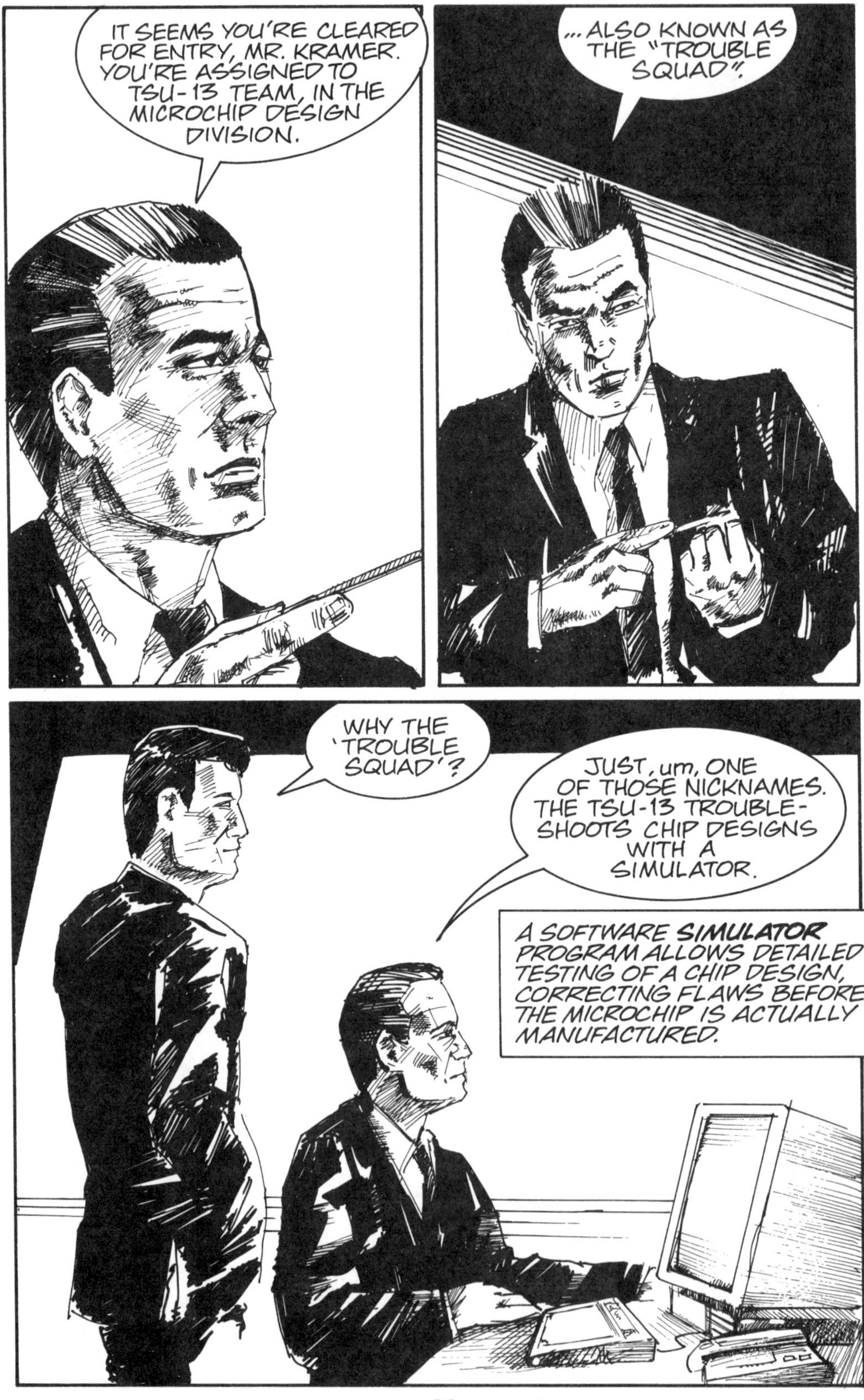
IT SEEMS YOU'RE CLEARED FOR ENTRY, MR. KRAMER. YOU'RE ASSIGNED TO TSU-13 TEAM, IN THE MICROCHIP DESIGN DIVISION.
...ALSO KNOWN AS THE "TROUBLE SQUAD".
WHY THE 'TROUBLE SQUAD'?
JUST, um, ONE OF THOSE NICKNAMES. THE TSU-13 TROUBLE-SHOOTS CHIP DESIGNS WITH A SIMULATOR.
A SOFTWARE **SIMULATOR** PROGRAM ALLOWS DETAILED TESTING OF A CHIP DESIGN, CORRECTING FLAWS BEFORE THE MICROCHIP IS ACTUALLY MANUFACTURED.

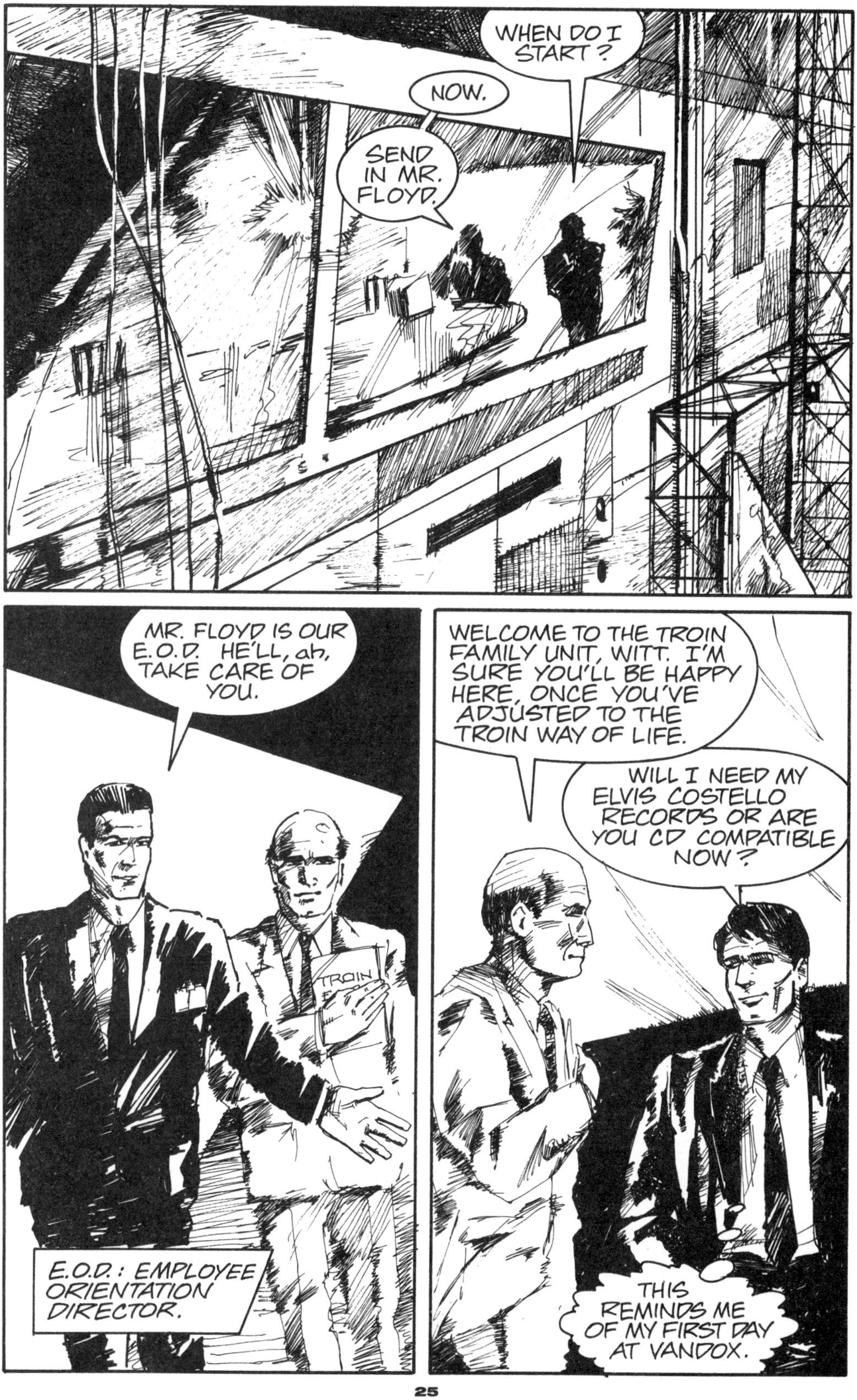
WHEN DO I START?
NOW.
SEND IN MR. FLOYD.
MR. FLOYD IS OUR E.O.D. HE'LL, ah, TAKE CARE OF YOU.
E.O.D.: EMPLOYEE ORIENTATION DIRECTOR.
TROIN
WELCOME TO THE TROIN FAMILY UNIT, WITT. I'M SURE YOU'LL BE HAPPY HERE, ONCE YOU'VE ADJUSTED TO THE TROIN WAY OF LIFE.
WILL I NEED MY ELVIS COSTELLO RECORDS OR ARE YOU CD COMPATIBLE NOW?
THIS REMINDS ME OF MY FIRST DAY AT VANDOX.

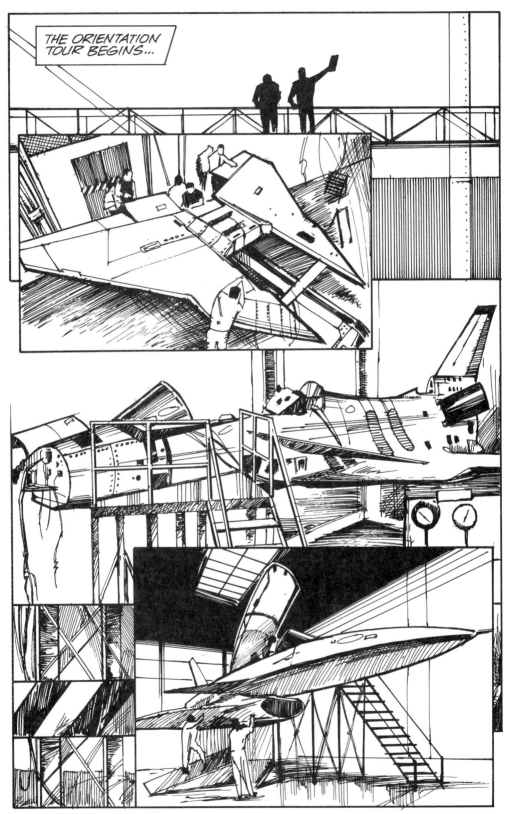

THE ORIENTATION TOUR BEGINS...

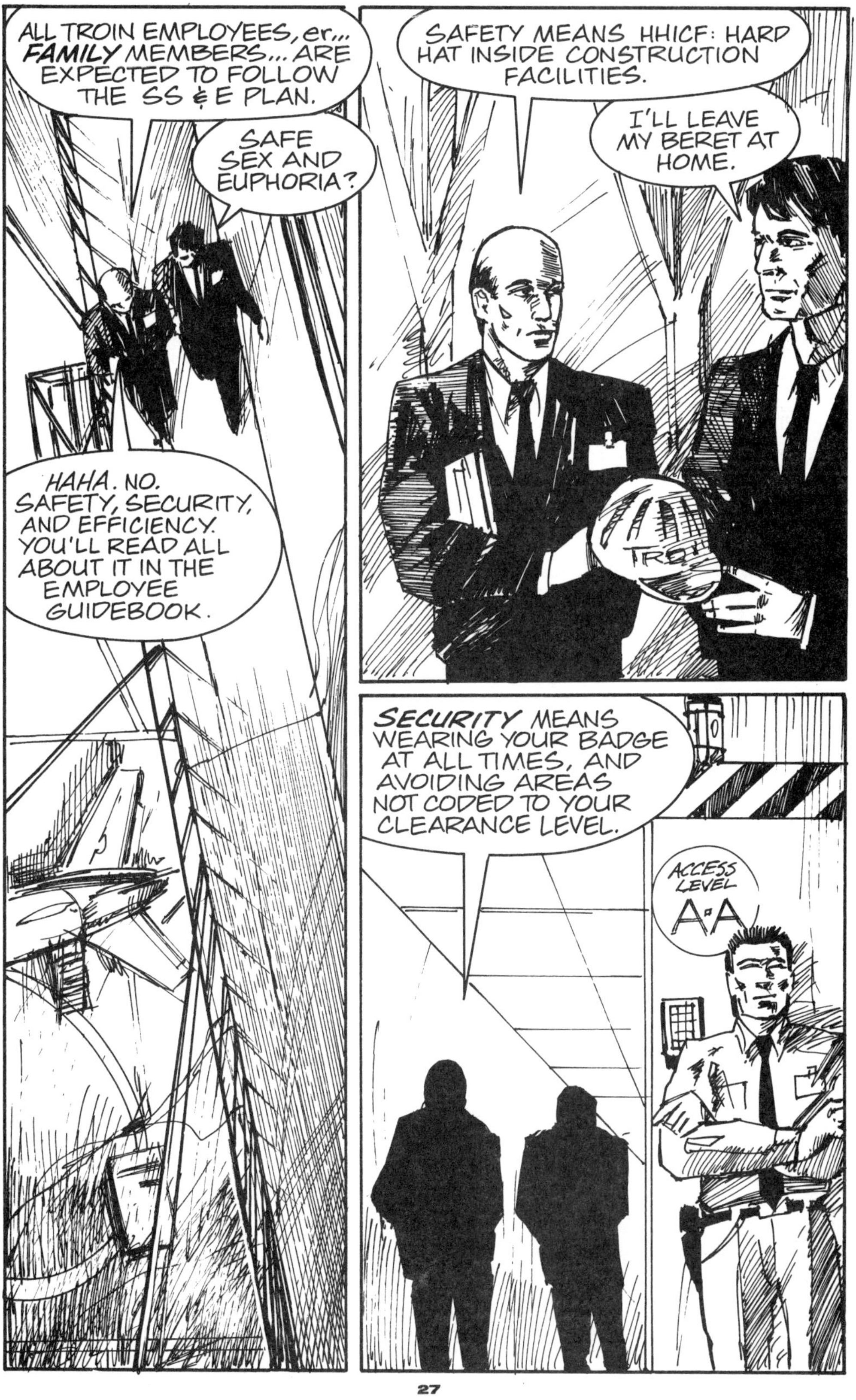
ALL TROIN EMPLOYEES, er... FAMILY MEMBERS... ARE EXPECTED TO FOLLOW THE SS & E PLAN.
SAFE SEX AND EUPHORIA?
HAHA. NO. SAFETY, SECURITY, AND EFFICIENCY. YOU'LL READ ALL ABOUT IT IN THE EMPLOYEE GUIDEBOOK.
SAFETY MEANS HHICF: HARD HAT INSIDE CONSTRUCTION FACILITIES.
I'LL LEAVE MY BERET AT HOME.
SECURITY MEANS WEARING YOUR BADGE AT ALL TIMES, AND AVOIDING AREAS NOT CODED TO YOUR CLEARANCE LEVEL.
ACCESS LEVEL A-A

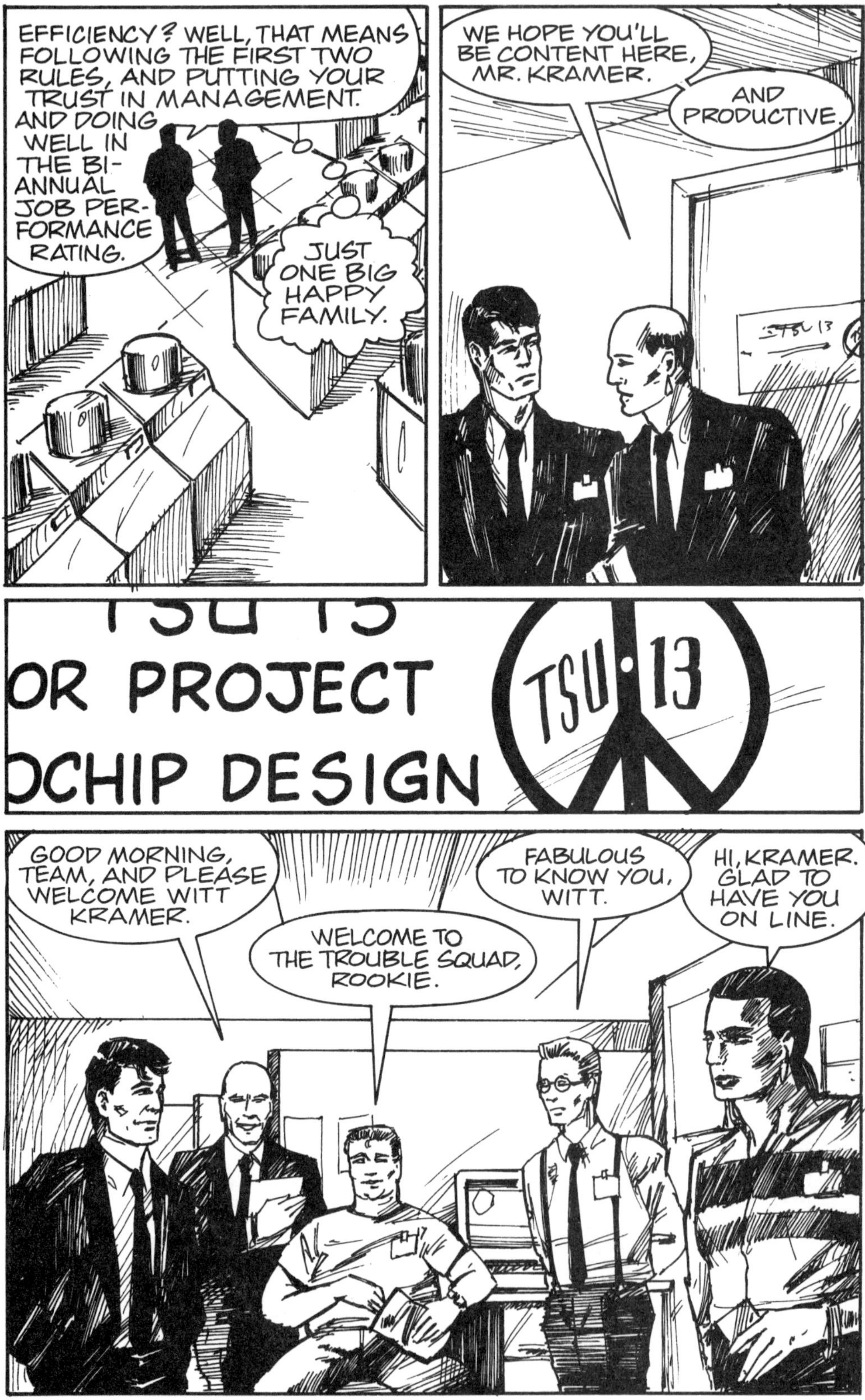
EFFICIENCY? WELL, THAT MEANS FOLLOWING THE FIRST TWO RULES, AND PUTTING YOUR TRUST IN MANAGEMENT. AND DOING WELL IN THE BI-ANNUAL JOB PERFORMANCE RATING.
JUST ONE BIG HAPPY FAMILY.
WE HOPE YOU'LL BE CONTENT HERE, MR. KRAMER.
AND PRODUCTIVE.
TSU 13
OR PROJECT
OCHIP DESIGN
TSU·13
GOOD MORNING, TEAM, AND PLEASE WELCOME WITT KRAMER.
WELCOME TO THE TROUBLE SQUAD, ROOKIE.
FABULOUS TO KNOW YOU, WITT.
HI, KRAMER. GLAD TO HAVE YOU ON LINE.

WE BEEN BEGGING 'EM TO ADD A FOURTH TEAM MEMBER FOR MONTHS, RIGHT, DANNY BOY?

THIS IS JUST SO EXCELLENT. DO YOU PLAY RACQUETBALL, BY ANY CHANCE?

LET'S, um, PROCEED WITH ORIENTATION, SHALL WE?

SURE THING, FLOYD.

CHOCKO, BOOT UP THE CHIP FLICK FOR MR. KRAMER.

CHIP FLICK?

REQUIRED VIEWING FOR ALL NEW EMPLOYEES, REGARDLESS OF EXPERIENCE...

AN INDUSTRIAL TRAINING FILM...

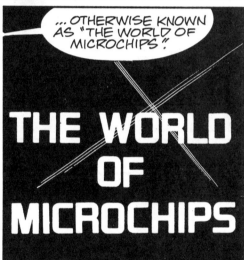

...OTHERWISE KNOWN AS "THE WORLD OF MICROCHIPS."

THE WORLD OF MICROCHIPS

COMPUTER CIRCUITRY WASN'T ALWAYS SMALL. EARLY COMPUTERS, WHICH USED VACUUM TUBES TO PROCESS AND STORE ELECTRONIC SIGNALS, TOOK UP WHOLE ROOMS AND GENERATED MORE HEAT THAN A PIZZA OVEN.

THESE PRIMITIVE CALCULATION MACHINES WERE, LIKE DINO-SAURS, GETTING BIGGER AND BIGGER—UNTIL A FUNNY THING HAPPENED.

THE TRANSISTOR RADIO!

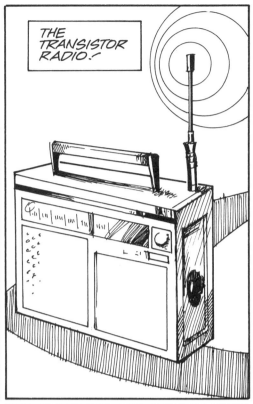

THE TRANSISTOR WAS THE FIRST BREAKTHROUGH IN MINIATUR-IZING ELECTRONIC CIRCUITRY.

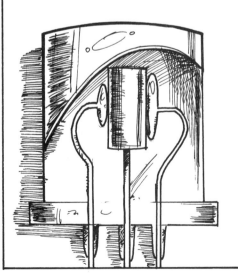

MADE FROM A CHIP OF CRYSTAL GERMANIUM, THESE NEW 'SEMICONDUCTORS' (SO CALLED BECAUSE THE MATERIAL EITHER CONDUCTS OR INSU-LATES, DEPENDING ON EXTERNAL CONDITIONS) WERE CHEAP TO MASS PRODUCE.

32 72.59
4
2830
937.4 Ge
5.32
$[Ar]3d^{10}4s^24p^2$
Germanium

THE NEXT STEP WAS TO FIND A WAY TO MAKE THE TRANSISTOR SMALLER SO IT WOULD REQUIRE LESS POWER, GIVE OFF LESS HEAT, AND PROCESS SIGNALS EVEN QUICKER.

THE IDEAL MATERIAL WAS SILICON CRYSTAL, MADE FROM ORDINARY BEACH SAND.

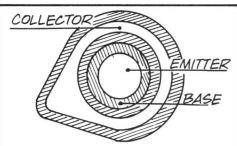

COLLECTOR
EMITTER
BASE

THE GATES, CONNECTING CIRCUITS, AND SWITCHES OF A TRANSISTOR COULD BE ETCHED DIRECTLY INTO THE SEMICONDUCTING SURFACE OF A SMALL PIECE OF SILICON CRYSTAL -- A CHIP.

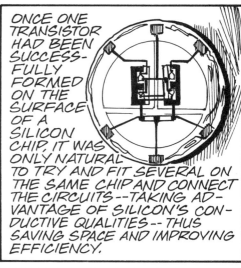

ONCE ONE TRANSISTOR HAD BEEN SUCCESSFULLY FORMED ON THE SURFACE OF A SILICON CHIP, IT WAS ONLY NATURAL TO TRY AND FIT SEVERAL ON THE SAME CHIP AND CONNECT THE CIRCUITS--TAKING ADVANTAGE OF SILICON'S CONDUCTIVE QUALITIES-- THUS SAVING SPACE AND IMPROVING EFFICIENCY.

THE INTEGRATED CIRCUIT WAS BORN! THE ELECTRONIC PROCESSING PREVIOUSLY DONE BY AN ENTIRE ARRAY OF BULKY VACUUM TUBES WAS REDUCED TO A CHIP OF CRYSTALIZED SAND SMALLER THAN A THUMBNAIL.

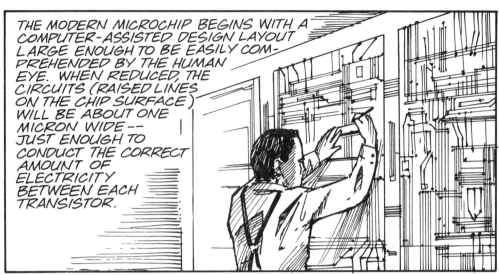

THE MODERN MICROCHIP BEGINS WITH A COMPUTER-ASSISTED DESIGN LAYOUT LARGE ENOUGH TO BE EASILY COMPREHENDED BY THE HUMAN EYE. WHEN REDUCED, THE CIRCUITS (RAISED LINES ON THE CHIP SURFACE) WILL BE ABOUT ONE MICRON WIDE-- JUST ENOUGH TO CONDUCT THE CORRECT AMOUNT OF ELECTRICITY BETWEEN EACH TRANSISTOR.

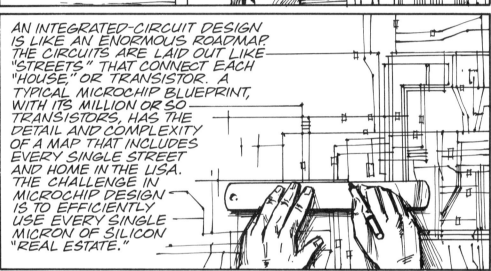

AN INTEGRATED-CIRCUIT DESIGN IS LIKE AN ENORMOUS ROADMAP. THE CIRCUITS ARE LAID OUT LIKE "STREETS" THAT CONNECT EACH "HOUSE," OR TRANSISTOR. A TYPICAL MICROCHIP BLUEPRINT, WITH ITS MILLION OR SO TRANSISTORS, HAS THE DETAIL AND COMPLEXITY OF A MAP THAT INCLUDES EVERY SINGLE STREET AND HOME IN THE LISA. THE CHALLENGE IN MICROCHIP DESIGN IS TO EFFICIENTLY USE EVERY SINGLE MICRON OF SILICON "REAL ESTATE."

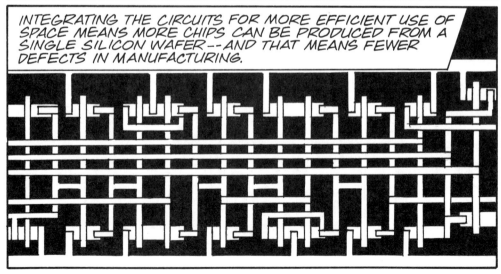

INTEGRATING THE CIRCUITS FOR MORE EFFICIENT USE OF SPACE MEANS MORE CHIPS CAN BE PRODUCED FROM A SINGLE SILICON WAFER--AND THAT MEANS FEWER DEFECTS IN MANUFACTURING.

THE DESIGN TEAM BEGINS WITH AN OVERVIEW OF WHAT TASK THE CHIP IS EXPECTED TO ACCOMPLISH. THEN INDIVIDUAL COMPONENTS ARE IDENTIFIED. OFTEN A PROCESS FLOWCHART IS DEVELOPED TO SHOW HOW AND IN WHAT ORDER A CHIP WILL PERFORM FUNCTIONS.

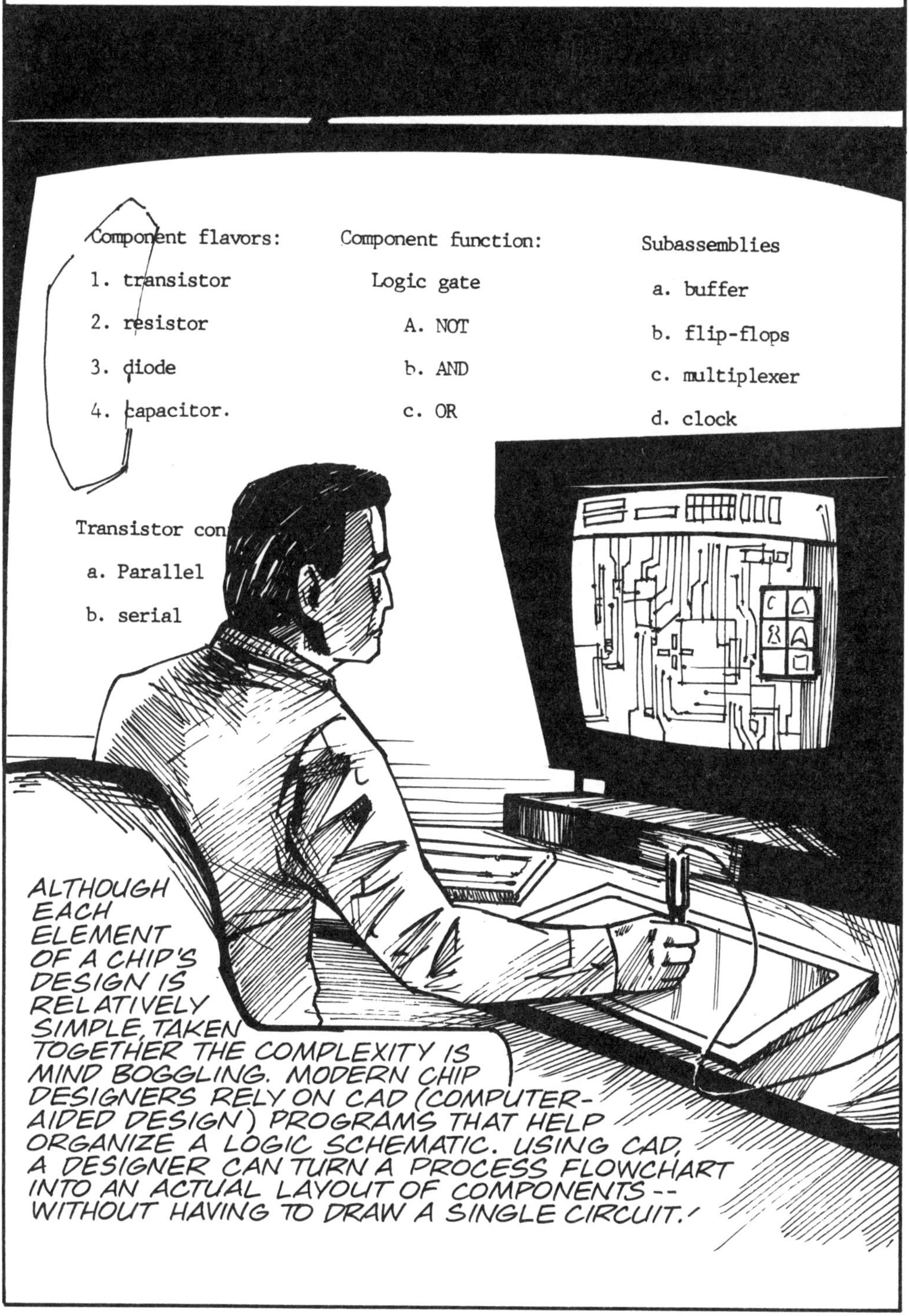
Component flavors:
1. transistor
2. resistor
3. diode
4. capacitor.
Component function:
Logic gate
A. NOT
b. AND
c. OR
Subassemblies
a. buffer
b. flip-flops
c. multiplexer
d. clock
Transistor con
a. Parallel
b. serial
ALTHOUGH EACH ELEMENT OF A CHIP'S DESIGN IS RELATIVELY SIMPLE, TAKEN TOGETHER THE COMPLEXITY IS MIND BOGGLING. MODERN CHIP DESIGNERS RELY ON CAD (COMPUTER-AIDED DESIGN) PROGRAMS THAT HELP ORGANIZE A LOGIC SCHEMATIC. USING CAD, A DESIGNER CAN TURN A PROCESS FLOWCHART INTO AN ACTUAL LAYOUT OF COMPONENTS -- WITHOUT HAVING TO DRAW A SINGLE CIRCUIT!

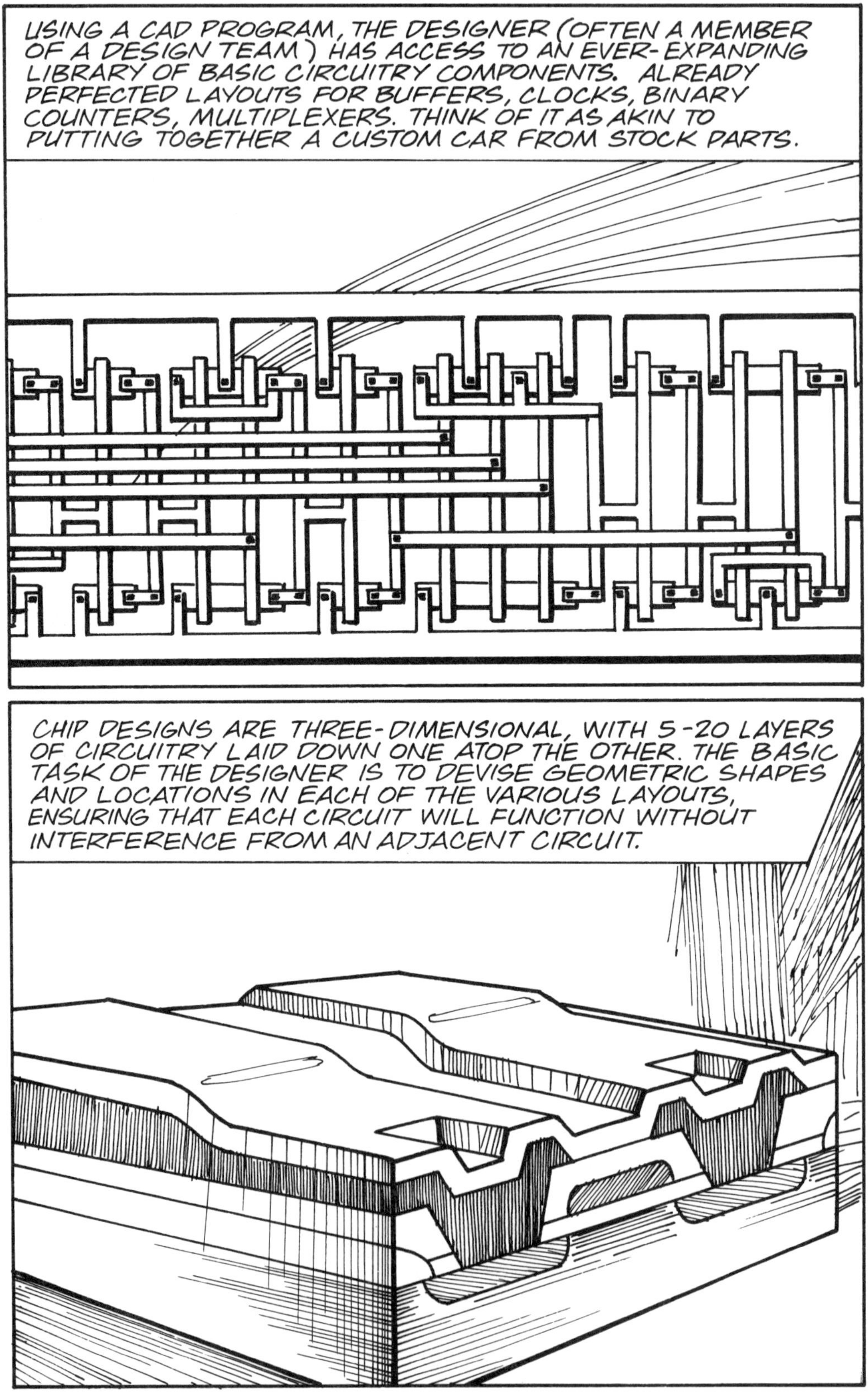

USING A CAD PROGRAM, THE DESIGNER (OFTEN A MEMBER OF A DESIGN TEAM) HAS ACCESS TO AN EVER-EXPANDING LIBRARY OF BASIC CIRCUITRY COMPONENTS. ALREADY PERFECTED LAYOUTS FOR BUFFERS, CLOCKS, BINARY COUNTERS, MULTIPLEXERS. THINK OF IT AS AKIN TO PUTTING TOGETHER A CUSTOM CAR FROM STOCK PARTS.

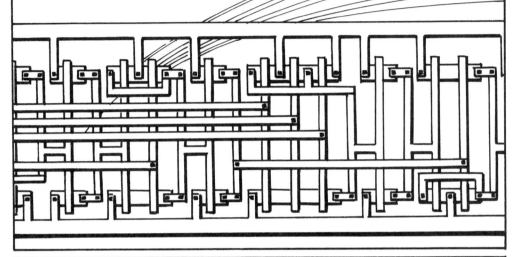

CHIP DESIGNS ARE THREE-DIMENSIONAL, WITH 5-20 LAYERS OF CIRCUITRY LAID DOWN ONE ATOP THE OTHER. THE BASIC TASK OF THE DESIGNER IS TO DEVISE GEOMETRIC SHAPES AND LOCATIONS IN EACH OF THE VARIOUS LAYOUTS, ENSURING THAT EACH CIRCUIT WILL FUNCTION WITHOUT INTERFERENCE FROM AN ADJACENT CIRCUIT.

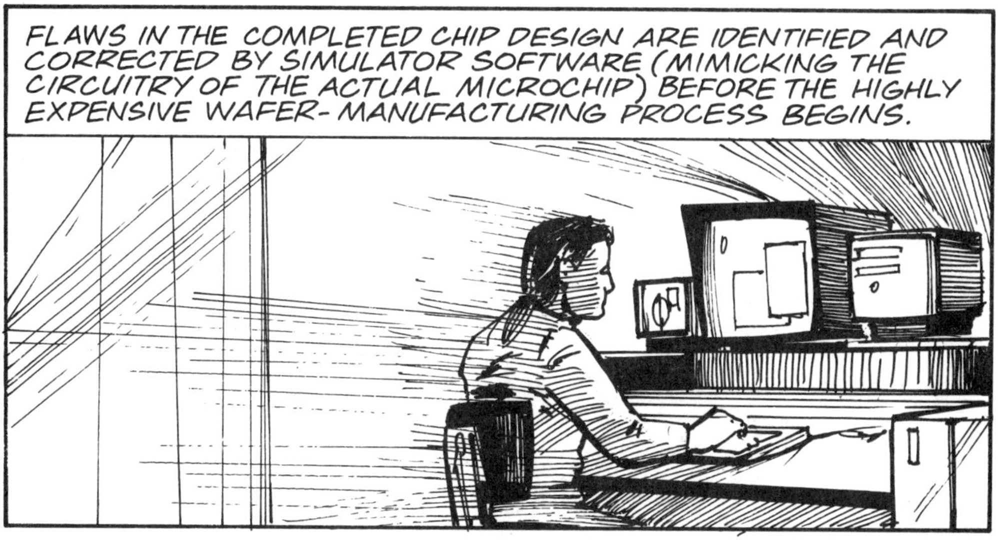
FLAWS IN THE COMPLETED CHIP DESIGN ARE IDENTIFIED AND CORRECTED BY SIMULATOR SOFTWARE (MIMICKING THE CIRCUITRY OF THE ACTUAL MICROCHIP) BEFORE THE HIGHLY EXPENSIVE WAFER-MANUFACTURING PROCESS BEGINS.

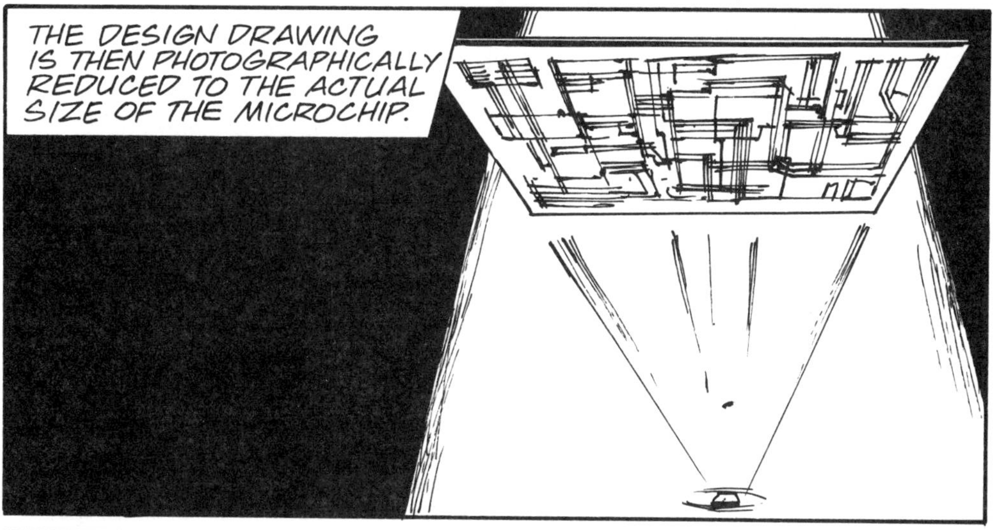
THE DESIGN DRAWING IS THEN PHOTOGRAPHICALLY REDUCED TO THE ACTUAL SIZE OF THE MICROCHIP.

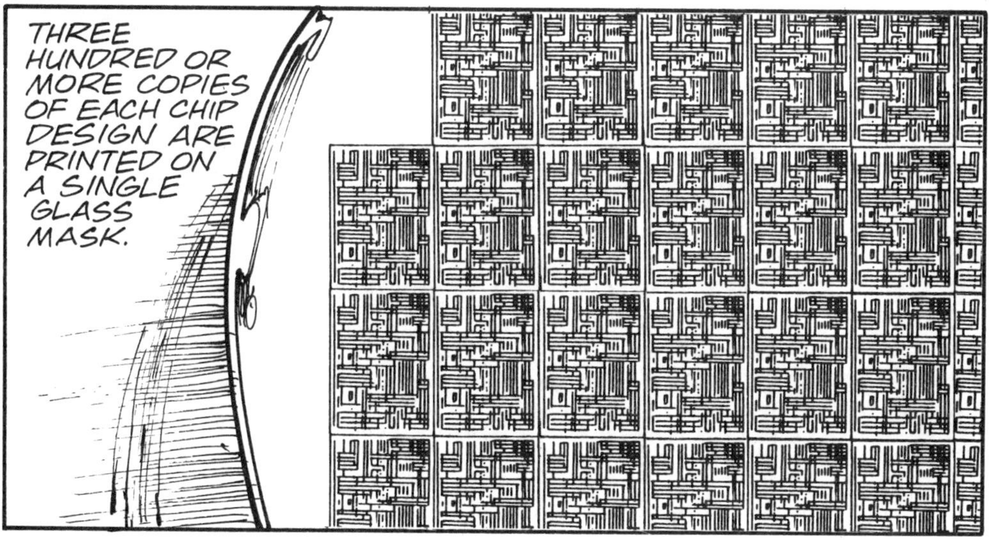
THREE HUNDRED OR MORE COPIES OF EACH CHIP DESIGN ARE PRINTED ON A SINGLE GLASS MASK.

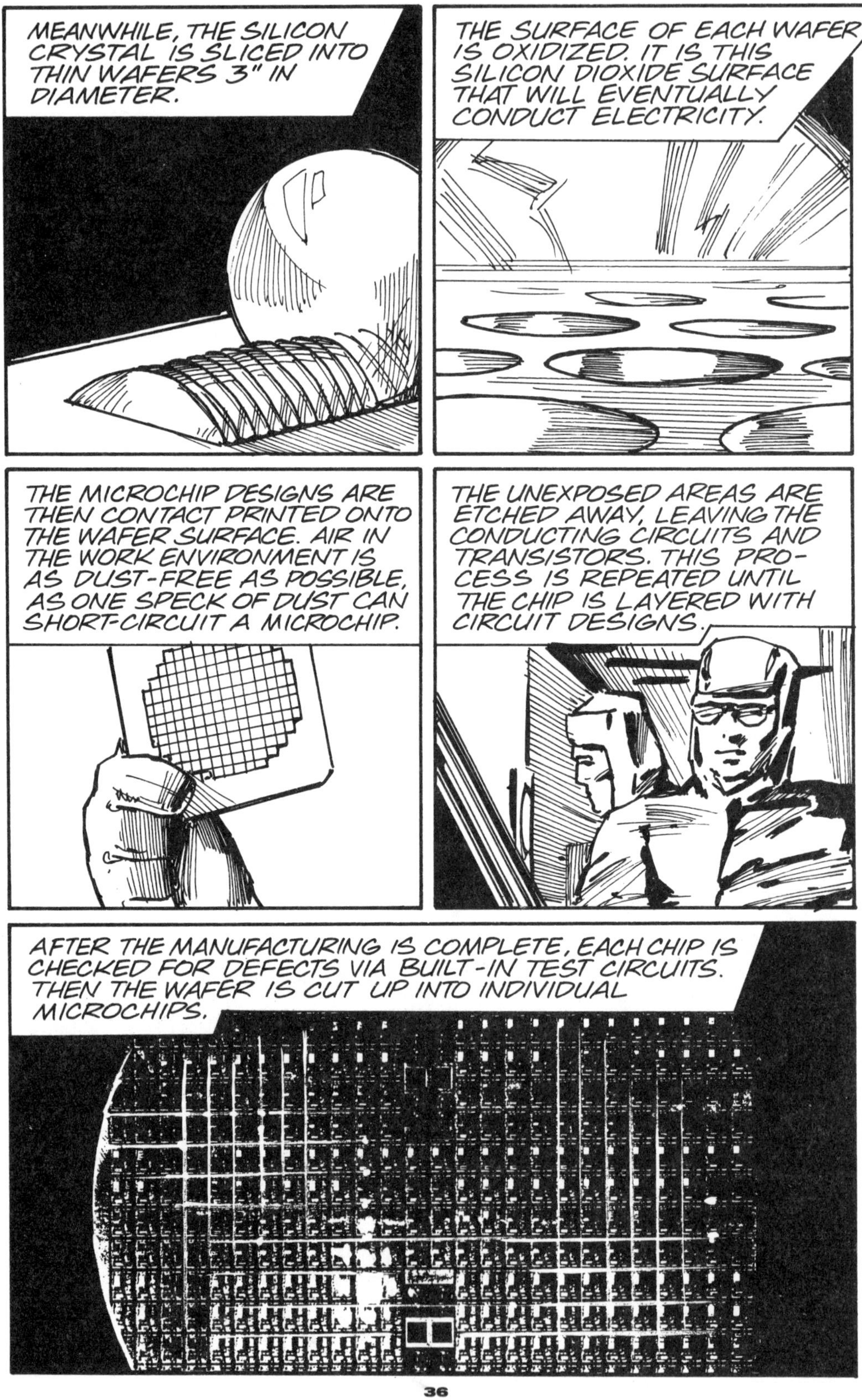
MEANWHILE, THE SILICON CRYSTAL IS SLICED INTO THIN WAFERS 3" IN DIAMETER.
THE SURFACE OF EACH WAFER IS OXIDIZED. IT IS THIS SILICON DIOXIDE SURFACE THAT WILL EVENTUALLY CONDUCT ELECTRICITY.
THE MICROCHIP DESIGNS ARE THEN CONTACT PRINTED ONTO THE WAFER SURFACE. AIR IN THE WORK ENVIRONMENT IS AS DUST-FREE AS POSSIBLE, AS ONE SPECK OF DUST CAN SHORT-CIRCUIT A MICROCHIP.
THE UNEXPOSED AREAS ARE ETCHED AWAY, LEAVING THE CONDUCTING CIRCUITS AND TRANSISTORS. THIS PROCESS IS REPEATED UNTIL THE CHIP IS LAYERED WITH CIRCUIT DESIGNS.
AFTER THE MANUFACTURING IS COMPLETE, EACH CHIP IS CHECKED FOR DEFECTS VIA BUILT-IN TEST CIRCUITS. THEN THE WAFER IS CUT UP INTO INDIVIDUAL MICROCHIPS.

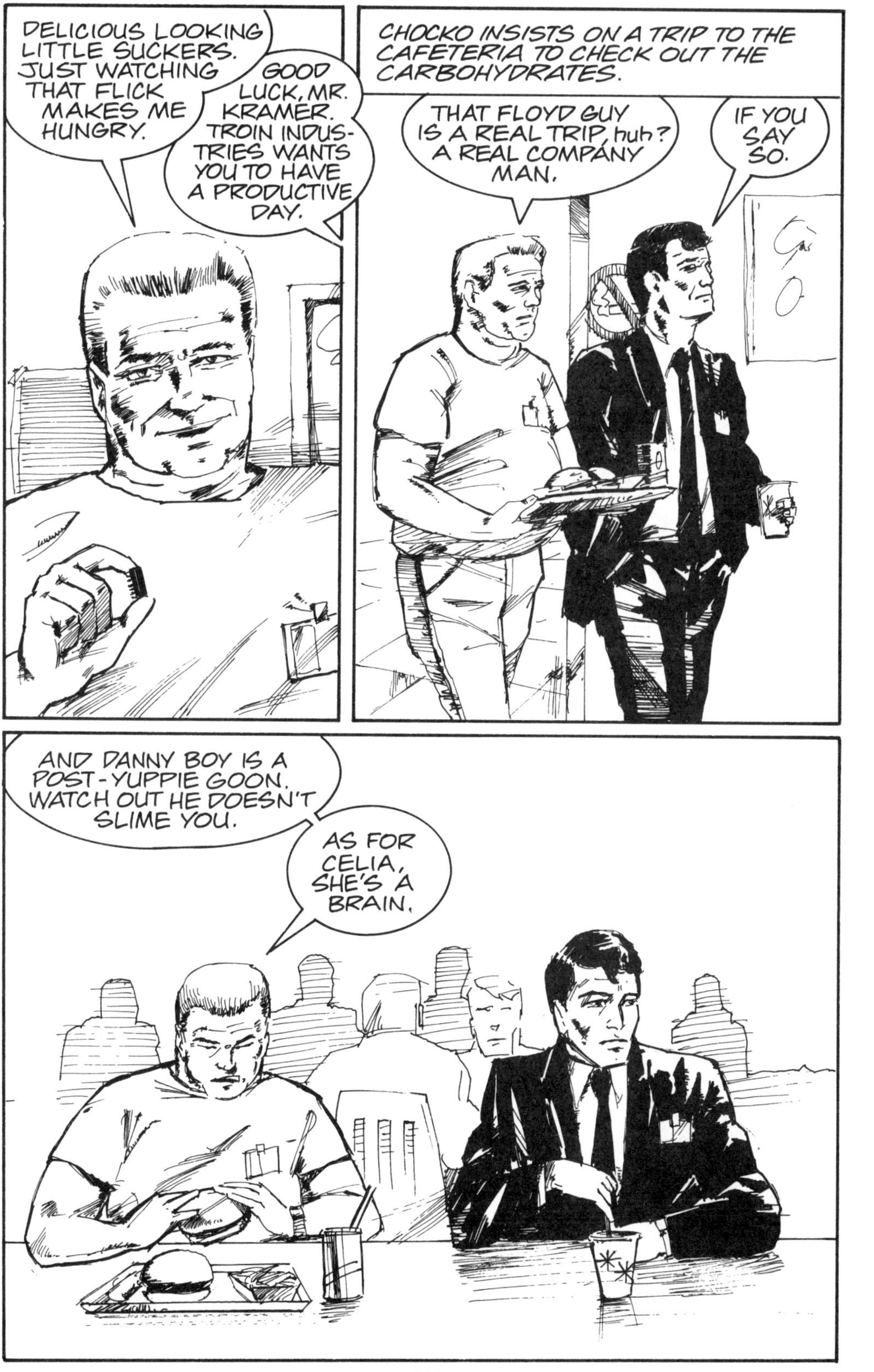
DELICIOUS LOOKING LITTLE SUCKERS. JUST WATCHING THAT FLICK MAKES ME HUNGRY.
GOOD LUCK, MR. KRAMER. TROIN INDUS-TRIES WANTS YOU TO HAVE A PRODUCTIVE DAY.
CHOCKO INSISTS ON A TRIP TO THE CAFETERIA TO CHECK OUT THE CARBOHYDRATES.
THAT FLOYD GUY IS A REAL TRIP, huh? A REAL COMPANY MAN.
IF YOU SAY SO.
AND DANNY BOY IS A POST-YUPPIE GOON. WATCH OUT HE DOESN'T SLIME YOU.
AS FOR CELIA, SHE'S A BRAIN.

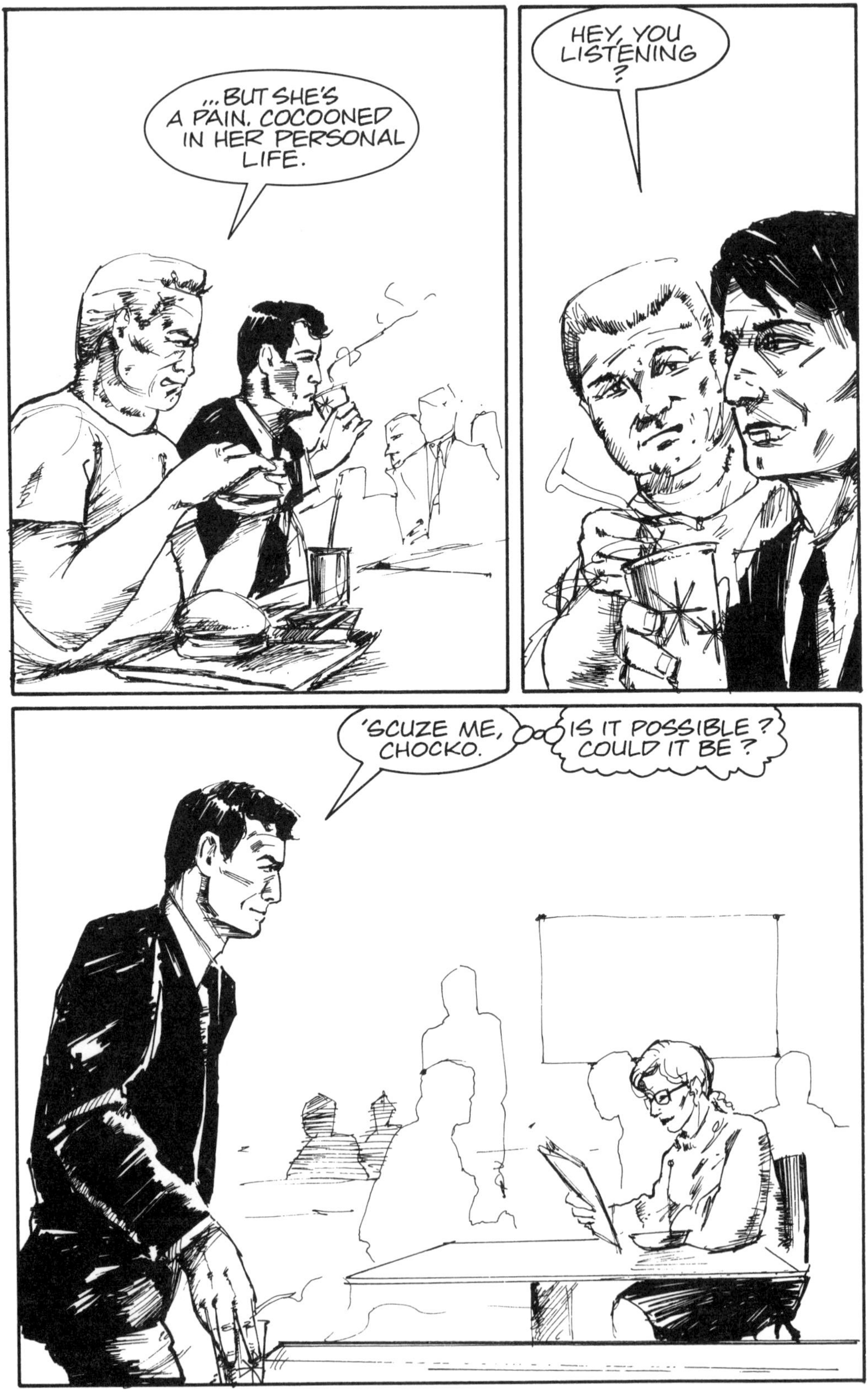
...BUT SHE'S A PAIN. COCOONED IN HER PERSONAL LIFE.
HEY, YOU LISTENING ?
'SCUZE ME, CHOCKO.
IS IT POSSIBLE ? COULD IT BE ?

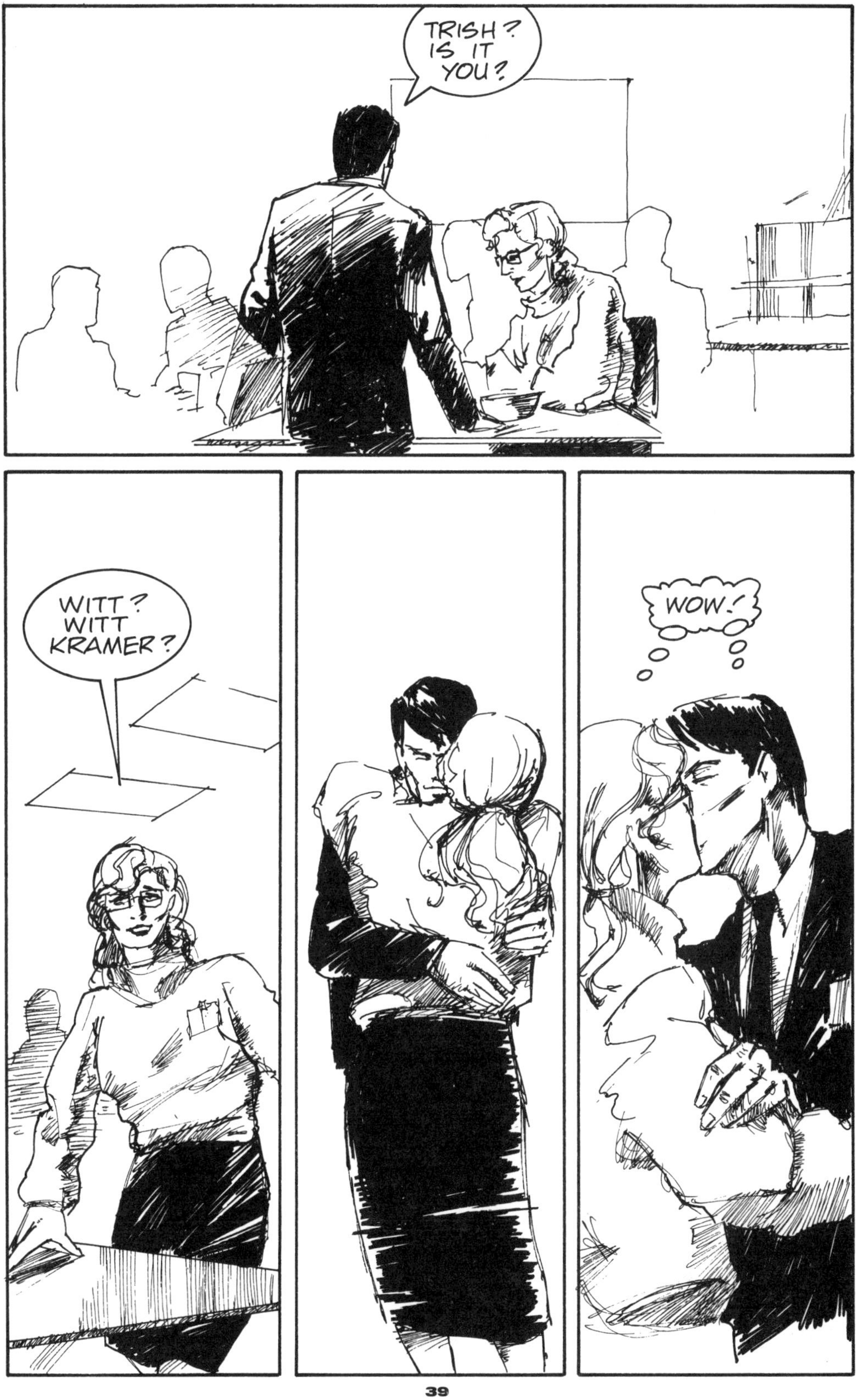
TRISH? IS IT YOU?
WITT? WITT KRAMER?
WOW!

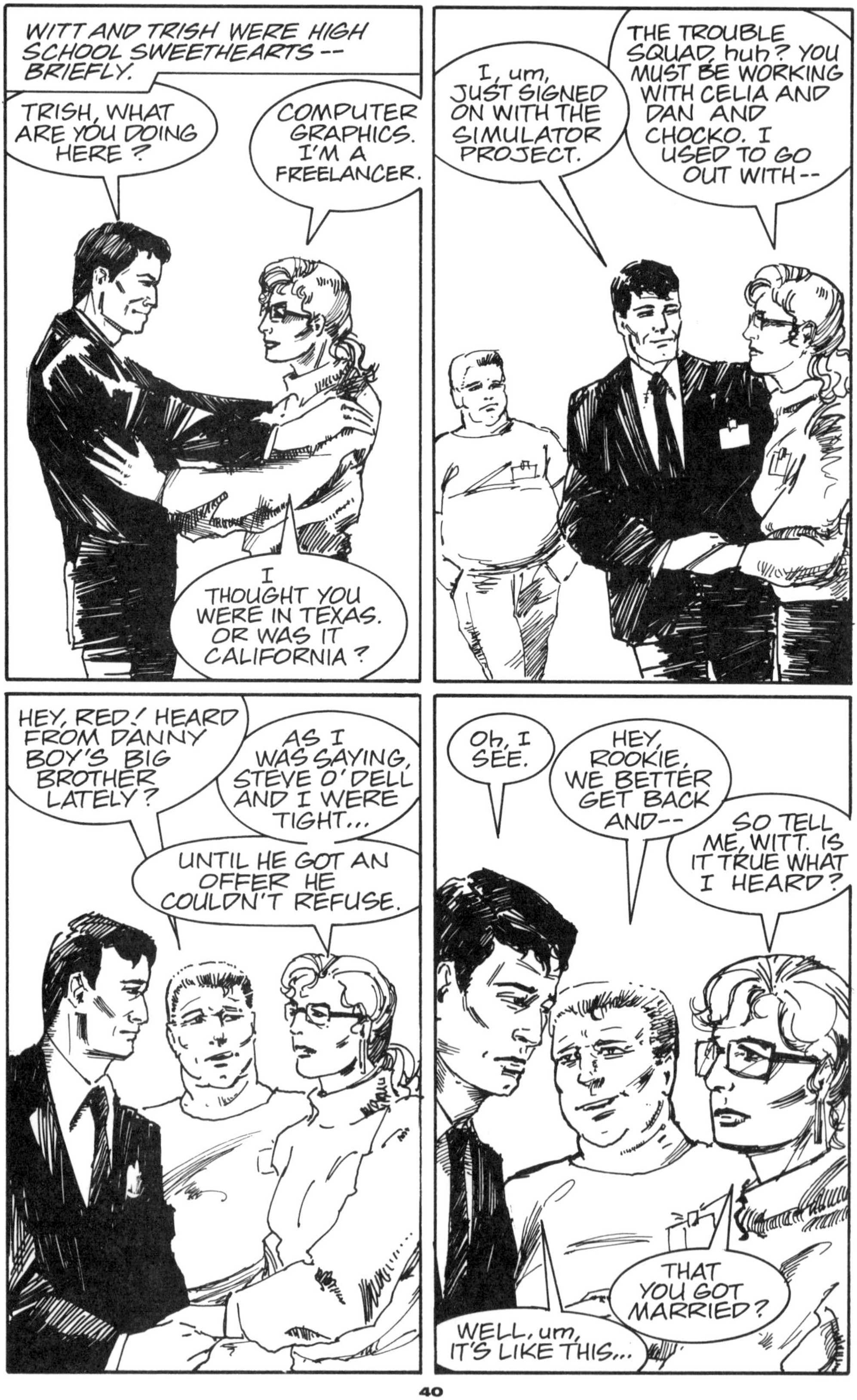
WITT AND TRISH WERE HIGH SCHOOL SWEETHEARTS -- BRIEFLY.
TRISH, WHAT ARE YOU DOING HERE?
COMPUTER GRAPHICS. I'M A FREELANCER.
I THOUGHT YOU WERE IN TEXAS. OR WAS IT CALIFORNIA?
I, um, JUST SIGNED ON WITH THE SIMULATOR PROJECT.
THE TROUBLE SQUAD, huh? YOU MUST BE WORKING WITH CELIA AND DAN AND CHOCKO. I USED TO GO OUT WITH--
HEY, RED! HEARD FROM DANNY BOY'S BIG BROTHER LATELY?
AS I WAS SAYING, STEVE O'DELL AND I WERE TIGHT...
UNTIL HE GOT AN OFFER HE COULDN'T REFUSE.
Oh, I SEE.
HEY, ROOKIE, WE BETTER GET BACK AND--
SO TELL ME, WITT. IS IT TRUE WHAT I HEARD?
THAT YOU GOT MARRIED?
WELL, um, IT'S LIKE THIS...

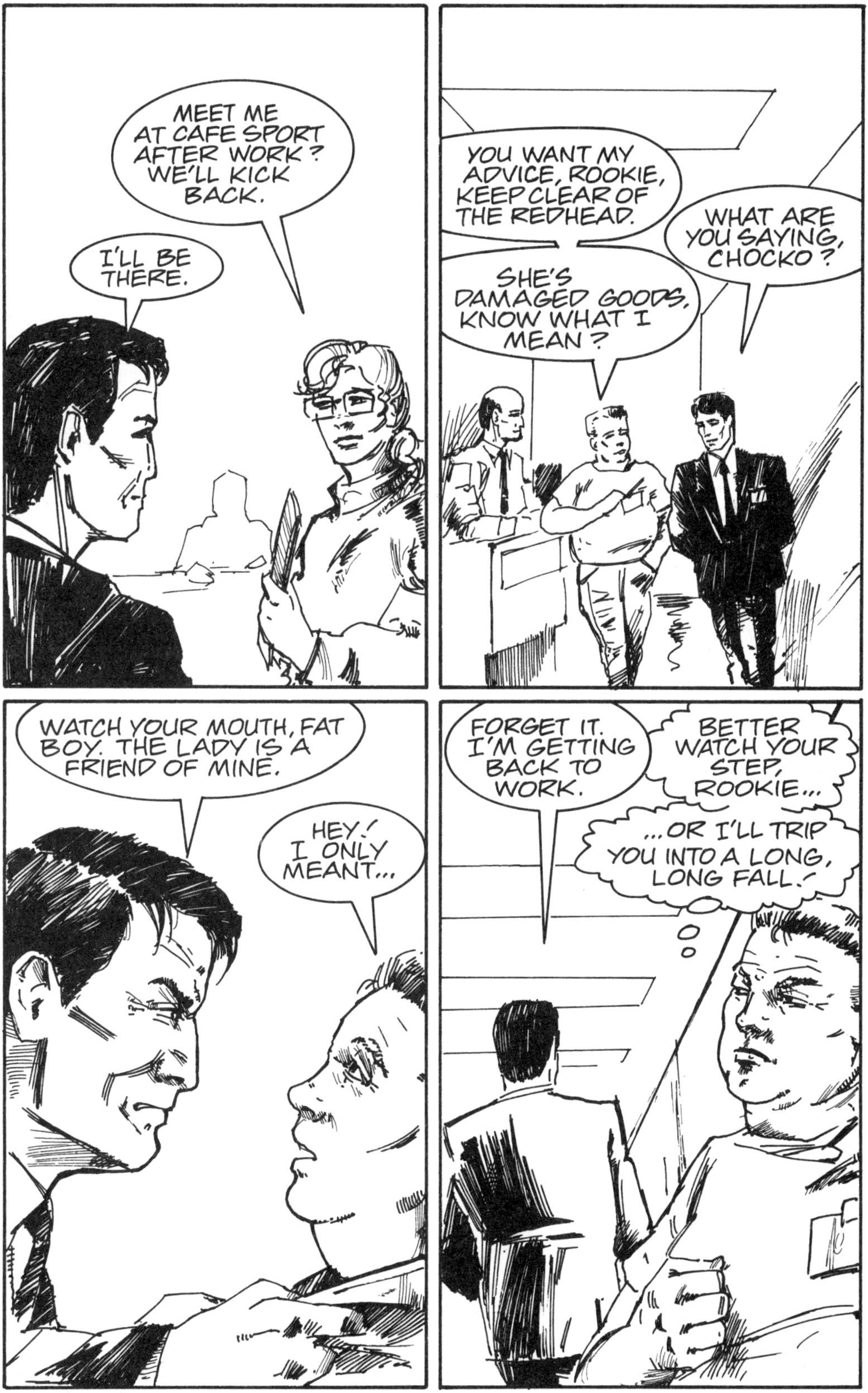
MEET ME AT CAFE SPORT AFTER WORK? WE'LL KICK BACK.
I'LL BE THERE.
YOU WANT MY ADVICE, ROOKIE, KEEP CLEAR OF THE REDHEAD.
SHE'S DAMAGED GOODS, KNOW WHAT I MEAN?
WHAT ARE YOU SAYING, CHOCKO?
WATCH YOUR MOUTH, FAT BOY. THE LADY IS A FRIEND OF MINE.
HEY! I ONLY MEANT...
FORGET IT. I'M GETTING BACK TO WORK.
BETTER WATCH YOUR STEP, ROOKIE...
...OR I'LL TRIP YOU INTO A LONG, LONG FALL!

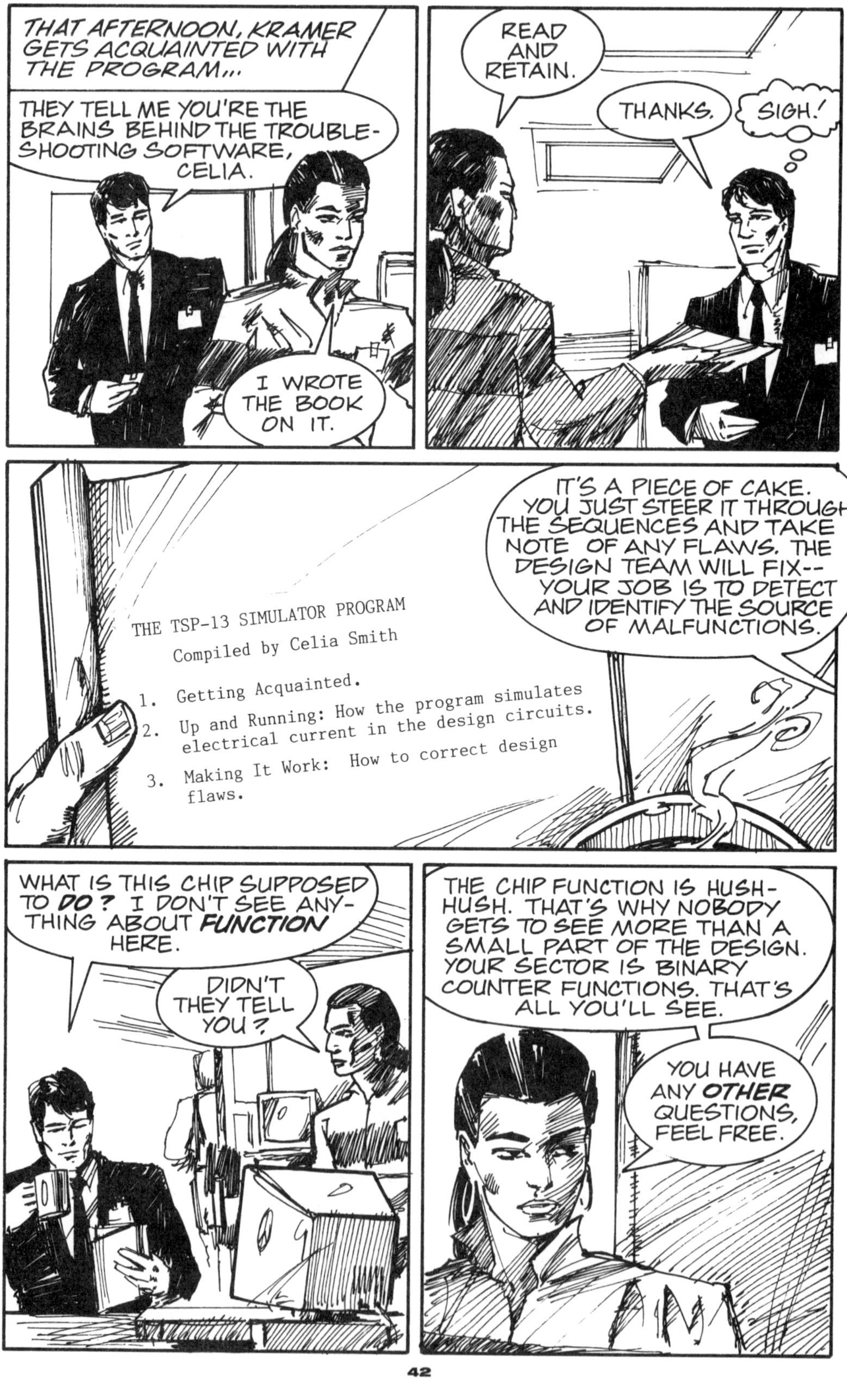
THAT AFTERNOON, KRAMER GETS ACQUAINTED WITH THE PROGRAM...
THEY TELL ME YOU'RE THE BRAINS BEHIND THE TROUBLE-SHOOTING SOFTWARE, CELIA.
I WROTE THE BOOK ON IT.
READ AND RETAIN.
THANKS.
SIGH!
THE TSP-13 SIMULATOR PROGRAM
Compiled by Celia Smith
1. Getting Acquainted.
2. Up and Running: How the program simulates electrical current in the design circuits.
3. Making It Work: How to correct design flaws.
IT'S A PIECE OF CAKE. YOU JUST STEER IT THROUGH THE SEQUENCES AND TAKE NOTE OF ANY FLAWS. THE DESIGN TEAM WILL FIX-- YOUR JOB IS TO DETECT AND IDENTIFY THE SOURCE OF MALFUNCTIONS.
WHAT IS THIS CHIP SUPPOSED TO *DO*? I DON'T SEE ANY-THING ABOUT *FUNCTION* HERE.
DIDN'T THEY TELL YOU?
THE CHIP FUNCTION IS HUSH-HUSH. THAT'S WHY NOBODY GETS TO SEE MORE THAN A SMALL PART OF THE DESIGN. YOUR SECTOR IS BINARY COUNTER FUNCTIONS. THAT'S ALL YOU'LL SEE.
YOU HAVE ANY *OTHER* QUESTIONS, FEEL FREE.

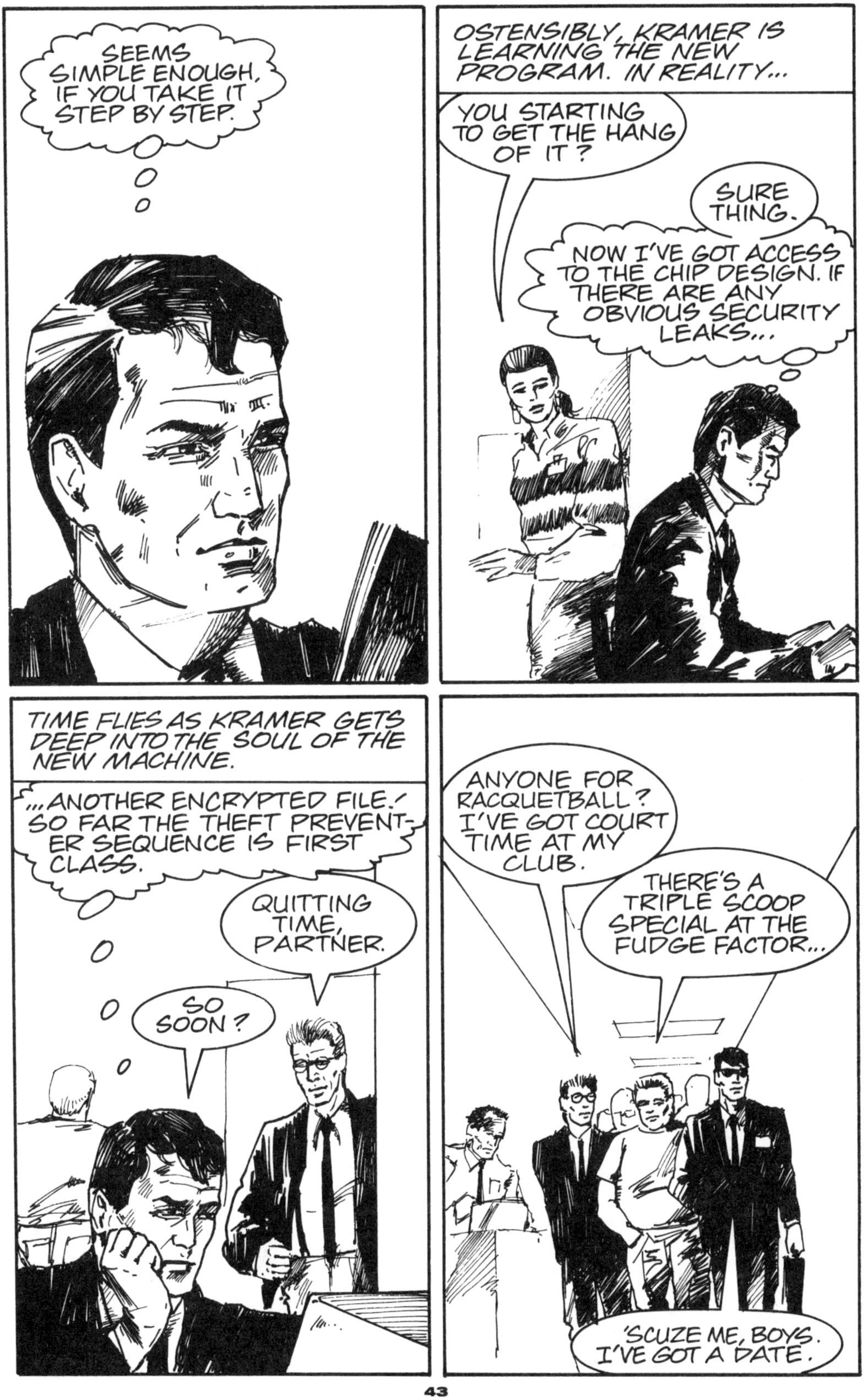
SEEMS SIMPLE ENOUGH, IF YOU TAKE IT STEP BY STEP.
OSTENSIBLY, KRAMER IS LEARNING THE NEW PROGRAM. IN REALITY...
YOU STARTING TO GET THE HANG OF IT?
SURE THING.
NOW I'VE GOT ACCESS TO THE CHIP DESIGN. IF THERE ARE ANY OBVIOUS SECURITY LEAKS...
TIME FLIES AS KRAMER GETS DEEP INTO THE SOUL OF THE NEW MACHINE.
...ANOTHER ENCRYPTED FILE! SO FAR THE THEFT PREVENTER SEQUENCE IS FIRST CLASS.
QUITTING TIME, PARTNER.
SO SOON?
ANYONE FOR RACQUETBALL? I'VE GOT COURT TIME AT MY CLUB.
THERE'S A TRIPLE SCOOP SPECIAL AT THE FUDGE FACTOR...
'SCUZE ME, BOYS. I'VE GOT A DATE.

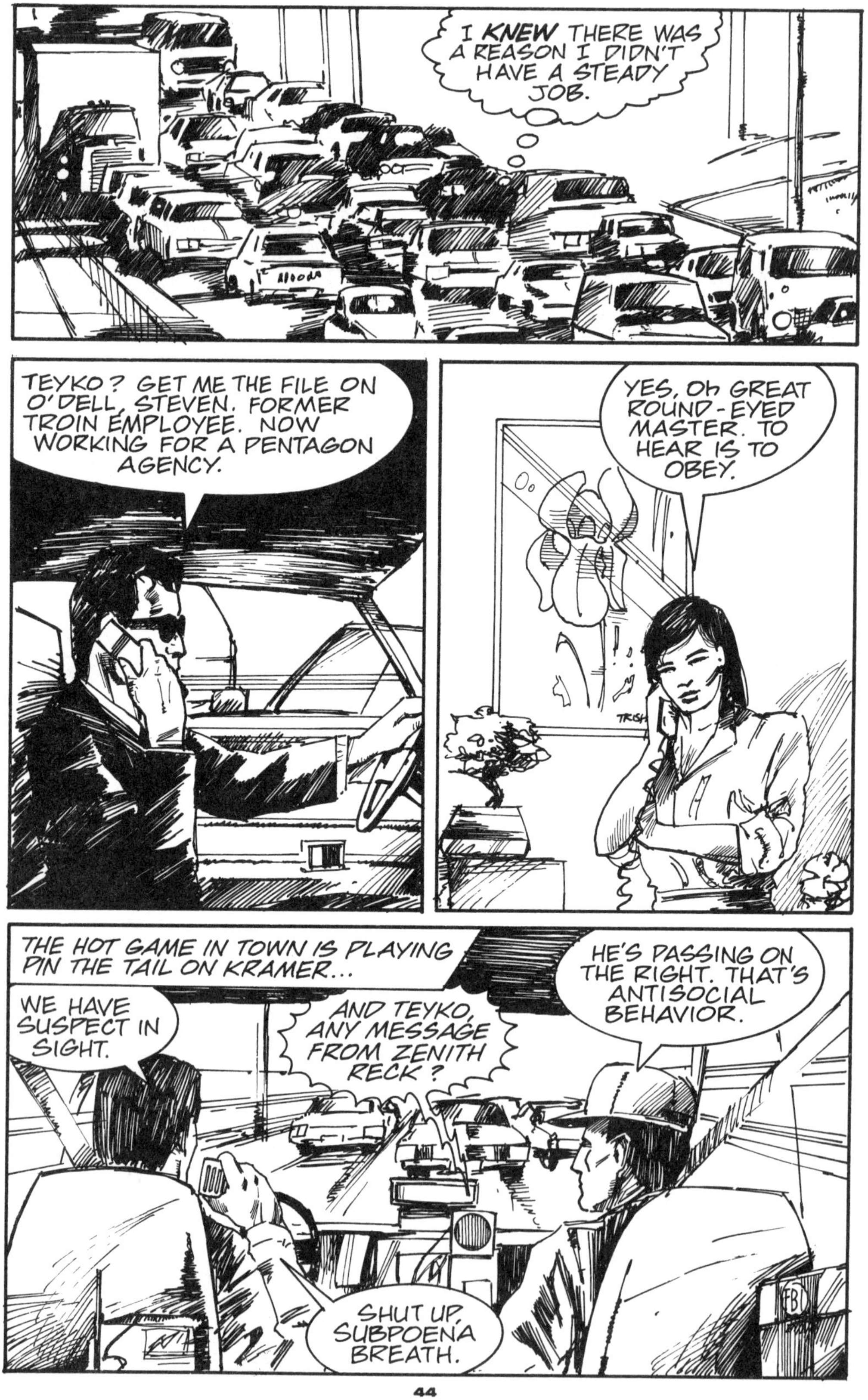
I KNEW THERE WAS A REASON I DIDN'T HAVE A STEADY JOB.
TEYKO? GET ME THE FILE ON O'DELL, STEVEN. FORMER TROIN EMPLOYEE. NOW WORKING FOR A PENTAGON AGENCY.
YES, Oh GREAT ROUND-EYED MASTER. TO HEAR IS TO OBEY.
THE HOT GAME IN TOWN IS PLAYING PIN THE TAIL ON KRAMER...
WE HAVE SUSPECT IN SIGHT.
AND TEYKO, ANY MESSAGE FROM ZENITH RECK?
HE'S PASSING ON THE RIGHT. THAT'S ANTISOCIAL BEHAVIOR.
SHUT UP, SUBPOENA BREATH.
FBI

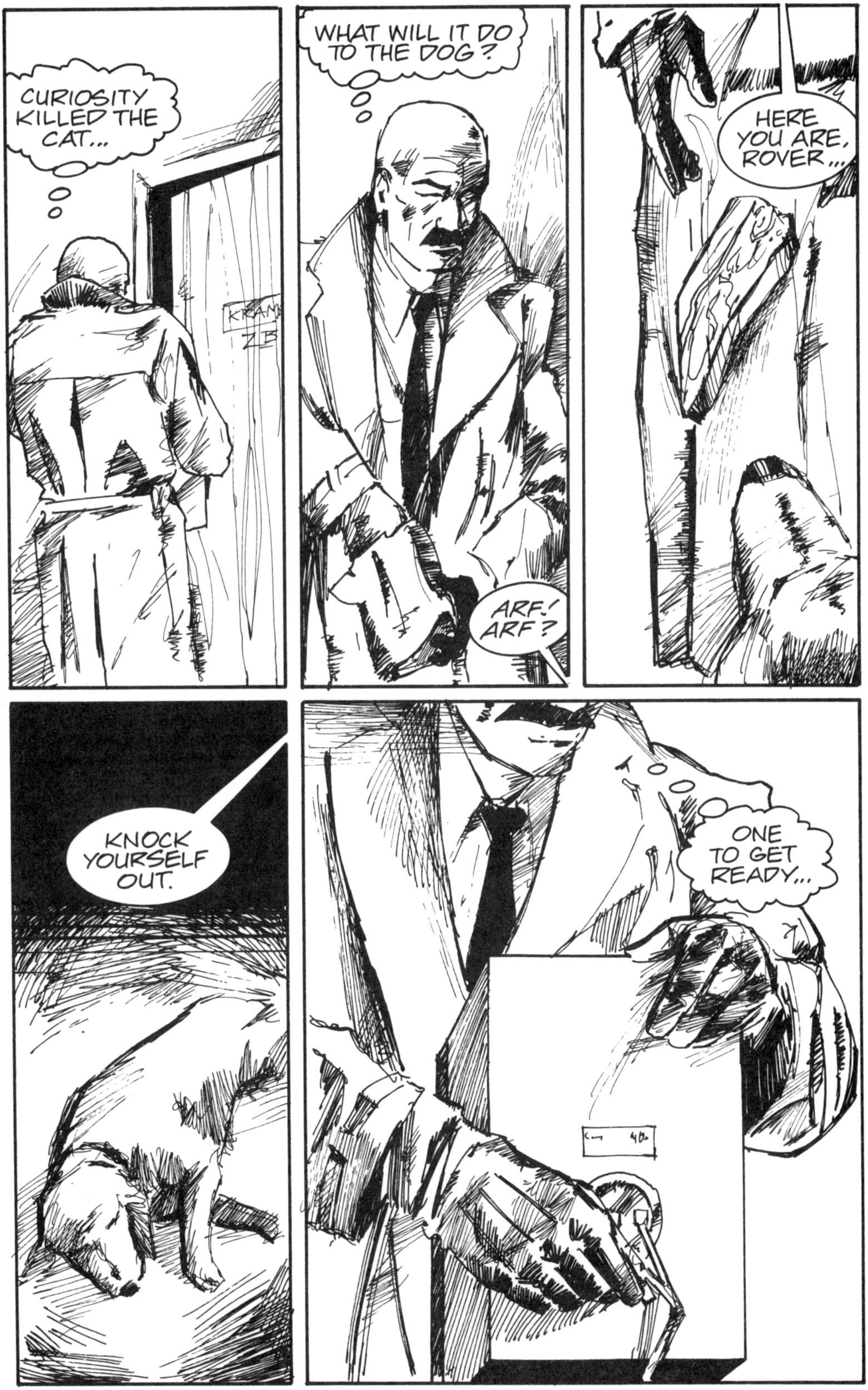
CURIOSITY KILLED THE CAT...
WHAT WILL IT DO TO THE DOG?
ARF! ARF?
HERE YOU ARE, ROVER...
KNOCK YOURSELF OUT.
ONE TO GET READY...

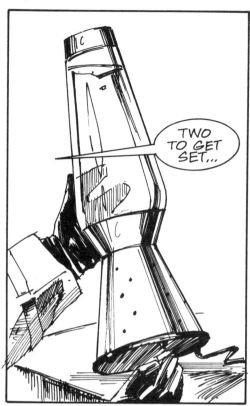

TWO TO GET SET...

AND THREE TO GO...

MEANWHILE, AT THE CAFE SPORT, ART-DECO HANGOUT FOR SEATTLE'S BEAUTIFUL PEOPLE AND AT LEAST ONE PRIVATE INVESTIGATOR...

VODKA BLAST OFF, PLEASE. HOLD THE NITRO.

MAKE IT TWO. AND HOLD THE VODKA.

TELL ME, WITT, DID THEY FALL FOR IT?

huh? FALL FOR WHAT?

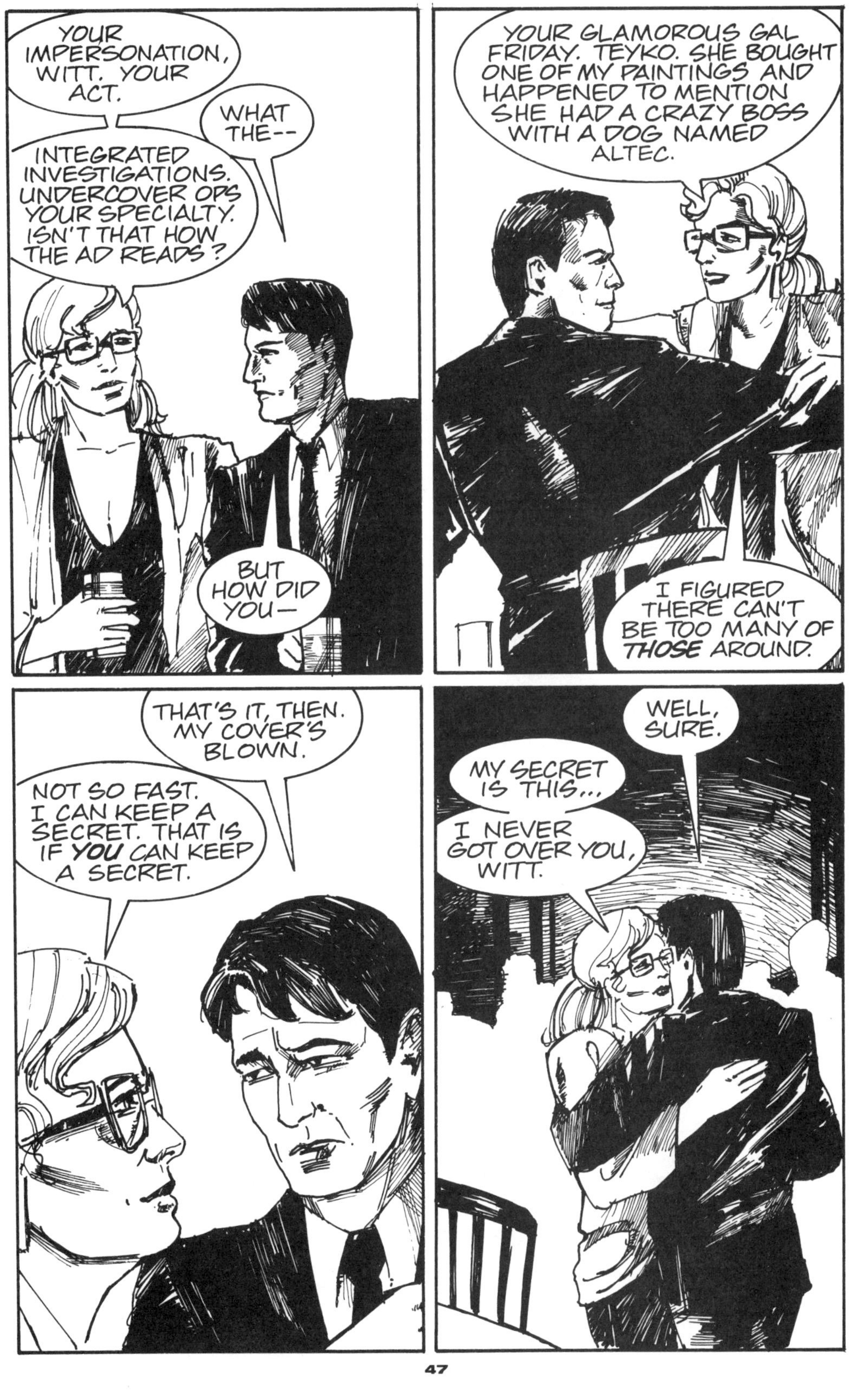
YOUR IMPERSONATION, WITT. YOUR ACT.
INTEGRATED INVESTIGATIONS. UNDERCOVER OPS YOUR SPECIALTY. ISN'T THAT HOW THE AD READS?
WHAT THE--
BUT HOW DID YOU—
YOUR GLAMOROUS GAL FRIDAY. TEYKO. SHE BOUGHT ONE OF MY PAINTINGS AND HAPPENED TO MENTION SHE HAD A CRAZY BOSS WITH A DOG NAMED ALTEC.
I FIGURED THERE CAN'T BE TOO MANY OF *THOSE* AROUND.
THAT'S IT, THEN. MY COVER'S BLOWN.
NOT SO FAST. I CAN KEEP A SECRET. THAT IS IF *YOU* CAN KEEP A SECRET.
WELL, SURE.
MY SECRET IS THIS...
I NEVER GOT OVER YOU, WITT.

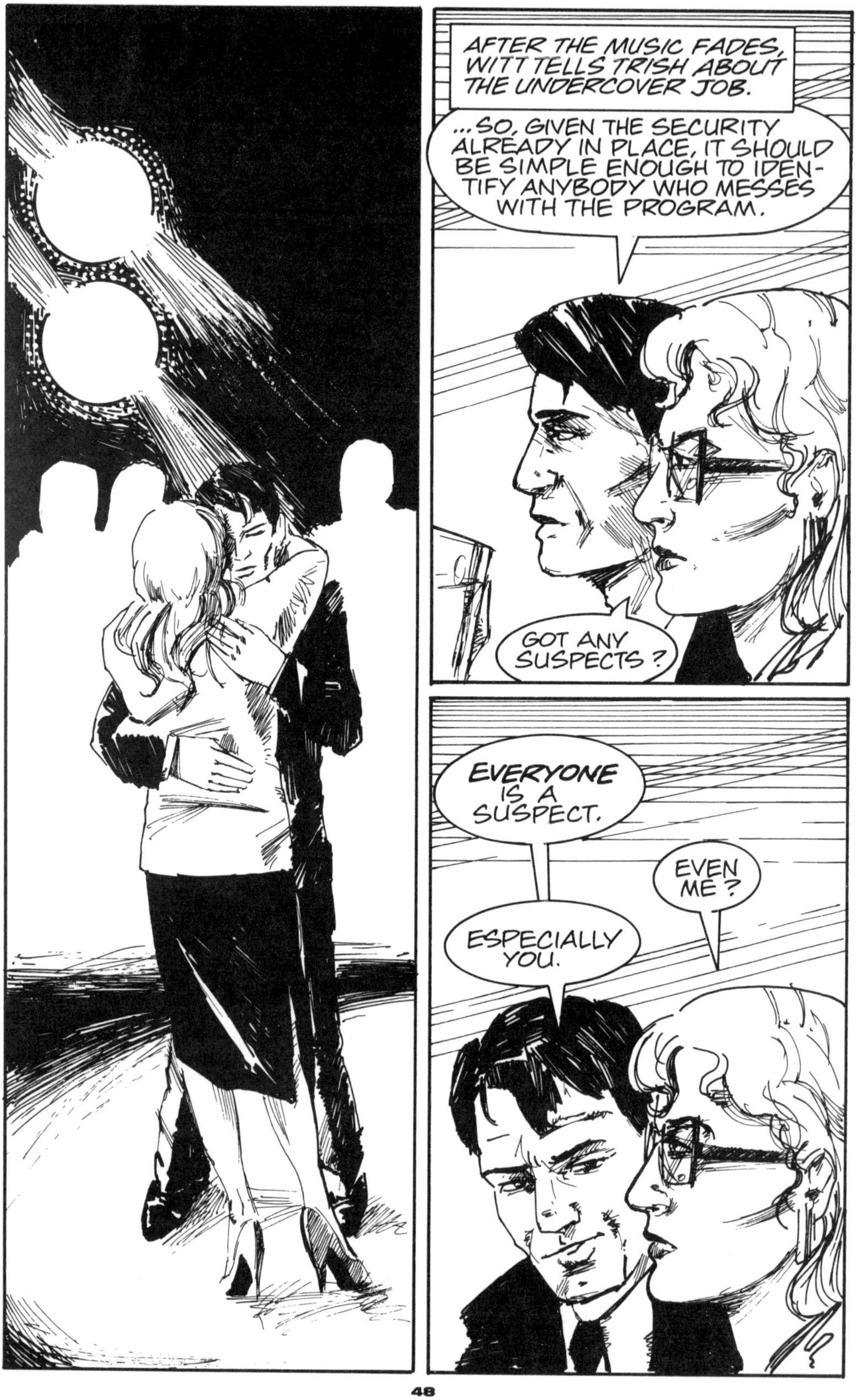
AFTER THE MUSIC FADES, WITT TELLS TRISH ABOUT THE UNDERCOVER JOB.
...SO, GIVEN THE SECURITY ALREADY IN PLACE, IT SHOULD BE SIMPLE ENOUGH TO IDENTIFY ANYBODY WHO MESSES WITH THE PROGRAM.
GOT ANY SUSPECTS?
EVERYONE IS A SUSPECT.
EVEN ME?
ESPECIALLY YOU.

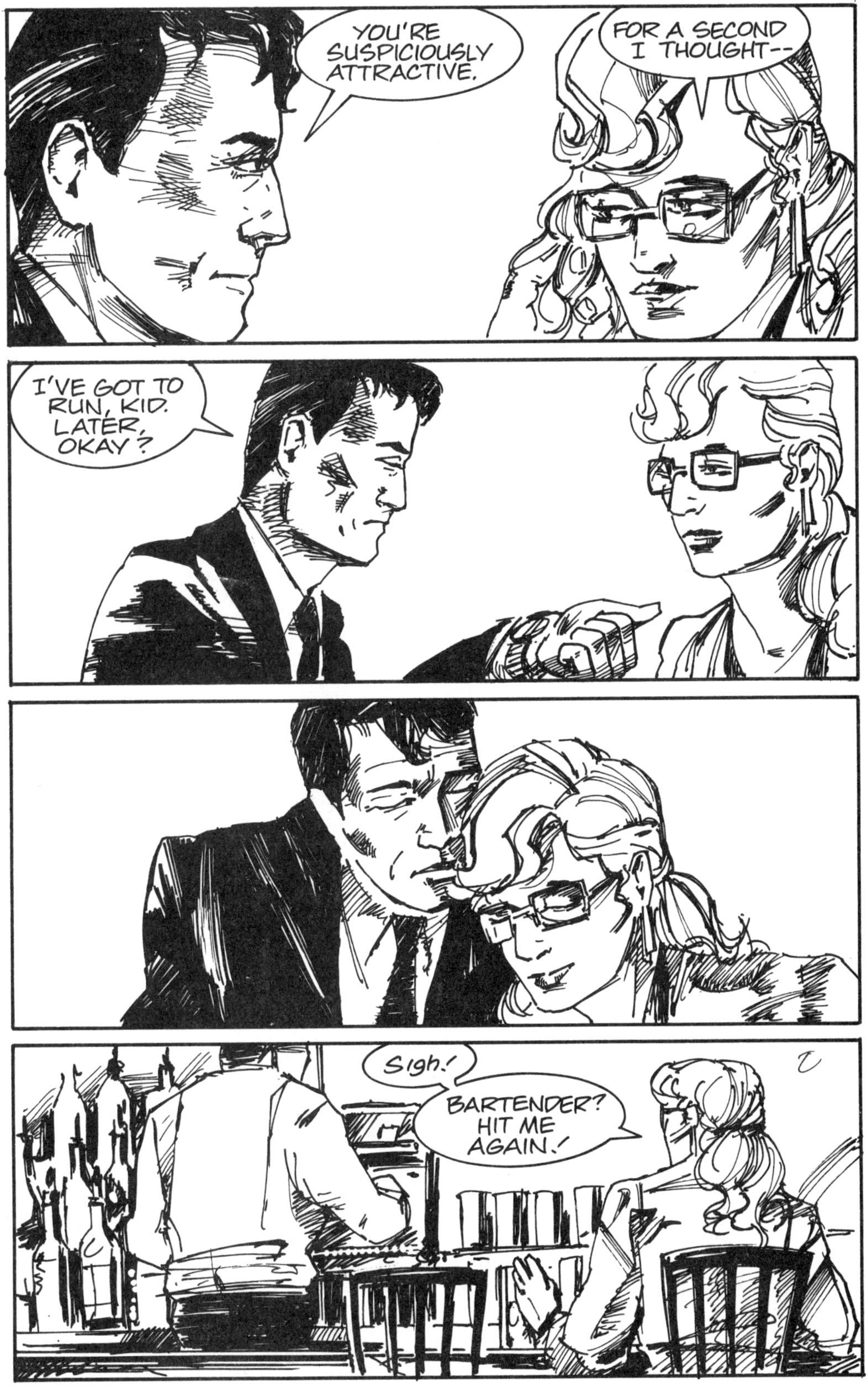
YOU'RE SUSPICIOUSLY ATTRACTIVE.
FOR A SECOND I THOUGHT--
I'VE GOT TO RUN, KID. LATER, OKAY?
Sigh!
BARTENDER? HIT ME AGAIN!

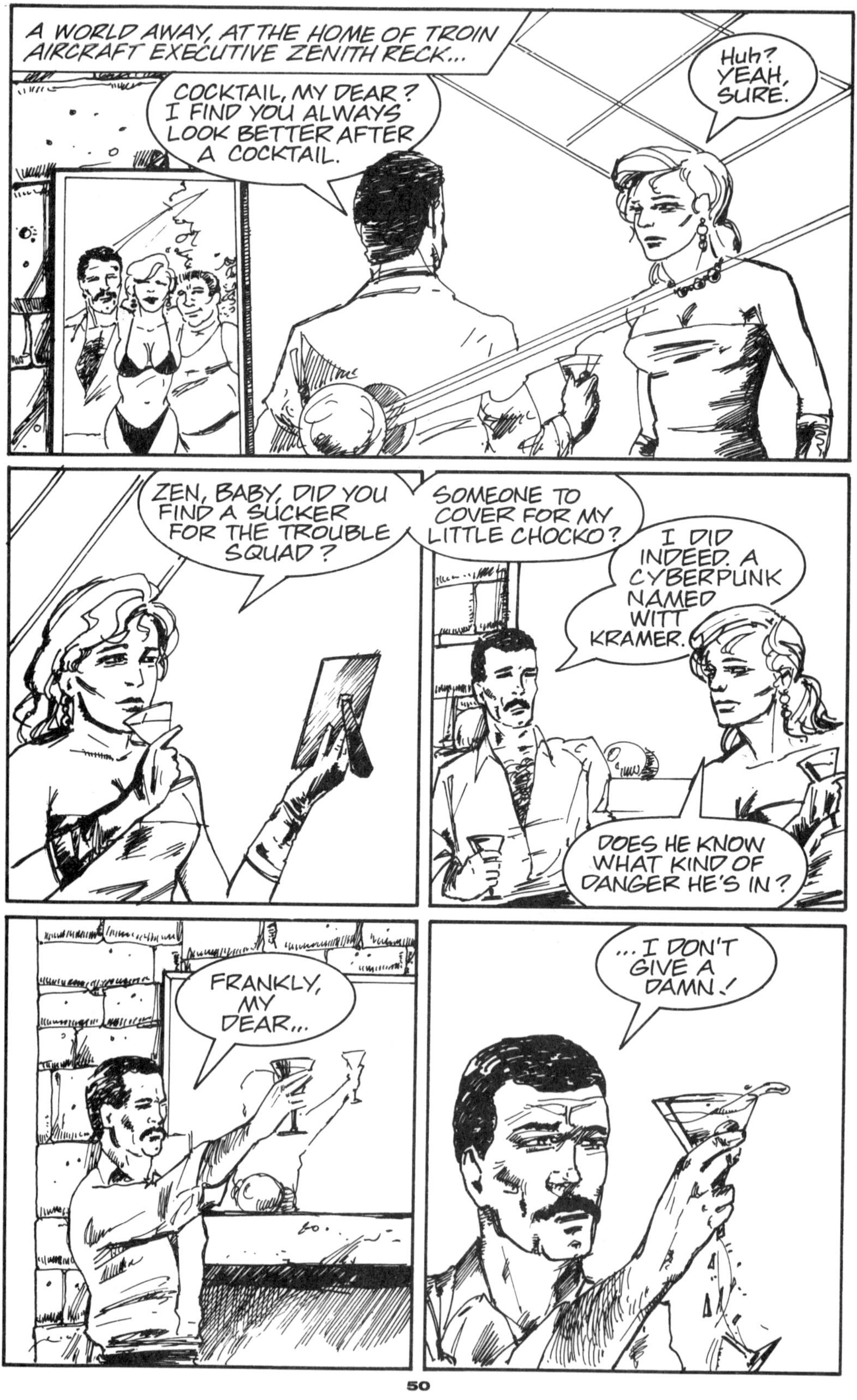
A WORLD AWAY, AT THE HOME OF TROIN AIRCRAFT EXECUTIVE ZENITH RECK...
COCKTAIL, MY DEAR? I FIND YOU ALWAYS LOOK BETTER AFTER A COCKTAIL.
Huh? YEAH, SURE.
ZEN, BABY, DID YOU FIND A SUCKER FOR THE TROUBLE SQUAD?
SOMEONE TO COVER FOR MY LITTLE CHOCKO?
I DID INDEED. A CYBERPUNK NAMED WITT KRAMER.
DOES HE KNOW WHAT KIND OF DANGER HE'S IN?
FRANKLY, MY DEAR...
...I DON'T GIVE A DAMN!

Driving back that evening, I had women in mind. Trish — what a blast from the past *she* was. Last time we clicked we'd been kids trying to grow up fast. Now we were both out there in the big, bad world, each with a past. It was tempting to fall back into the kid routine again, all fever kisses and bumping hearts.

Then there was Layne, the lovely, living-in-Palo-Alto Layne. She hadn't called in months and every time I reached for the phone it felt too hot to handle.

Keep both hands on the wheel, Kramer, and your eye on the road. Don't get fooled by the curves again.

Before you start feeling sorry for yourself, remember you've already got a loyal female waiting at home. . .

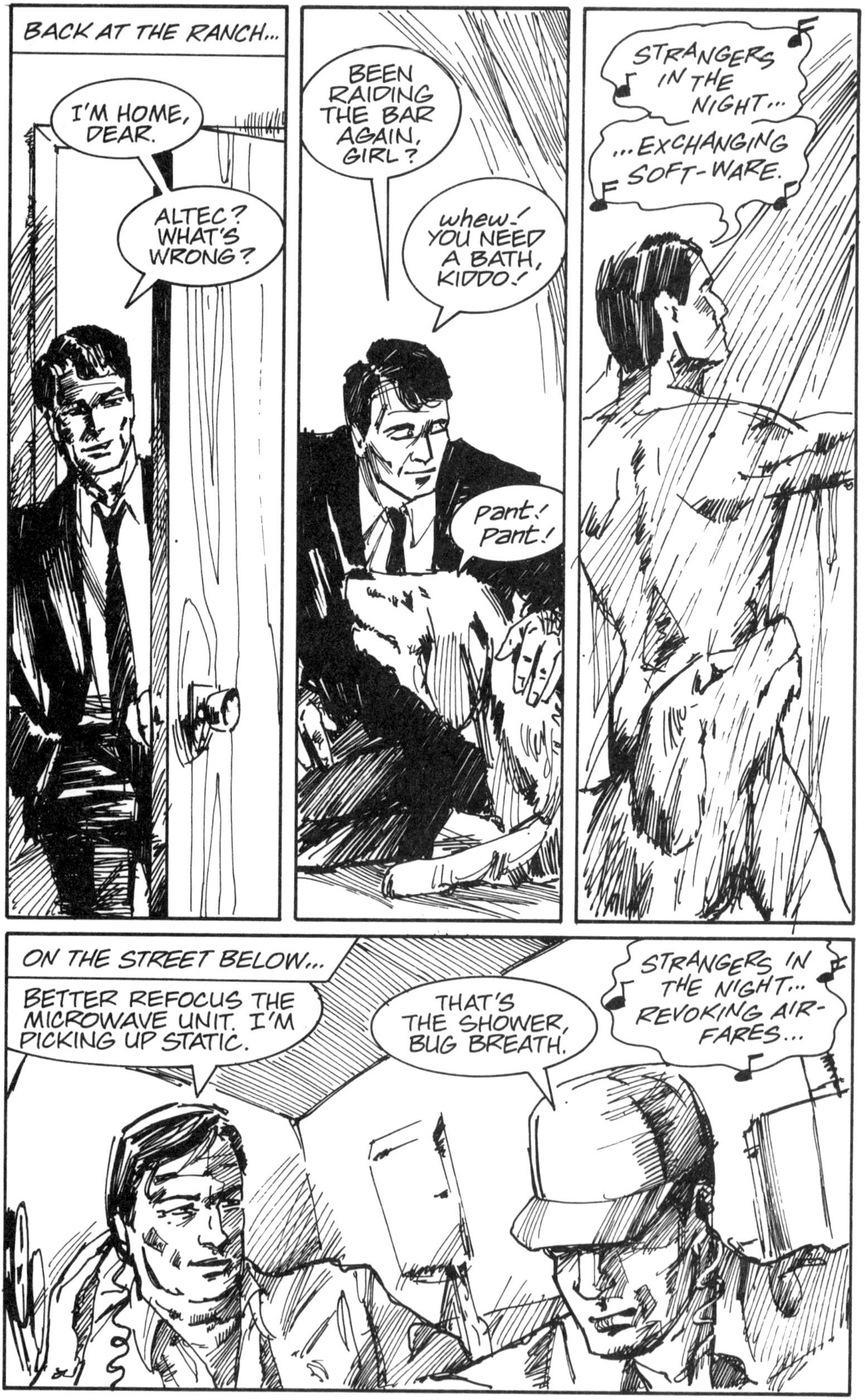
BACK AT THE RANCH...
I'M HOME, DEAR.
ALTEC? WHAT'S WRONG?
BEEN RAIDING THE BAR AGAIN, GIRL?
whew! YOU NEED A BATH, KIDDO!
pant! pant!
STRANGERS IN THE NIGHT...
...EXCHANGING SOFT-WARE.
ON THE STREET BELOW...
BETTER REFOCUS THE MICROWAVE UNIT. I'M PICKING UP STATIC.
THAT'S THE SHOWER, BUG BREATH.
STRANGERS IN THE NIGHT... REVOKING AIR-FARES...

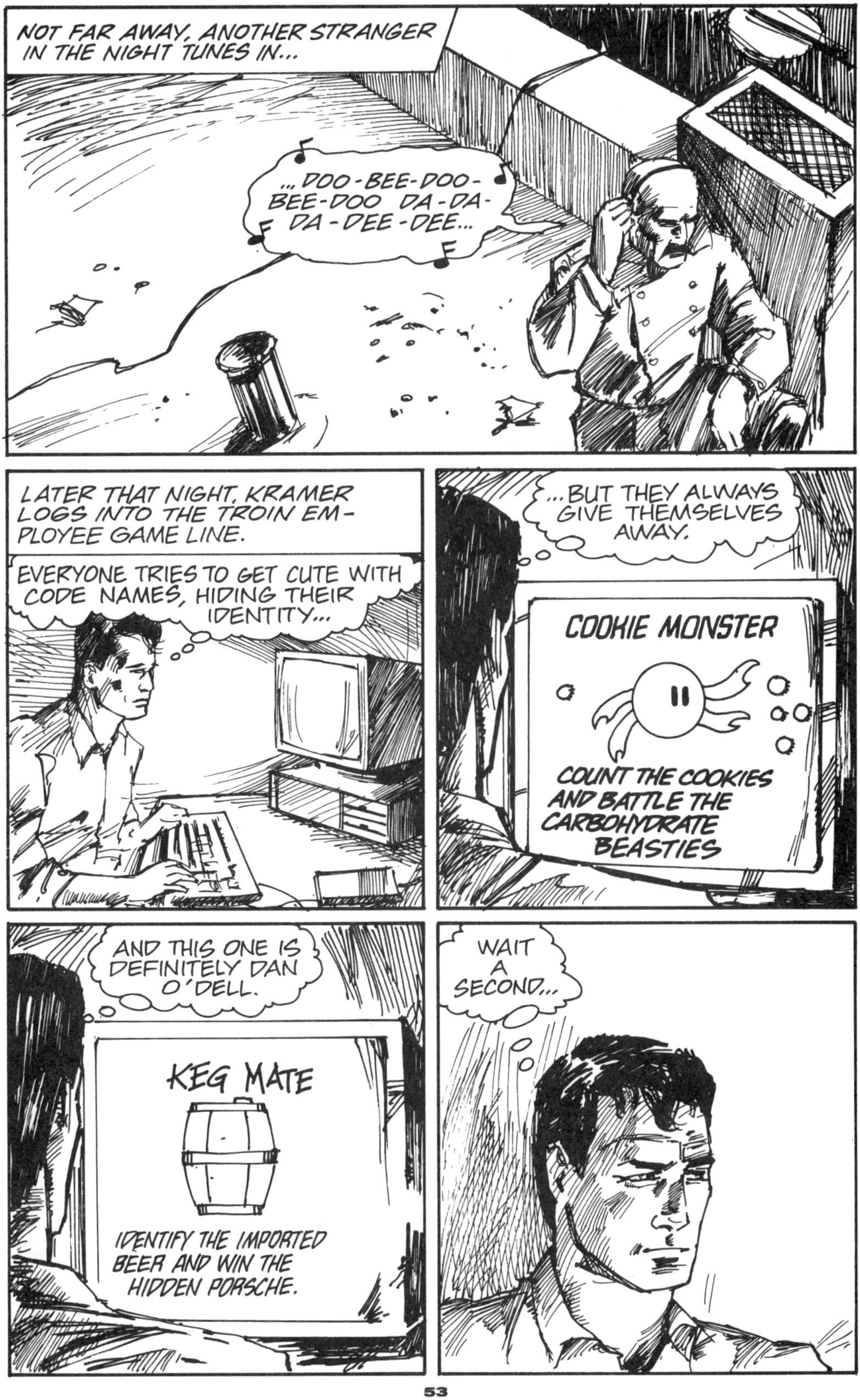
NOT FAR AWAY, ANOTHER STRANGER IN THE NIGHT TUNES IN...
..., DOO-BEE-DOO-BEE-DOO DA-DA-DA-DEE-DEE...
LATER THAT NIGHT, KRAMER LOGS INTO THE TROIN EMPLOYEE GAME LINE.
EVERYONE TRIES TO GET CUTE WITH CODE NAMES, HIDING THEIR IDENTITY...
...BUT THEY ALWAYS GIVE THEMSELVES AWAY.
COOKIE MONSTER
COUNT THE COOKIES AND BATTLE THE CARBOHYDRATE BEASTIES
AND THIS ONE IS DEFINITELY DAN O'DELL.
KEG MATE
IDENTIFY THE IMPORTED BEER AND WIN THE HIDDEN PORSCHE.
WAIT A SECOND...

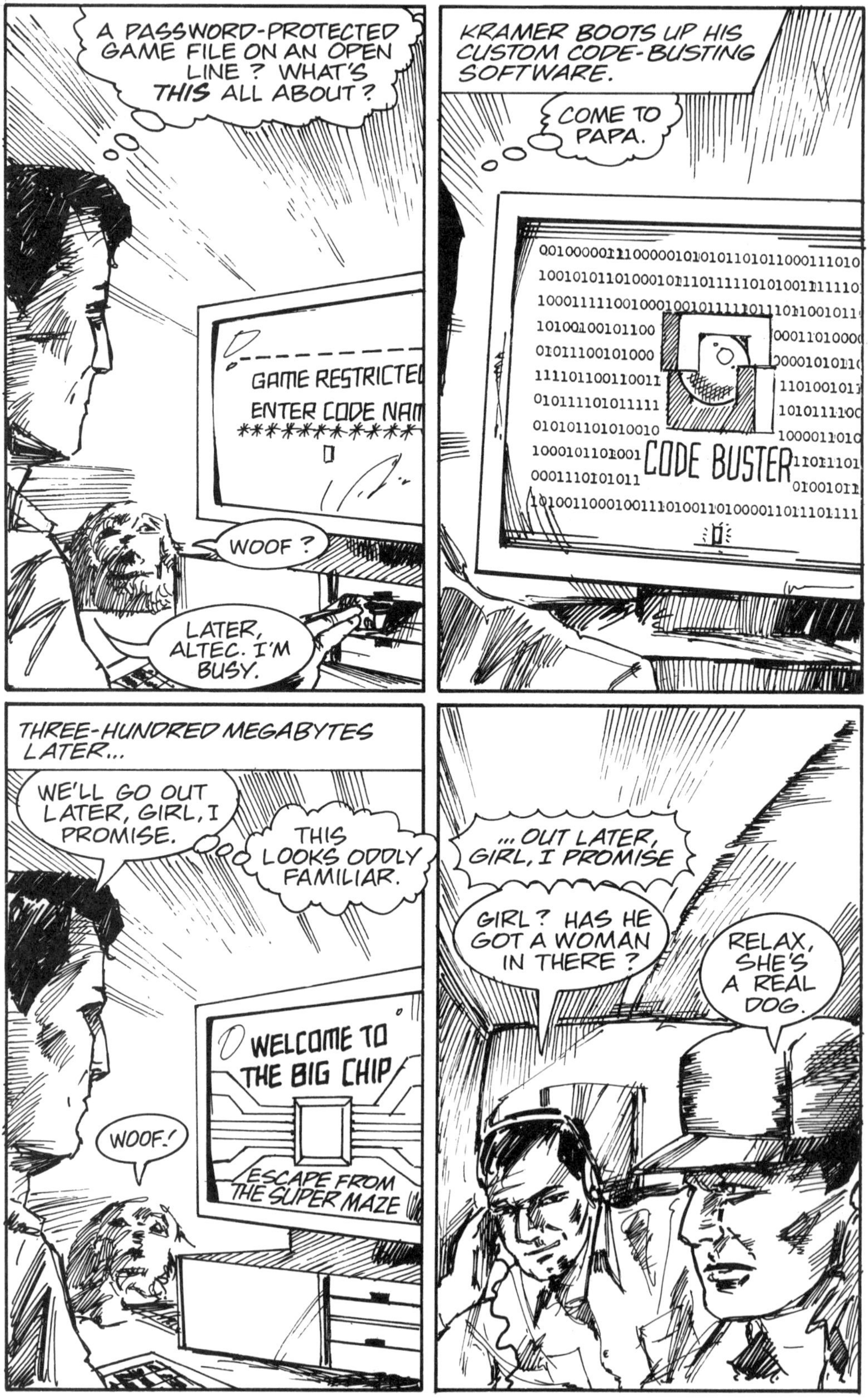
A PASSWORD-PROTECTED GAME FILE ON AN OPEN LINE ? WHAT'S *THIS* ALL ABOUT ?
GAME RESTRICTED
ENTER CODE NAM
WOOF ?
LATER, ALTEC. I'M BUSY.
KRAMER BOOTS UP HIS CUSTOM CODE-BUSTING SOFTWARE.
COME TO PAPA.
CODE BUSTER
THREE-HUNDRED MEGABYTES LATER...
WE'LL GO OUT LATER, GIRL, I PROMISE.
THIS LOOKS ODDLY FAMILIAR.
WELCOME TO THE BIG CHIP
ESCAPE FROM THE SUPER MAZE
WOOF!
...OUT LATER, GIRL, I PROMISE
GIRL ? HAS HE GOT A WOMAN IN THERE ?
RELAX, SHE'S A REAL DOG.

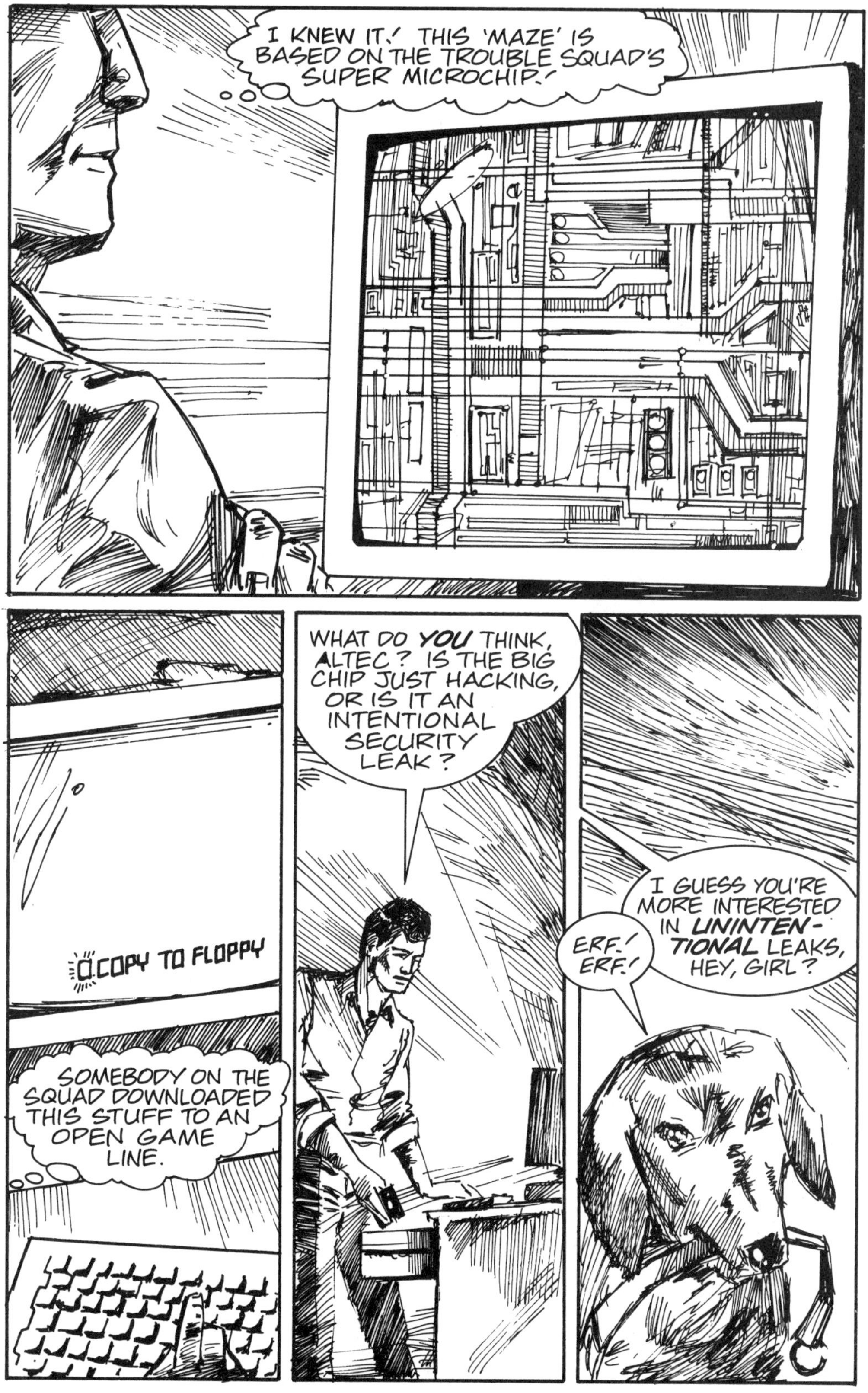
I KNEW IT! THIS 'MAZE' IS BASED ON THE TROUBLE SQUAD'S SUPER MICROCHIP!
COPY TO FLOPPY
SOMEBODY ON THE SQUAD DOWNLOADED THIS STUFF TO AN OPEN GAME LINE.
WHAT DO ***YOU*** THINK, ALTEC? IS THE BIG CHIP JUST HACKING, OR IS IT AN INTENTIONAL SECURITY LEAK?
I GUESS YOU'RE MORE INTERESTED IN ***UNINTENTIONAL*** LEAKS, HEY, GIRL?
ERF! ERF!

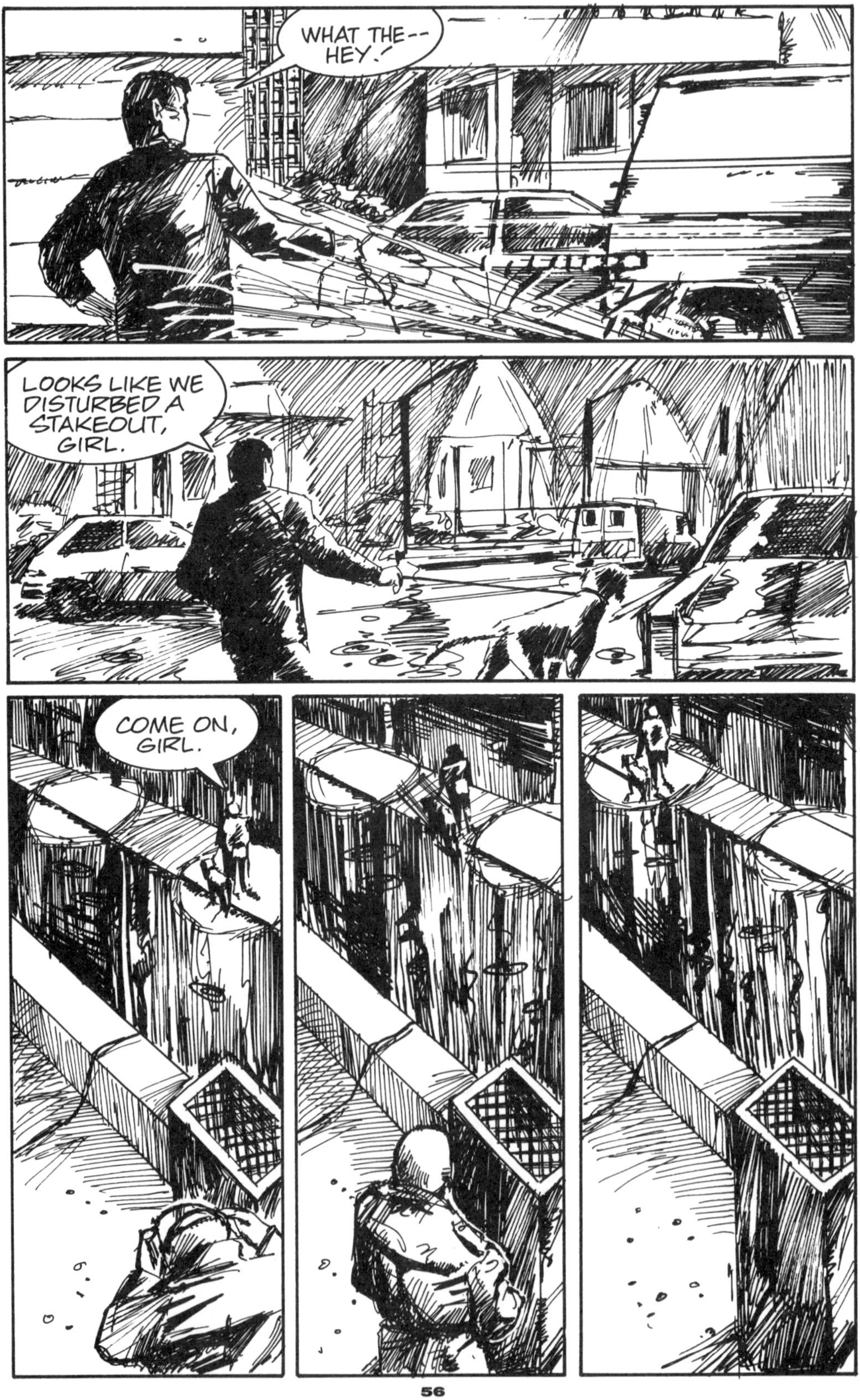
WHAT THE--
HEY.!
LOOKS LIKE WE DISTURBED A STAKEOUT, GIRL.
COME ON, GIRL.

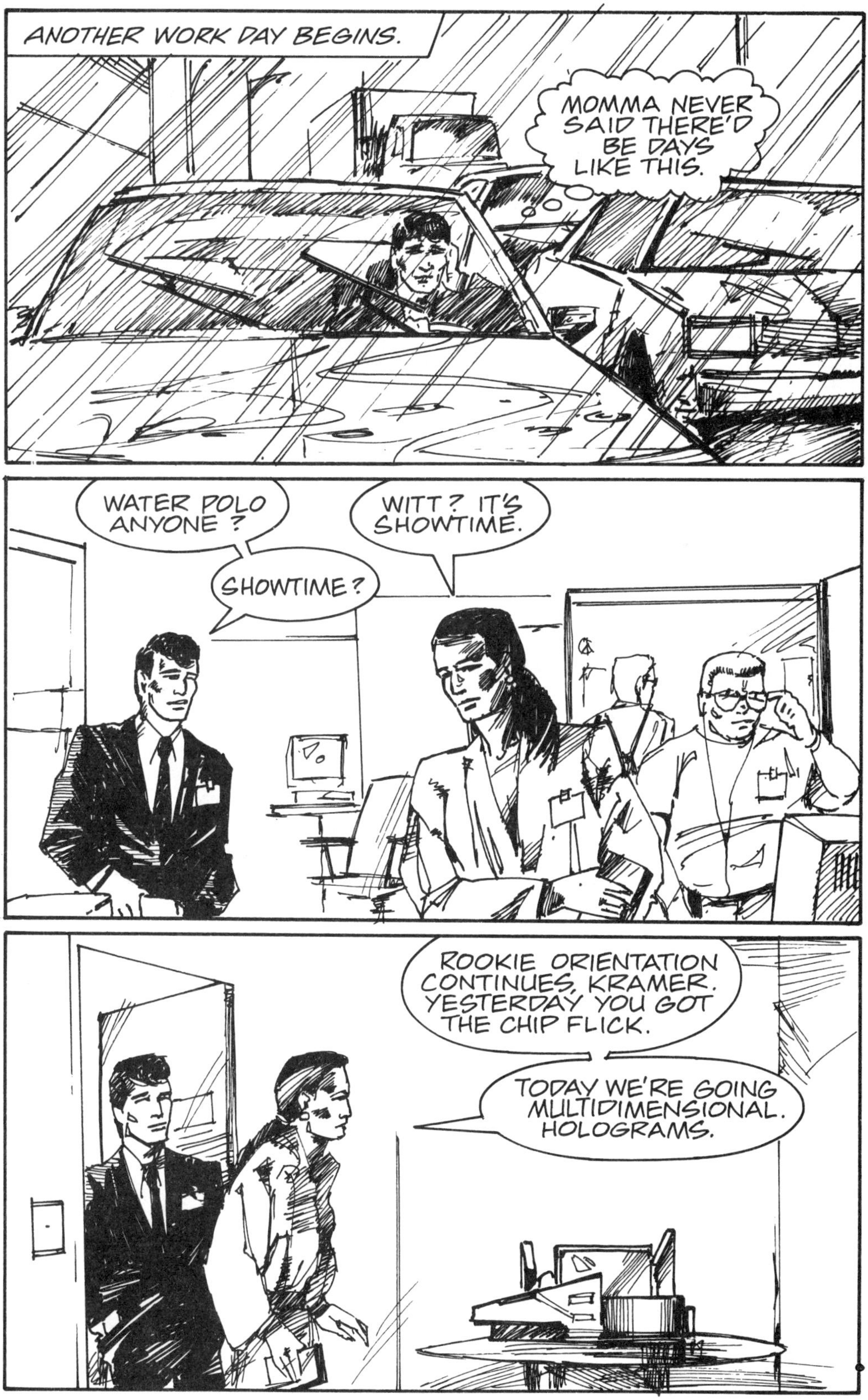
ANOTHER WORK DAY BEGINS.
MOMMA NEVER SAID THERE'D BE DAYS LIKE THIS.
WATER POLO ANYONE ?
WITT ? IT'S SHOWTIME.
SHOWTIME ?
ROOKIE ORIENTATION CONTINUES, KRAMER. YESTERDAY YOU GOT THE CHIP FLICK.
TODAY WE'RE GOING MULTIDIMENSIONAL. HOLOGRAMS.

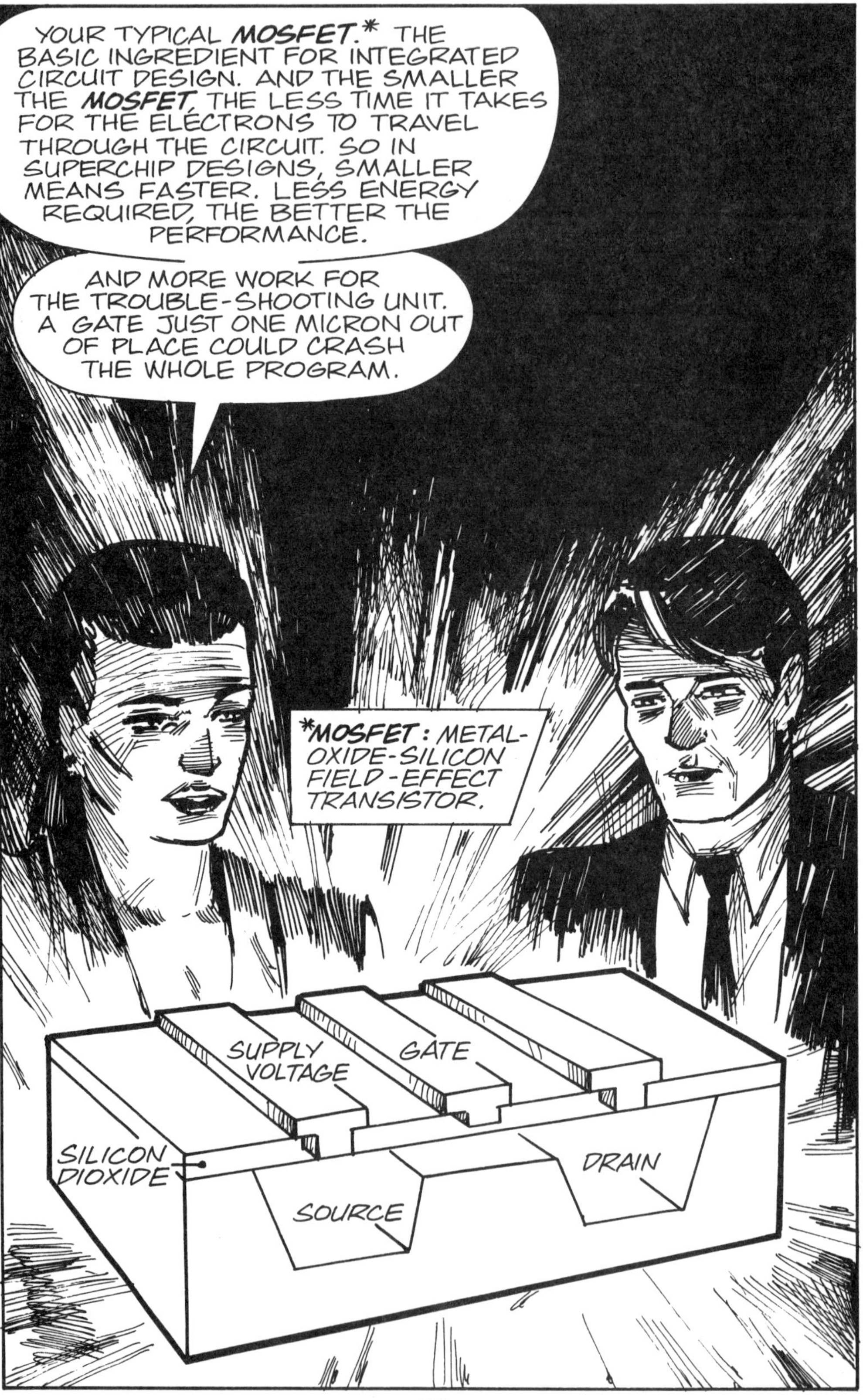
YOUR TYPICAL MOSFET.* THE BASIC INGREDIENT FOR INTEGRATED CIRCUIT DESIGN. AND THE SMALLER THE MOSFET, THE LESS TIME IT TAKES FOR THE ELECTRONS TO TRAVEL THROUGH THE CIRCUIT. SO IN SUPERCHIP DESIGNS, SMALLER MEANS FASTER. LESS ENERGY REQUIRED, THE BETTER THE PERFORMANCE.
AND MORE WORK FOR THE TROUBLE-SHOOTING UNIT. A GATE JUST ONE MICRON OUT OF PLACE COULD CRASH THE WHOLE PROGRAM.
*MOSFET: METAL-OXIDE-SILICON FIELD-EFFECT TRANSISTOR.
SUPPLY VOLTAGE
GATE
SILICON DIOXIDE
DRAIN
SOURCE

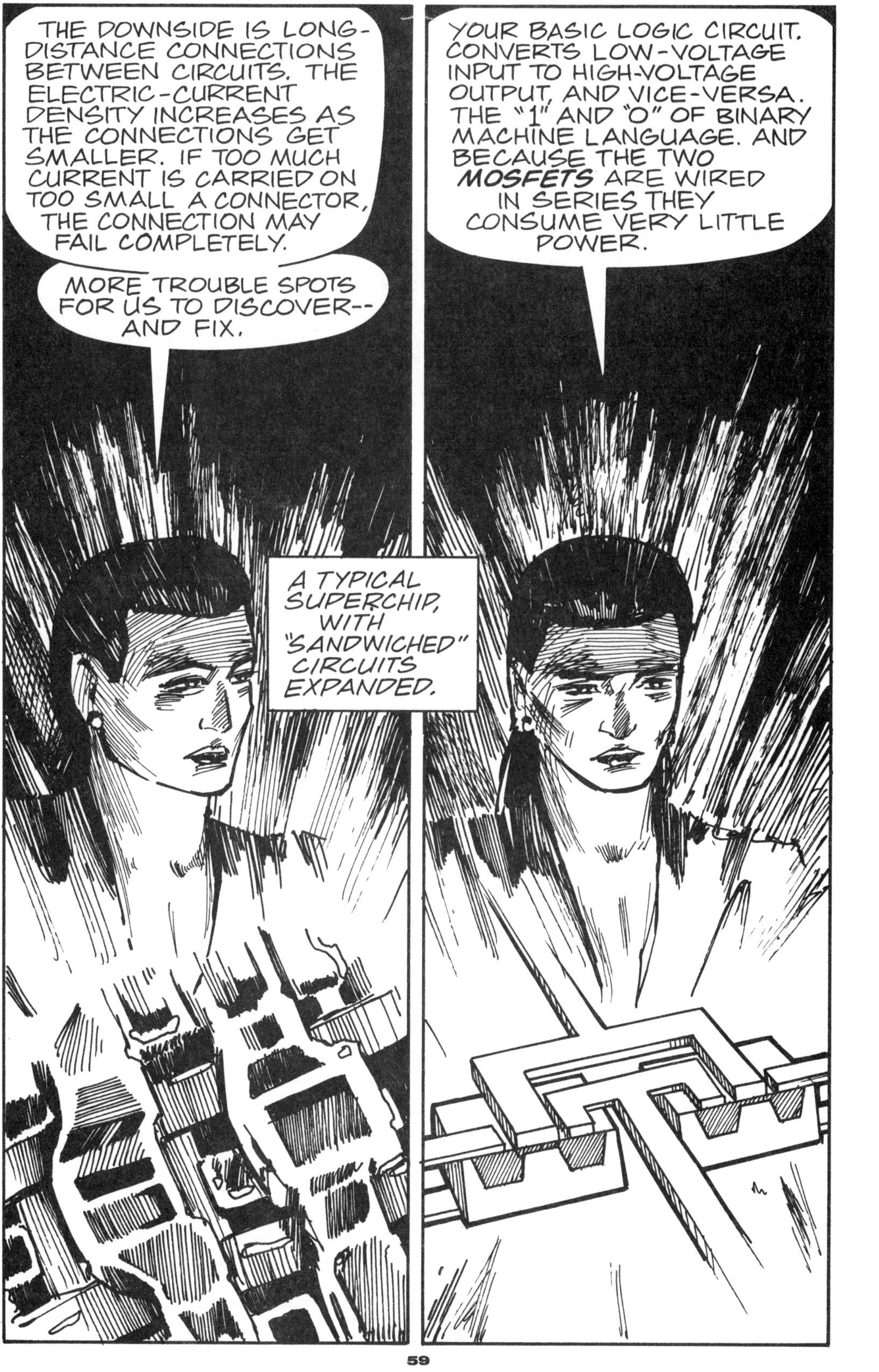
THE DOWNSIDE IS LONG-DISTANCE CONNECTIONS BETWEEN CIRCUITS. THE ELECTRIC-CURRENT DENSITY INCREASES AS THE CONNECTIONS GET SMALLER. IF TOO MUCH CURRENT IS CARRIED ON TOO SMALL A CONNECTOR, THE CONNECTION MAY FAIL COMPLETELY.
MORE TROUBLE SPOTS FOR US TO DISCOVER-- AND FIX.
A TYPICAL SUPERCHIP, WITH "SANDWICHED" CIRCUITS EXPANDED.
YOUR BASIC LOGIC CIRCUIT. CONVERTS LOW-VOLTAGE INPUT TO HIGH-VOLTAGE OUTPUT, AND VICE-VERSA. THE "1" AND "0" OF BINARY MACHINE LANGUAGE. AND BECAUSE THE TWO MOSFETS ARE WIRED IN SERIES THEY CONSUME VERY LITTLE POWER.

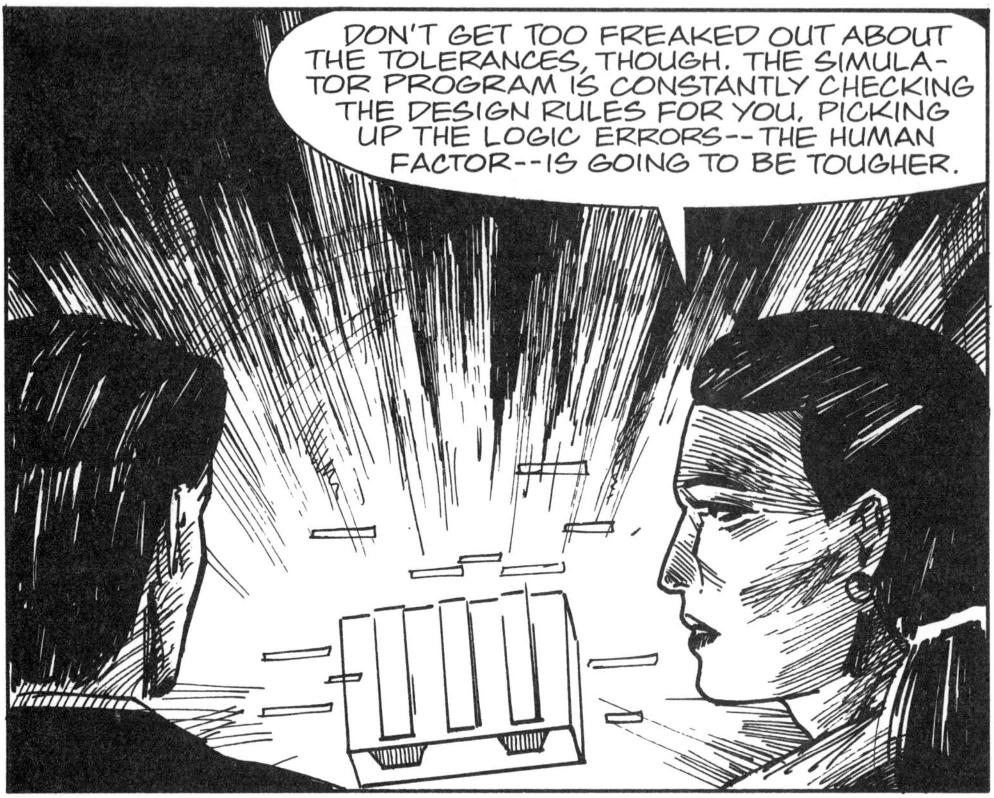
DON'T GET TOO FREAKED OUT ABOUT THE TOLERANCES, THOUGH. THE SIMULATOR PROGRAM IS CONSTANTLY CHECKING THE DESIGN RULES FOR YOU, PICKING UP THE LOGIC ERRORS--THE HUMAN FACTOR--IS GOING TO BE TOUGHER.

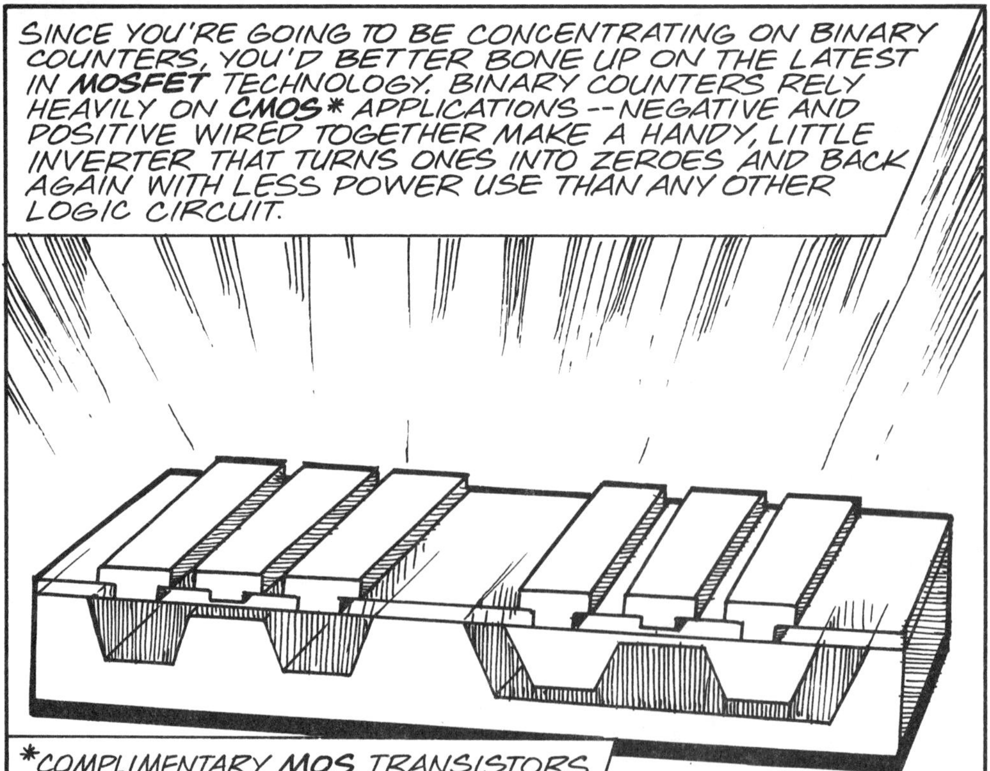
SINCE YOU'RE GOING TO BE CONCENTRATING ON BINARY COUNTERS, YOU'D BETTER BONE UP ON THE LATEST IN **MOSFET** TECHNOLOGY. BINARY COUNTERS RELY HEAVILY ON **CMOS*** APPLICATIONS--NEGATIVE AND POSITIVE WIRED TOGETHER MAKE A HANDY, LITTLE INVERTER THAT TURNS ONES INTO ZEROES AND BACK AGAIN WITH LESS POWER USE THAN ANY OTHER LOGIC CIRCUIT.
*COMPLIMENTARY **MOS** TRANSISTORS.

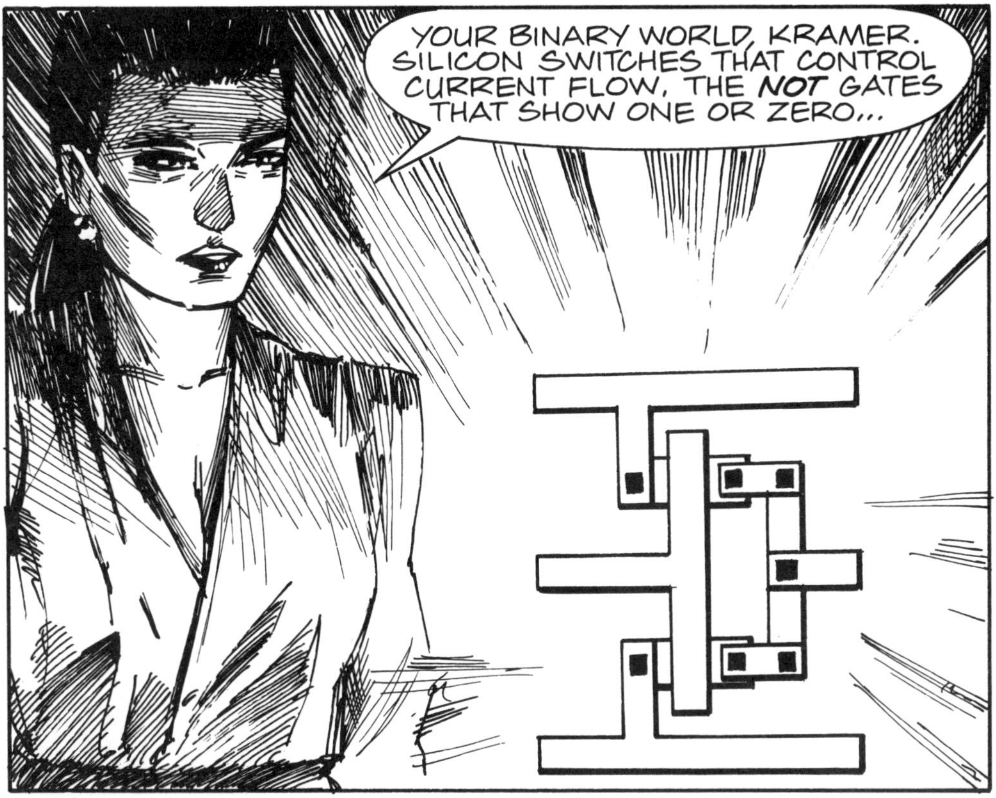
YOUR BINARY WORLD, KRAMER. SILICON SWITCHES THAT CONTROL CURRENT FLOW, THE **NOT** GATES THAT SHOW ONE OR ZERO...

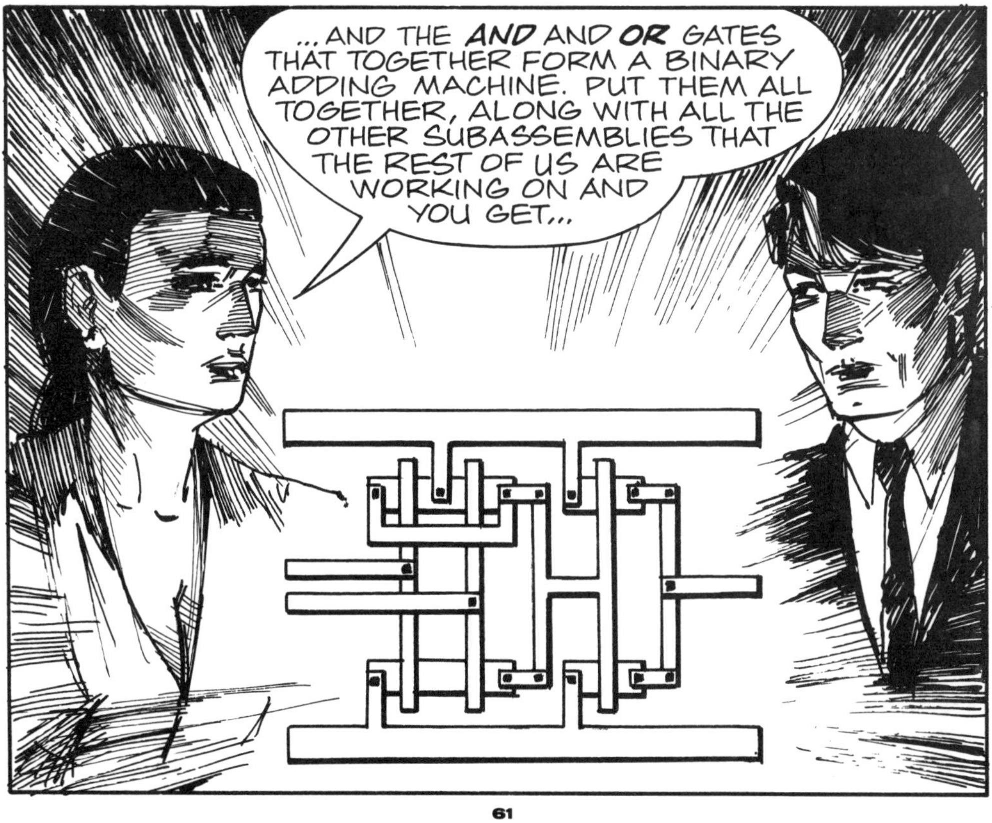
...AND THE **AND** AND **OR** GATES THAT TOGETHER FORM A BINARY ADDING MACHINE. PUT THEM ALL TOGETHER, ALONG WITH ALL THE OTHER SUBASSEMBLIES THAT THE REST OF US ARE WORKING ON AND YOU GET...

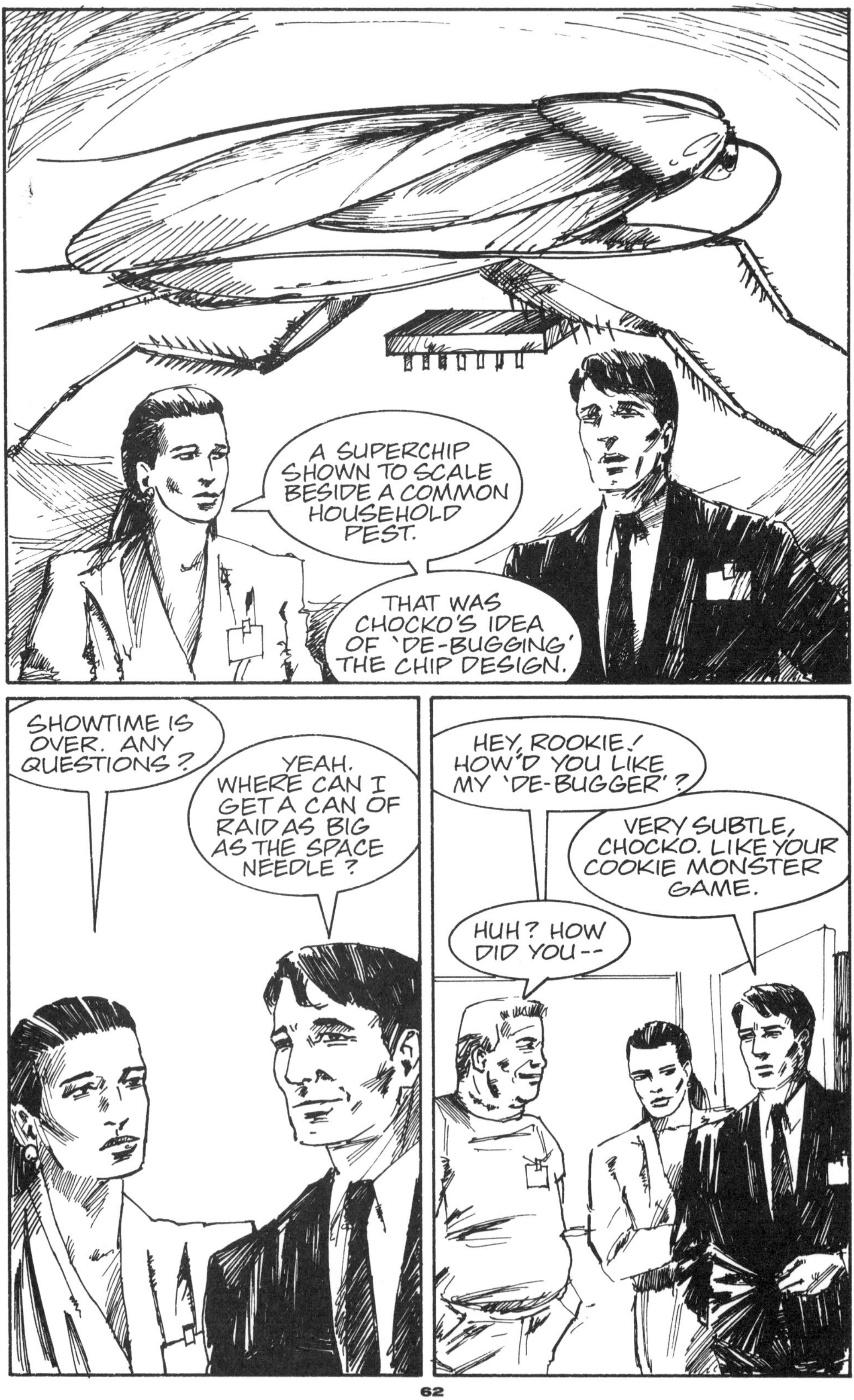
A SUPERCHIP SHOWN TO SCALE BESIDE A COMMON HOUSEHOLD PEST.
THAT WAS CHOCKO'S IDEA OF 'DE-BUGGING' THE CHIP DESIGN.
SHOWTIME IS OVER. ANY QUESTIONS?
YEAH. WHERE CAN I GET A CAN OF RAID AS BIG AS THE SPACE NEEDLE?
HEY, ROOKIE! HOW'D YOU LIKE MY 'DE-BUGGER'?
VERY SUBTLE, CHOCKO. LIKE YOUR COOKIE MONSTER GAME.
HUH? HOW DID YOU--

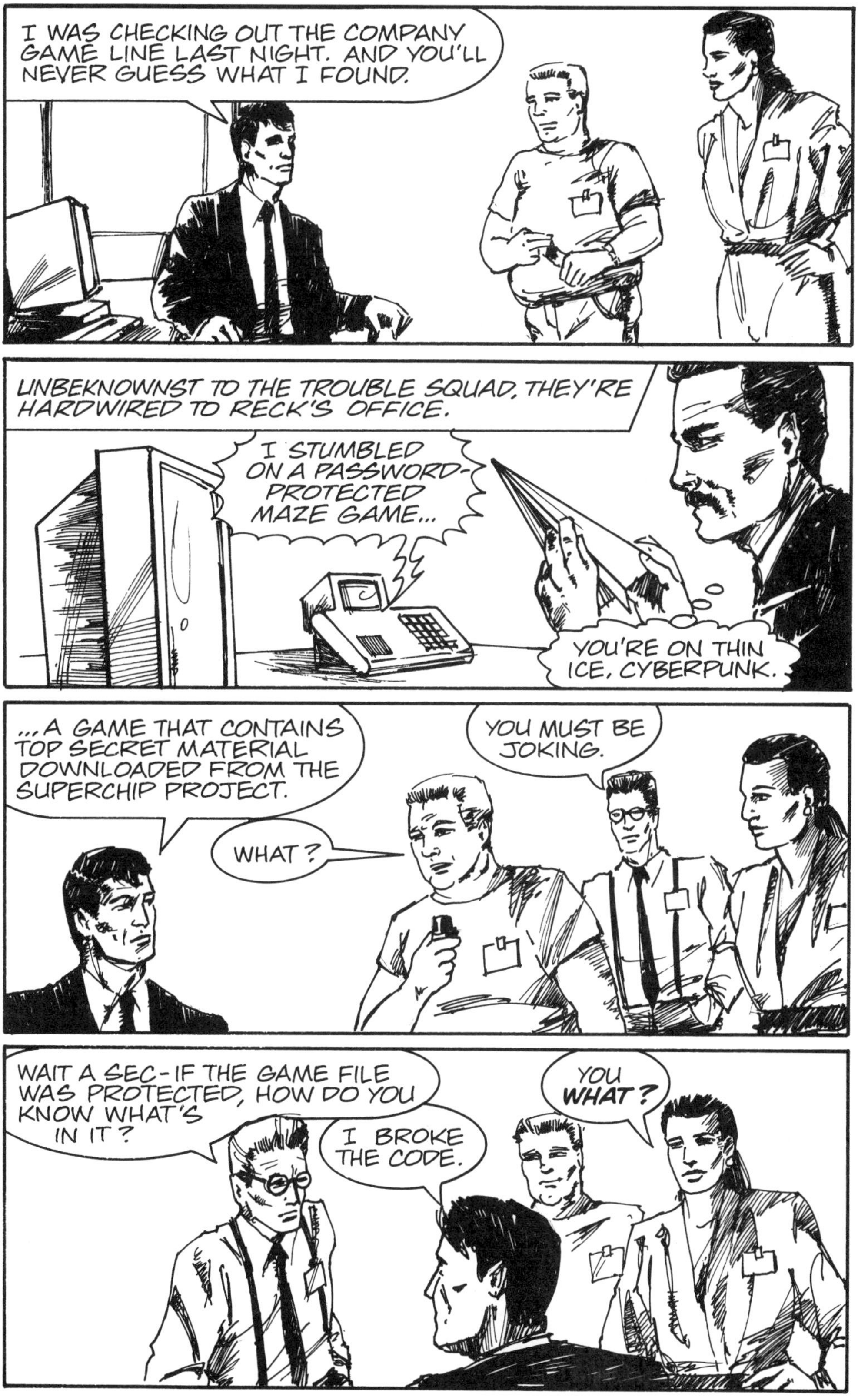
I WAS CHECKING OUT THE COMPANY GAME LINE LAST NIGHT. AND YOU'LL NEVER GUESS WHAT I FOUND.
UNBEKNOWNST TO THE TROUBLE SQUAD, THEY'RE HARDWIRED TO RECK'S OFFICE.
I STUMBLED ON A PASSWORD-PROTECTED MAZE GAME...
YOU'RE ON THIN ICE, CYBERPUNK.
...A GAME THAT CONTAINS TOP SECRET MATERIAL DOWNLOADED FROM THE SUPERCHIP PROJECT.
YOU MUST BE JOKING.
WHAT?
WAIT A SEC-IF THE GAME FILE WAS PROTECTED, HOW DO YOU KNOW WHAT'S IN IT?
I BROKE THE CODE.
YOU **WHAT?**

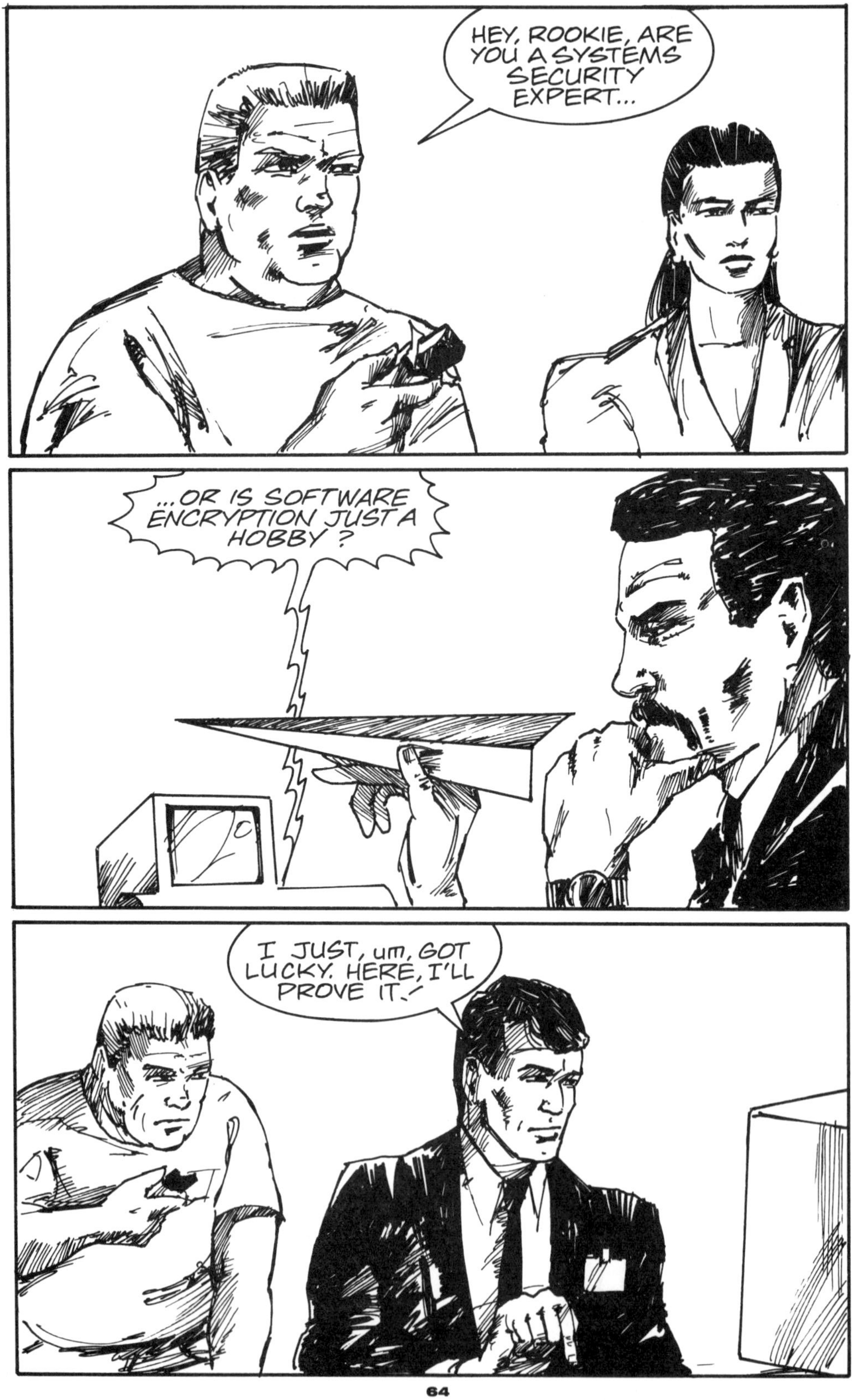
HEY, ROOKIE, ARE YOU A SYSTEMS SECURITY EXPERT...
...OR IS SOFTWARE ENCRYPTION JUST A HOBBY ?
I JUST, um, GOT LUCKY. HERE, I'LL PROVE IT.

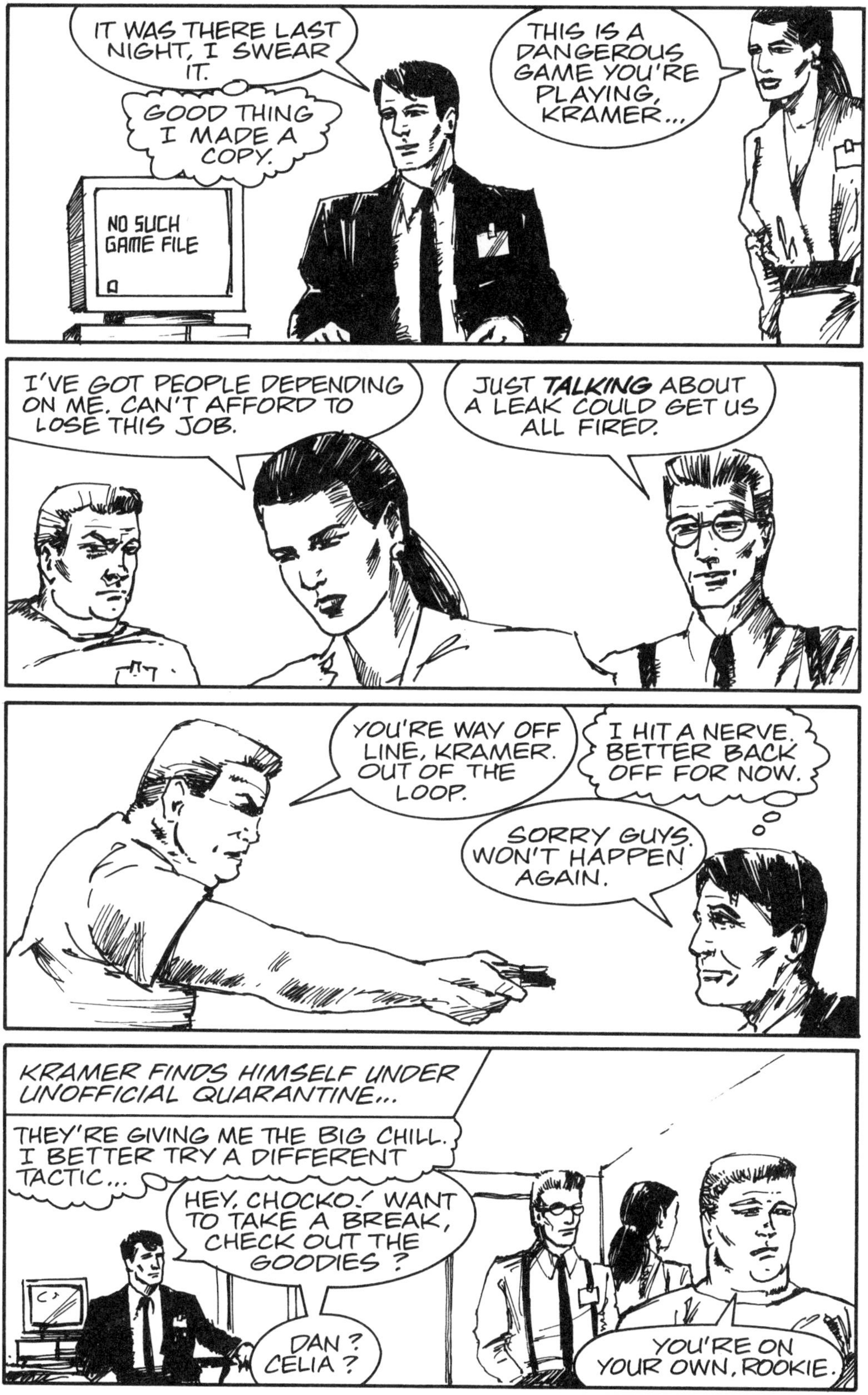
IT WAS THERE LAST NIGHT, I SWEAR IT.
GOOD THING I MADE A COPY.
NO SUCH GAME FILE
THIS IS A DANGEROUS GAME YOU'RE PLAYING, KRAMER...
I'VE GOT PEOPLE DEPENDING ON ME. CAN'T AFFORD TO LOSE THIS JOB.
JUST **TALKING** ABOUT A LEAK COULD GET US ALL FIRED.
YOU'RE WAY OFF LINE, KRAMER. OUT OF THE LOOP.
I HIT A NERVE. BETTER BACK OFF FOR NOW.
SORRY GUYS. WON'T HAPPEN AGAIN.
KRAMER FINDS HIMSELF UNDER UNOFFICIAL QUARANTINE...
THEY'RE GIVING ME THE BIG CHILL. I BETTER TRY A DIFFERENT TACTIC...
HEY, CHOCKO! WANT TO TAKE A BREAK, CHECK OUT THE GOODIES?
DAN? CELIA?
YOU'RE ON YOUR OWN, ROOKIE.

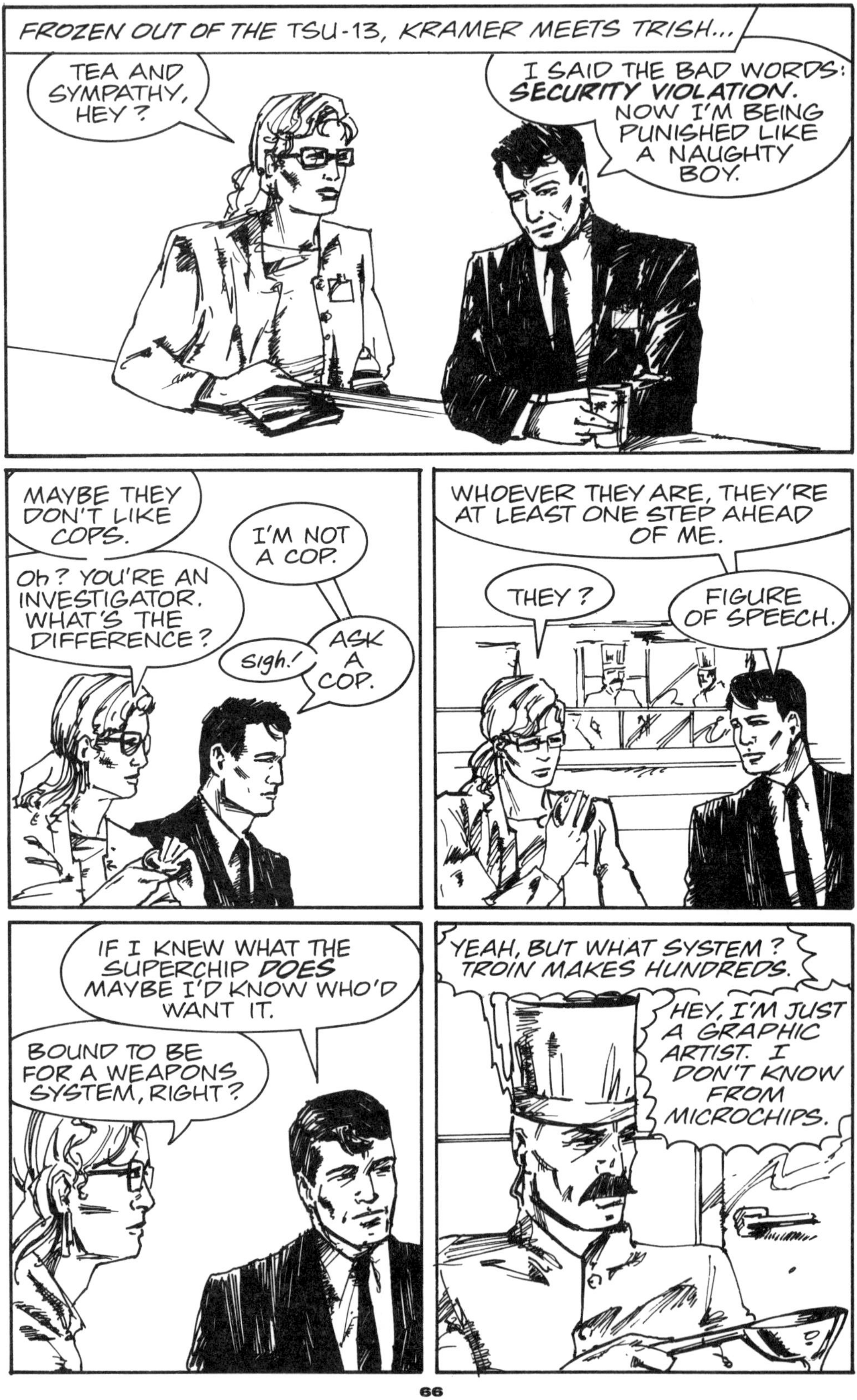
FROZEN OUT OF THE TSU-13, KRAMER MEETS TRISH...
TEA AND SYMPATHY, HEY?
I SAID THE BAD WORDS: **SECURITY VIOLATION.** NOW I'M BEING PUNISHED LIKE A NAUGHTY BOY.
MAYBE THEY DON'T LIKE COPS.
I'M NOT A COP.
Oh? YOU'RE AN INVESTIGATOR. WHAT'S THE DIFFERENCE?
Sigh.!
ASK A COP.
WHOEVER THEY ARE, THEY'RE AT LEAST ONE STEP AHEAD OF ME.
THEY?
FIGURE OF SPEECH.
IF I KNEW WHAT THE SUPERCHIP **DOES** MAYBE I'D KNOW WHO'D WANT IT.
BOUND TO BE FOR A WEAPONS SYSTEM, RIGHT?
YEAH, BUT WHAT SYSTEM? TROIN MAKES HUNDREDS.
HEY, I'M JUST A GRAPHIC ARTIST. I DON'T KNOW FROM MICROCHIPS.

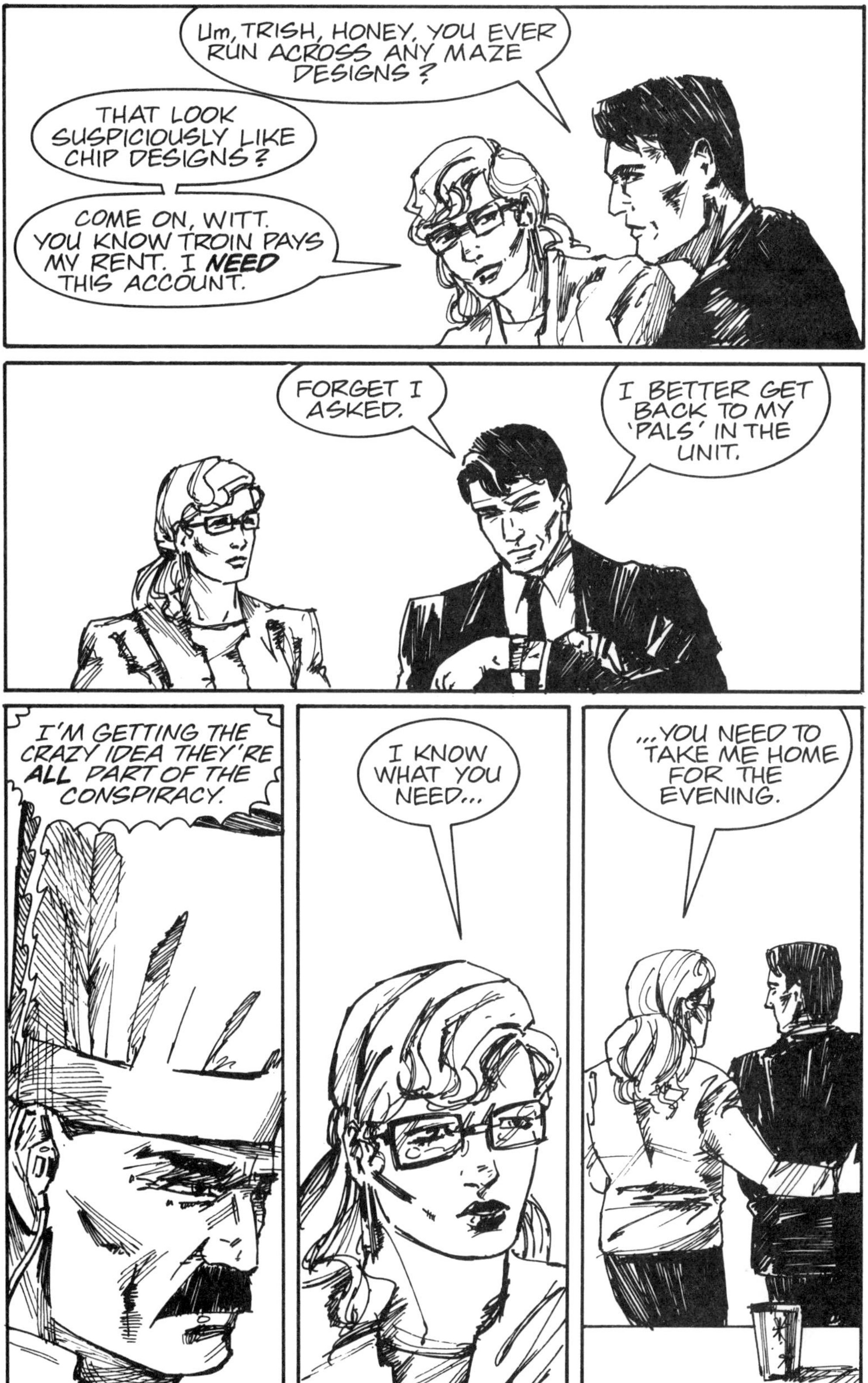
Um, TRISH, HONEY, YOU EVER RUN ACROSS ANY MAZE DESIGNS?
THAT LOOK SUSPICIOUSLY LIKE CHIP DESIGNS?
COME ON, WITT. YOU KNOW TROIN PAYS MY RENT. I NEED THIS ACCOUNT.
FORGET I ASKED.
I BETTER GET BACK TO MY 'PALS' IN THE UNIT.
I'M GETTING THE CRAZY IDEA THEY'RE ALL PART OF THE CONSPIRACY.
I KNOW WHAT YOU NEED...
...YOU NEED TO TAKE ME HOME FOR THE EVENING.

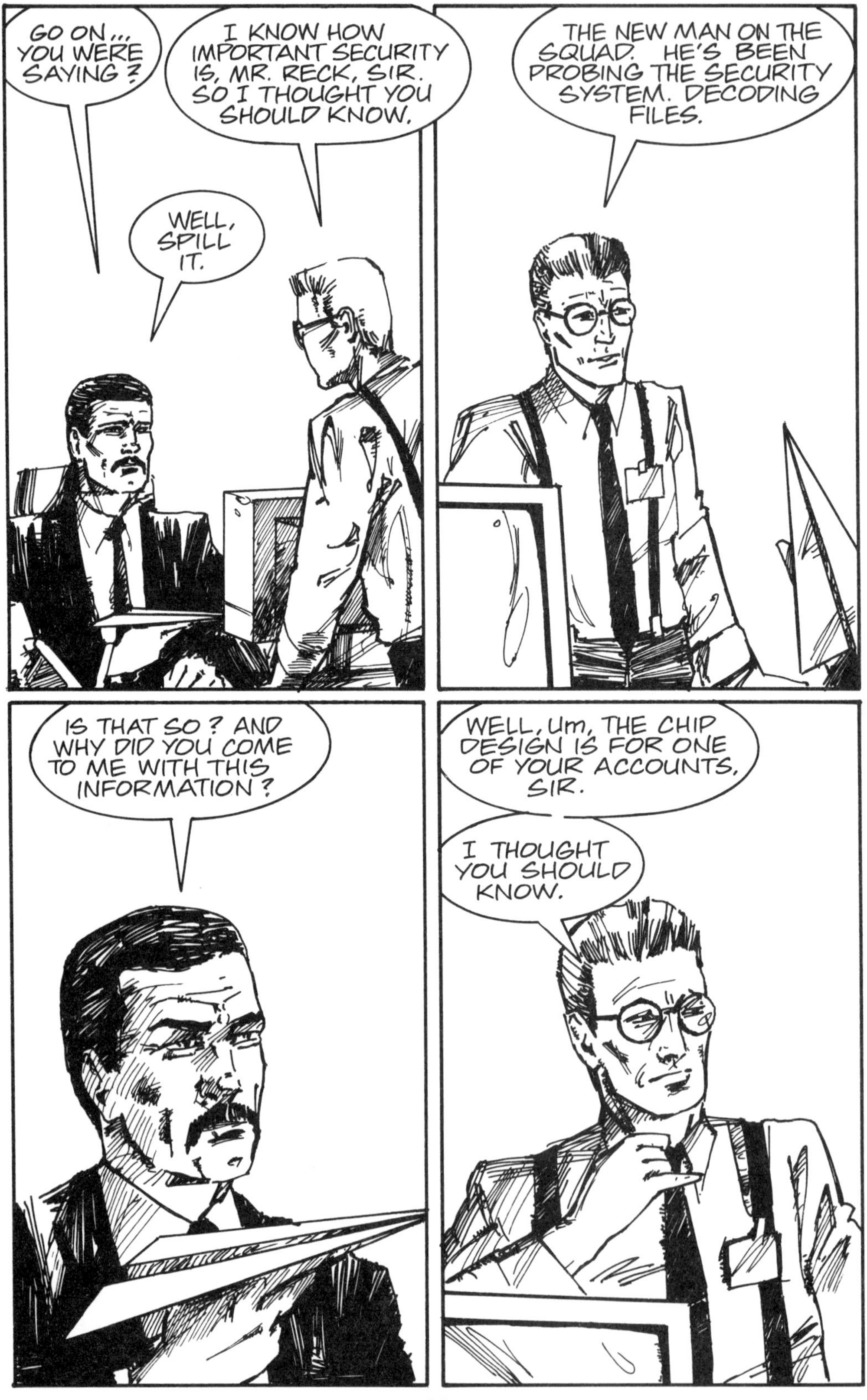
GO ON... YOU WERE SAYING?
I KNOW HOW IMPORTANT SECURITY IS, MR. RECK, SIR. SO I THOUGHT YOU SHOULD KNOW.
WELL, SPILL IT.
THE NEW MAN ON THE SQUAD. HE'S BEEN PROBING THE SECURITY SYSTEM. DECODING FILES.
IS THAT SO? AND WHY DID YOU COME TO ME WITH THIS INFORMATION?
WELL, Um, THE CHIP DESIGN IS FOR ONE OF YOUR ACCOUNTS, SIR.
I THOUGHT YOU SHOULD KNOW.

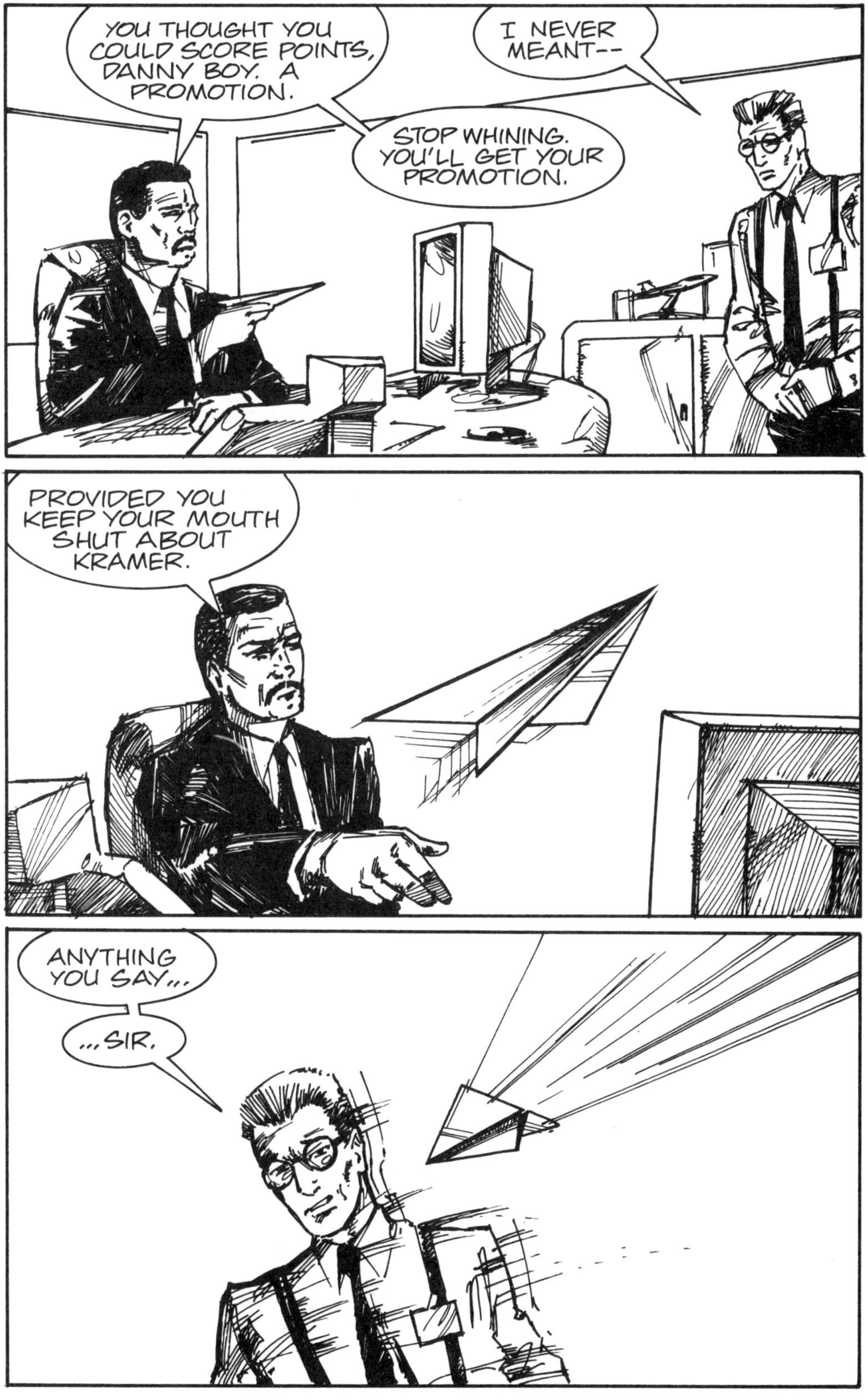
YOU THOUGHT YOU COULD SCORE POINTS, DANNY BOY. A PROMOTION.
I NEVER MEANT--
STOP WHINING. YOU'LL GET YOUR PROMOTION.
PROVIDED YOU KEEP YOUR MOUTH SHUT ABOUT KRAMER.
ANYTHING YOU SAY...
...SIR.

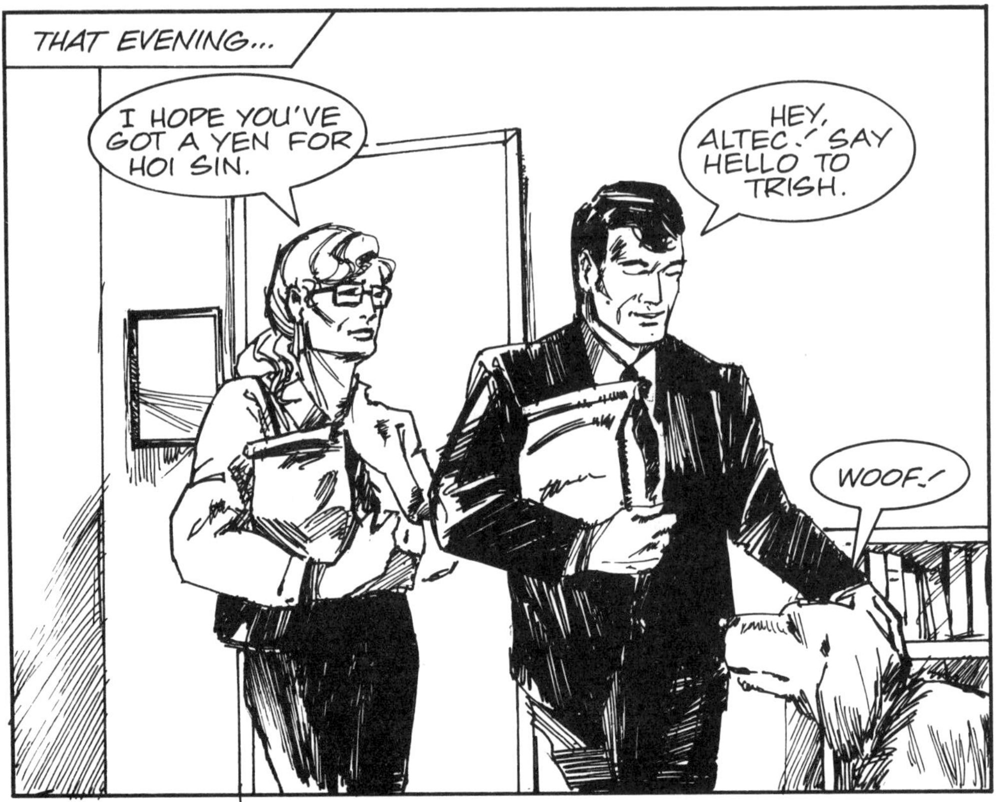
THAT EVENING...
I HOPE YOU'VE GOT A YEN FOR HOI SIN.
HEY, ALTEC.! SAY HELLO TO TRISH.
WOOF.!

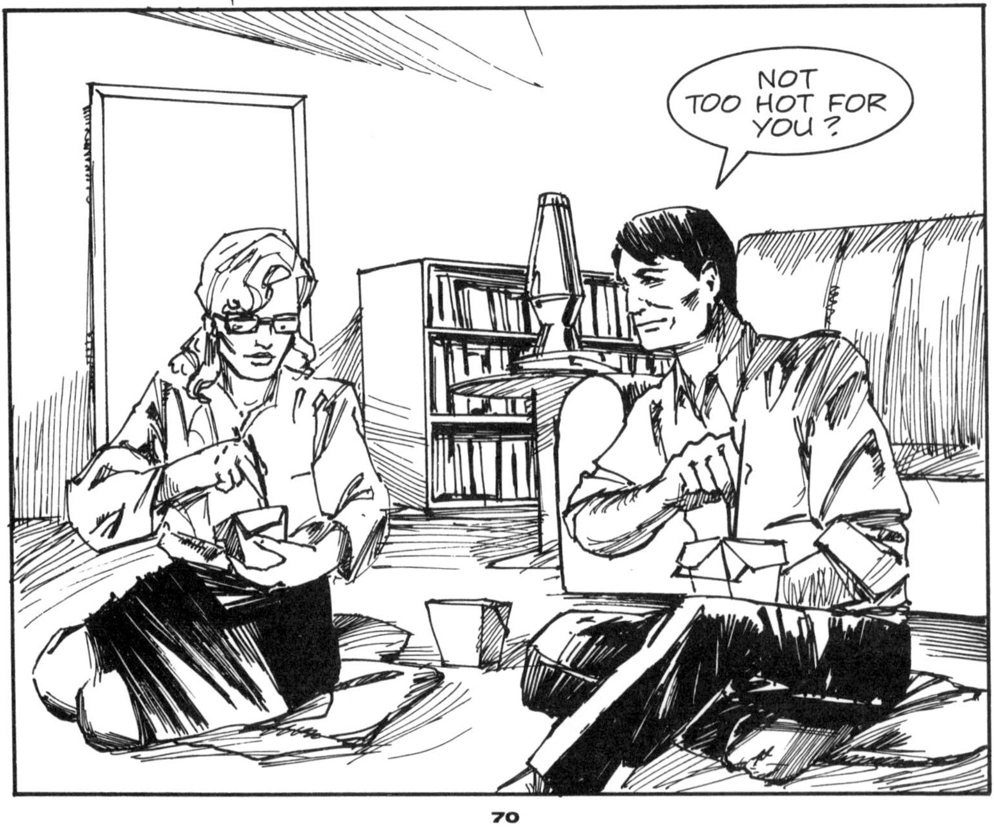
NOT TOO HOT FOR YOU ?

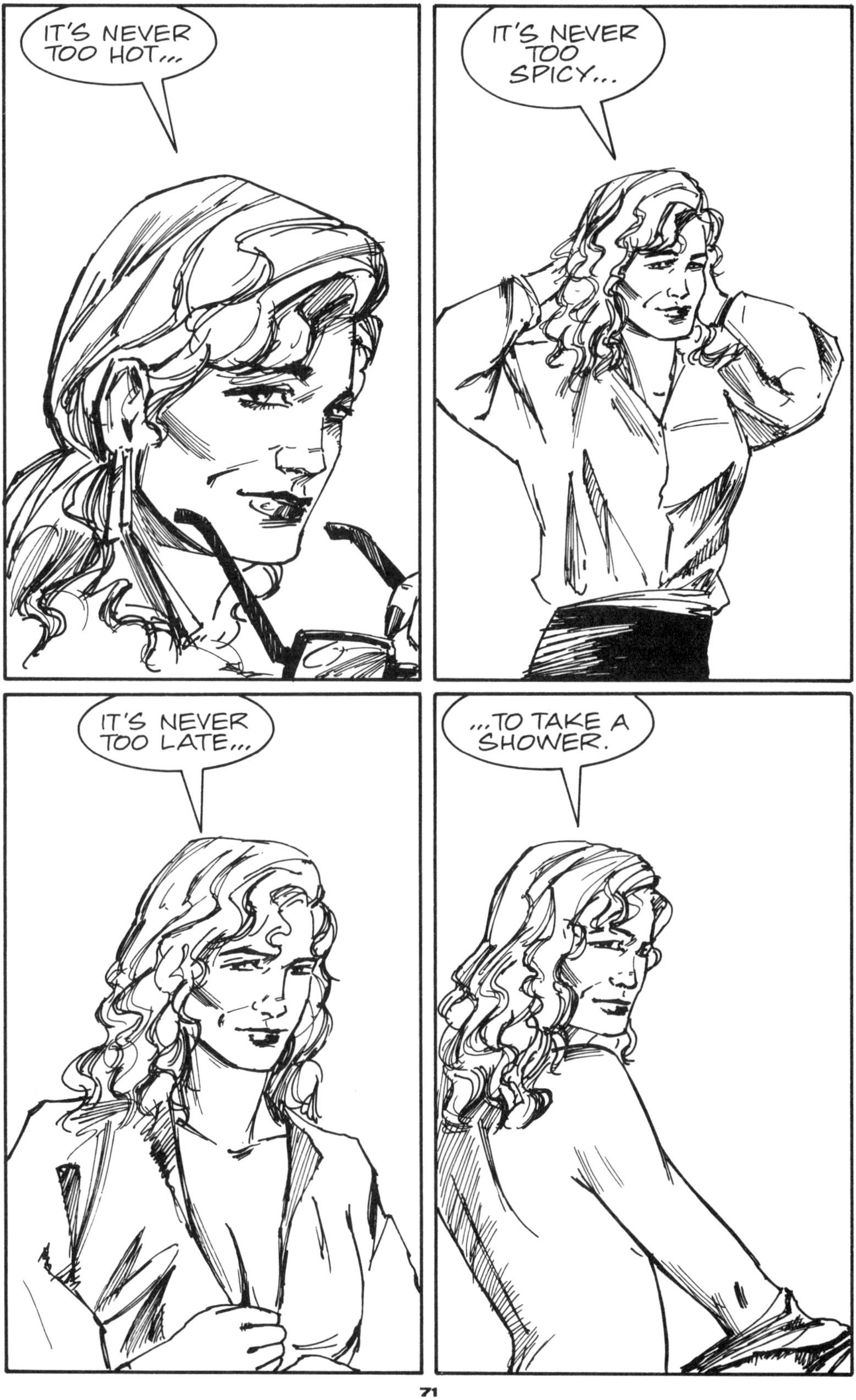
IT'S NEVER TOO HOT...
IT'S NEVER TOO SPICY...
IT'S NEVER TOO LATE...
...TO TAKE A SHOWER.

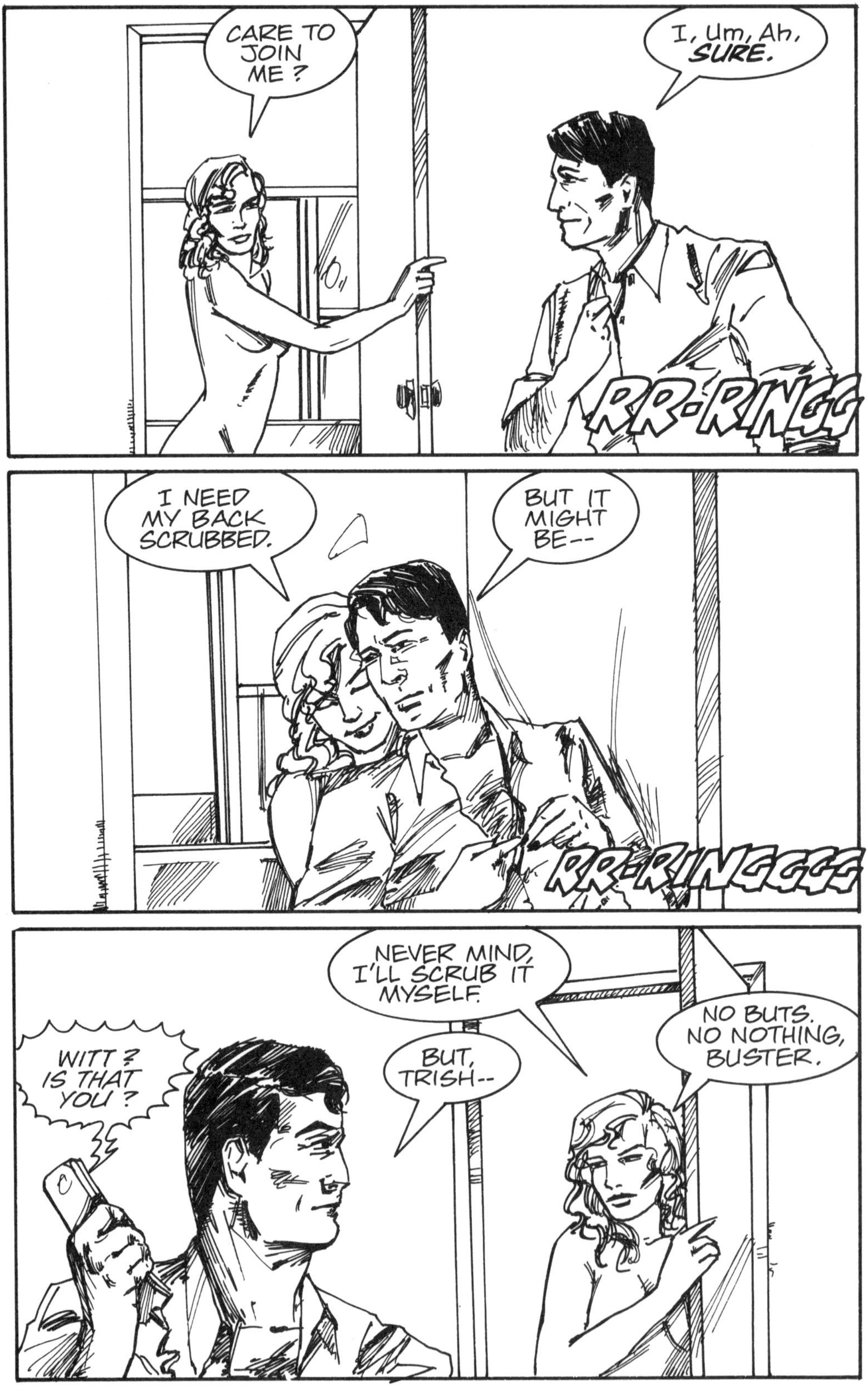
CARE TO JOIN ME ?
I, Um, Ah, SURE.
RR-RINGG
I NEED MY BACK SCRUBBED.
BUT IT MIGHT BE--
RR-RINGGGG
NEVER MIND, I'LL SCRUB IT MYSELF.
BUT, TRISH--
NO BUTS. NO NOTHING, BUSTER.
WITT ? IS THAT YOU ?

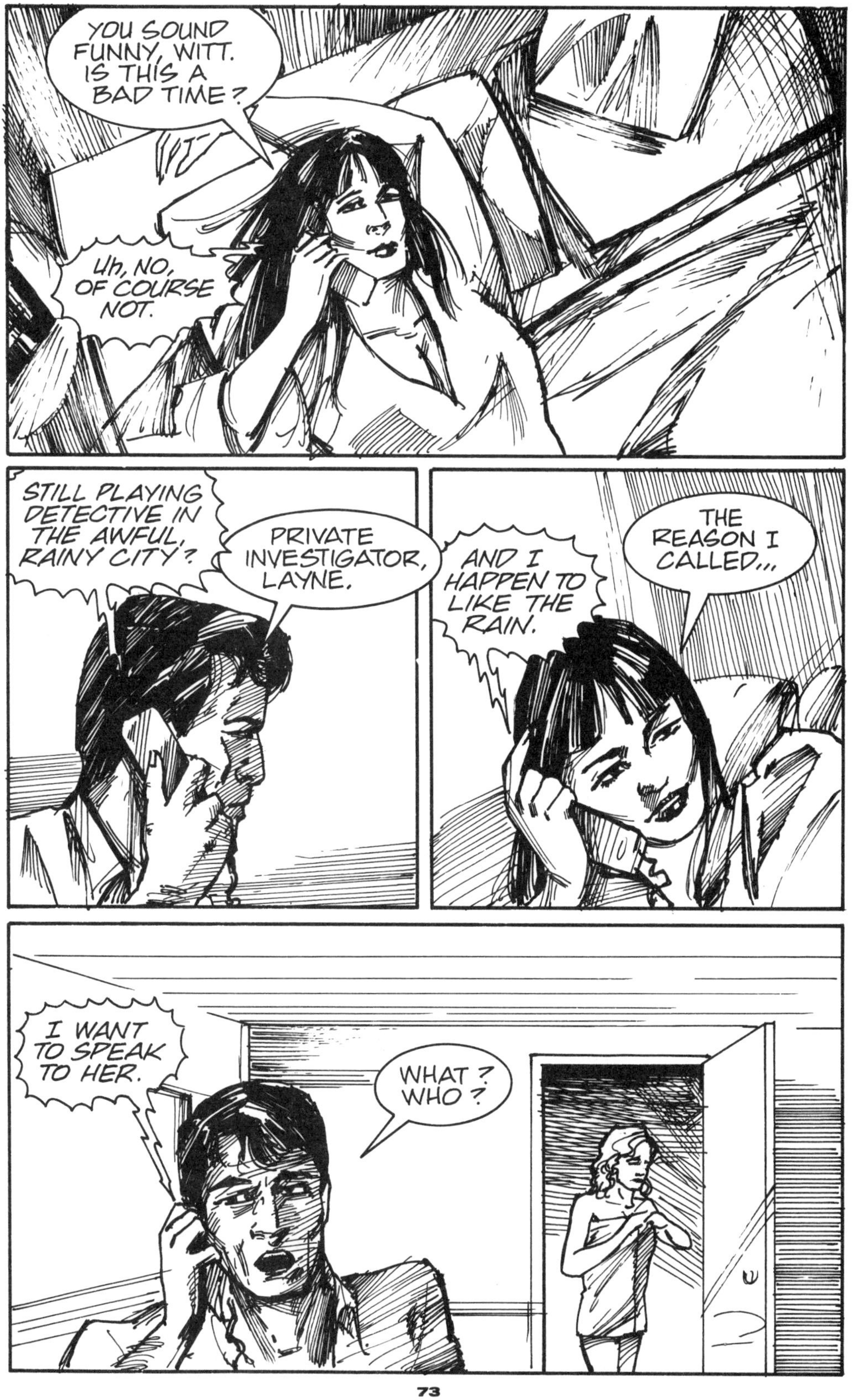
YOU SOUND FUNNY, WITT. IS THIS A BAD TIME?
Uh, NO, OF COURSE NOT.
STILL PLAYING DETECTIVE IN THE AWFUL, RAINY CITY?
PRIVATE INVESTIGATOR, LAYNE.
AND I HAPPEN TO LIKE THE RAIN.
THE REASON I CALLED...
I WANT TO SPEAK TO HER.
WHAT? WHO?

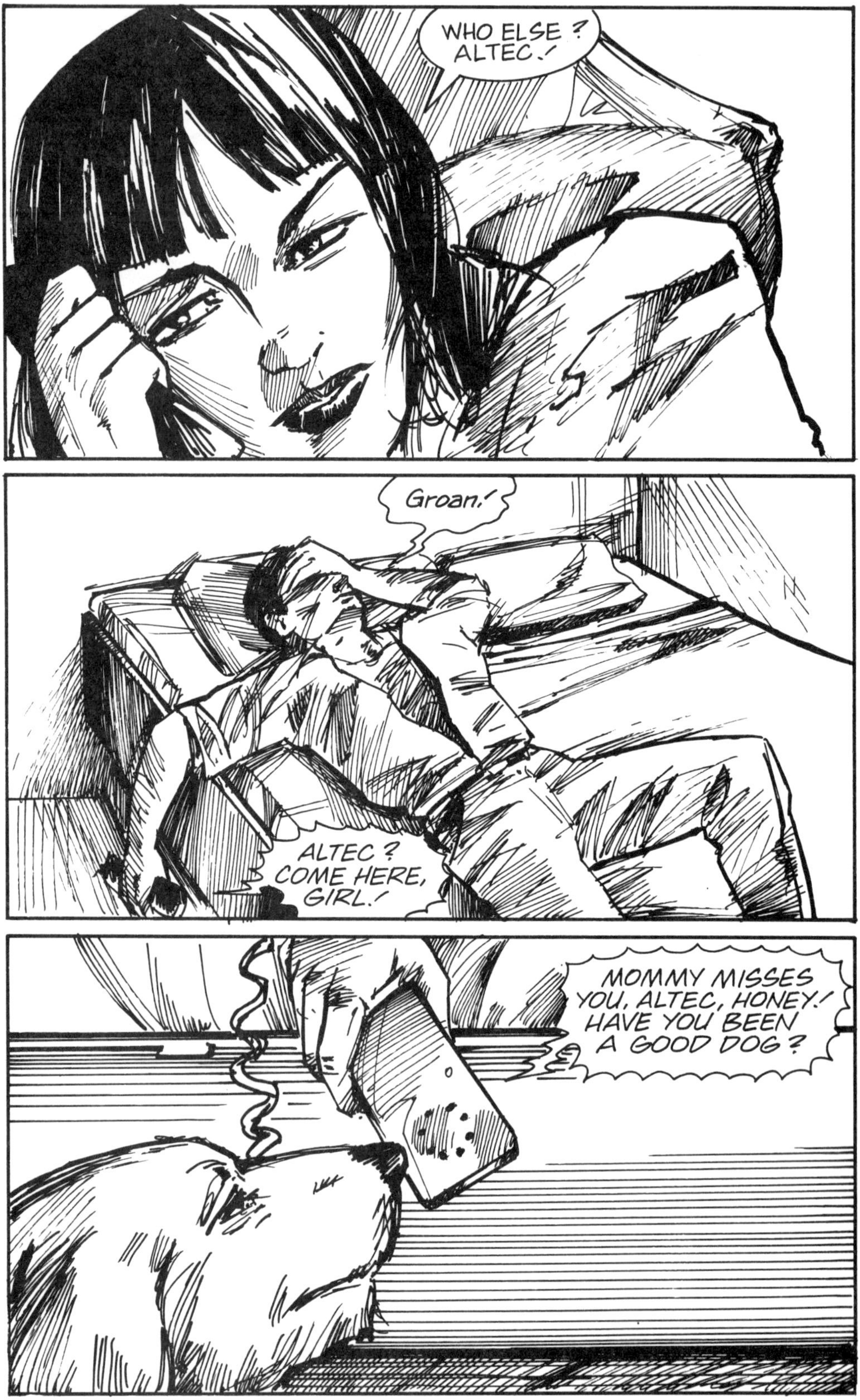

WHO ELSE ? ALTEC.!
Groan.!
ALTEC ? COME HERE, GIRL.!
MOMMY MISSES YOU, ALTEC, HONEY.! HAVE YOU BEEN A GOOD DOG ?

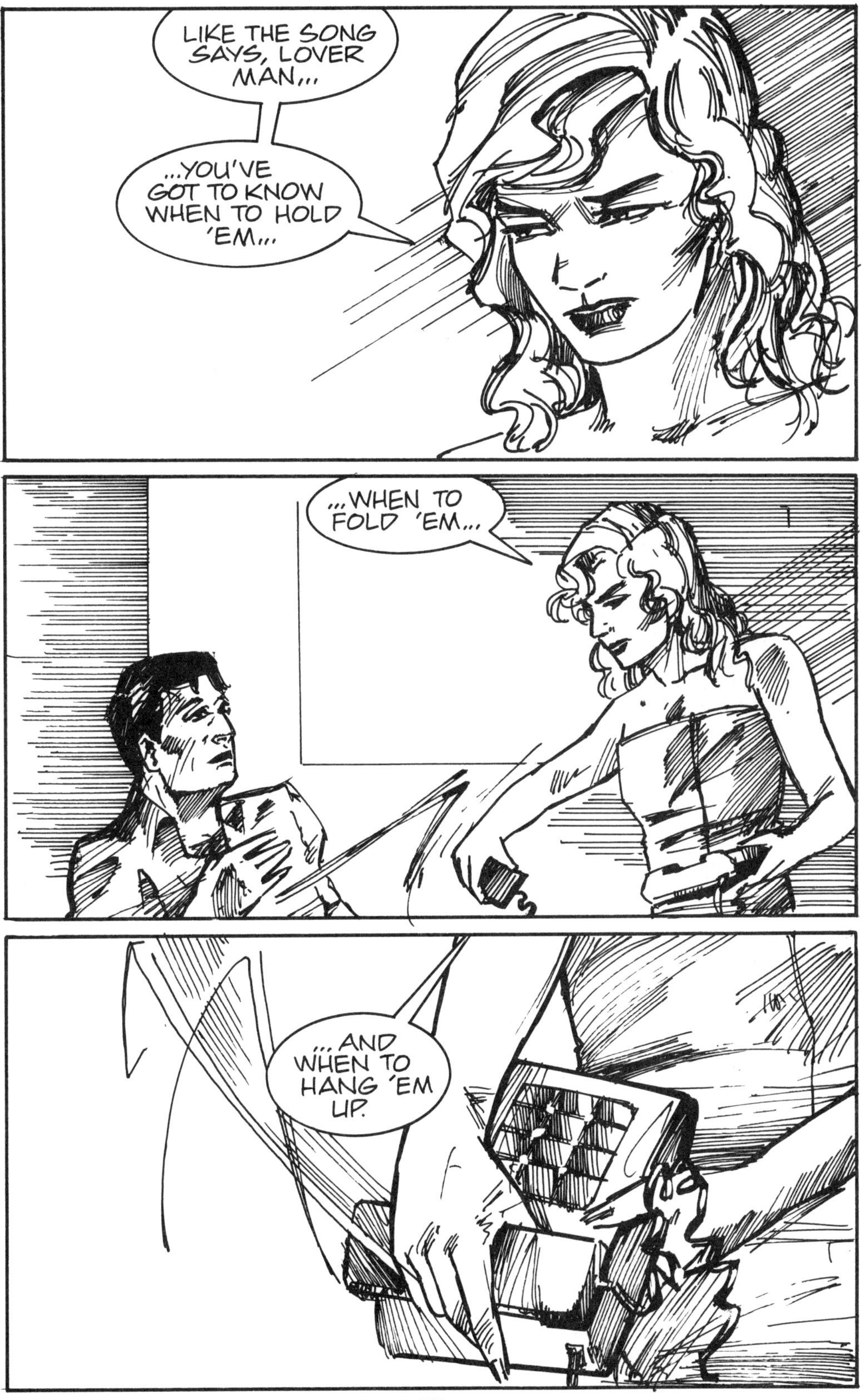
LIKE THE SONG SAYS, LOVER MAN...
...YOU'VE GOT TO KNOW WHEN TO HOLD 'EM...
...WHEN TO FOLD 'EM...
...AND WHEN TO HANG 'EM UP.

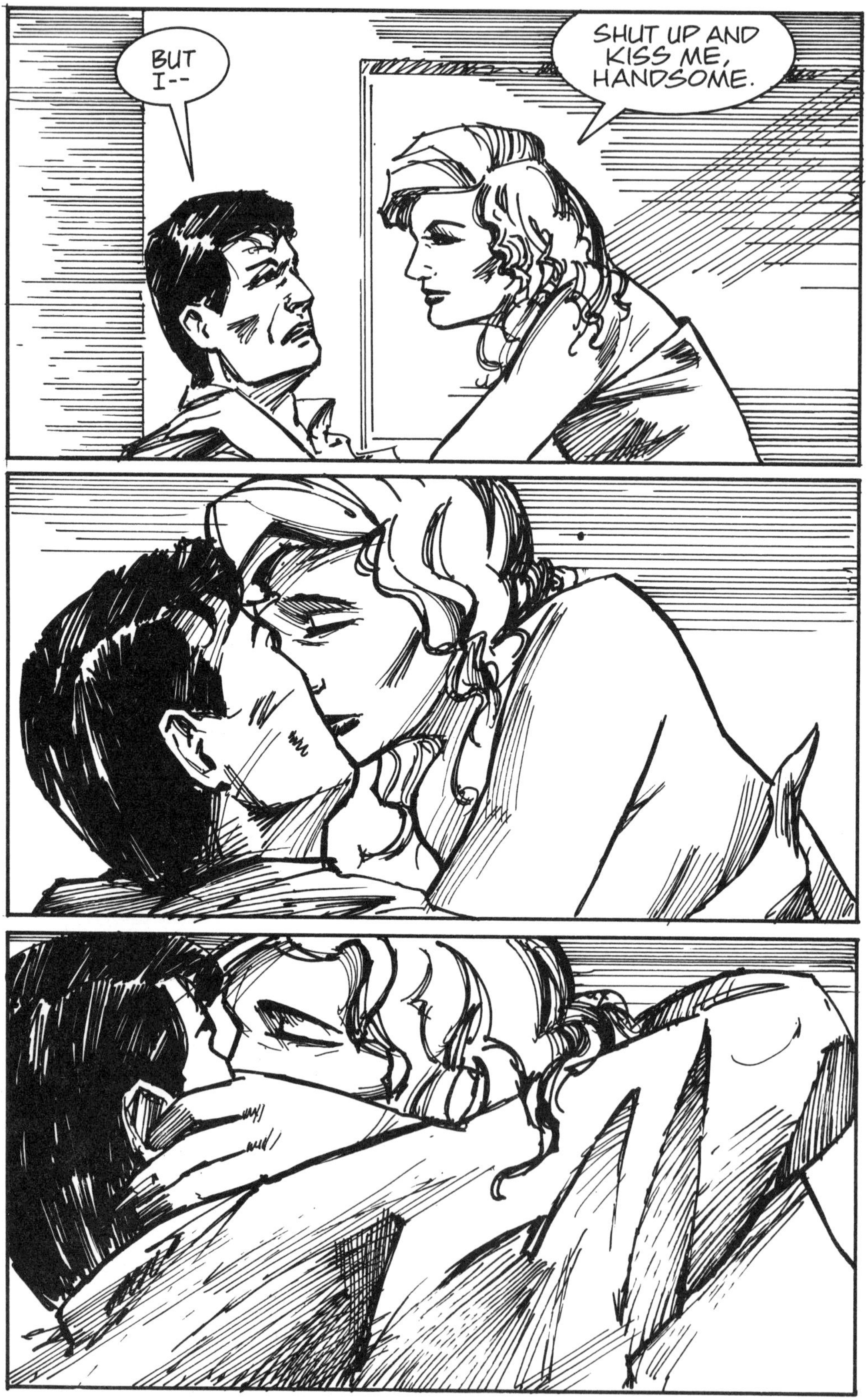
BUT I--
SHUT UP AND KISS ME, HANDSOME.

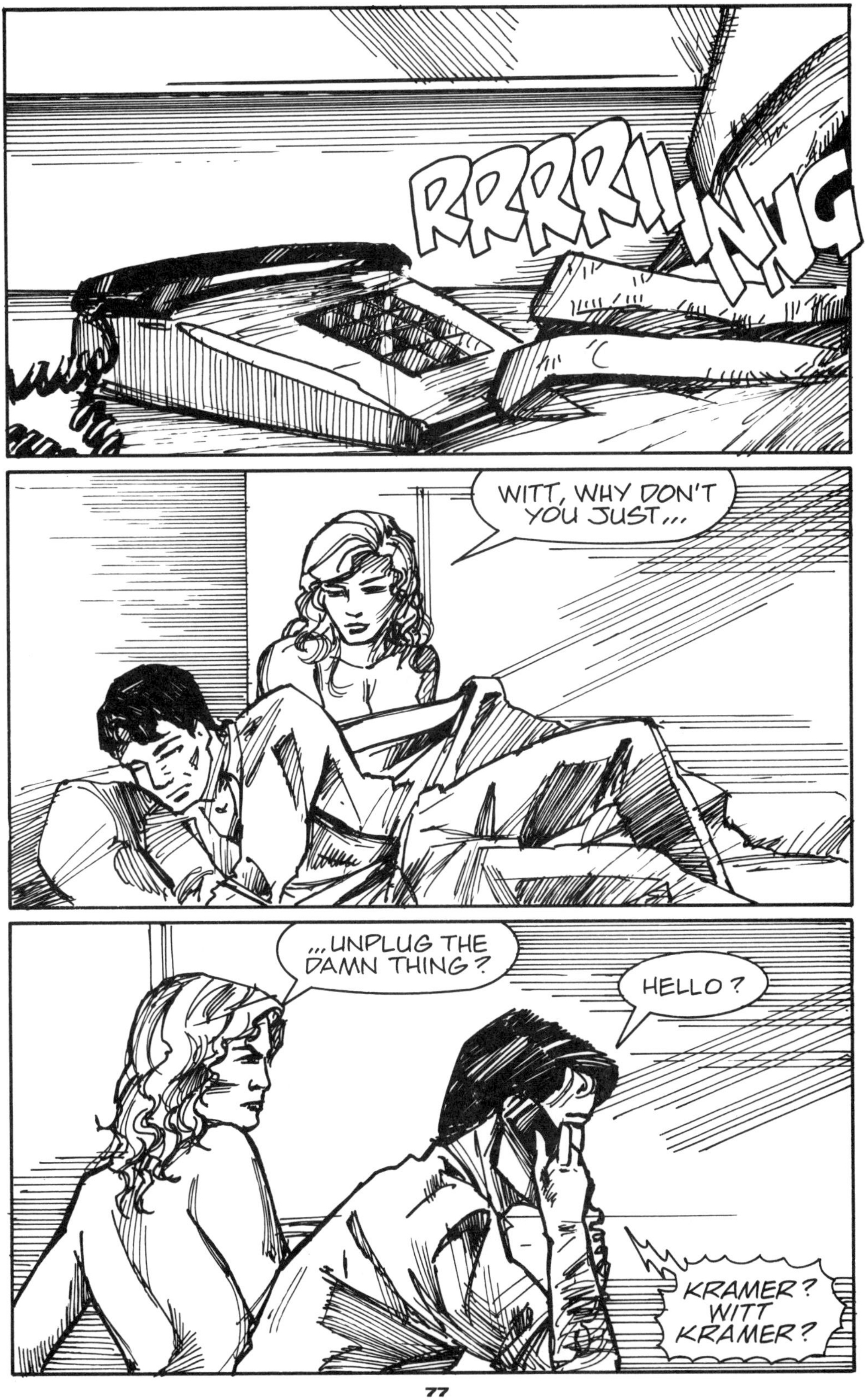
RRRRIINNG
WITT, WHY DON'T YOU JUST...
...UNPLUG THE DAMN THING?
HELLO?
KRAMER? WITT KRAMER?

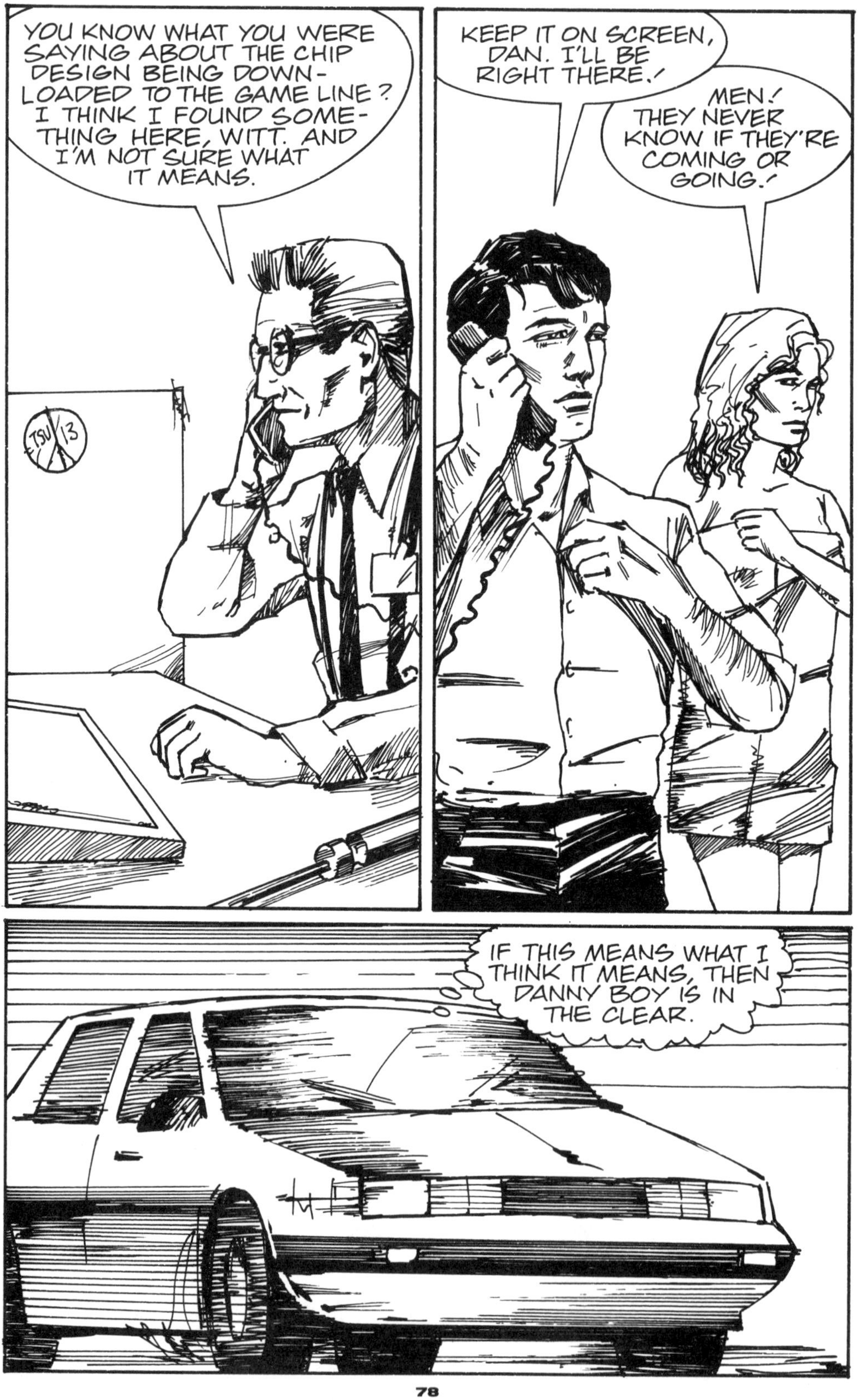
YOU KNOW WHAT YOU WERE SAYING ABOUT THE CHIP DESIGN BEING DOWN-LOADED TO THE GAME LINE? I THINK I FOUND SOME-THING HERE, WITT. AND I'M NOT SURE WHAT IT MEANS.
KEEP IT ON SCREEN, DAN. I'LL BE RIGHT THERE.!
MEN! THEY NEVER KNOW IF THEY'RE COMING OR GOING.!
IF THIS MEANS WHAT I THINK IT MEANS, THEN DANNY BOY IS IN THE CLEAR.

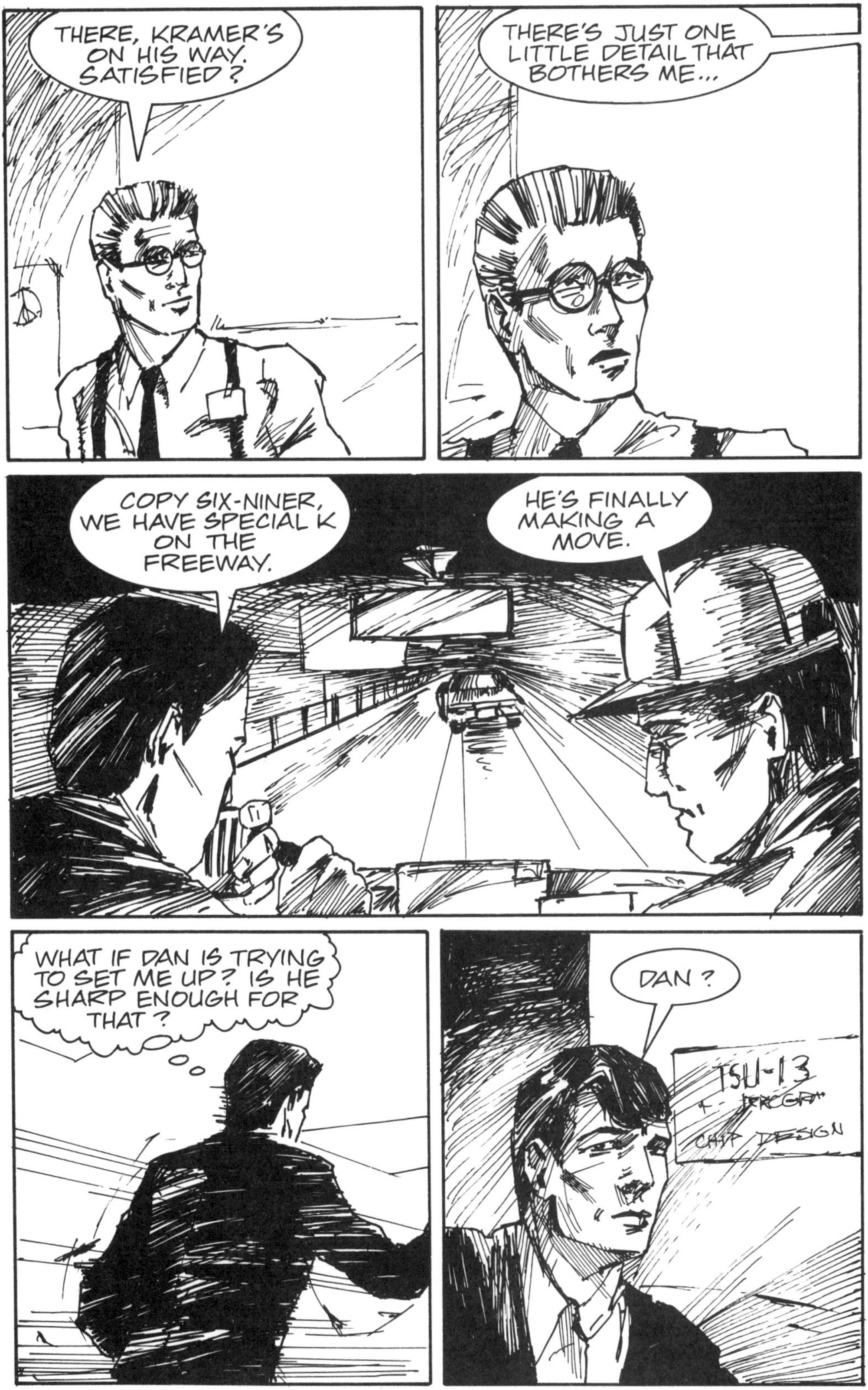
THERE, KRAMER'S ON HIS WAY. SATISFIED?
THERE'S JUST ONE LITTLE DETAIL THAT BOTHERS ME...
COPY SIX-NINER, WE HAVE SPECIAL K ON THE FREEWAY.
HE'S FINALLY MAKING A MOVE.
WHAT IF DAN IS TRYING TO SET ME UP? IS HE SHARP ENOUGH FOR THAT?
DAN?
TSU-13
CHIP DESIGN

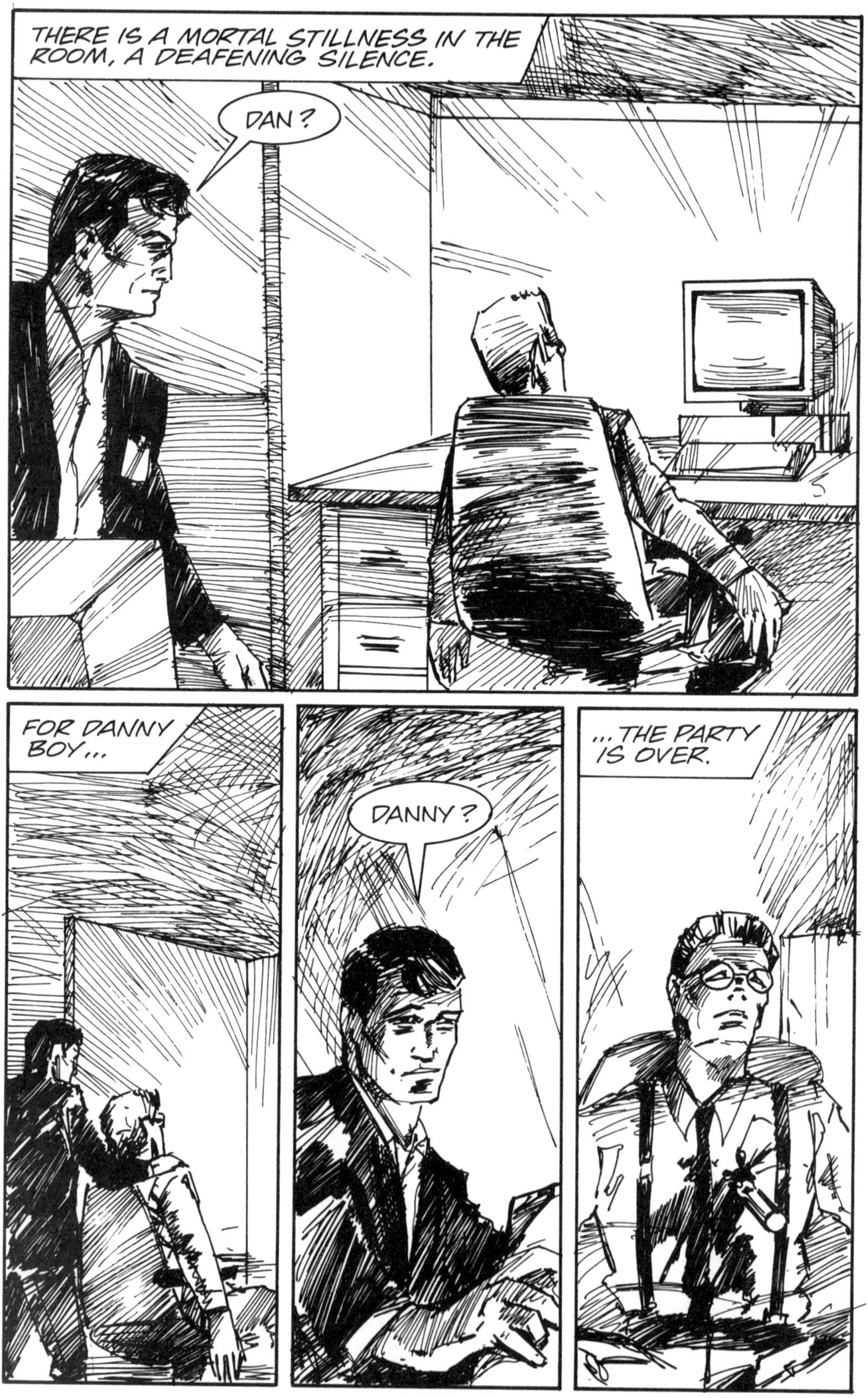
THERE IS A MORTAL STILLNESS IN THE ROOM, A DEAFENING SILENCE.
DAN?
FOR DANNY BOY...
DANNY?
...THE PARTY IS OVER.

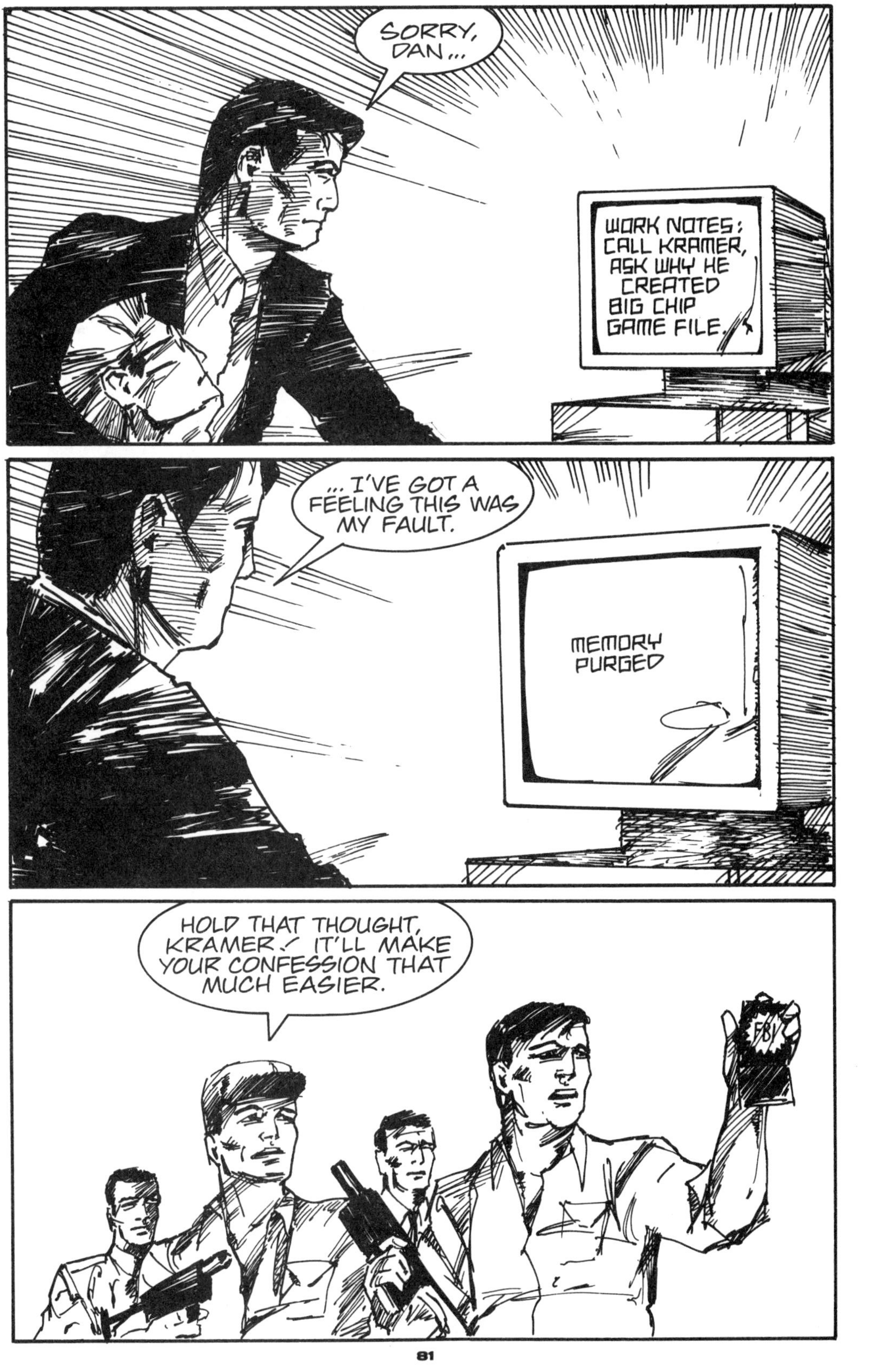
SORRY, DAN...
WORK NOTES: CALL KRAMER, ASK WHY HE CREATED BIG CHIP GAME FILE.
...I'VE GOT A FEELING THIS WAS MY FAULT.
MEMORY PURGED
HOLD THAT THOUGHT, KRAMER! IT'LL MAKE YOUR CONFESSION THAT MUCH EASIER.
FBI

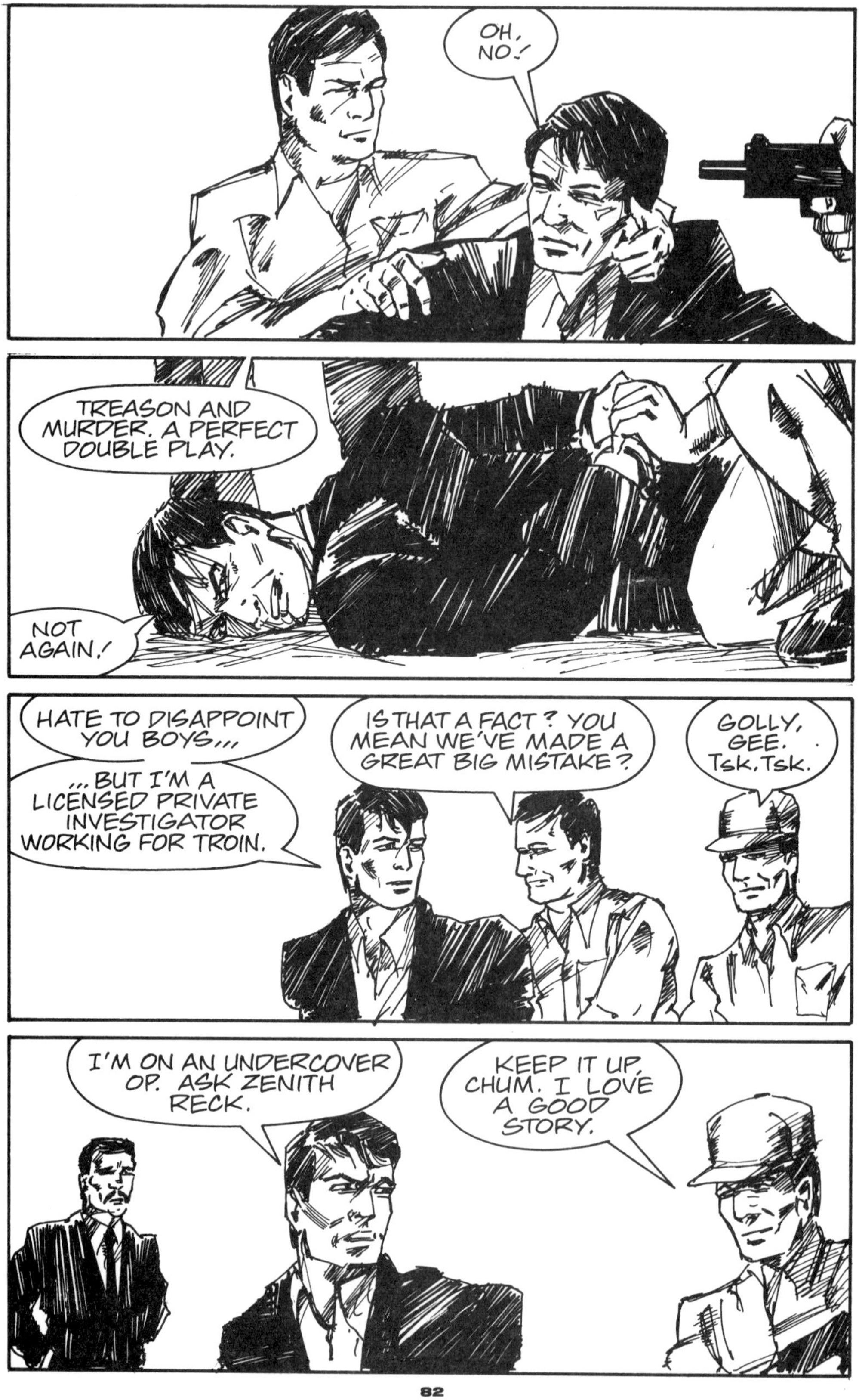
OH, NO.!
TREASON AND MURDER. A PERFECT DOUBLE PLAY.
NOT AGAIN.!
HATE TO DISAPPOINT YOU BOYS...
...BUT I'M A LICENSED PRIVATE INVESTIGATOR WORKING FOR TROIN.
IS THAT A FACT? YOU MEAN WE'VE MADE A GREAT BIG MISTAKE?
GOLLY, GEE. Tsk, Tsk.
I'M ON AN UNDERCOVER OP. ASK ZENITH RECK.
KEEP IT UP, CHUM. I LOVE A GOOD STORY.

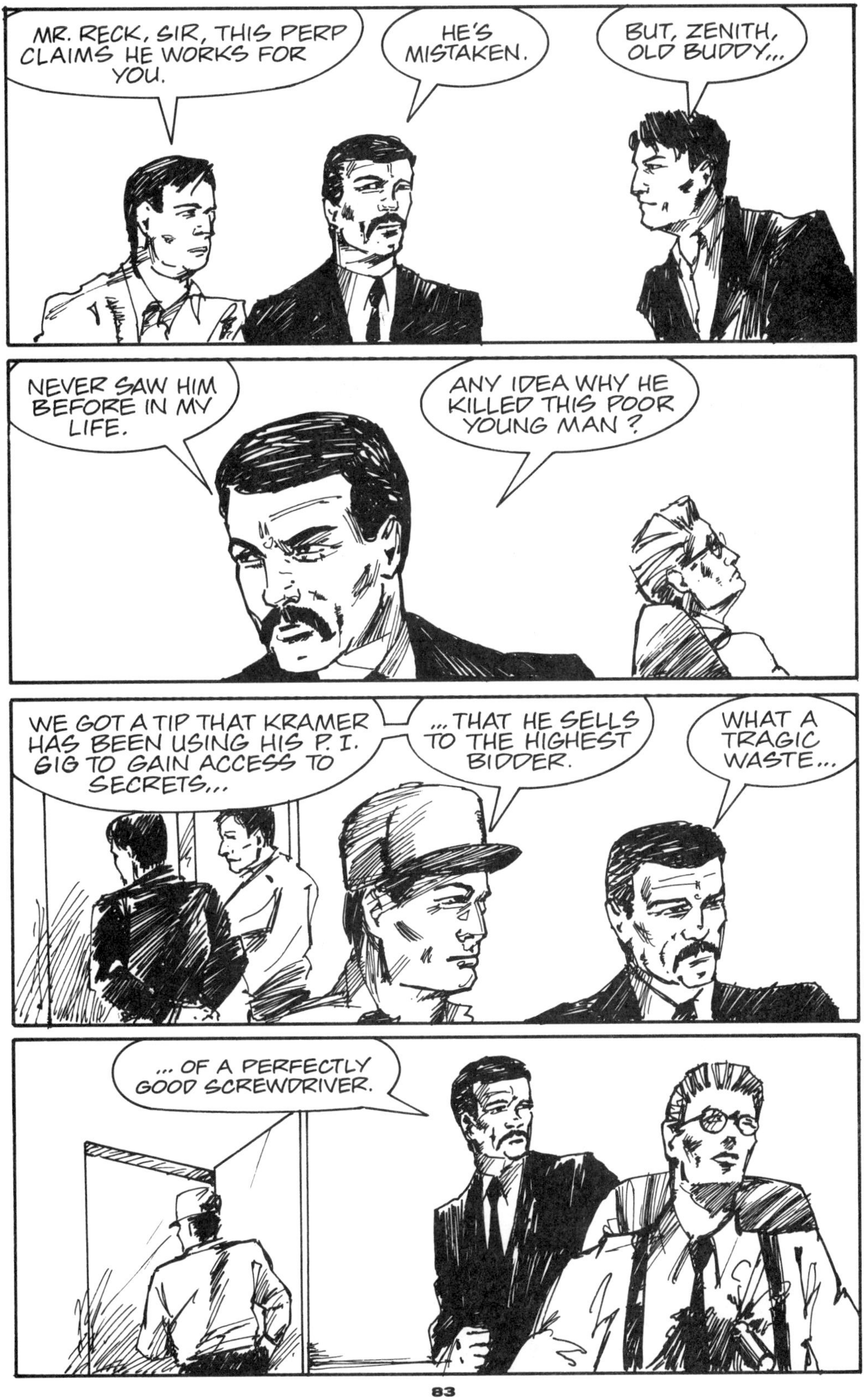
MR. RECK, SIR, THIS PERP CLAIMS HE WORKS FOR YOU.
HE'S MISTAKEN.
BUT, ZENITH, OLD BUDDY...
NEVER SAW HIM BEFORE IN MY LIFE.
ANY IDEA WHY HE KILLED THIS POOR YOUNG MAN ?
WE GOT A TIP THAT KRAMER HAS BEEN USING HIS P. I. GIG TO GAIN ACCESS TO SECRETS...
...THAT HE SELLS TO THE HIGHEST BIDDER.
WHAT A TRAGIC WASTE...
... OF A PERFECTLY GOOD SCREWDRIVER.

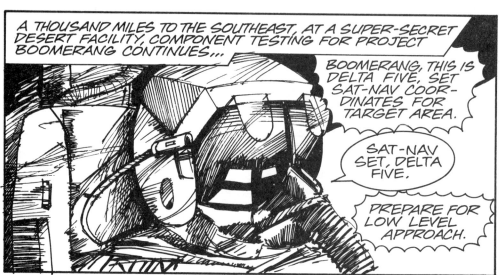

A THOUSAND MILES TO THE SOUTHEAST, AT A SUPER-SECRET DESERT FACILITY, COMPONENT TESTING FOR PROJECT BOOMERANG CONTINUES...

BOOMERANG, THIS IS DELTA FIVE, SET SAT-NAV COORDINATES FOR TARGET AREA.

SAT-NAV SET, DELTA FIVE.

PREPARE FOR LOW LEVEL APPROACH.

LAS LOCKED IN, DELTA FIVE. RANGE 10.7 MILES. REQUEST CLEARANCE TO OVERRIDE.

CLEARANCE GRANTED. SHE'S ALL YOURS, BOOMERANG.

AND GOOD LUCK.

ALL SYSTEMS GO. TARGET RANGE 7.4 MILES.

BOOMERANG HAS THE BONE IN HER TEETH, DELTA FIVE.

LAS WORKING PERFECTLY! CLEARED PEAK 9!

HE'S GOING TO MAKE IT.

UNLESS THAT NAVIGATION CONTROL MICROCHIP SCREWS UP AGAIN.

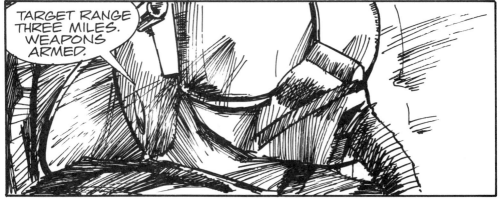

TARGET RANGE THREE MILES. WEAPONS ARMED.

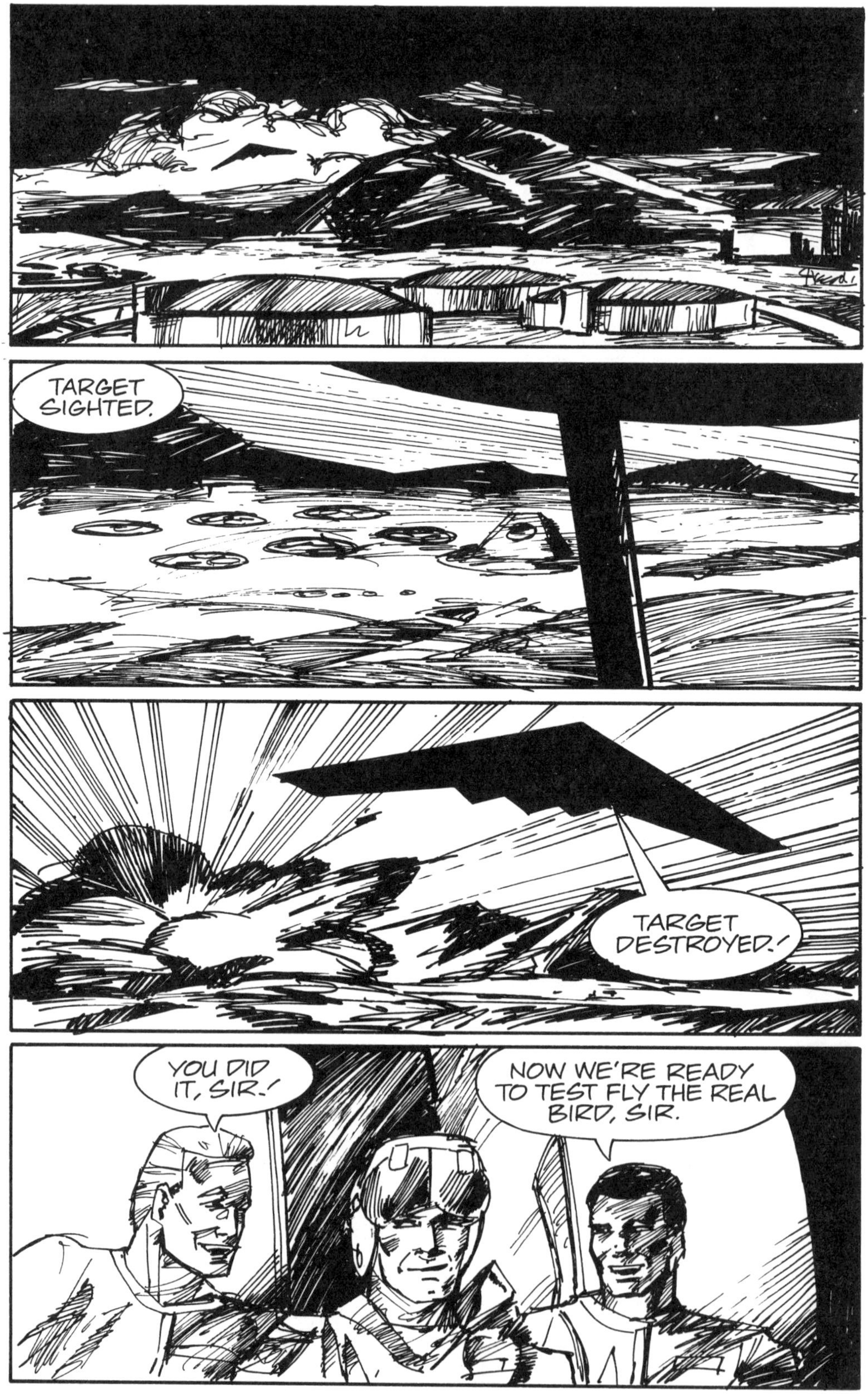
TARGET SIGHTED.
TARGET DESTROYED!
YOU DID IT, SIR!
NOW WE'RE READY TO TEST FLY THE REAL BIRD, SIR.

There's nothing like a night in jail to hone the senses. I'd been stuck on a narrow focus, unable to see the big picture. Get your nose too close to the screen and you lose sight of what's happening all around you — especially behind your back!

Zenith Reck. He'd had a world of high priced, hi-tech security firms to choose from and he'd picked on me.

Why?

I'd never bothered to get a straight answer. Maybe Dan O'Dell knew, and that's why he wasn't talking, not ever again. Had Reck set me up for a fall, or was he just writing me off as a bad investment? So far my best clue was the message left on O'Dell's screen: *Call Kramer, ask why he created the Big Chip game file.*

I hadn't created that file and O'Dell knew it. Therefore the message had been left by his killer, as a way to implicate me.

Why me?

And if I hadn't created The Big Chip file, who had?

The answer was still eluding me when the sun came — but then it's hard to concentrate when your cellmate smells like he's been skindiving in a vat of Mad Dog wine. . .

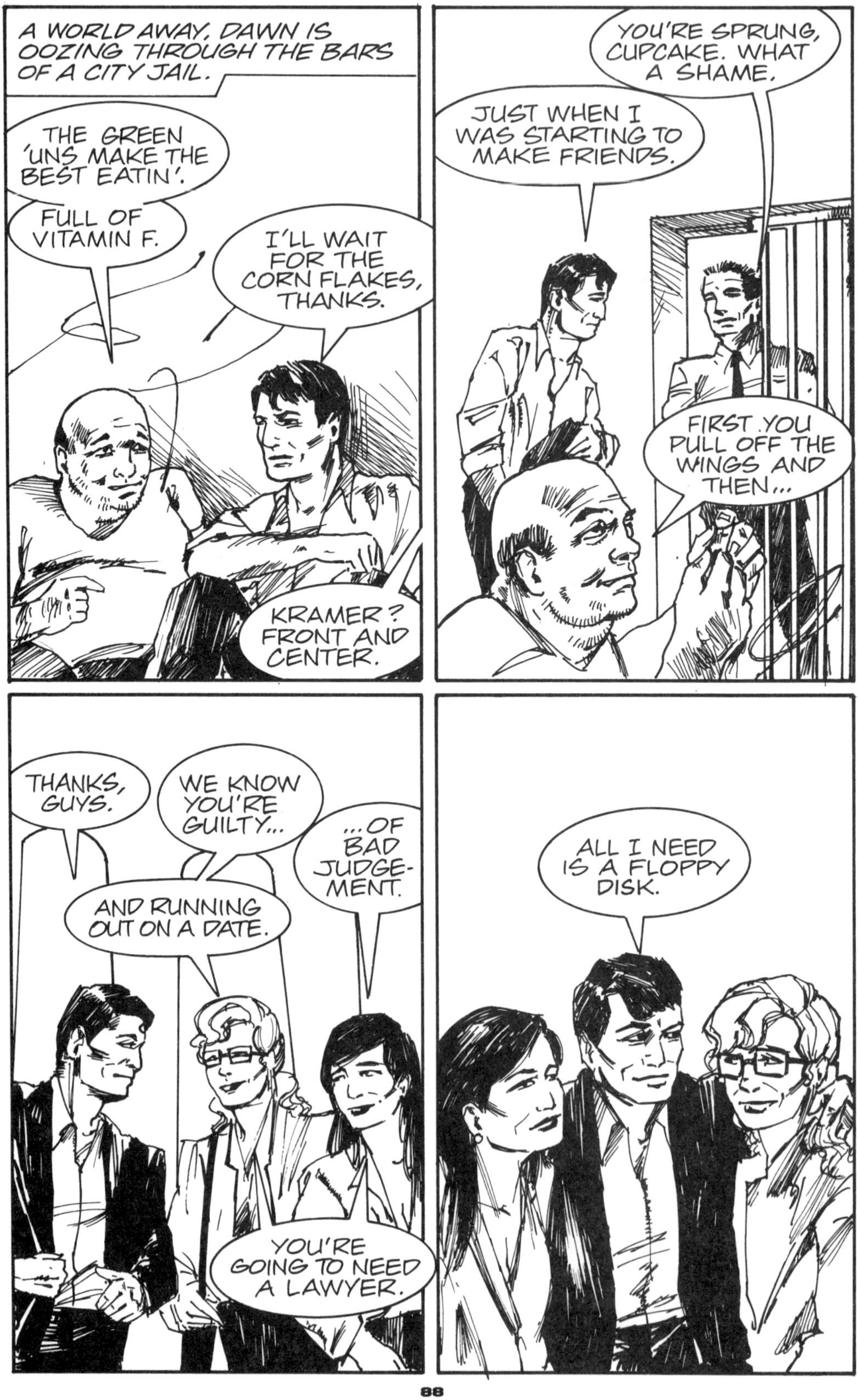
A WORLD AWAY, DAWN IS OOZING THROUGH THE BARS OF A CITY JAIL.
THE GREEN 'UNS MAKE THE BEST EATIN'.
FULL OF VITAMIN F.
I'LL WAIT FOR THE CORN FLAKES, THANKS.
KRAMER? FRONT AND CENTER.
YOU'RE SPRUNG, CUPCAKE. WHAT A SHAME.
JUST WHEN I WAS STARTING TO MAKE FRIENDS.
FIRST YOU PULL OFF THE WINGS AND THEN...
THANKS, GUYS.
WE KNOW YOU'RE GUILTY...
...OF BAD JUDGE-MENT.
AND RUNNING OUT ON A DATE.
YOU'RE GOING TO NEED A LAWYER.
ALL I NEED IS A FLOPPY DISK.

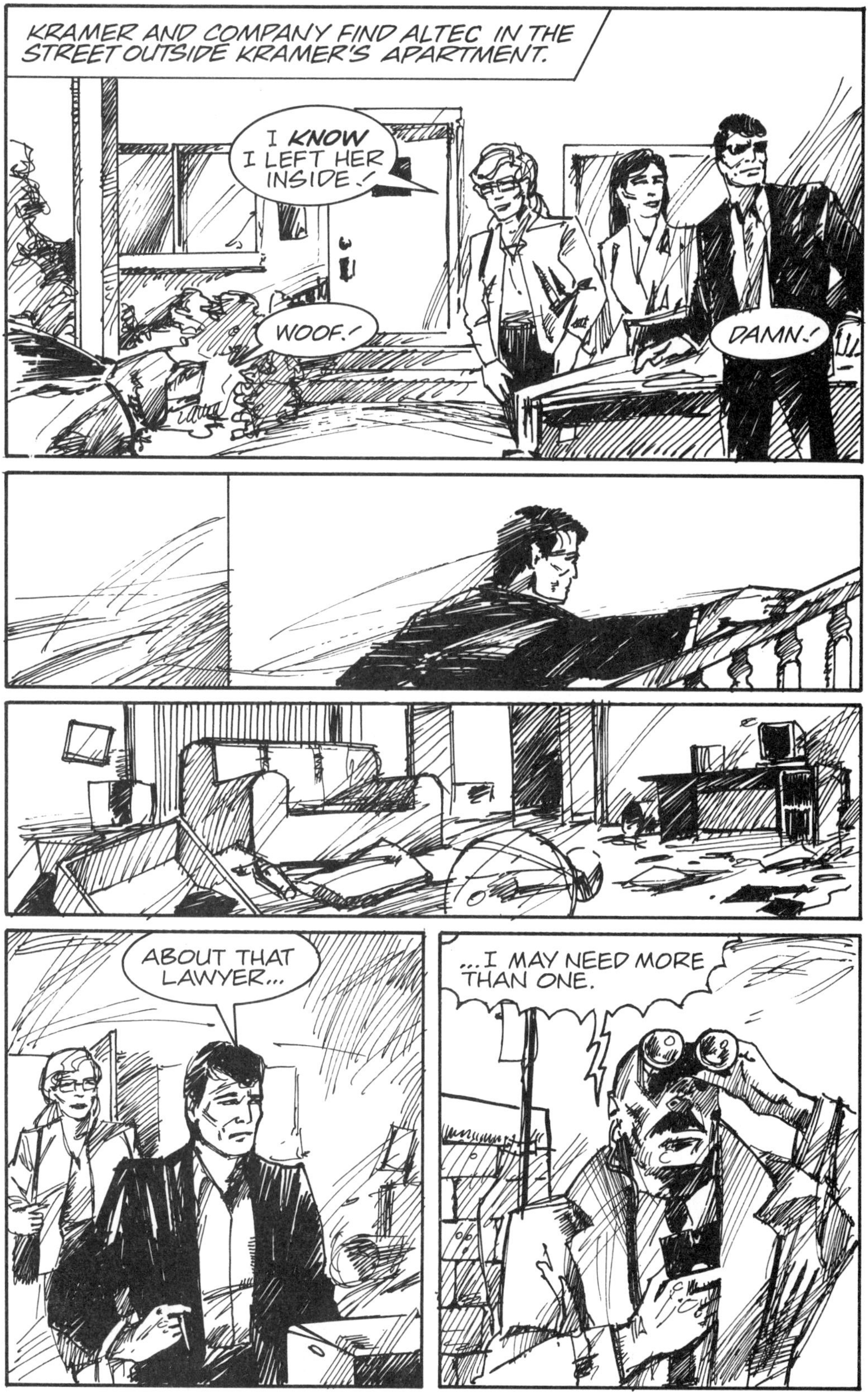
KRAMER AND COMPANY FIND ALTEC IN THE STREET OUTSIDE KRAMER'S APARTMENT.
I KNOW I LEFT HER INSIDE!
WOOF!
DAMN!
ABOUT THAT LAWYER...
...I MAY NEED MORE THAN ONE.

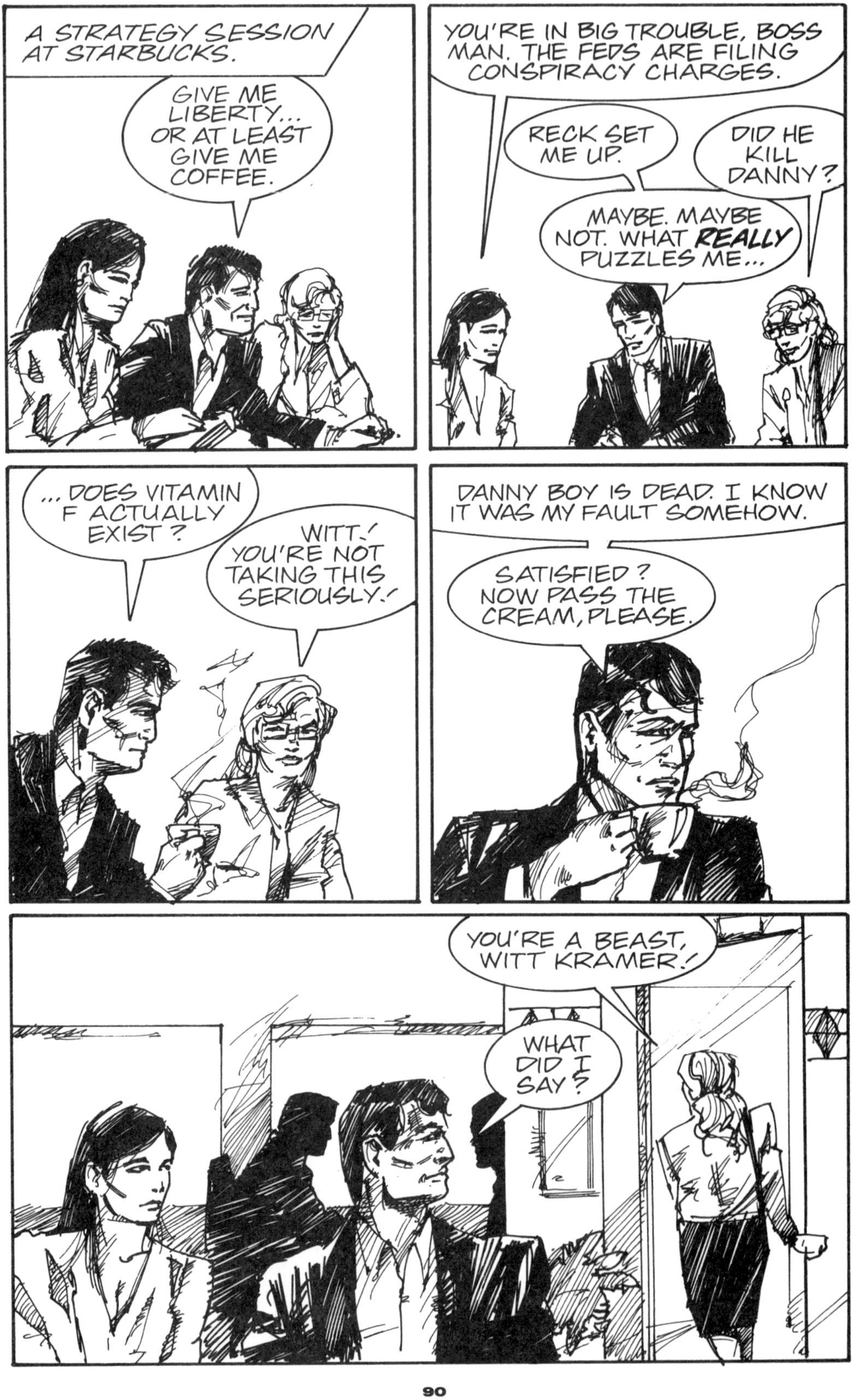
A STRATEGY SESSION AT STARBUCKS.
GIVE ME LIBERTY... OR AT LEAST GIVE ME COFFEE.
YOU'RE IN BIG TROUBLE, BOSS MAN. THE FEDS ARE FILING CONSPIRACY CHARGES.
RECK SET ME UP.
DID HE KILL DANNY?
MAYBE. MAYBE NOT. WHAT **REALLY** PUZZLES ME...
...DOES VITAMIN F ACTUALLY EXIST?
WITT! YOU'RE NOT TAKING THIS SERIOUSLY!
DANNY BOY IS DEAD. I KNOW IT WAS MY FAULT SOMEHOW.
SATISFIED? NOW PASS THE CREAM, PLEASE.
YOU'RE A BEAST, WITT KRAMER!
WHAT DID I SAY?

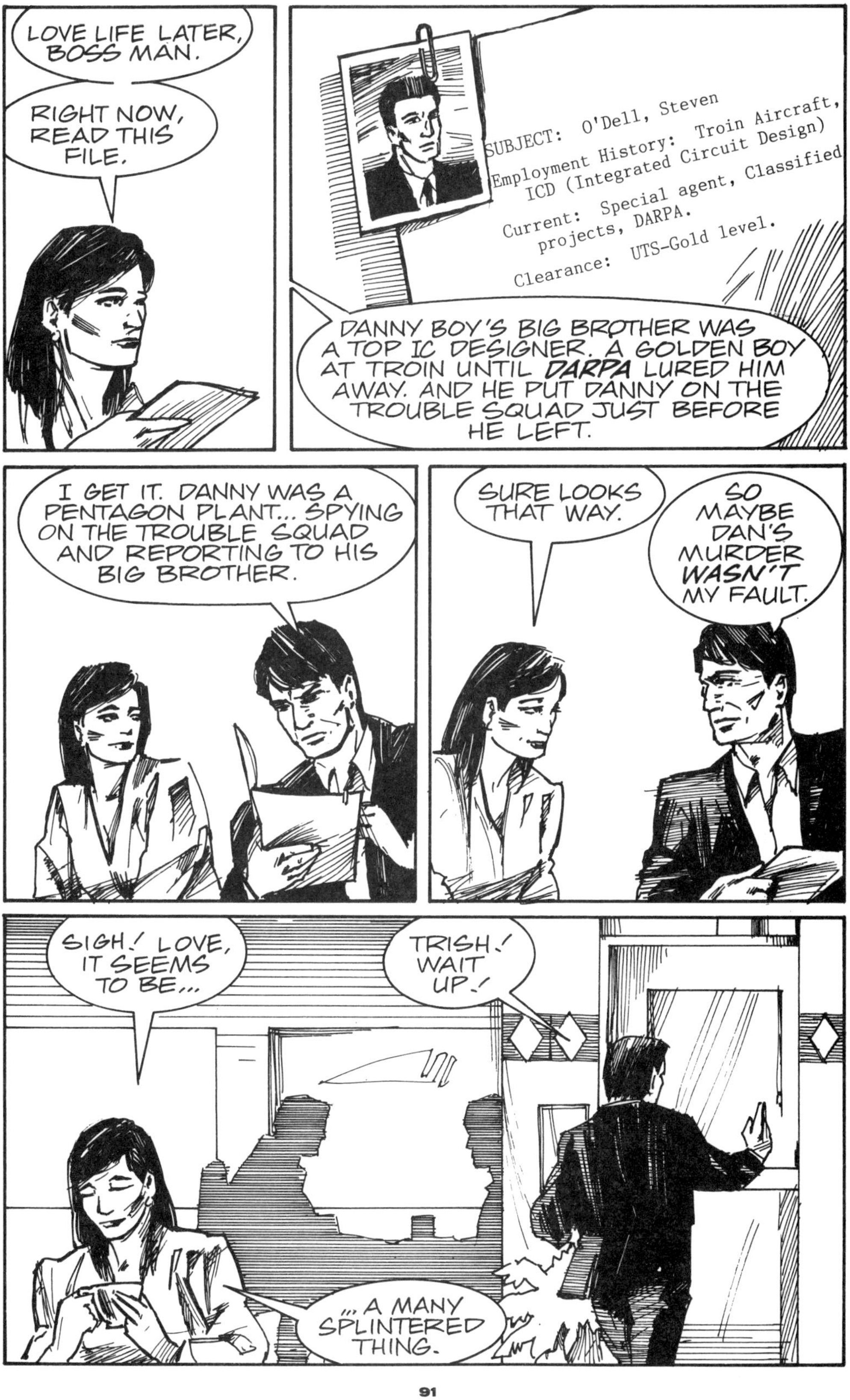
LOVE LIFE LATER, BOSS MAN.
RIGHT NOW, READ THIS FILE.
SUBJECT: O'Dell, Steven
Employment History: Troin Aircraft, ICD (Integrated Circuit Design)
Current: Special agent, Classified projects, DARPA.
Clearance: UTS-Gold level.
DANNY BOY'S BIG BROTHER WAS A TOP IC DESIGNER. A GOLDEN BOY AT TROIN UNTIL DARPA LURED HIM AWAY. AND HE PUT DANNY ON THE TROUBLE SQUAD JUST BEFORE HE LEFT.
I GET IT. DANNY WAS A PENTAGON PLANT... SPYING ON THE TROUBLE SQUAD AND REPORTING TO HIS BIG BROTHER.
SURE LOOKS THAT WAY.
SO MAYBE DAN'S MURDER WASN'T MY FAULT.
SIGH! LOVE, IT SEEMS TO BE...
TRISH! WAIT UP!
...A MANY SPLINTERED THING.

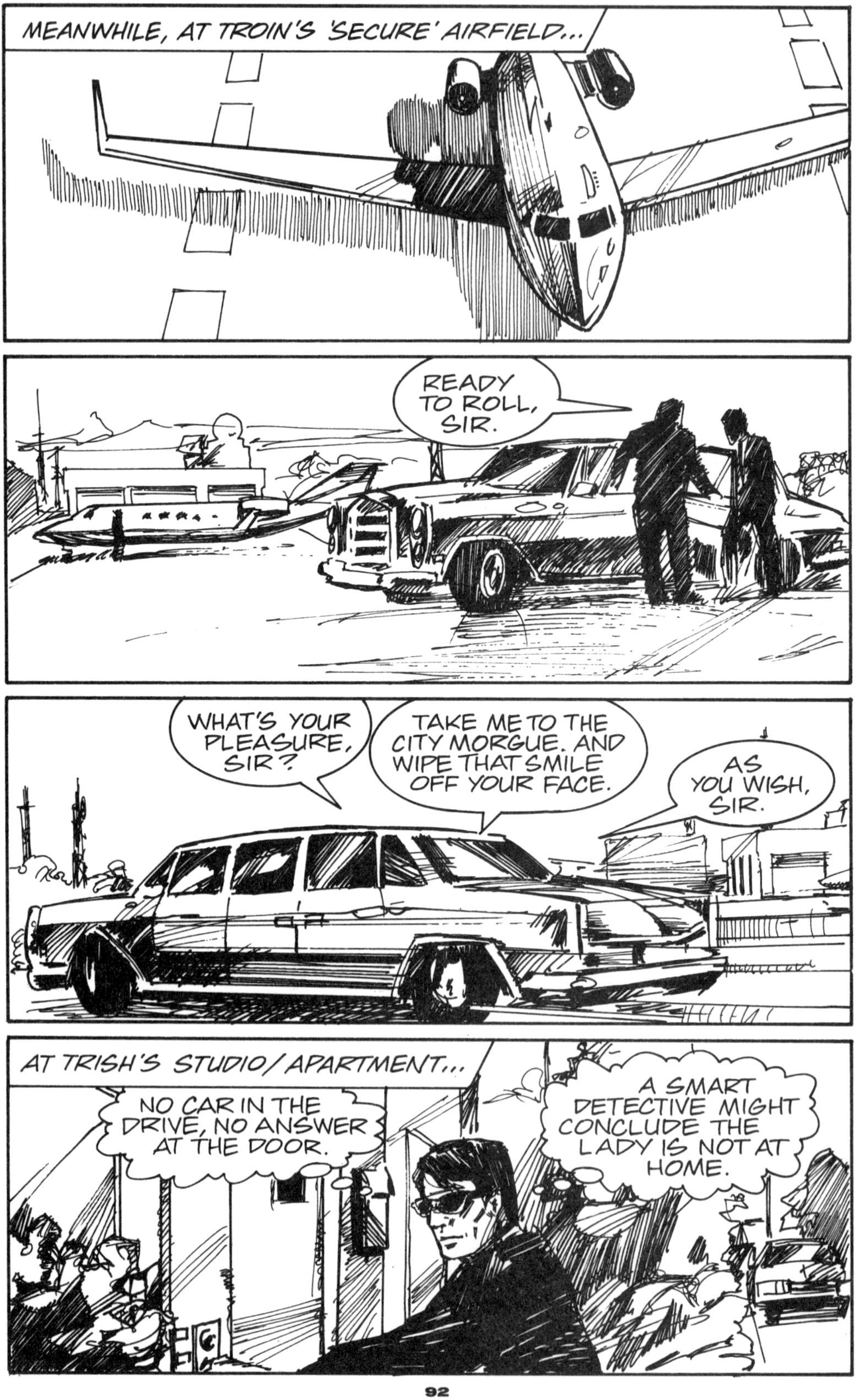
MEANWHILE, AT TROIN'S 'SECURE' AIRFIELD...
READY TO ROLL, SIR.
WHAT'S YOUR PLEASURE, SIR?
TAKE ME TO THE CITY MORGUE. AND WIPE THAT SMILE OFF YOUR FACE.
AS YOU WISH, SIR.
AT TRISH'S STUDIO/APARTMENT...
NO CAR IN THE DRIVE, NO ANSWER AT THE DOOR.
A SMART DETECTIVE MIGHT CONCLUDE THE LADY IS NOT AT HOME.

AND A SMART DETECTIVE WOULDN'T PHONE THE SCENE OF THE CRIME.

HELLO, CHOCKO? I'M TRYING TO GET AHOLD OF TRISH.

KRAMER? WHAT'S GOING ON? I'M ALL ALONE HERE. NO ROOKIE, NO DANNY BOY, NO CELIA...

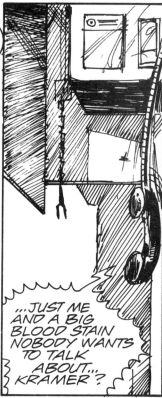

...JUST ME AND A BIG BLOOD STAIN NOBODY WANTS TO TALK ABOUT... KRAMER?

CELIA! I NEVER GAVE HER A THOUGHT!

SHE'S THE BRAINS OF THE TROUBLE SQUAD! A PERFECT TARGET!

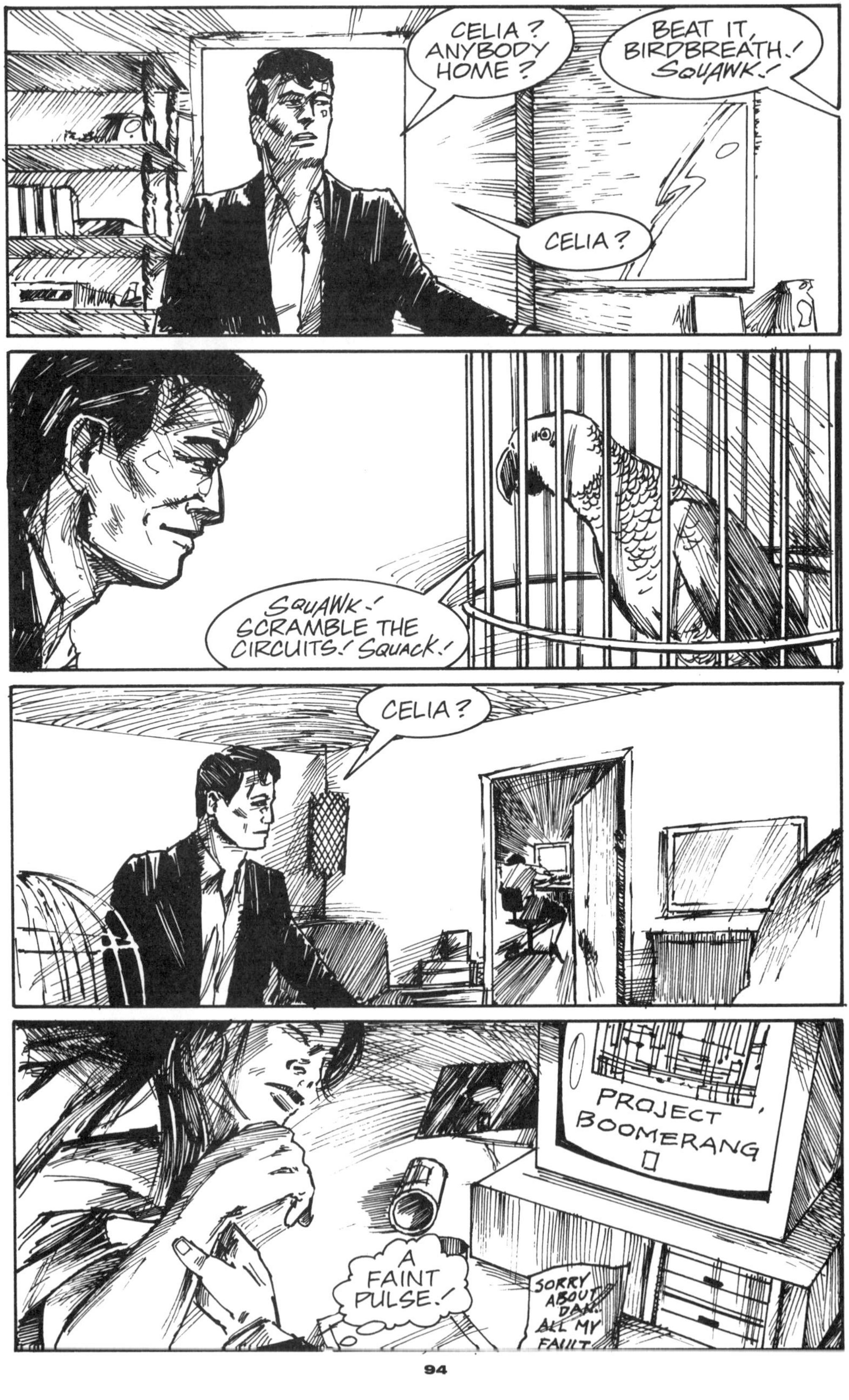
CELIA? ANYBODY HOME?
BEAT IT, BIRDBREATH! SQUAWK!
CELIA?
SQUAWK! SCRAMBLE THE CIRCUITS! SQUACK!
CELIA?
PROJECT BOOMERANG
A FAINT PULSE!
SORRY ABOUT DAN. ALL MY FAULT

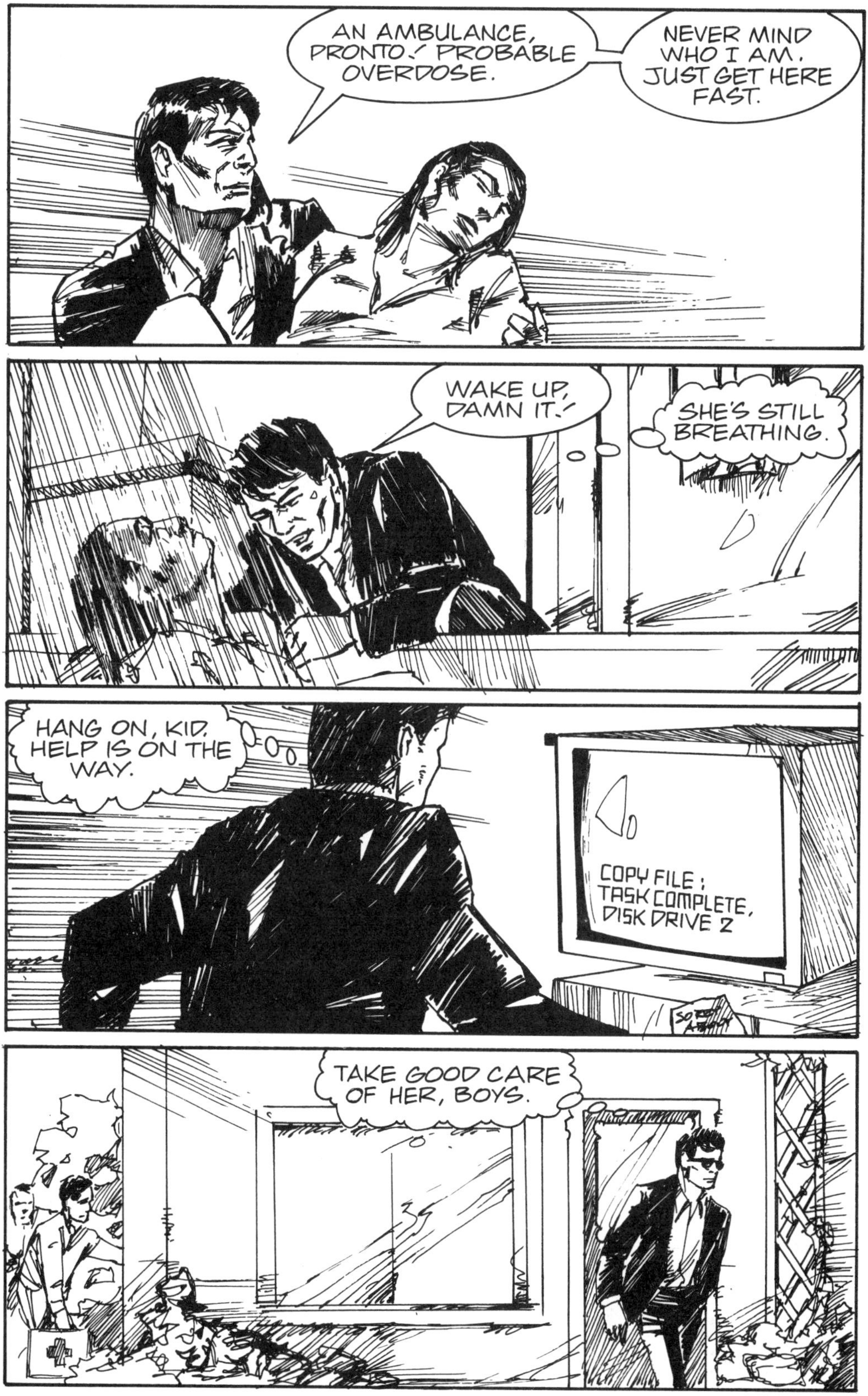
AN AMBULANCE, PRONTO! PROBABLE OVERDOSE.
NEVER MIND WHO I AM. JUST GET HERE FAST.
WAKE UP, DAMN IT!
SHE'S STILL BREATHING.
HANG ON, KID. HELP IS ON THE WAY.
COPY FILE: TASK COMPLETE, DISK DRIVE 2
TAKE GOOD CARE OF HER, BOYS.

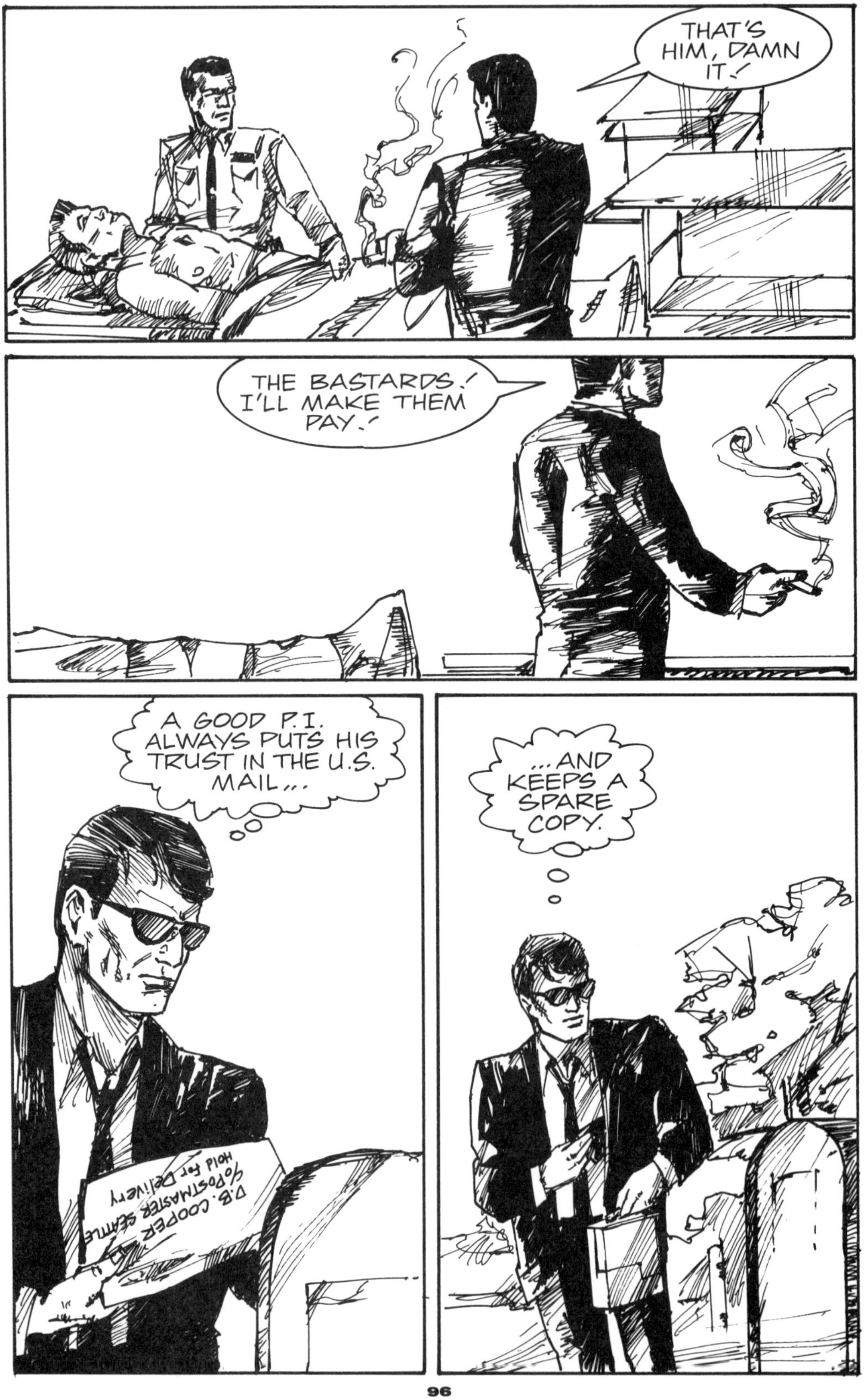
THAT'S HIM, DAMN IT!
THE BASTARDS! I'LL MAKE THEM PAY!
A GOOD P.I. ALWAYS PUTS HIS TRUST IN THE U.S. MAIL...
D.B. COOPER SEATTLE
c/o POSTMASTER
Hold for Delivery
...AND KEEPS A SPARE COPY.

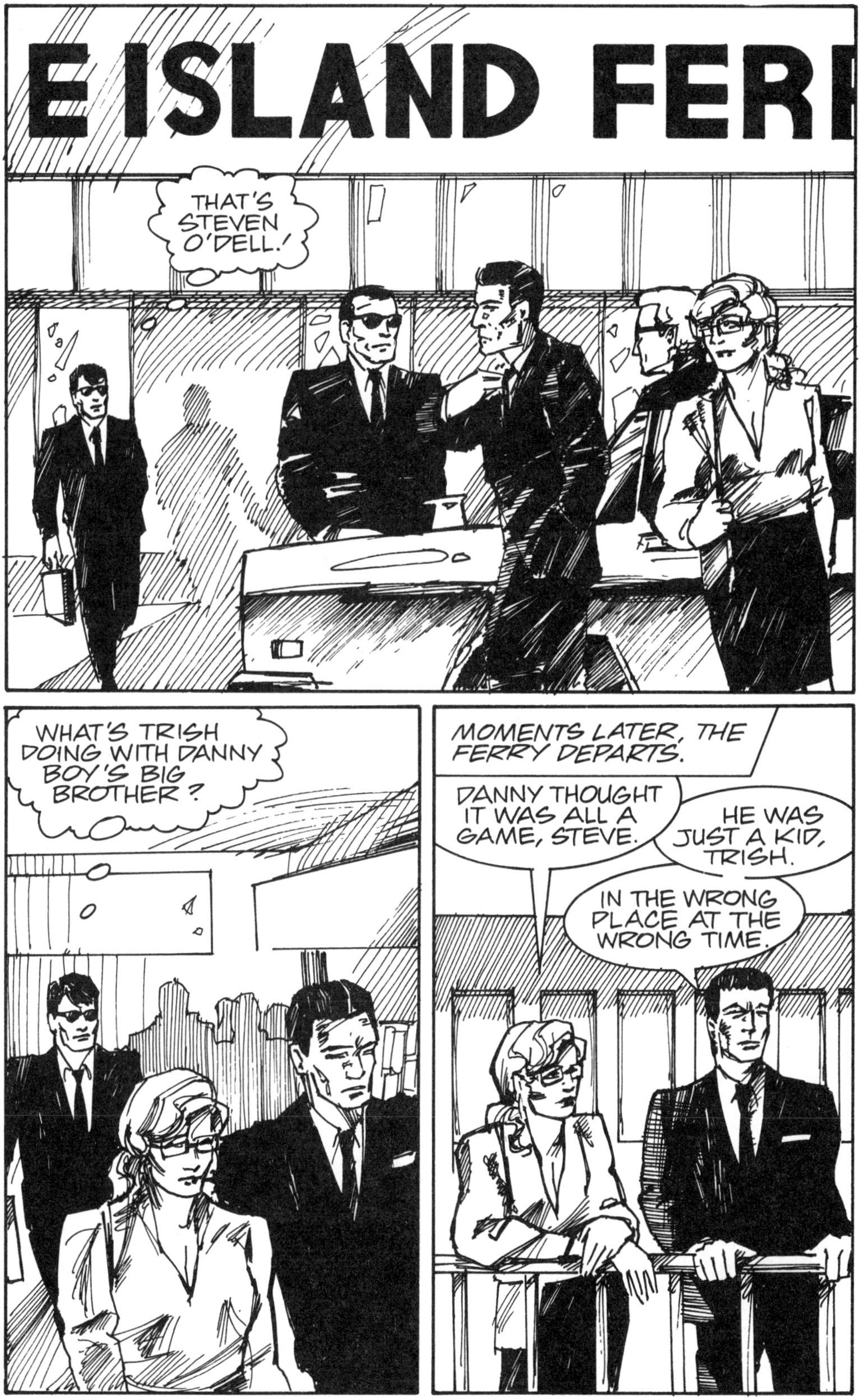
E ISLAND FER
THAT'S STEVEN O'DELL.!
WHAT'S TRISH DOING WITH DANNY BOY'S BIG BROTHER?
MOMENTS LATER, THE FERRY DEPARTS.
DANNY THOUGHT IT WAS ALL A GAME, STEVE.
HE WAS JUST A KID, TRISH.
IN THE WRONG PLACE AT THE WRONG TIME.

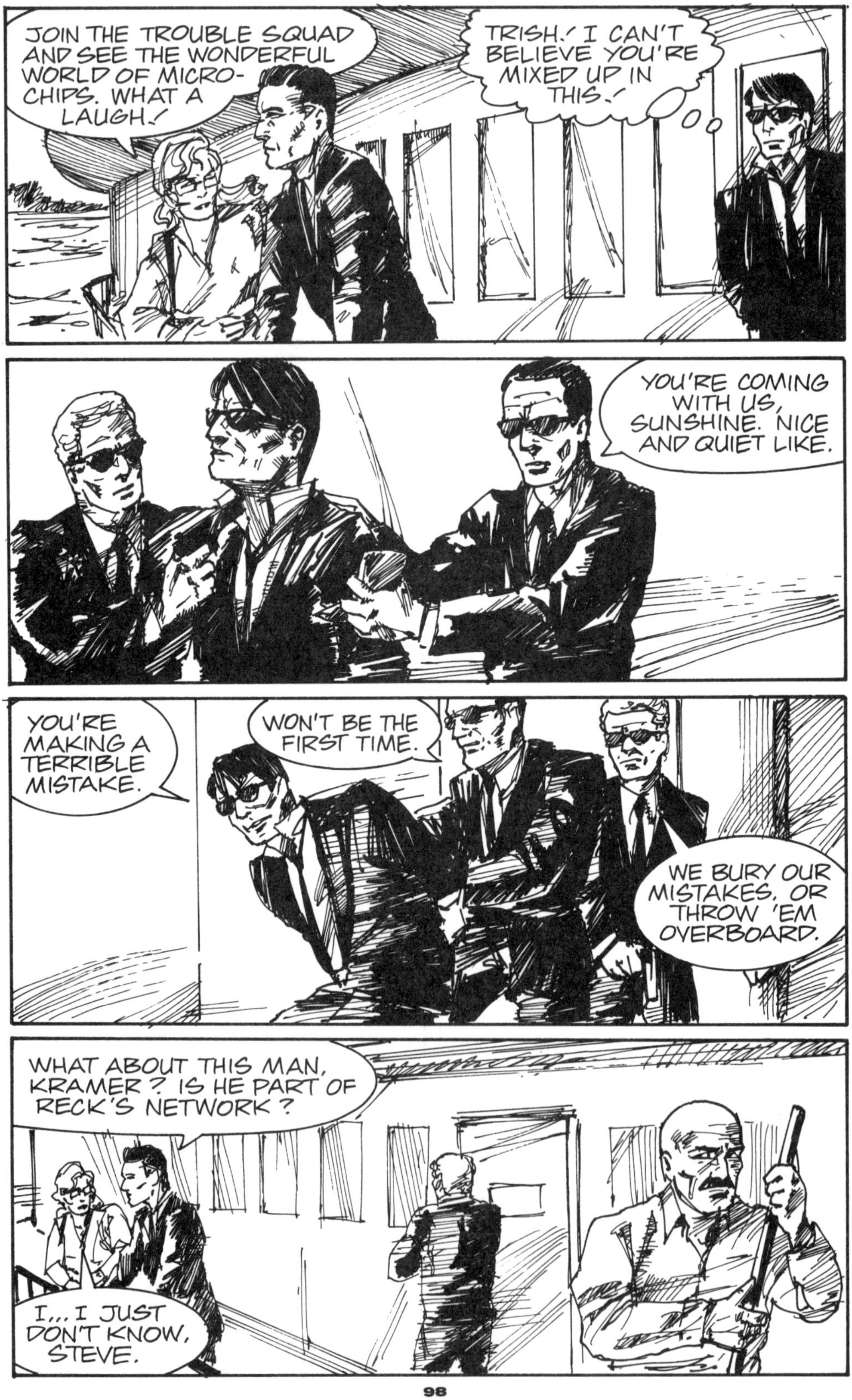
JOIN THE TROUBLE SQUAD AND SEE THE WONDERFUL WORLD OF MICRO-CHIPS. WHAT A LAUGH!
TRISH! I CAN'T BELIEVE YOU'RE MIXED UP IN THIS!
YOU'RE COMING WITH US, SUNSHINE. NICE AND QUIET LIKE.
YOU'RE MAKING A TERRIBLE MISTAKE.
WON'T BE THE FIRST TIME.
WE BURY OUR MISTAKES, OR THROW 'EM OVERBOARD.
WHAT ABOUT THIS MAN, KRAMER? IS HE PART OF RECK'S NETWORK?
I... I JUST DON'T KNOW, STEVE.

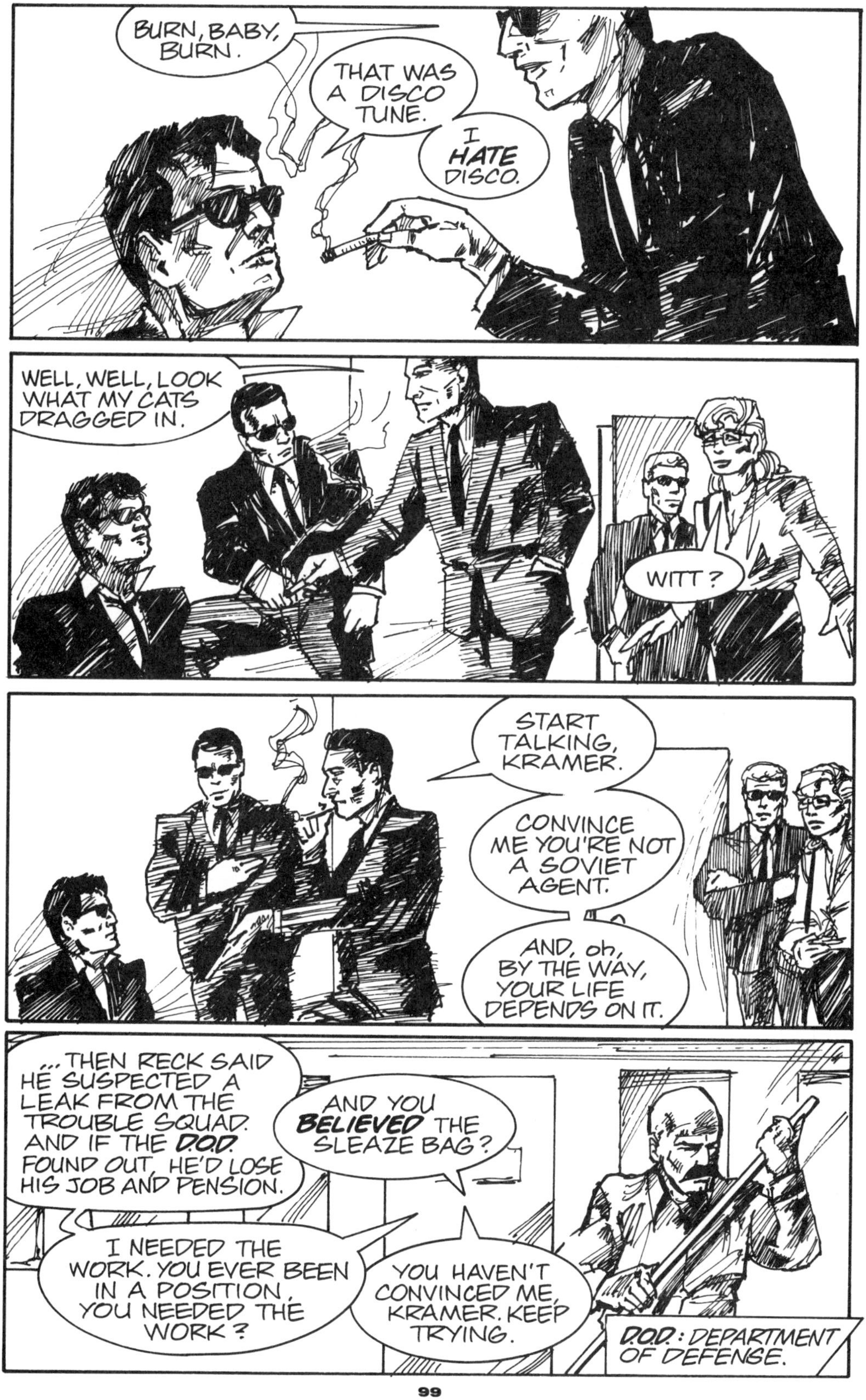
BURN, BABY, BURN.
THAT WAS A DISCO TUNE.
I HATE DISCO.
WELL, WELL, LOOK WHAT MY CATS DRAGGED IN.
WITT?
START TALKING, KRAMER.
CONVINCE ME YOU'RE NOT A SOVIET AGENT.
AND, oh, BY THE WAY, YOUR LIFE DEPENDS ON IT.
...THEN RECK SAID HE SUSPECTED A LEAK FROM THE TROUBLE SQUAD. AND IF THE D.O.D. FOUND OUT, HE'D LOSE HIS JOB AND PENSION.
AND YOU BELIEVED THE SLEAZE BAG?
I NEEDED THE WORK. YOU EVER BEEN IN A POSITION, YOU NEEDED THE WORK?
YOU HAVEN'T CONVINCED ME, KRAMER. KEEP TRYING.
D.O.D.: DEPARTMENT OF DEFENSE.

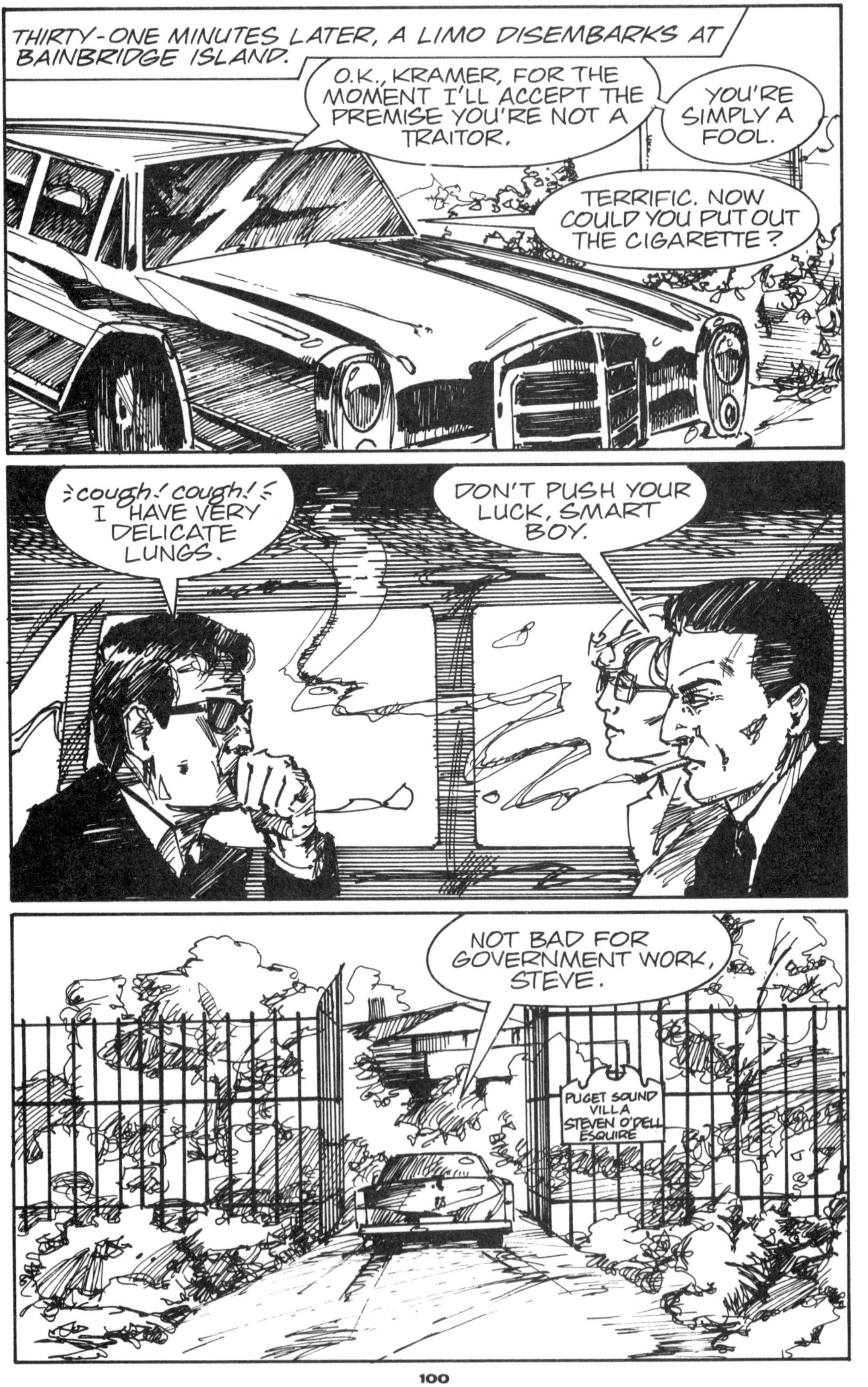
THIRTY-ONE MINUTES LATER, A LIMO DISEMBARKS AT BAINBRIDGE ISLAND.
O.K., KRAMER, FOR THE MOMENT I'LL ACCEPT THE PREMISE YOU'RE NOT A TRAITOR.
YOU'RE SIMPLY A FOOL.
TERRIFIC. NOW COULD YOU PUT OUT THE CIGARETTE?
cough! cough! I HAVE VERY DELICATE LUNGS.
DON'T PUSH YOUR LUCK, SMART BOY.
NOT BAD FOR GOVERNMENT WORK, STEVE.
PUGET SOUND VILLA STEVEN O'DELL ESQUIRE

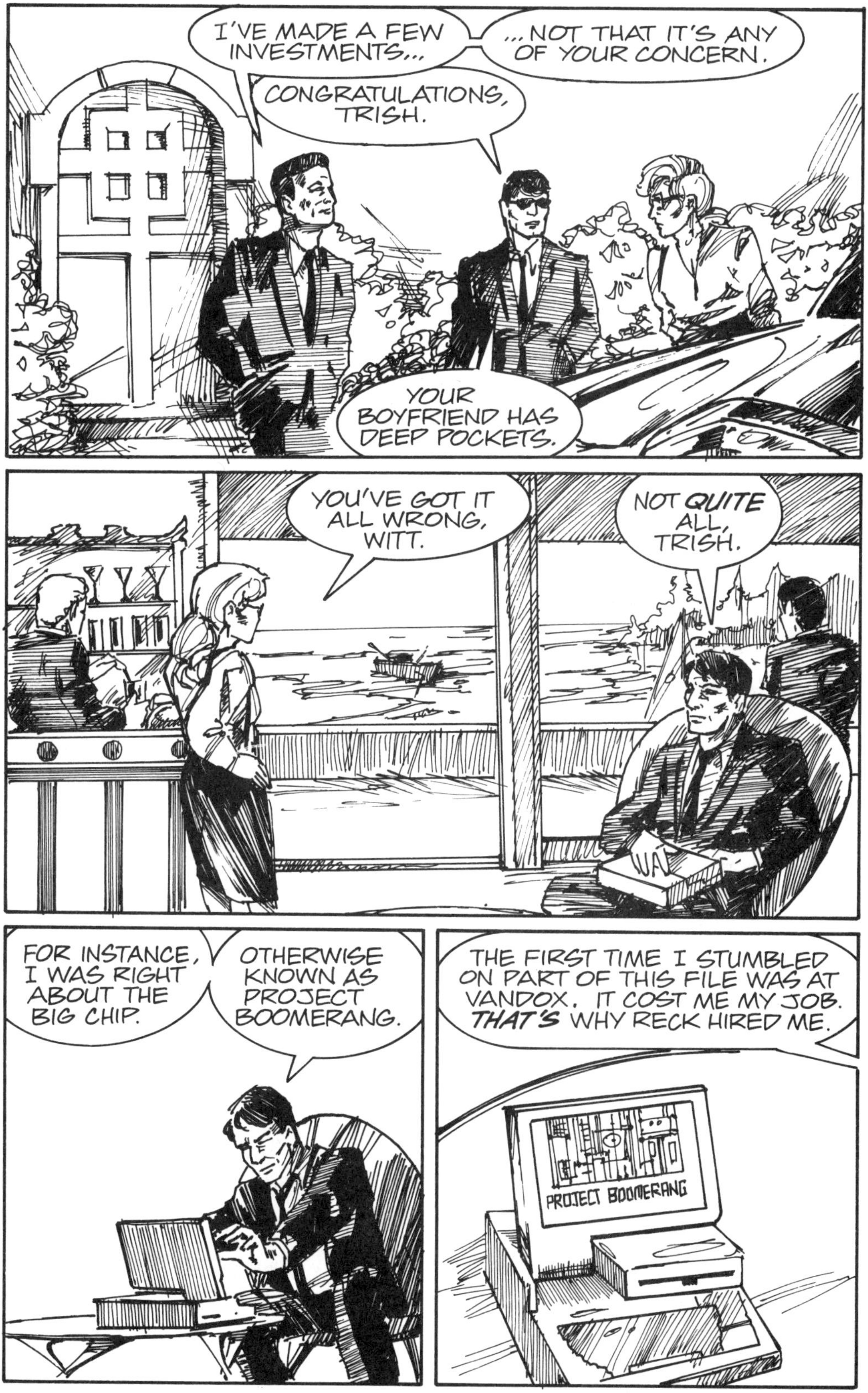
I'VE MADE A FEW INVESTMENTS...
...NOT THAT IT'S ANY OF YOUR CONCERN.
CONGRATULATIONS, TRISH.
YOUR BOYFRIEND HAS DEEP POCKETS.
YOU'VE GOT IT ALL WRONG, WITT.
NOT QUITE ALL, TRISH.
FOR INSTANCE, I WAS RIGHT ABOUT THE BIG CHIP.
OTHERWISE KNOWN AS PROJECT BOOMERANG.
THE FIRST TIME I STUMBLED ON PART OF THIS FILE WAS AT VANDOX. IT COST ME MY JOB. THAT'S WHY RECK HIRED ME.
PROJECT BOOMERANG

RECK NEEDED A FALL GUY IN THE TROUBLE SQUAD, TO COVER HIS INVOLVEMENT IN DOWNLOADING THE DESIGN INTO AN OPEN GAMELINE. I THOUGHT DAN WAS HIS ACCOMPLICE, OR MAYBE CHOCKO.

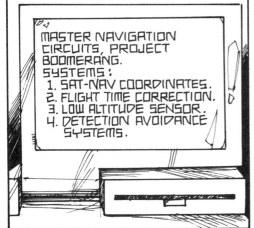

MASTER NAVIGATION CIRCUITS, PROJECT BOOMERANG.
SYSTEMS:
1. SAT-NAV COORDINATES.
2. FLIGHT TIME CORRECTION.
3. LOW ALTITUDE SENSOR.
4. DETECTION AVOIDANCE SYSTEMS.

I NEVER SUSPECTED CELIA.

MY MISTAKE. CELIA WAS THE ONLY ONE ON THE SQUAD WITH THE EXPERTISE TO ACCESS THE ENTIRE CHIP DESIGN.

WAS?

HAVEN'T YOU HEARD?

CELIA FELT RESPONSIBLE FOR DAN'S MURDER. SHE TRIED TO KILL HERSELF.

CELIA? OH, MY GOD!

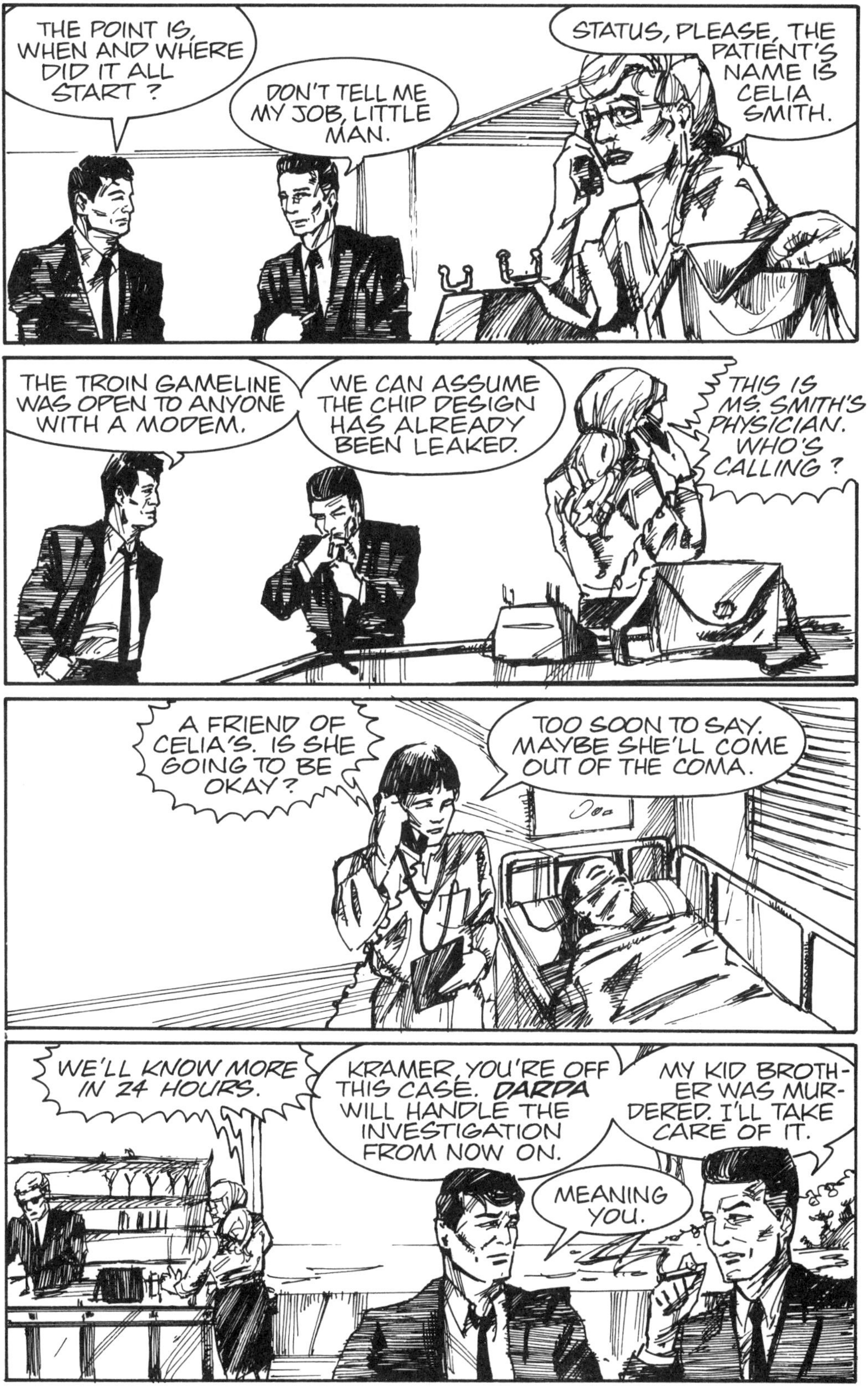
THE POINT IS, WHEN AND WHERE DID IT ALL START ?
DON'T TELL ME MY JOB, LITTLE MAN.
STATUS, PLEASE, THE PATIENT'S NAME IS CELIA SMITH.
THE TROIN GAMELINE WAS OPEN TO ANYONE WITH A MODEM.
WE CAN ASSUME THE CHIP DESIGN HAS ALREADY BEEN LEAKED.
THIS IS MS. SMITH'S PHYSICIAN. WHO'S CALLING ?
A FRIEND OF CELIA'S. IS SHE GOING TO BE OKAY ?
TOO SOON TO SAY. MAYBE SHE'LL COME OUT OF THE COMA.
WE'LL KNOW MORE IN 24 HOURS.
KRAMER, YOU'RE OFF THIS CASE. DARPA WILL HANDLE THE INVESTIGATION FROM NOW ON.
MY KID BROTH-ER WAS MUR-DERED. I'LL TAKE CARE OF IT.
MEANING YOU.

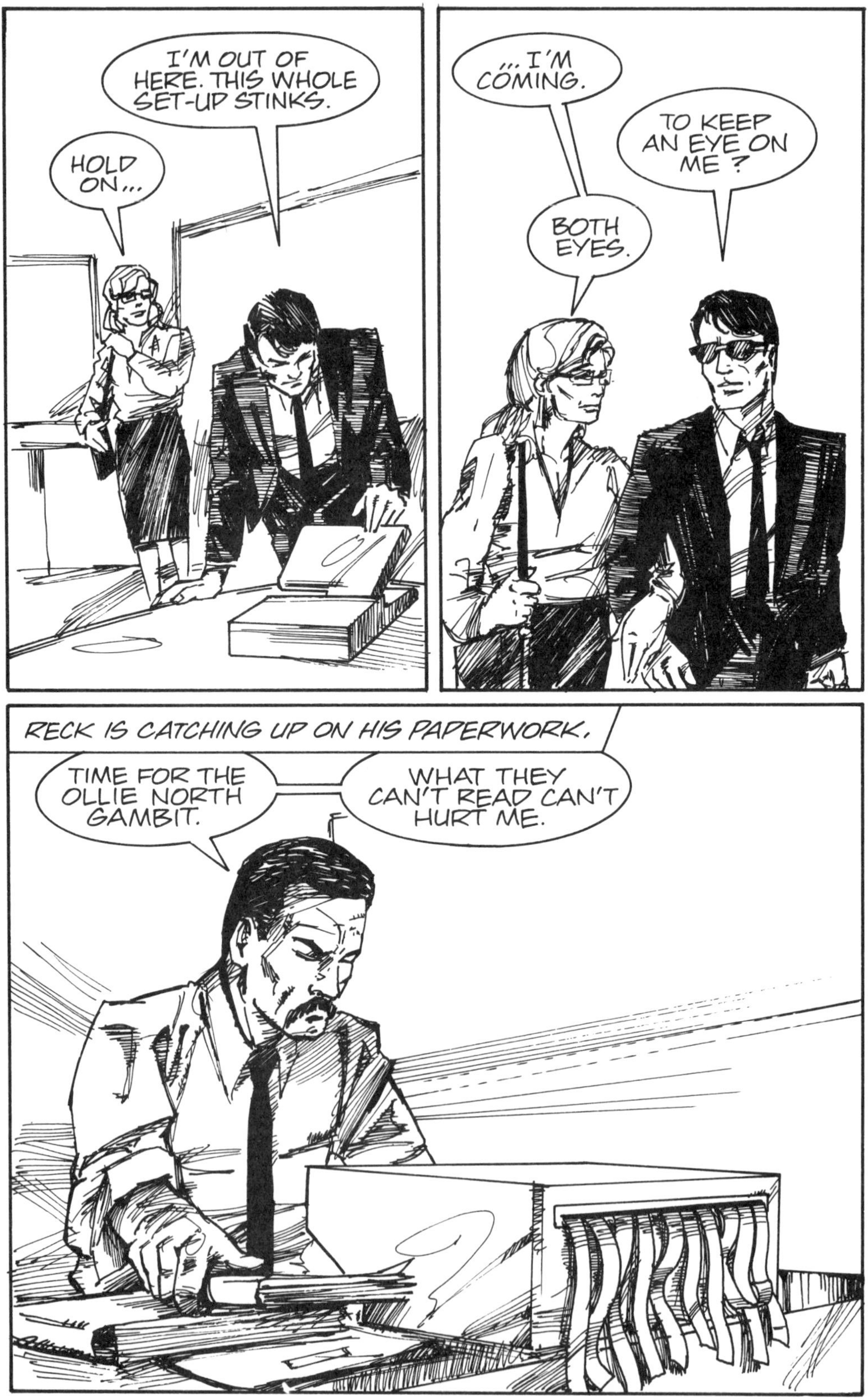
I'M OUT OF HERE. THIS WHOLE SET-UP STINKS.
HOLD ON...
...I'M COMING.
TO KEEP AN EYE ON ME?
BOTH EYES.
RECK IS CATCHING UP ON HIS PAPERWORK.
TIME FOR THE OLLIE NORTH GAMBIT.
WHAT THEY CAN'T READ CAN'T HURT ME.

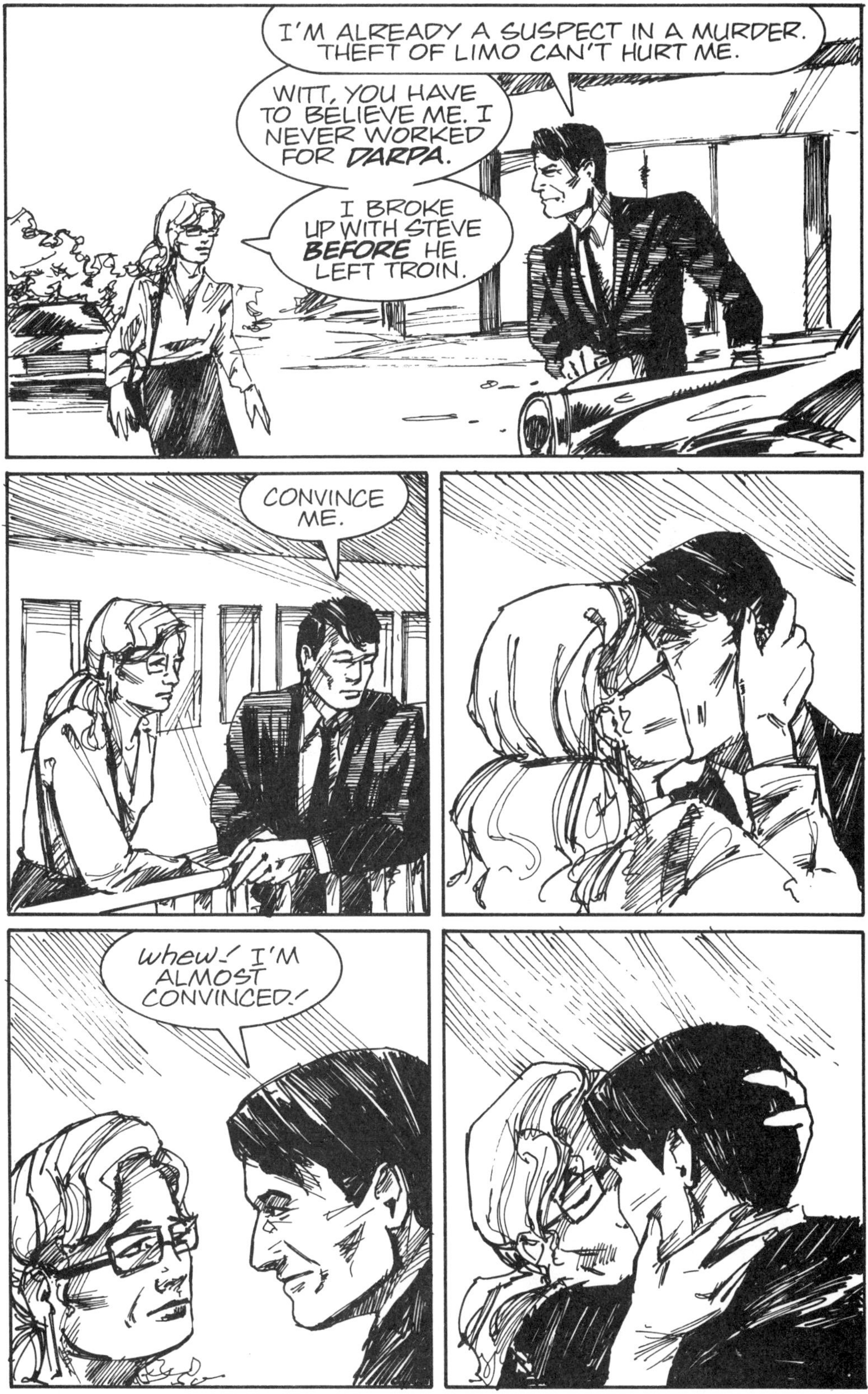
I'M ALREADY A SUSPECT IN A MURDER. THEFT OF LIMO CAN'T HURT ME.
WITT, YOU HAVE TO BELIEVE ME. I NEVER WORKED FOR DARPA.
I BROKE UP WITH STEVE BEFORE HE LEFT TROIN.
CONVINCE ME.
whew! I'M ALMOST CONVINCED!

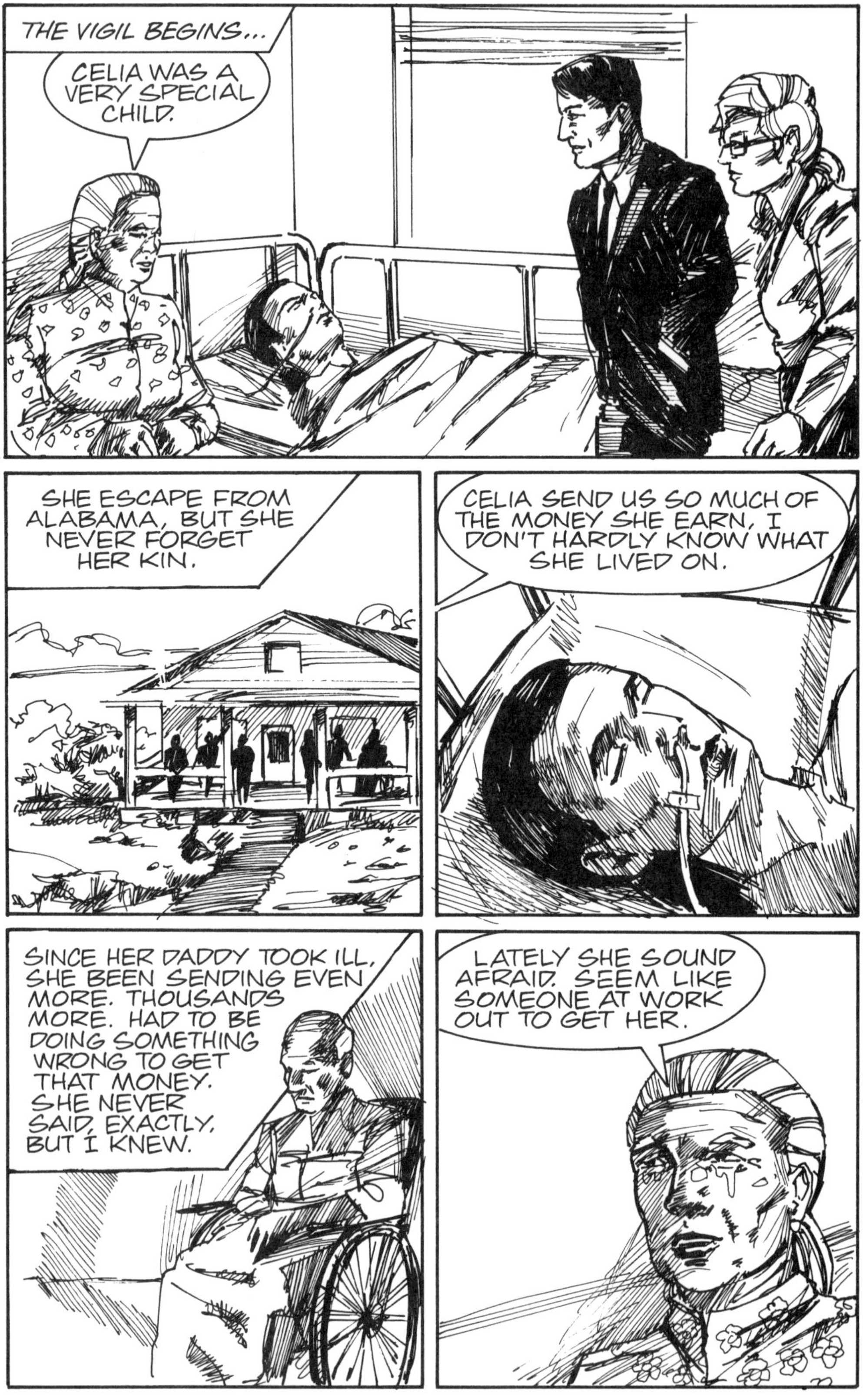
THE VIGIL BEGINS...
CELIA WAS A VERY SPECIAL CHILD.
SHE ESCAPE FROM ALABAMA, BUT SHE NEVER FORGET HER KIN.
CELIA SEND US SO MUCH OF THE MONEY SHE EARN, I DON'T HARDLY KNOW WHAT SHE LIVED ON.
SINCE HER DADDY TOOK ILL, SHE BEEN SENDING EVEN MORE. THOUSANDS MORE. HAD TO BE DOING SOMETHING WRONG TO GET THAT MONEY. SHE NEVER SAID, EXACTLY, BUT I KNEW.
LATELY SHE SOUND AFRAID. SEEM LIKE SOMEONE AT WORK OUT TO GET HER.

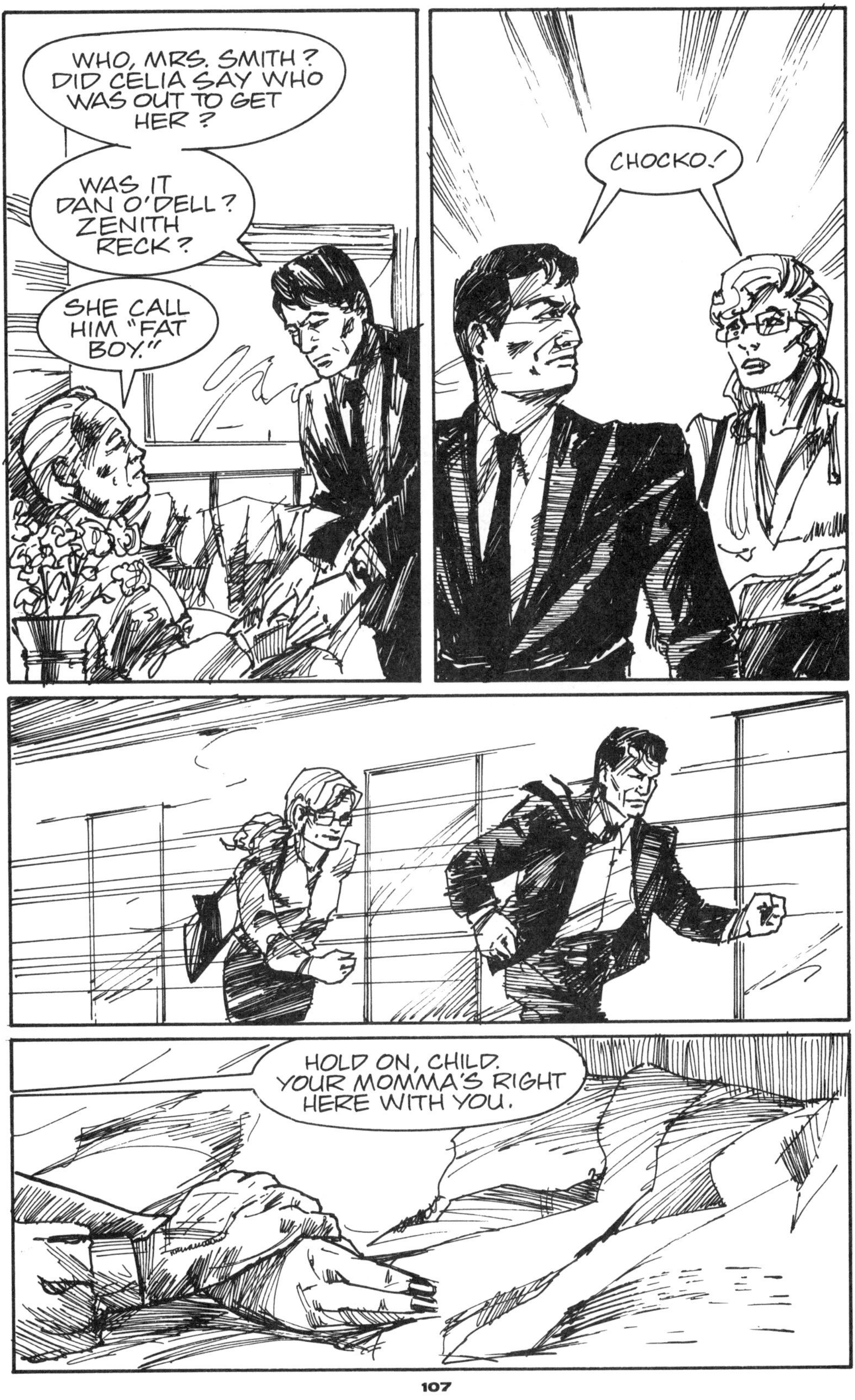
WHO, MRS. SMITH? DID CELIA SAY WHO WAS OUT TO GET HER?
WAS IT DAN O'DELL? ZENITH RECK?
SHE CALL HIM "FAT BOY."
CHOCKO!
HOLD ON, CHILD. YOUR MOMMA'S RIGHT HERE WITH YOU.

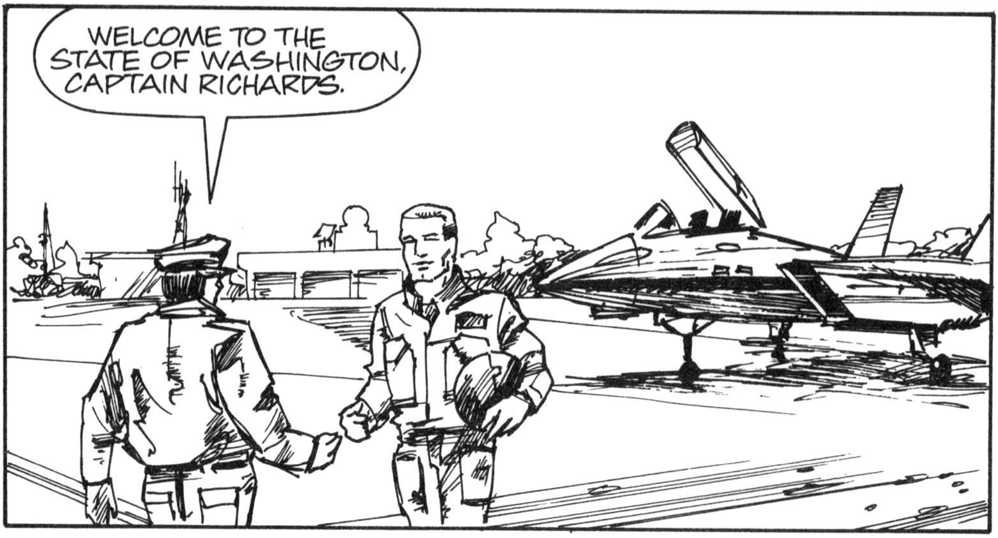
WELCOME TO THE STATE OF WASHINGTON, CAPTAIN RICHARDS.

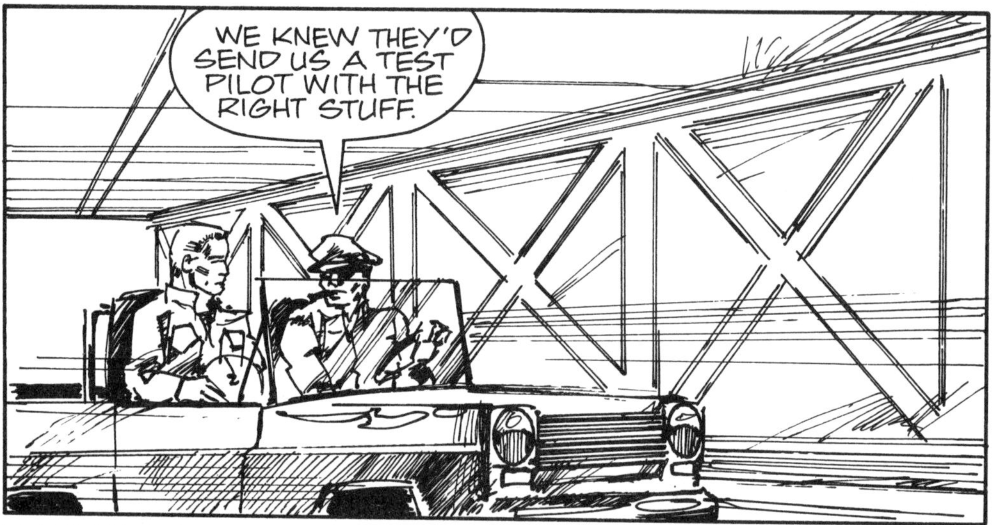
WE KNEW THEY'D SEND US A TEST PILOT WITH THE RIGHT STUFF.

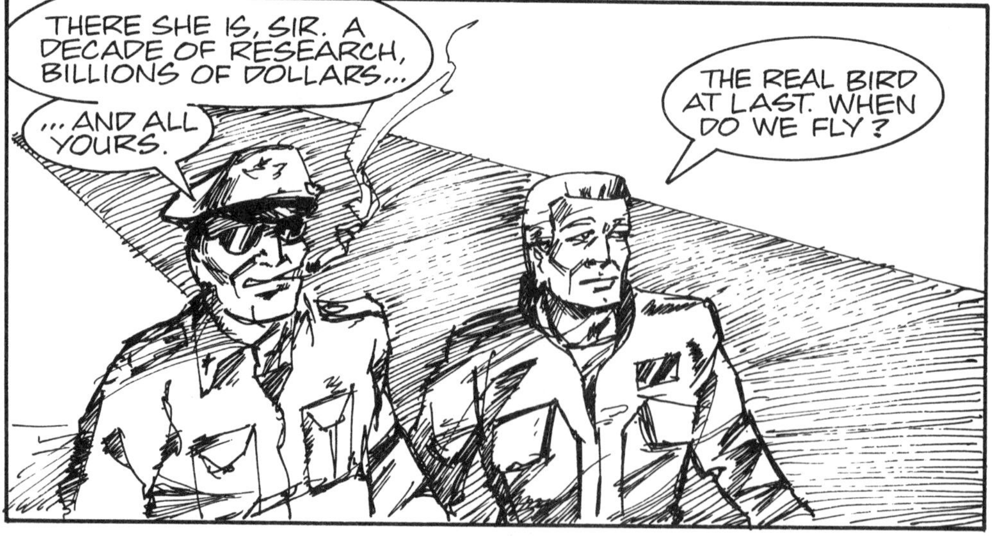
THERE SHE IS, SIR. A DECADE OF RESEARCH, BILLIONS OF DOLLARS...
...AND ALL YOURS.
THE REAL BIRD AT LAST. WHEN DO WE FLY?

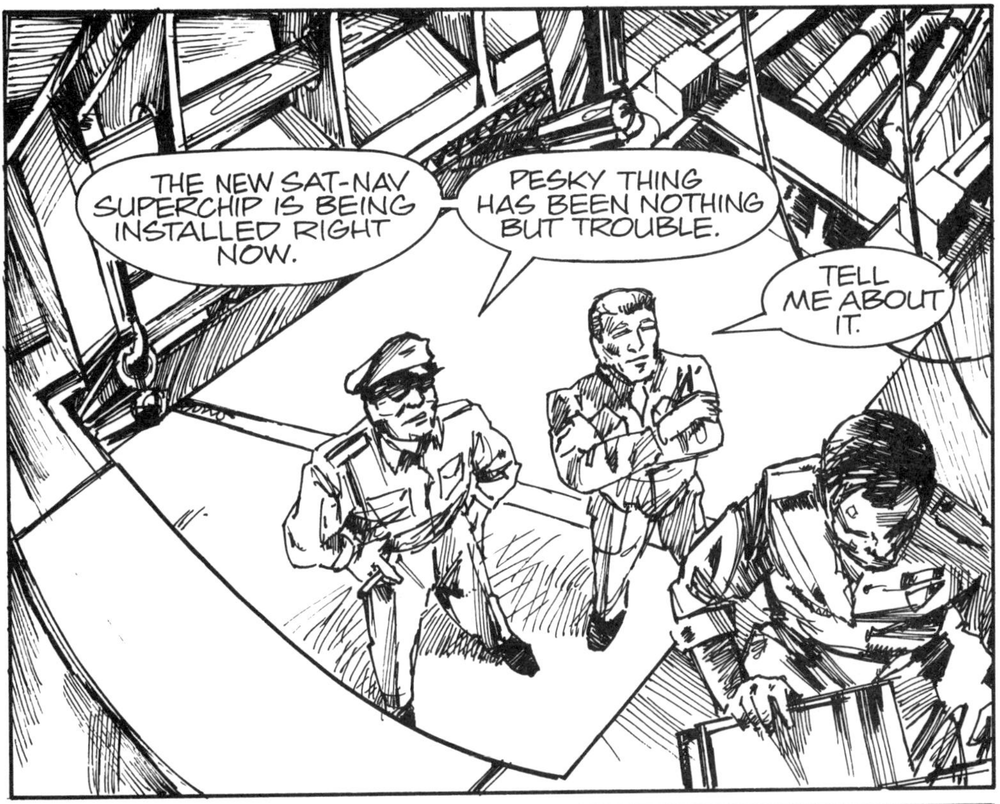
THE NEW SAT-NAV SUPERCHIP IS BEING INSTALLED RIGHT NOW.
PESKY THING HAS BEEN NOTHING BUT TROUBLE.
TELL ME ABOUT IT.

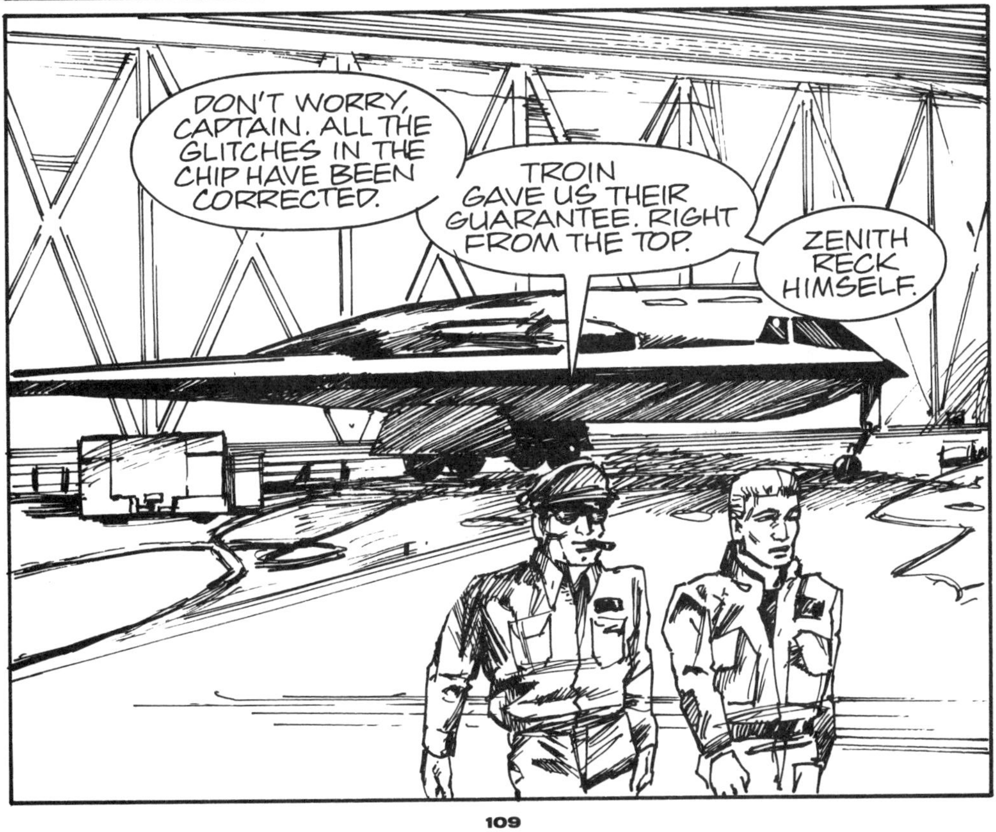
DON'T WORRY, CAPTAIN. ALL THE GLITCHES IN THE CHIP HAVE BEEN CORRECTED.
TROIN GAVE US THEIR GUARANTEE. RIGHT FROM THE TOP.
ZENITH RECK HIMSELF.

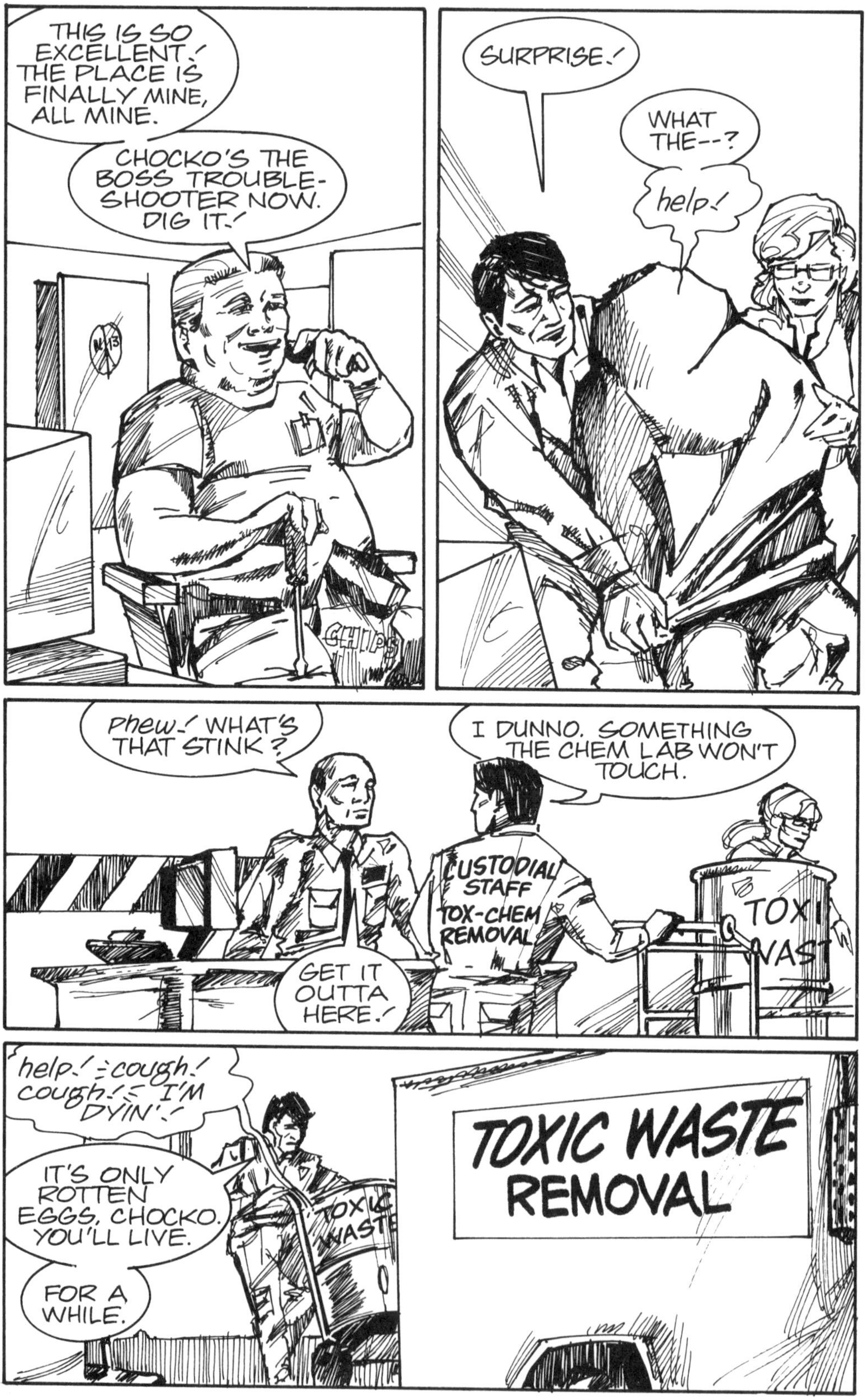
THIS IS SO EXCELLENT! THE PLACE IS FINALLY MINE, ALL MINE.
CHOCKO'S THE BOSS TROUBLE-SHOOTER NOW. DIG IT!
CHIPS
SURPRISE!
WHAT THE--?
help!
phew! WHAT'S THAT STINK?
I DUNNO. SOMETHING THE CHEM LAB WON'T TOUCH.
CUSTODIAL STAFF TOX-CHEM REMOVAL
GET IT OUTTA HERE!
help! cough! cough! I'M DYIN'!
IT'S ONLY ROTTEN EGGS, CHOCKO. YOU'LL LIVE.
FOR A WHILE.
TOXIC WASTE REMOVAL

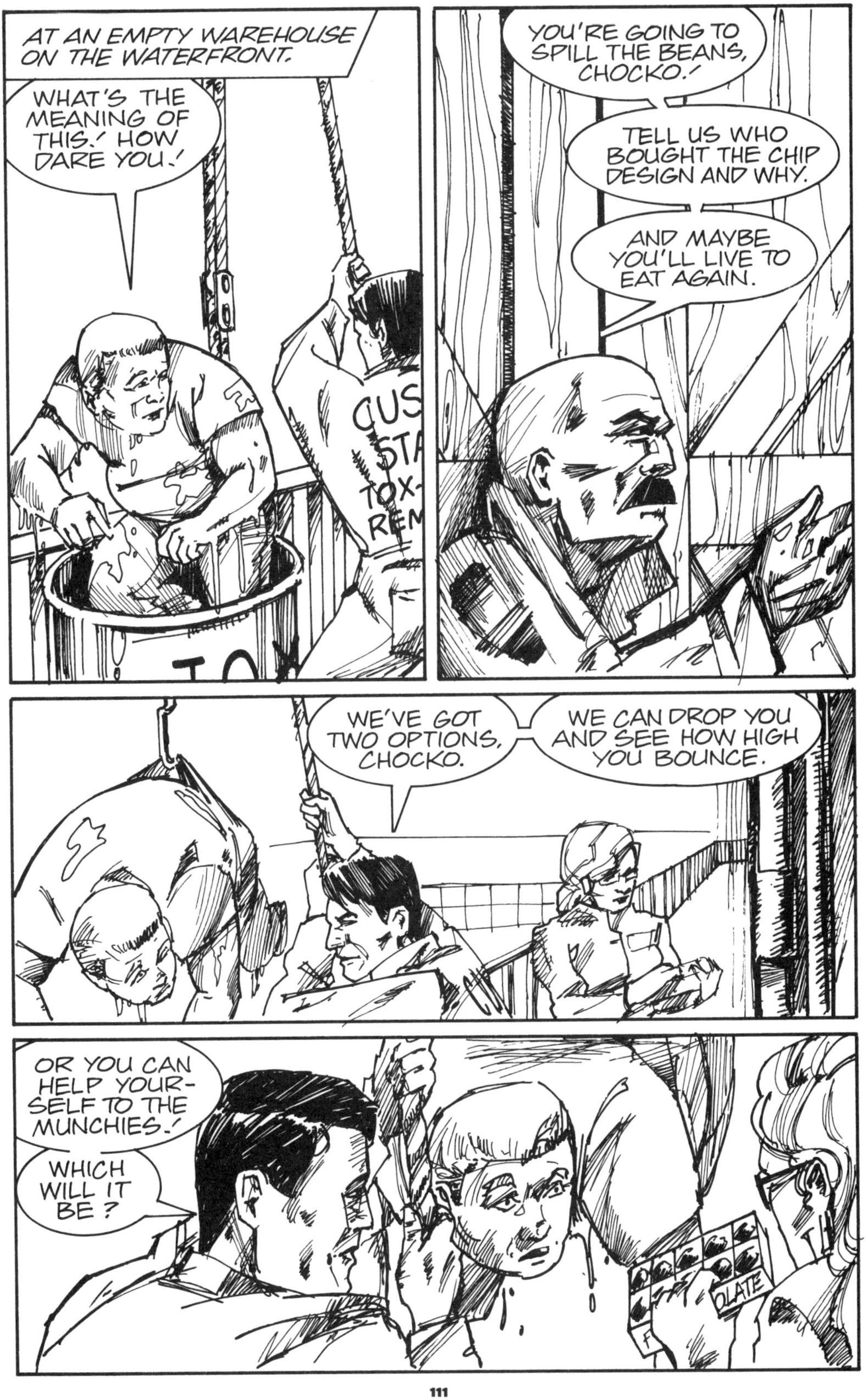
AT AN EMPTY WAREHOUSE ON THE WATERFRONT.
WHAT'S THE MEANING OF THIS! HOW DARE YOU!
YOU'RE GOING TO SPILL THE BEANS, CHOCKO!
TELL US WHO BOUGHT THE CHIP DESIGN AND WHY.
AND MAYBE YOU'LL LIVE TO EAT AGAIN.
WE'VE GOT TWO OPTIONS, CHOCKO.
WE CAN DROP YOU AND SEE HOW HIGH YOU BOUNCE.
OR YOU CAN HELP YOURSELF TO THE MUNCHIES!
WHICH WILL IT BE ?

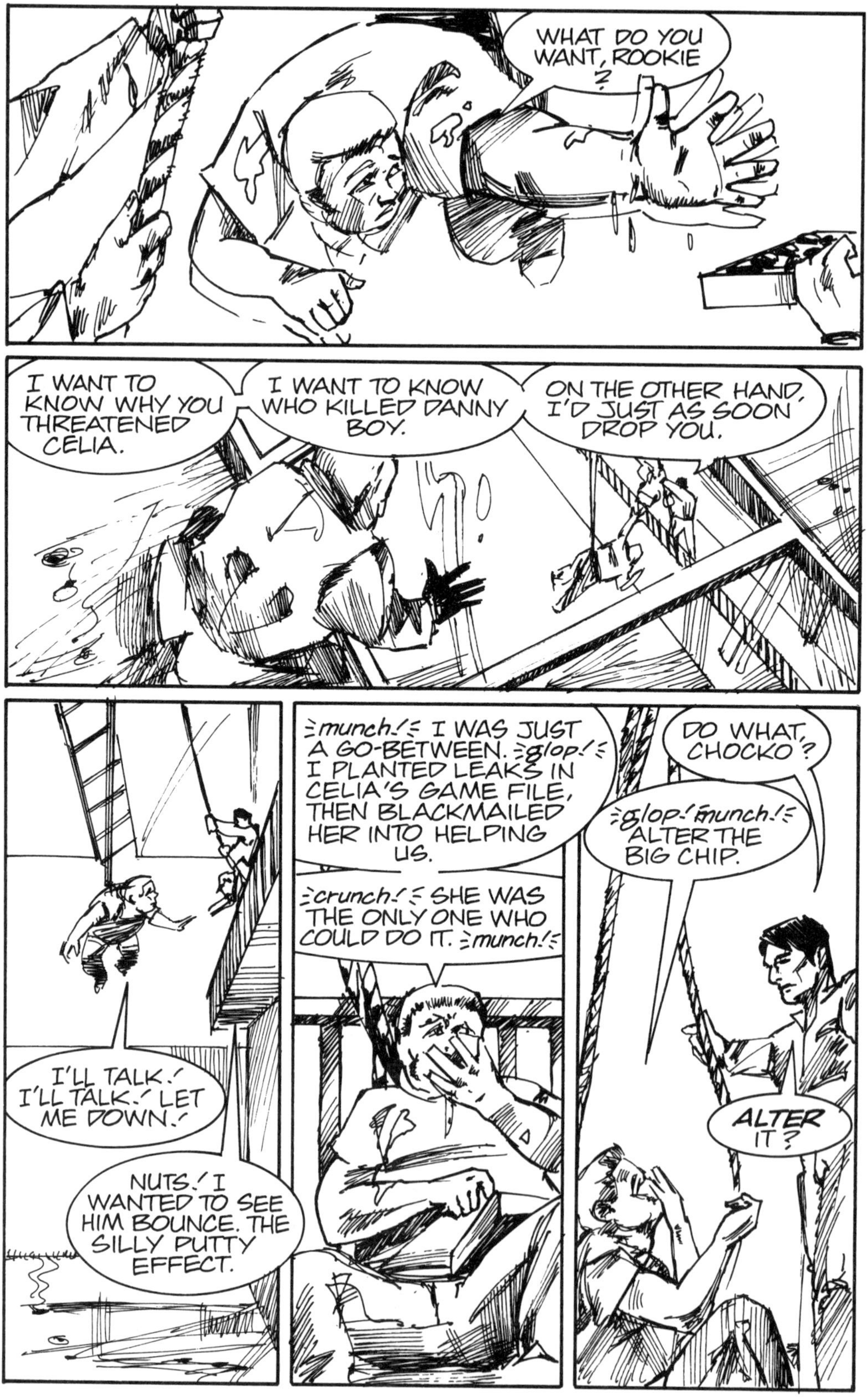
WHAT DO YOU WANT, ROOKIE?
I WANT TO KNOW WHY YOU THREATENED CELIA.
I WANT TO KNOW WHO KILLED DANNY BOY.
ON THE OTHER HAND, I'D JUST AS SOON DROP YOU.
I'LL TALK! I'LL TALK! LET ME DOWN!
NUTS! I WANTED TO SEE HIM BOUNCE. THE SILLY PUTTY EFFECT.
munch! I WAS JUST A GO-BETWEEN. glop! I PLANTED LEAKS IN CELIA'S GAME FILE, THEN BLACKMAILED HER INTO HELPING US.
crunch! SHE WAS THE ONLY ONE WHO COULD DO IT. munch!
DO WHAT, CHOCKO?
glop! munch! ALTER THE BIG CHIP.
ALTER IT?

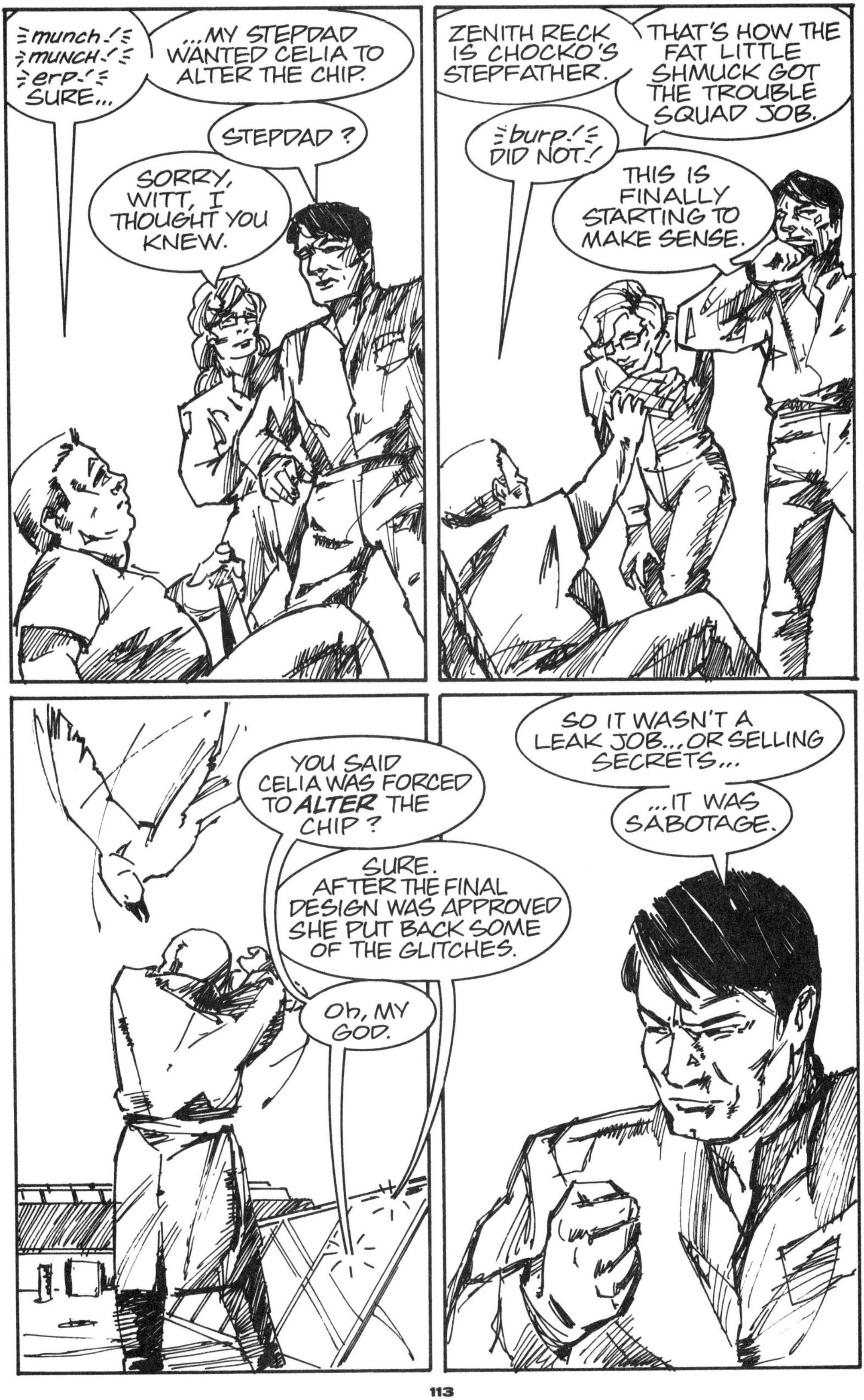
munch! munch! erp! SURE...
...MY STEPDAD WANTED CELIA TO ALTER THE CHIP.
STEPDAD?
SORRY, WITT, I THOUGHT YOU KNEW.
ZENITH RECK IS CHOCKO'S STEPFATHER.
THAT'S HOW THE FAT LITTLE SHMUCK GOT THE TROUBLE SQUAD JOB.
burp! DID NOT!
THIS IS FINALLY STARTING TO MAKE SENSE.
YOU SAID CELIA WAS FORCED TO ALTER THE CHIP?
SURE. AFTER THE FINAL DESIGN WAS APPROVED SHE PUT BACK SOME OF THE GLITCHES.
Oh, MY GOD.
SO IT WASN'T A LEAK JOB..., OR SELLING SECRETS...
...IT WAS SABOTAGE.

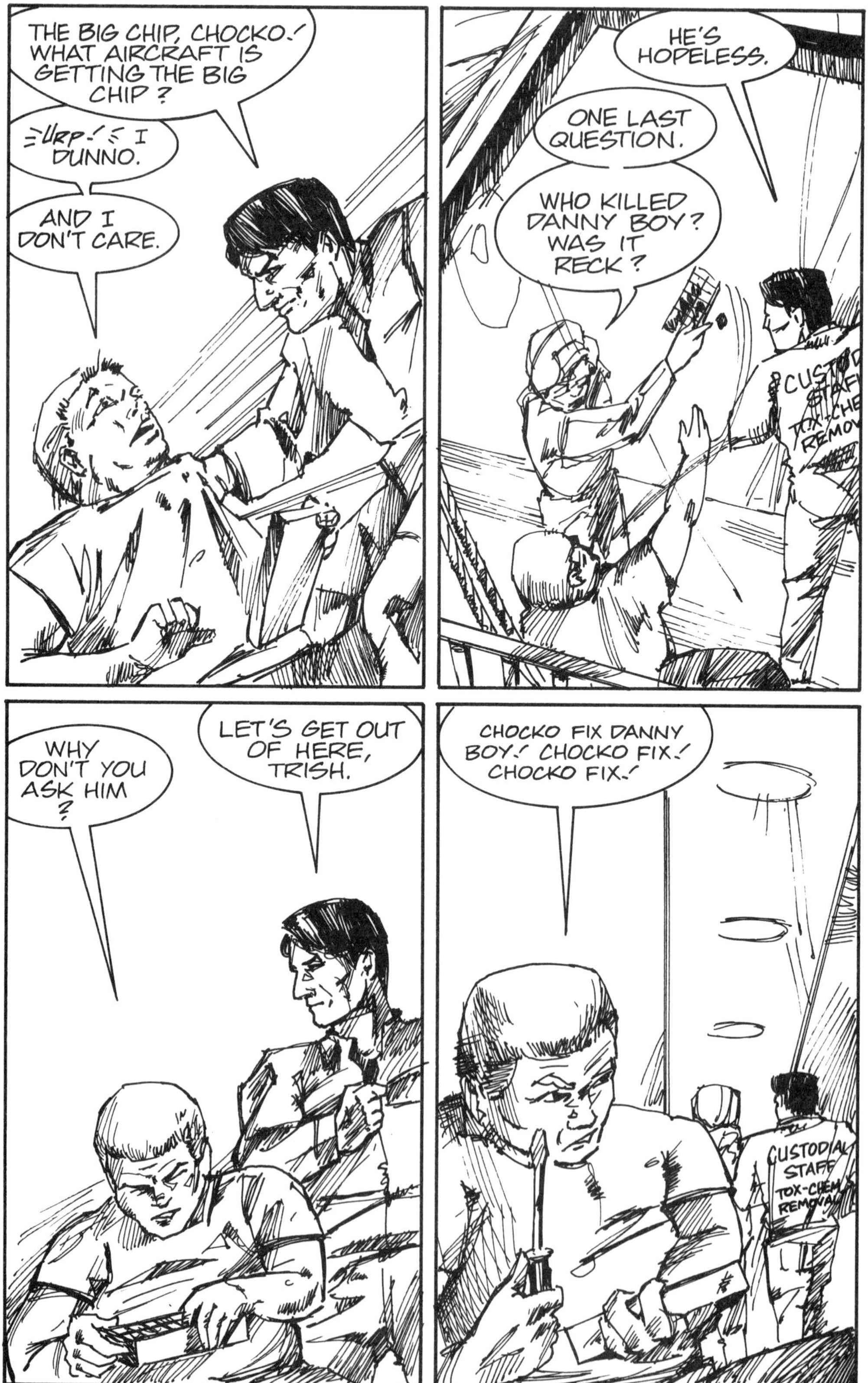
THE BIG CHIP, CHOCKO! WHAT AIRCRAFT IS GETTING THE BIG CHIP?
URP! I DUNNO.
AND I DON'T CARE.
HE'S HOPELESS.
ONE LAST QUESTION.
WHO KILLED DANNY BOY? WAS IT RECK?
CUSTODIAL STAFF TOX-CHEM REMOVAL
WHY DON'T YOU ASK HIM?
LET'S GET OUT OF HERE, TRISH.
CHOCKO FIX DANNY BOY! CHOCKO FIX! CHOCKO FIX!
CUSTODIAL STAFF TOX-CHEM REMOVAL

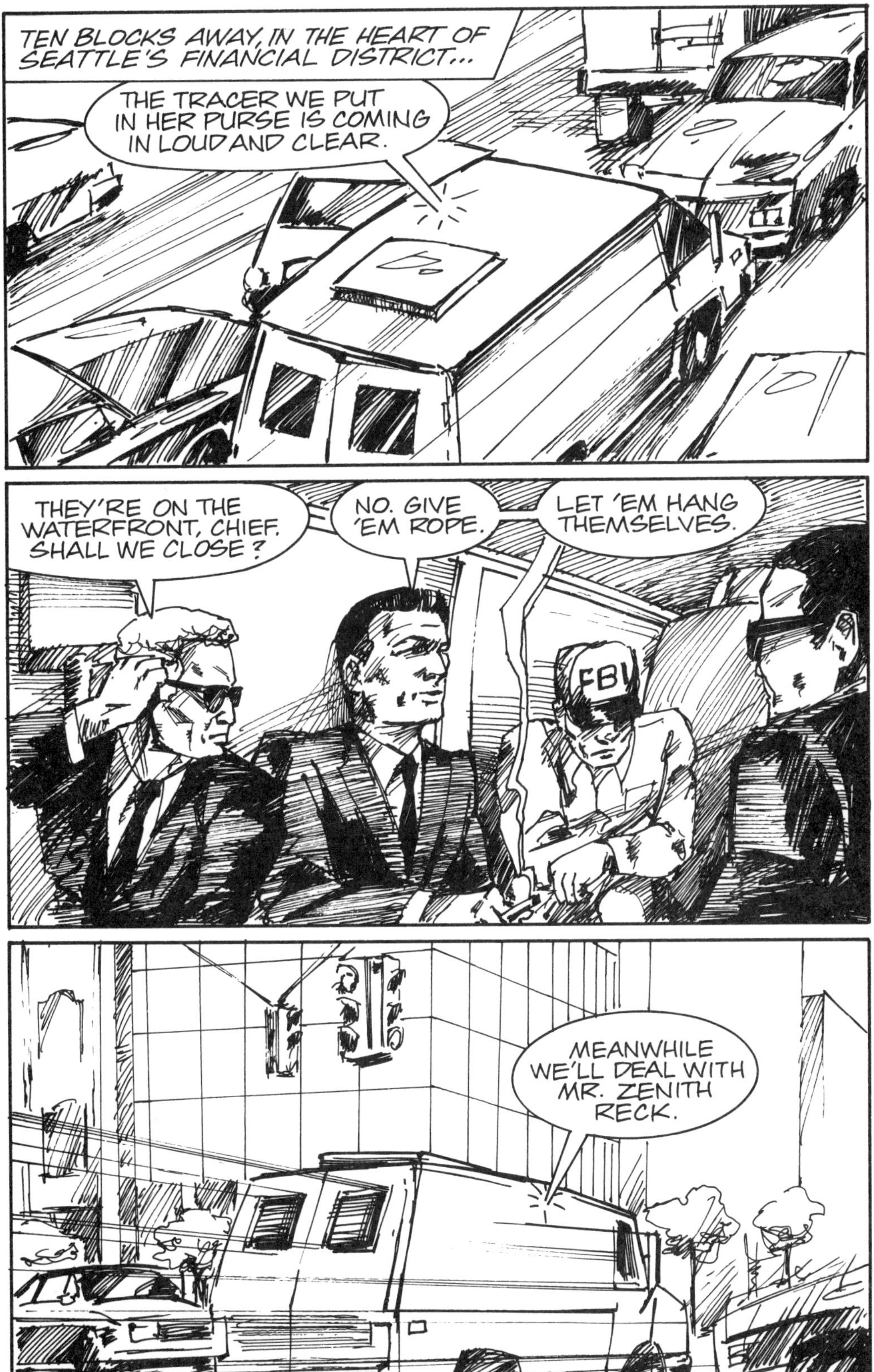
TEN BLOCKS AWAY, IN THE HEART OF SEATTLE'S FINANCIAL DISTRICT...
THE TRACER WE PUT IN HER PURSE IS COMING IN LOUD AND CLEAR.
THEY'RE ON THE WATERFRONT, CHIEF. SHALL WE CLOSE?
NO. GIVE 'EM ROPE.
LET 'EM HANG THEMSELVES.
FBI
MEANWHILE WE'LL DEAL WITH MR. ZENITH RECK.

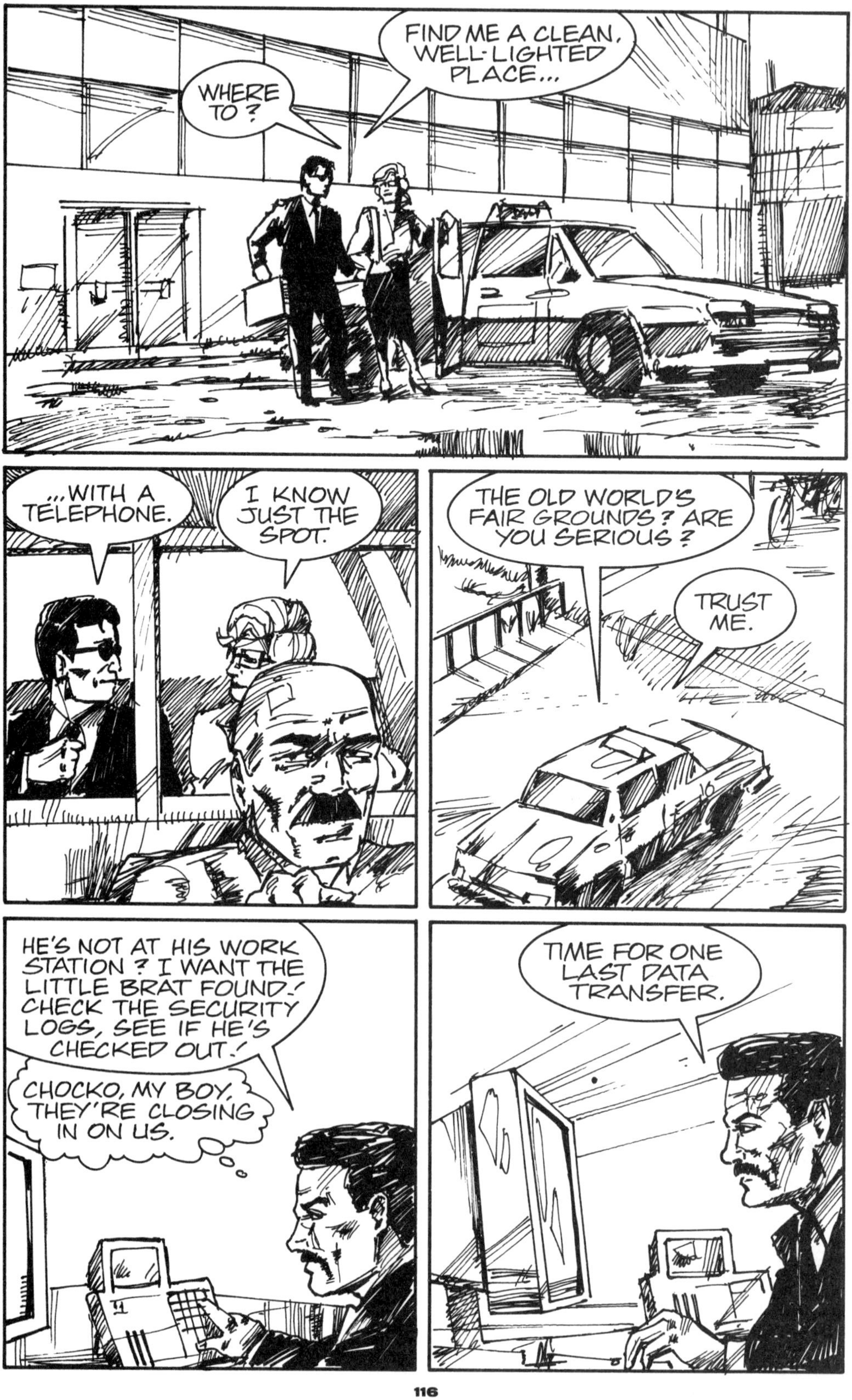
WHERE TO ?
FIND ME A CLEAN, WELL-LIGHTED PLACE...
...WITH A TELEPHONE.
I KNOW JUST THE SPOT.
THE OLD WORLD'S FAIR GROUNDS ? ARE YOU SERIOUS ?
TRUST ME.
HE'S NOT AT HIS WORK STATION ? I WANT THE LITTLE BRAT FOUND! CHECK THE SECURITY LOGS, SEE IF HE'S CHECKED OUT!
CHOCKO, MY BOY, THEY'RE CLOSING IN ON US.
TIME FOR ONE LAST DATA TRANSFER.

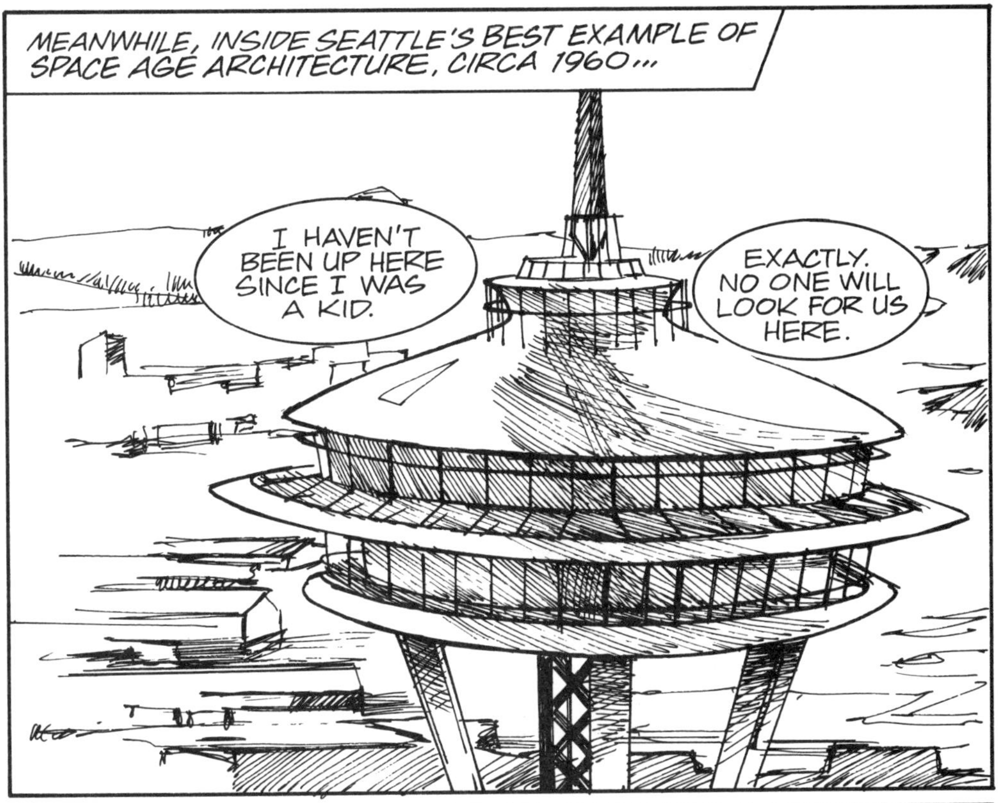
MEANWHILE, INSIDE SEATTLE'S BEST EXAMPLE OF SPACE AGE ARCHITECTURE, CIRCA 1960...
I HAVEN'T BEEN UP HERE SINCE I WAS A KID.
EXACTLY. NO ONE WILL LOOK FOR US HERE.

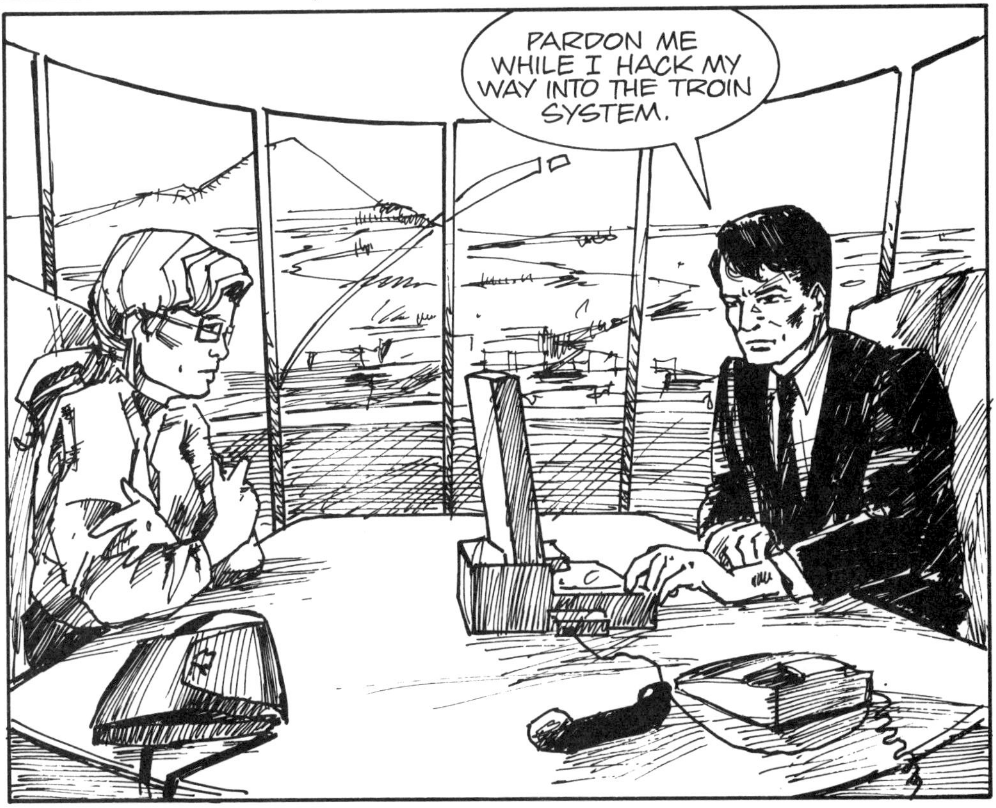
PARDON ME WHILE I HACK MY WAY INTO THE TROIN SYSTEM.

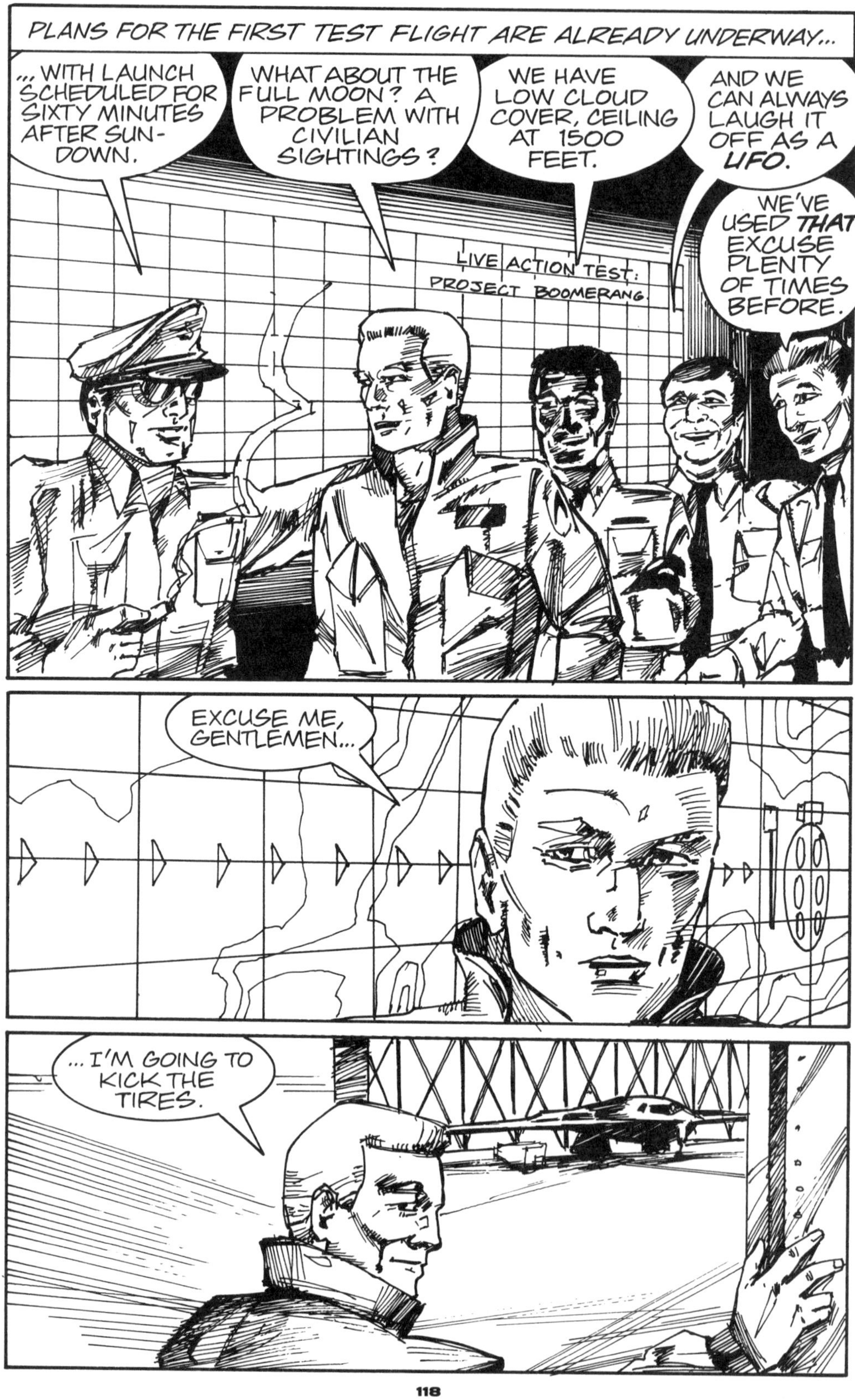
PLANS FOR THE FIRST TEST FLIGHT ARE ALREADY UNDERWAY...
...WITH LAUNCH SCHEDULED FOR SIXTY MINUTES AFTER SUN-DOWN.
WHAT ABOUT THE FULL MOON? A PROBLEM WITH CIVILIAN SIGHTINGS?
WE HAVE LOW CLOUD COVER, CEILING AT 1500 FEET.
AND WE CAN ALWAYS LAUGH IT OFF AS A UFO.
WE'VE USED THAT EXCUSE PLENTY OF TIMES BEFORE.
LIVE ACTION TEST: PROJECT BOOMERANG.
EXCUSE ME, GENTLEMEN...
...I'M GOING TO KICK THE TIRES.

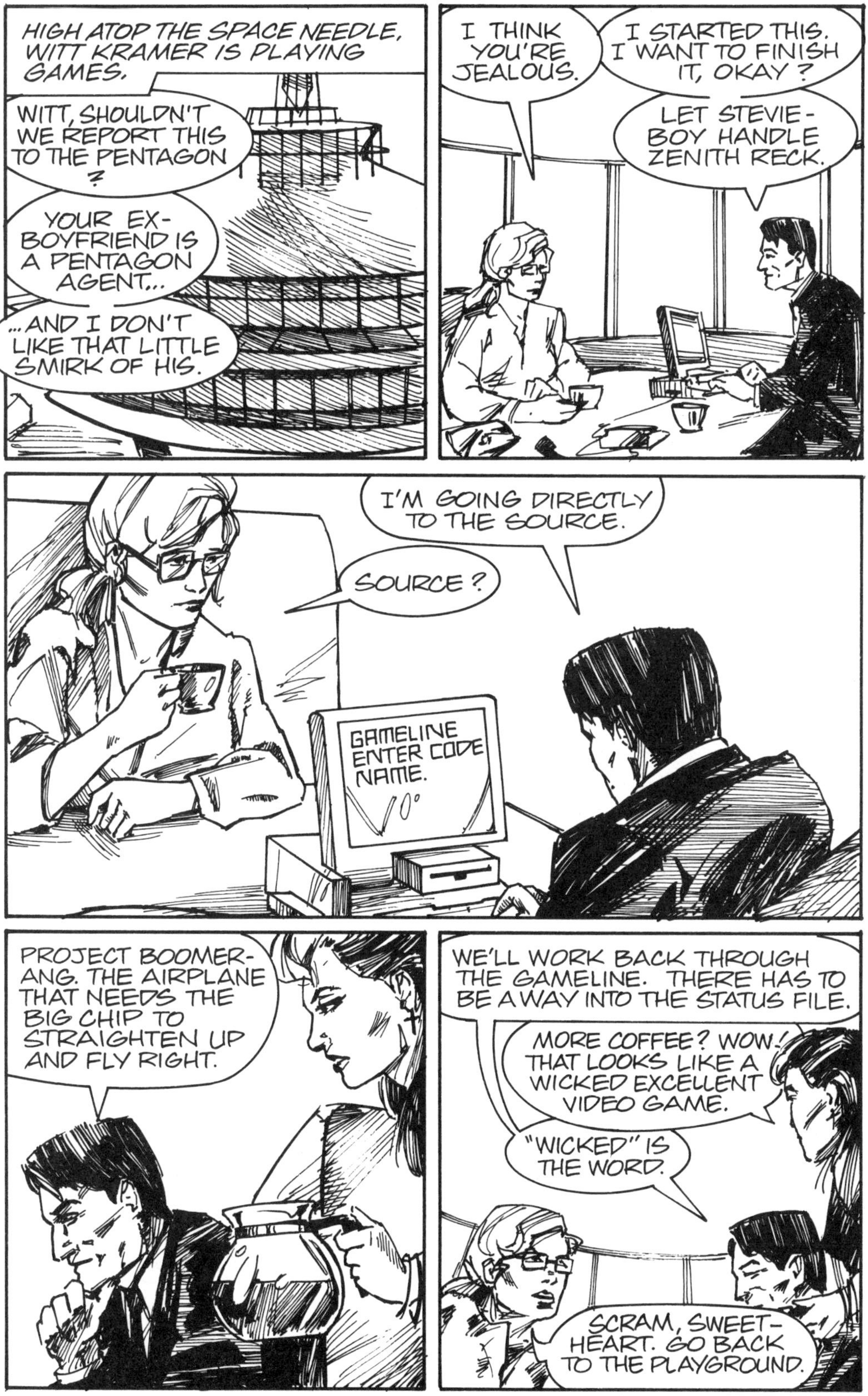
HIGH ATOP THE SPACE NEEDLE, WITT KRAMER IS PLAYING GAMES.
WITT, SHOULDN'T WE REPORT THIS TO THE PENTAGON ?
YOUR EX-BOYFRIEND IS A PENTAGON AGENT...
...AND I DON'T LIKE THAT LITTLE SMIRK OF HIS.
I THINK YOU'RE JEALOUS.
I STARTED THIS. I WANT TO FINISH IT, OKAY ?
LET STEVIE-BOY HANDLE ZENITH RECK.
I'M GOING DIRECTLY TO THE SOURCE.
SOURCE ?
GAMELINE ENTER CODE NAME.
PROJECT BOOMERANG. THE AIRPLANE THAT NEEDS THE BIG CHIP TO STRAIGHTEN UP AND FLY RIGHT.
WE'LL WORK BACK THROUGH THE GAMELINE. THERE HAS TO BE A WAY INTO THE STATUS FILE.
MORE COFFEE? WOW! THAT LOOKS LIKE A WICKED EXCELLENT VIDEO GAME.
"WICKED" IS THE WORD.
SCRAM, SWEETHEART. GO BACK TO THE PLAYGROUND.

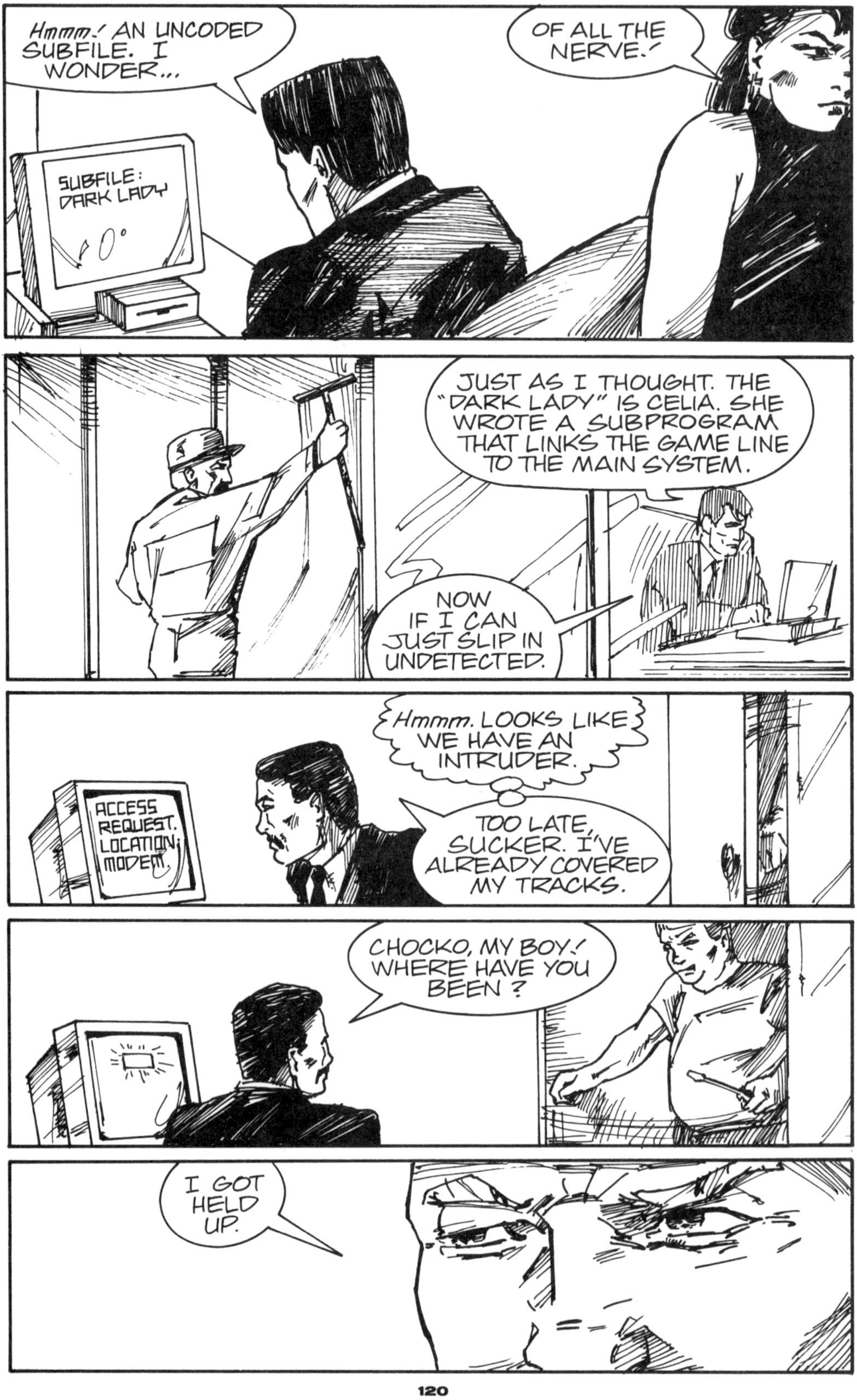
Hmmm! AN UNCODED SUBFILE. I WONDER...
SUBFILE: DARK LADY
OF ALL THE NERVE!
JUST AS I THOUGHT. THE "DARK LADY" IS CELIA. SHE WROTE A SUBPROGRAM THAT LINKS THE GAME LINE TO THE MAIN SYSTEM.
NOW IF I CAN JUST SLIP IN UNDETECTED.
Hmmm. LOOKS LIKE WE HAVE AN INTRUDER.
ACCESS REQUEST. LOCATION: MODEM.
TOO LATE, SUCKER. I'VE ALREADY COVERED MY TRACKS.
CHOCKO, MY BOY! WHERE HAVE YOU BEEN?
I GOT HELD UP.

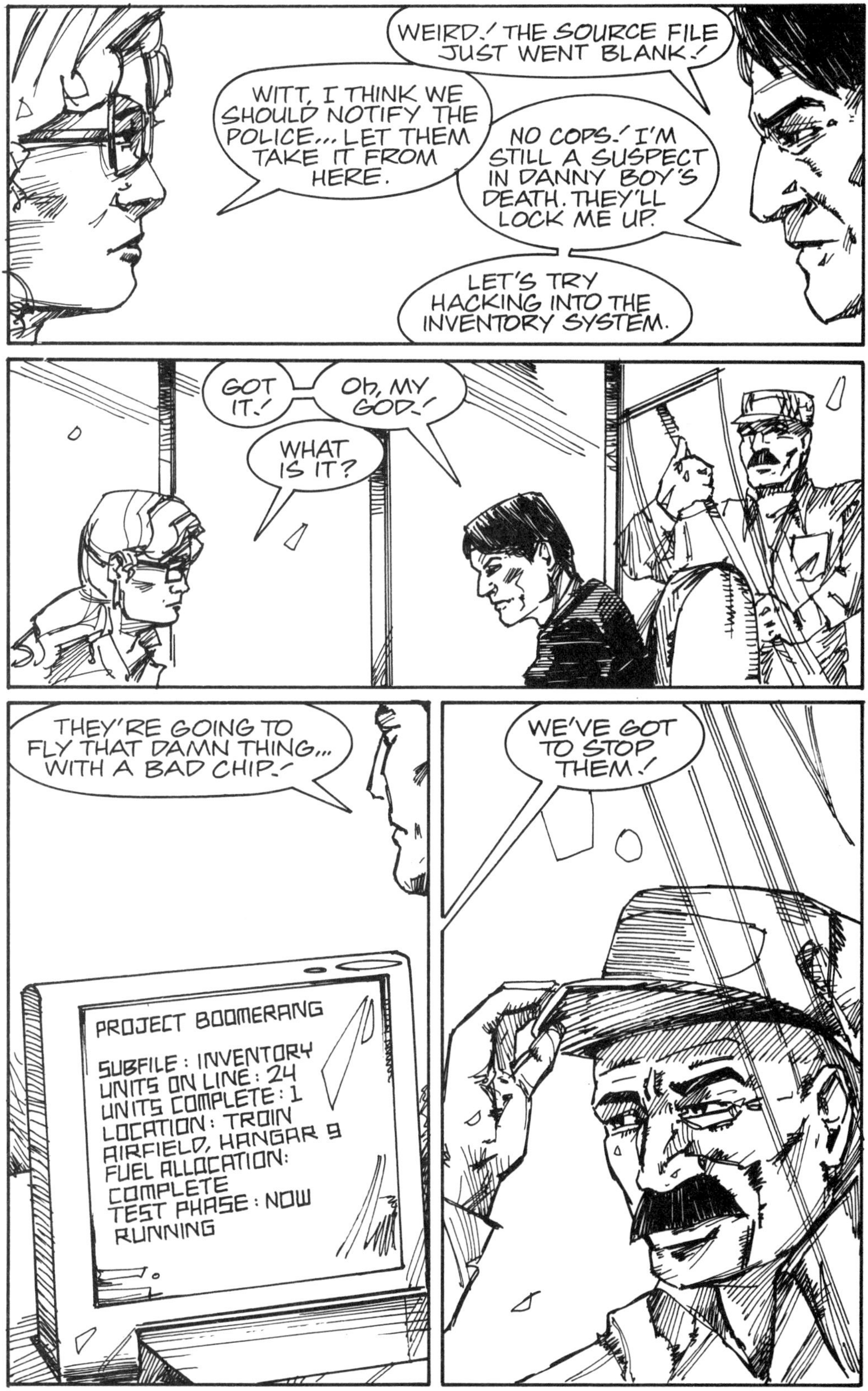
WEIRD! THE SOURCE FILE JUST WENT BLANK!
WITT, I THINK WE SHOULD NOTIFY THE POLICE... LET THEM TAKE IT FROM HERE.
NO COPS! I'M STILL A SUSPECT IN DANNY BOY'S DEATH. THEY'LL LOCK ME UP.
LET'S TRY HACKING INTO THE INVENTORY SYSTEM.
GOT IT!
OH, MY GOD!
WHAT IS IT?
THEY'RE GOING TO FLY THAT DAMN THING... WITH A BAD CHIP!
PROJECT BOOMERANG
SUBFILE: INVENTORY
UNITS ON LINE: 24
UNITS COMPLETE: 1
LOCATION: TROIN AIRFIELD, HANGAR 9
FUEL ALLOCATION: COMPLETE
TEST PHASE: NOW RUNNING
WE'VE GOT TO STOP THEM!

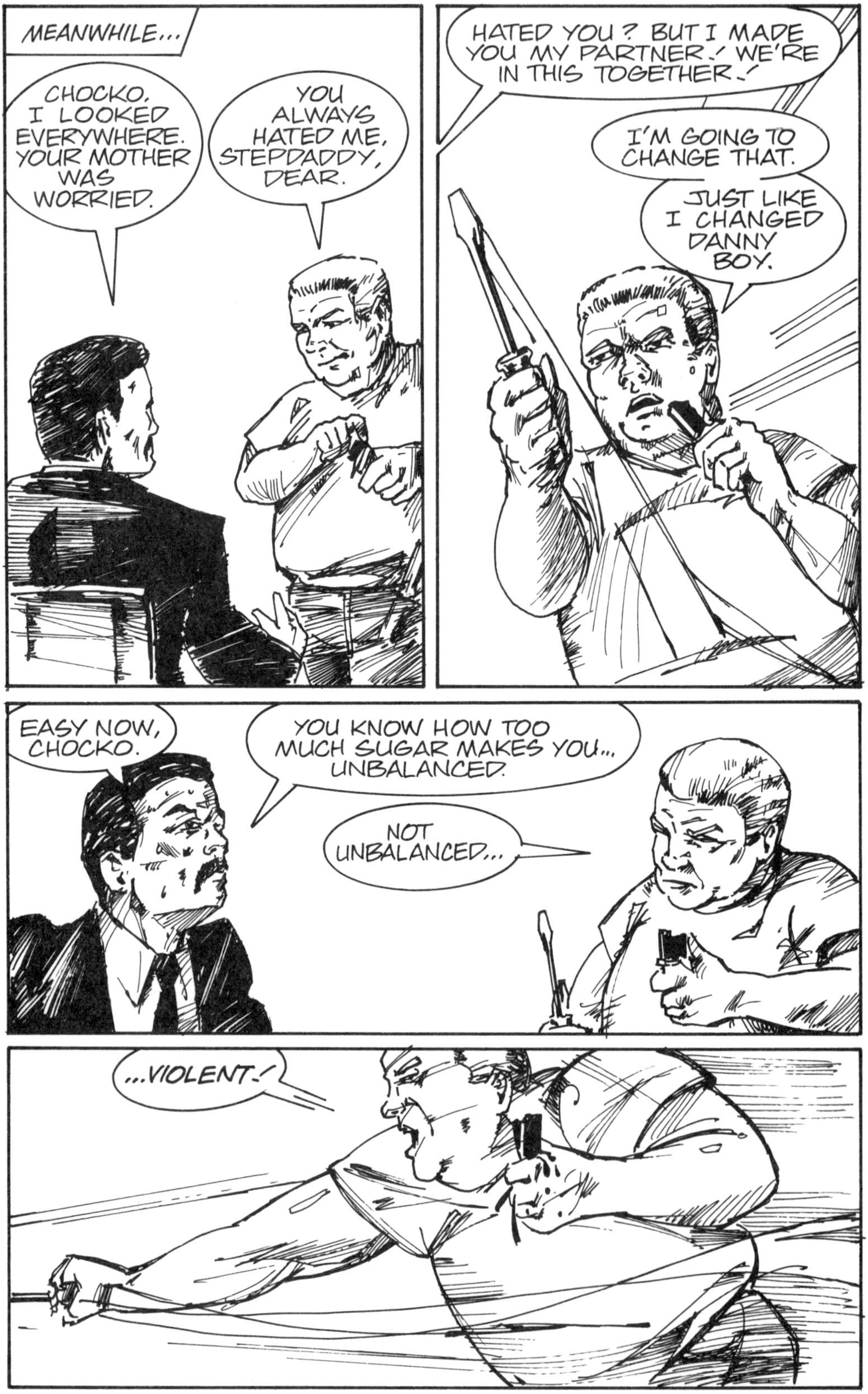
MEANWHILE...
CHOCKO. I LOOKED EVERYWHERE. YOUR MOTHER WAS WORRIED.
YOU ALWAYS HATED ME, STEPDADDY, DEAR.
HATED YOU? BUT I MADE YOU MY PARTNER! WE'RE IN THIS TOGETHER!
I'M GOING TO CHANGE THAT.
JUST LIKE I CHANGED DANNY BOY.
EASY NOW, CHOCKO.
YOU KNOW HOW TOO MUCH SUGAR MAKES YOU... UNBALANCED.
NOT UNBALANCED...
...VIOLENT!

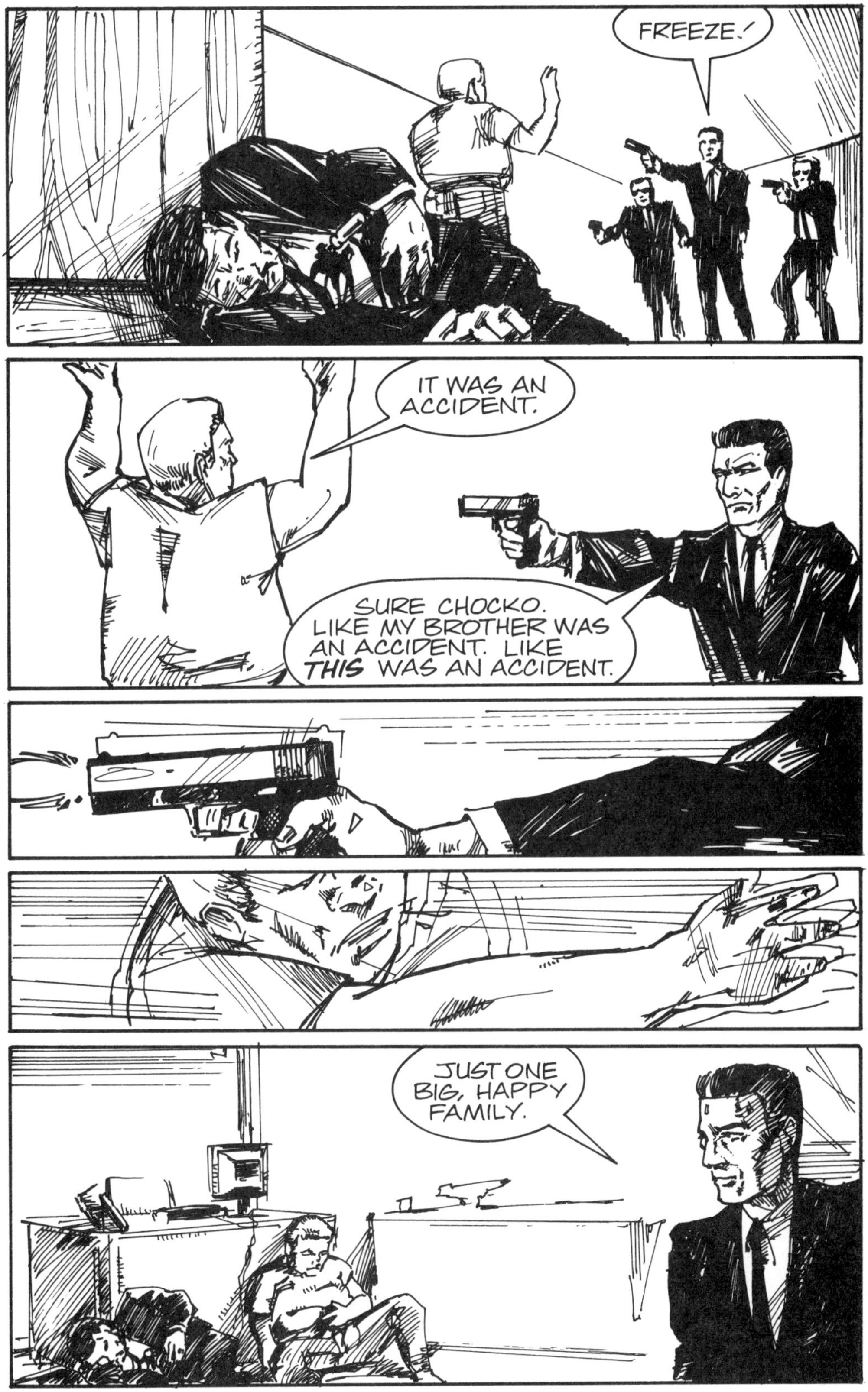
FREEZE!
IT WAS AN ACCIDENT.
SURE CHOCKO. LIKE MY BROTHER WAS AN ACCIDENT. LIKE **THIS** WAS AN ACCIDENT.
JUST ONE BIG, HAPPY FAMILY.

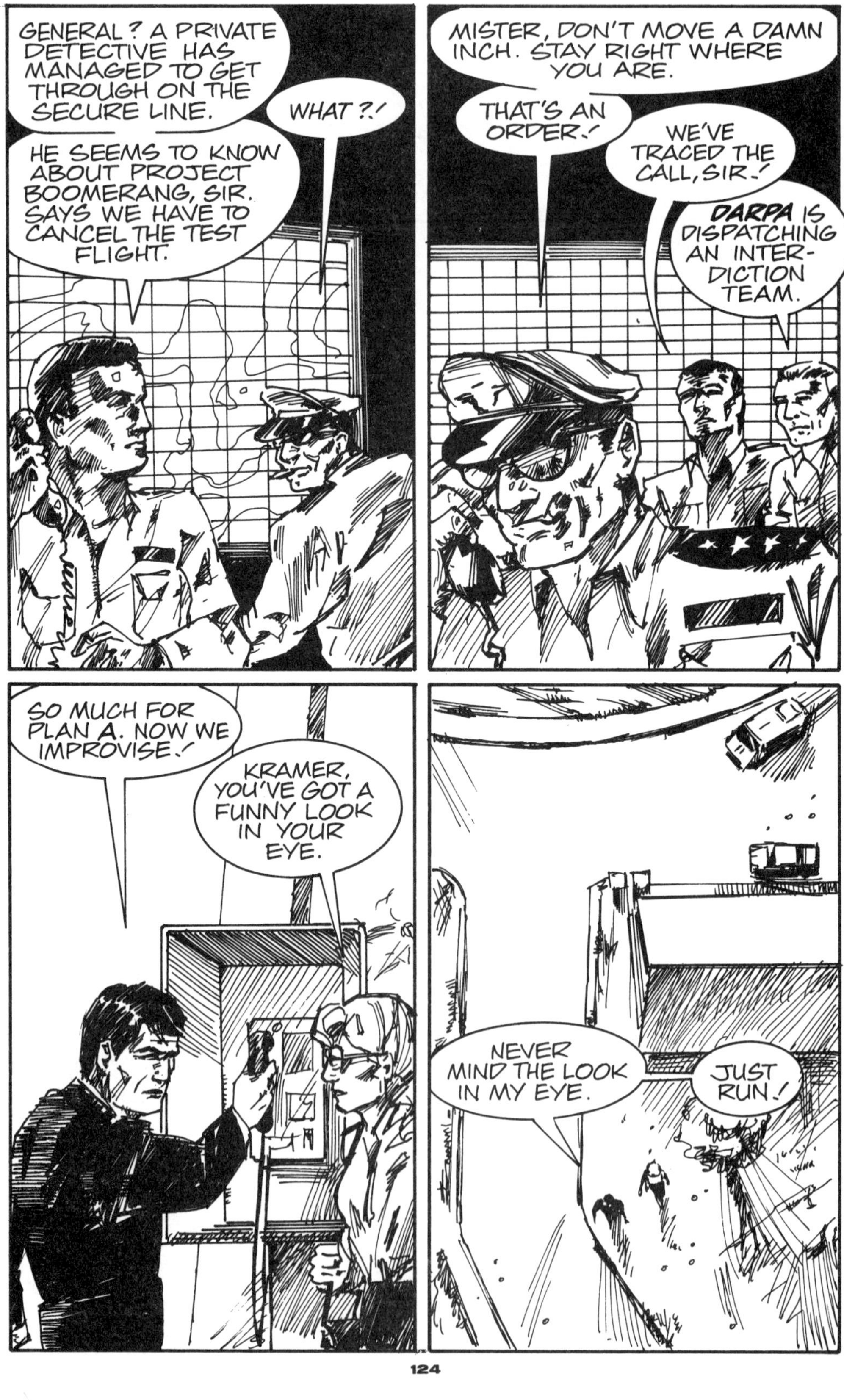
GENERAL? A PRIVATE DETECTIVE HAS MANAGED TO GET THROUGH ON THE SECURE LINE.
HE SEEMS TO KNOW ABOUT PROJECT BOOMERANG, SIR. SAYS WE HAVE TO CANCEL THE TEST FLIGHT.
WHAT?!
MISTER, DON'T MOVE A DAMN INCH. STAY RIGHT WHERE YOU ARE.
THAT'S AN ORDER!
WE'VE TRACED THE CALL, SIR!
DARPA IS DISPATCHING AN INTERDICTION TEAM.
SO MUCH FOR PLAN A. NOW WE IMPROVISE!
KRAMER, YOU'VE GOT A FUNNY LOOK IN YOUR EYE.
NEVER MIND THE LOOK IN MY EYE.
JUST RUN!

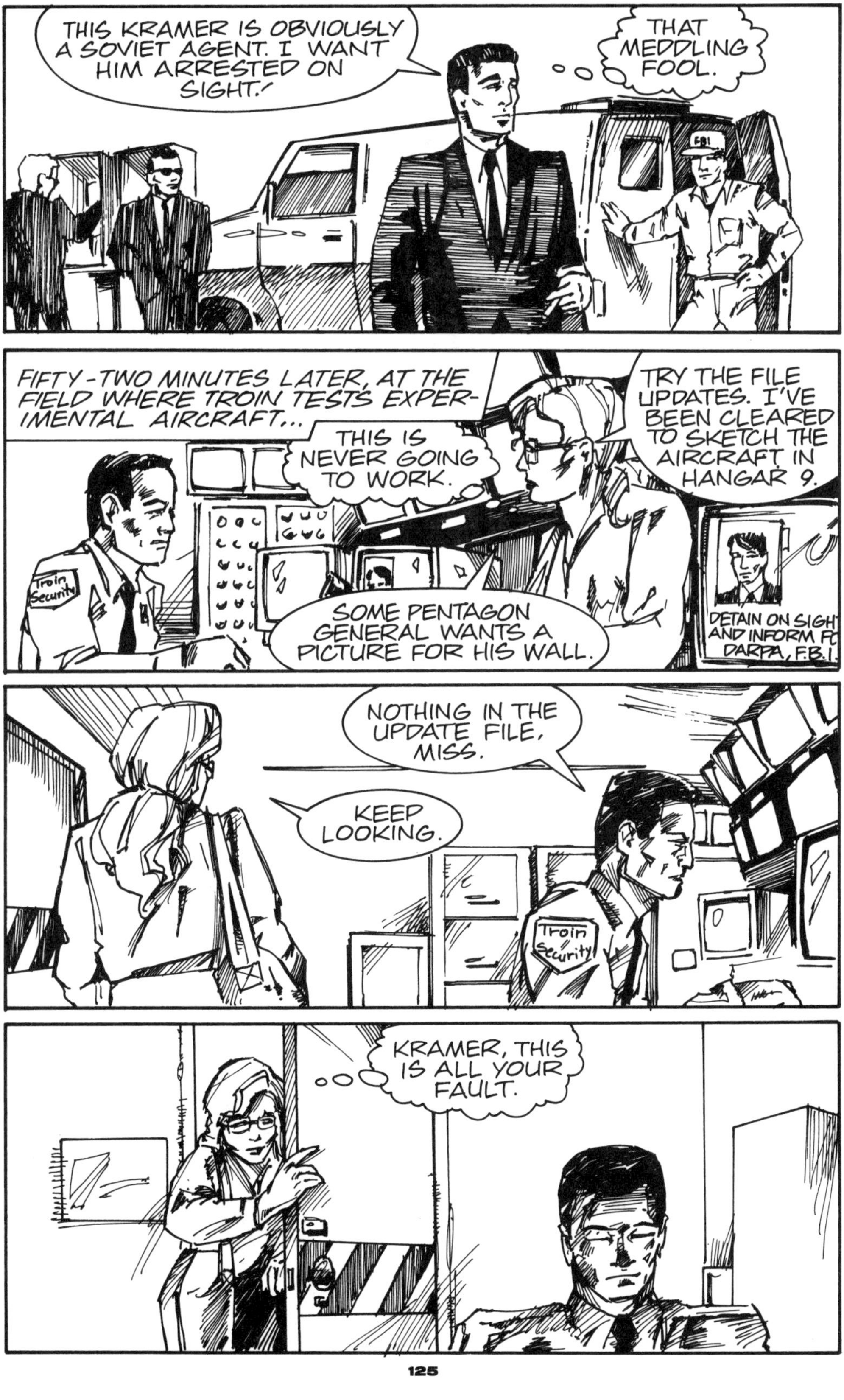
THIS KRAMER IS OBVIOUSLY A SOVIET AGENT. I WANT HIM ARRESTED ON SIGHT!
THAT MEDDLING FOOL.
FBI
FIFTY-TWO MINUTES LATER, AT THE FIELD WHERE TROIN TESTS EXPERIMENTAL AIRCRAFT...
THIS IS NEVER GOING TO WORK.
TRY THE FILE UPDATES. I'VE BEEN CLEARED TO SKETCH THE AIRCRAFT IN HANGAR 9.
Troin Security
SOME PENTAGON GENERAL WANTS A PICTURE FOR HIS WALL.
DETAIN ON SIGHT AND INFORM
DARPA, F.B.I.
NOTHING IN THE UPDATE FILE, MISS.
KEEP LOOKING.
Troin Security
KRAMER, THIS IS ALL YOUR FAULT.

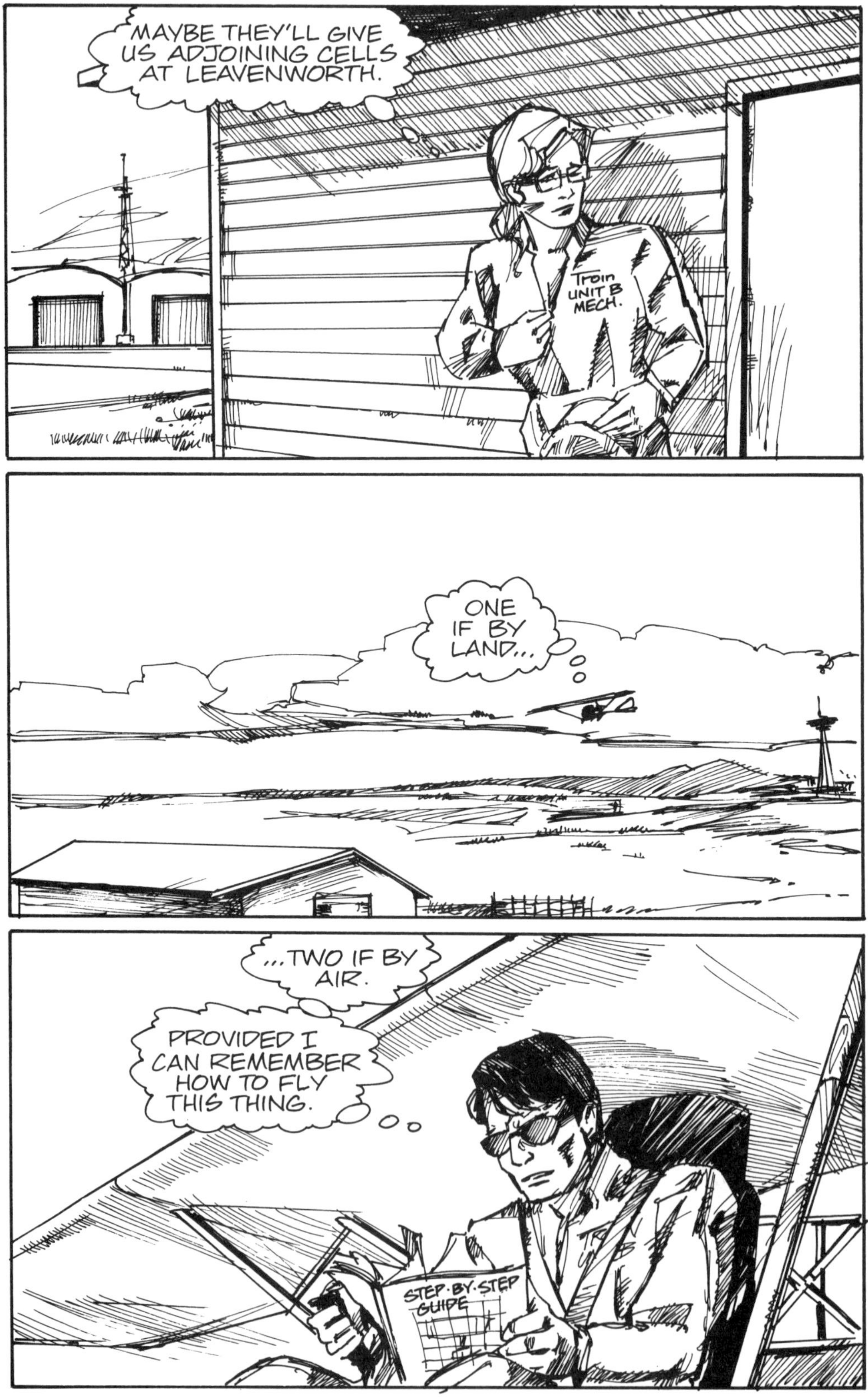
MAYBE THEY'LL GIVE US ADJOINING CELLS AT LEAVENWORTH.
Train UNIT B MECH.
ONE IF BY LAND...
...TWO IF BY AIR.
PROVIDED I CAN REMEMBER HOW TO FLY THIS THING.
STEP·BY·STEP GUIDE

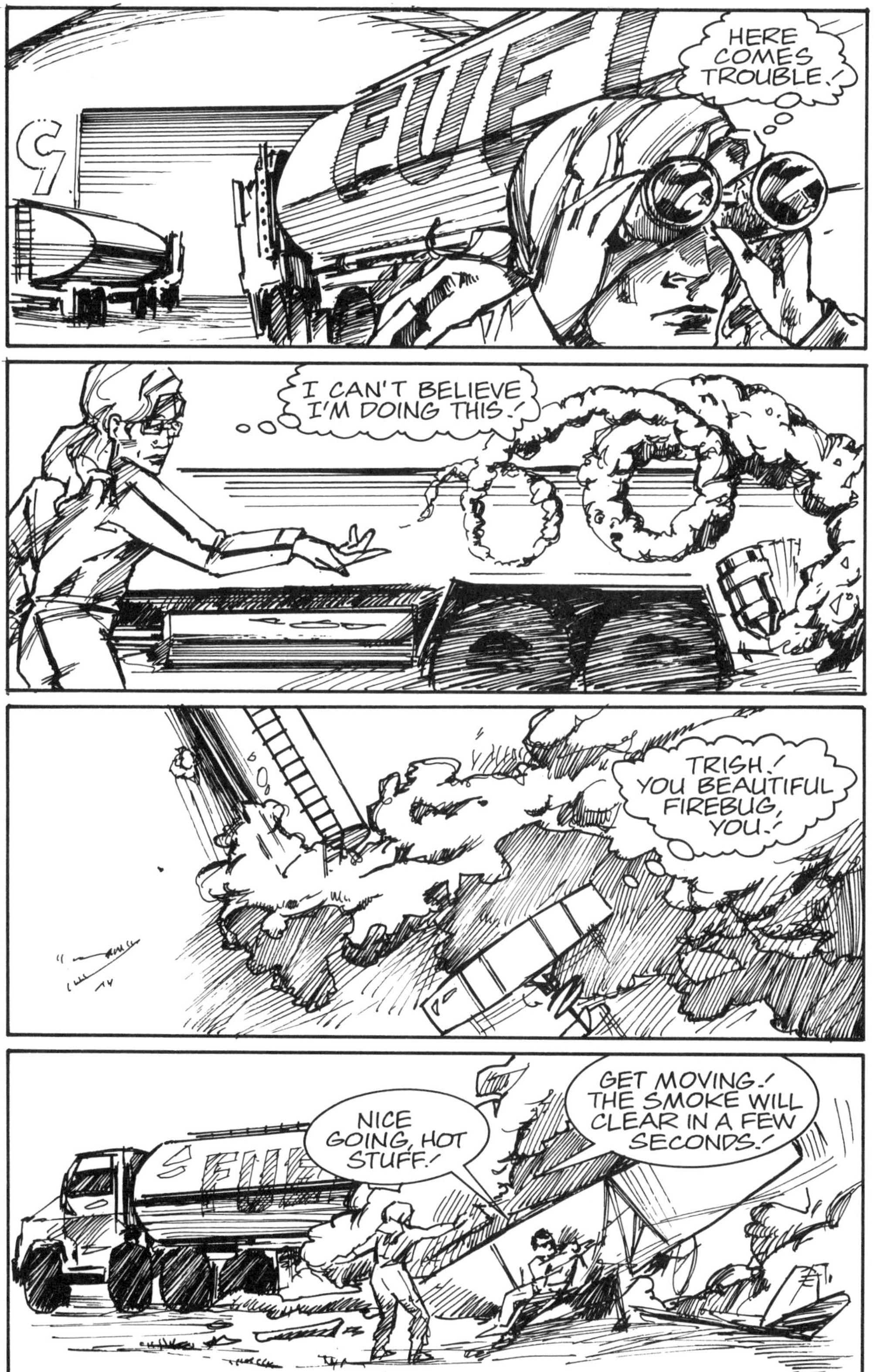
HERE COMES TROUBLE.!
I CAN'T BELIEVE I'M DOING THIS.!
TRISH.! YOU BEAUTIFUL FIREBUG, YOU.!
NICE GOING, HOT STUFF.!
GET MOVING.! THE SMOKE WILL CLEAR IN A FEW SECONDS.!

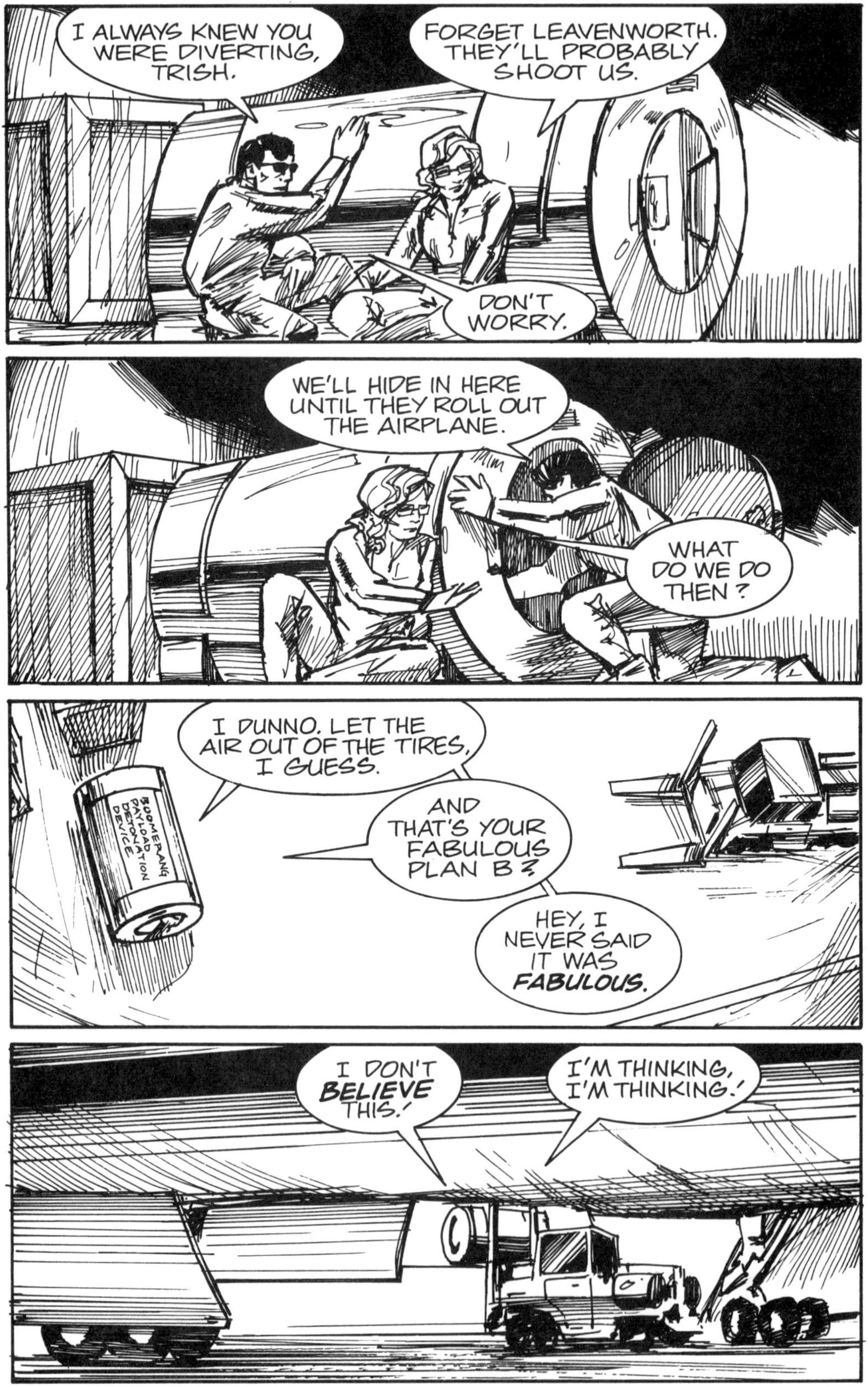
I ALWAYS KNEW YOU WERE DIVERTING, TRISH.
FORGET LEAVENWORTH. THEY'LL PROBABLY SHOOT US.
DON'T WORRY.
WE'LL HIDE IN HERE UNTIL THEY ROLL OUT THE AIRPLANE.
WHAT DO WE DO THEN?
I DUNNO. LET THE AIR OUT OF THE TIRES, I GUESS.
BOOMERANG PAYLOAD DETONATION DEVICE
AND THAT'S YOUR FABULOUS PLAN B?!
HEY, I NEVER SAID IT WAS FABULOUS.
I DON'T BELIEVE THIS!
I'M THINKING, I'M THINKING!

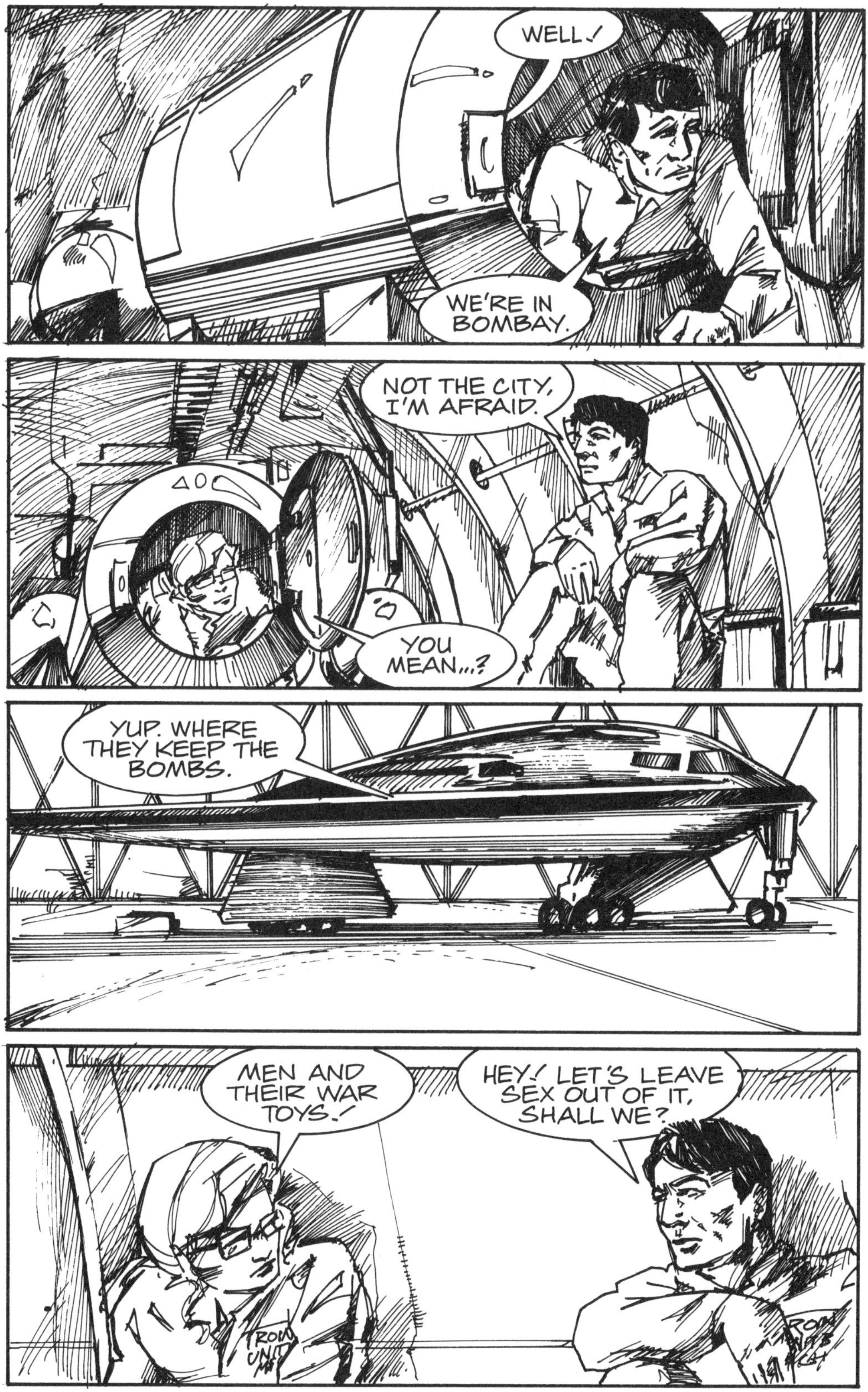
WELL!
WE'RE IN BOMBAY.
NOT THE CITY, I'M AFRAID.
YOU MEAN...?
YUP. WHERE THEY KEEP THE BOMBS.
MEN AND THEIR WAR TOYS!
HEY! LET'S LEAVE SEX OUT OF IT, SHALL WE?

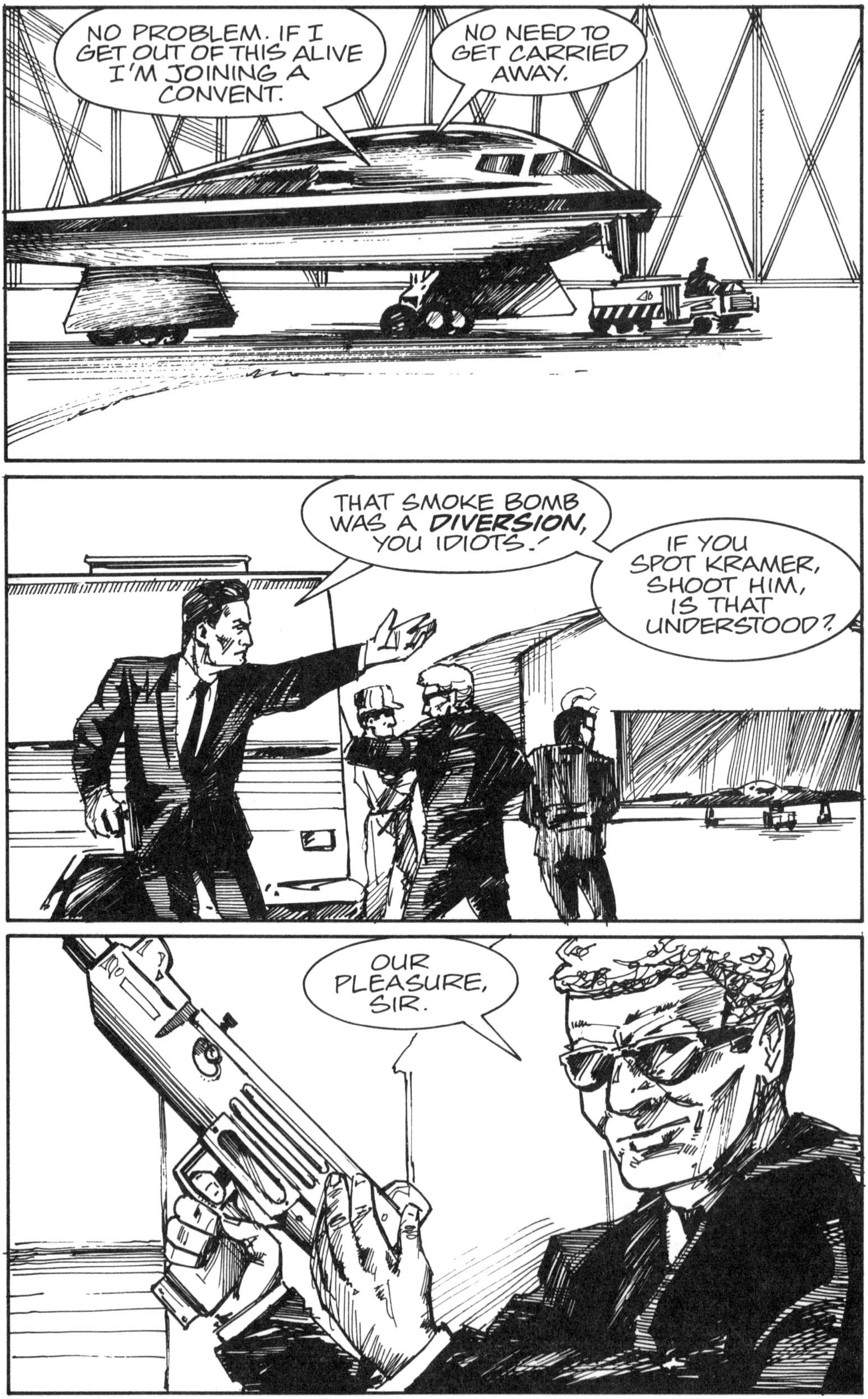
NO PROBLEM. IF I GET OUT OF THIS ALIVE I'M JOINING A CONVENT.
NO NEED TO GET CARRIED AWAY.
THAT SMOKE BOMB WAS A DIVERSION, YOU IDIOTS!
IF YOU SPOT KRAMER, SHOOT HIM, IS THAT UNDERSTOOD?
OUR PLEASURE, SIR.

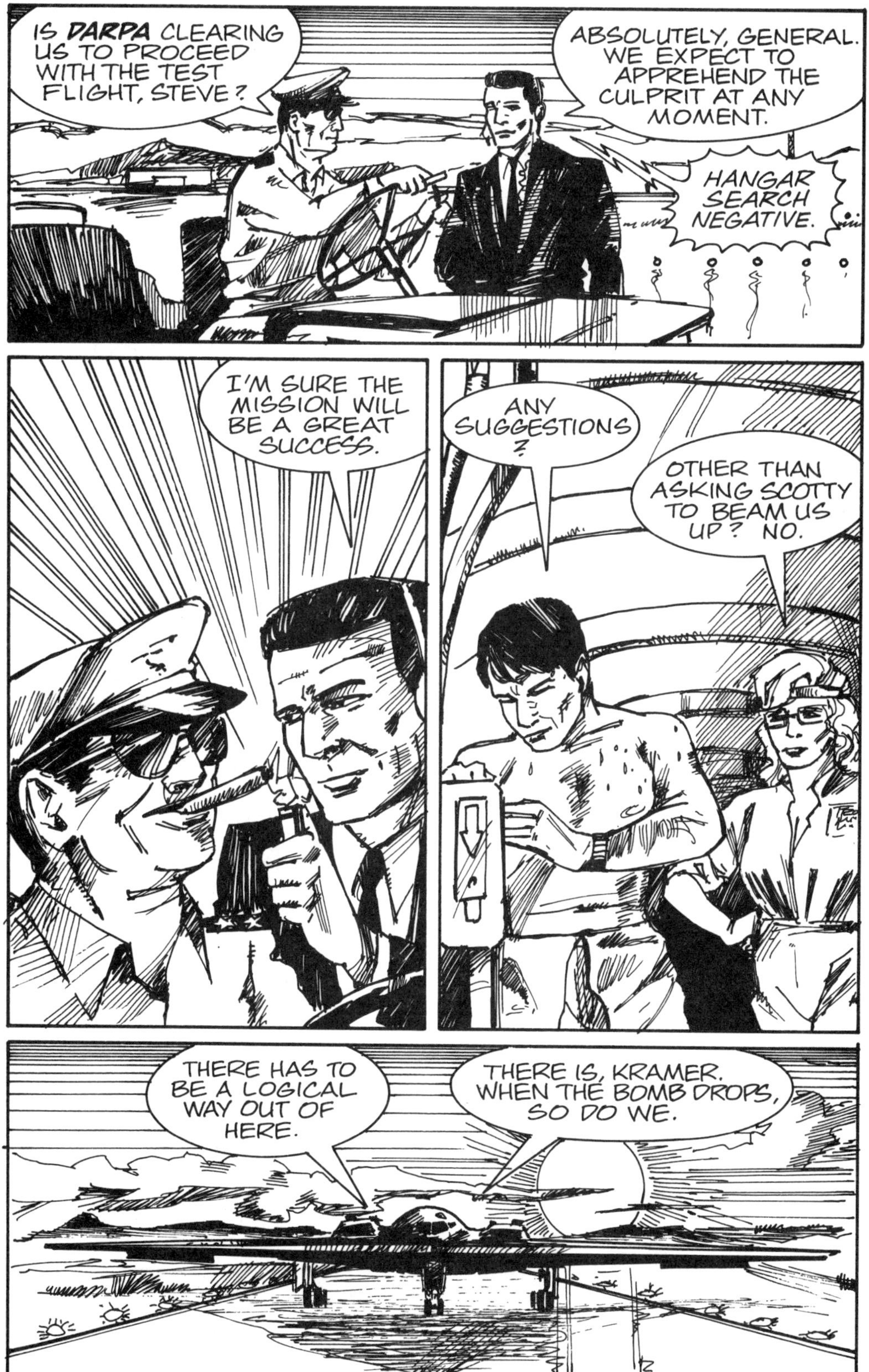
IS DARPA CLEARING US TO PROCEED WITH THE TEST FLIGHT, STEVE?
ABSOLUTELY, GENERAL. WE EXPECT TO APPREHEND THE CULPRIT AT ANY MOMENT.
HANGAR SEARCH NEGATIVE.
I'M SURE THE MISSION WILL BE A GREAT SUCCESS.
ANY SUGGESTIONS?
OTHER THAN ASKING SCOTTY TO BEAM US UP? NO.
THERE HAS TO BE A LOGICAL WAY OUT OF HERE.
THERE IS, KRAMER. WHEN THE BOMB DROPS, SO DO WE.

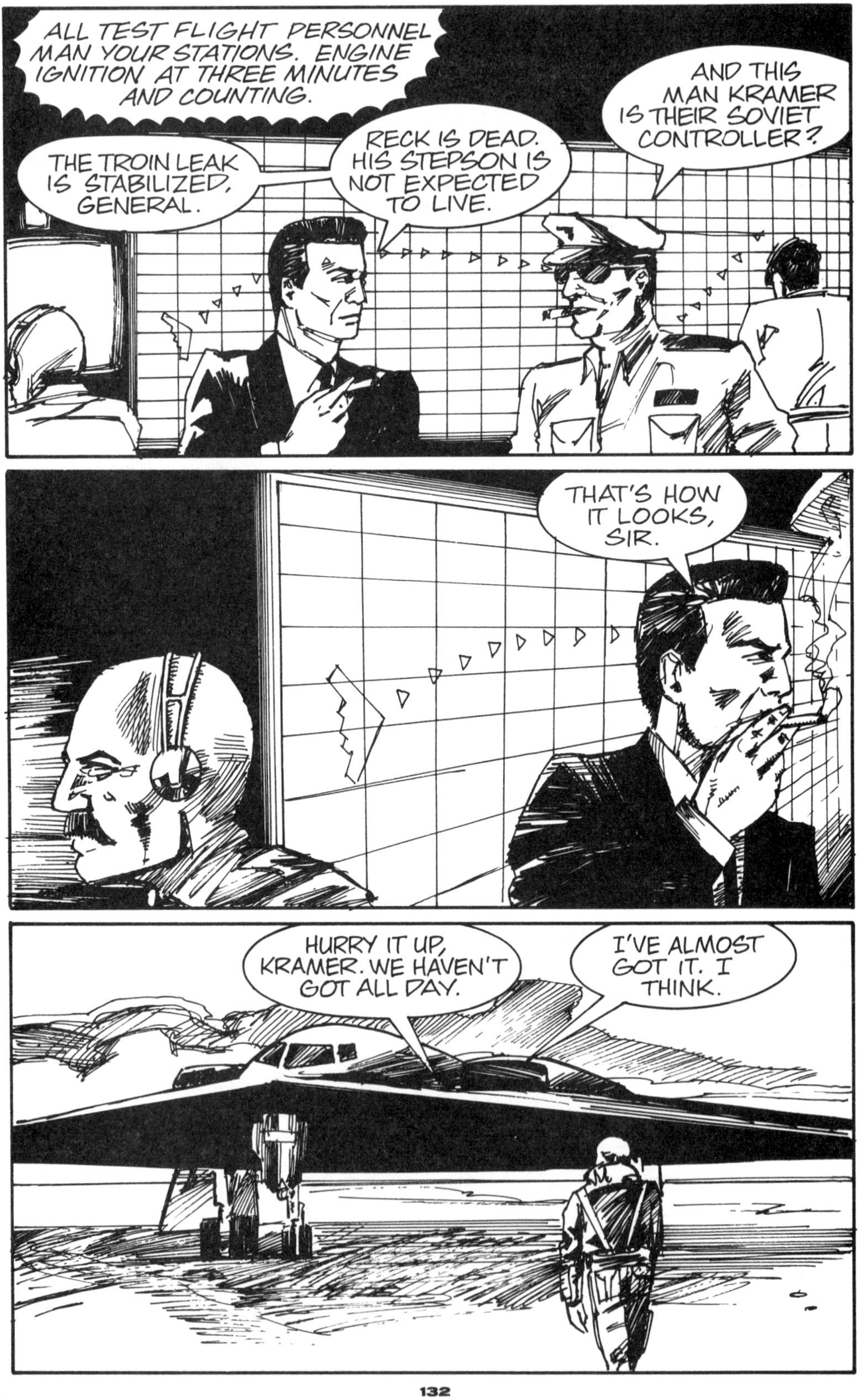
ALL TEST FLIGHT PERSONNEL MAN YOUR STATIONS. ENGINE IGNITION AT THREE MINUTES AND COUNTING.
THE TROIN LEAK IS STABILIZED, GENERAL.
RECK IS DEAD. HIS STEPSON IS NOT EXPECTED TO LIVE.
AND THIS MAN KRAMER IS THEIR SOVIET CONTROLLER?
THAT'S HOW IT LOOKS, SIR.
HURRY IT UP, KRAMER. WE HAVEN'T GOT ALL DAY.
I'VE ALMOST GOT IT. I THINK.

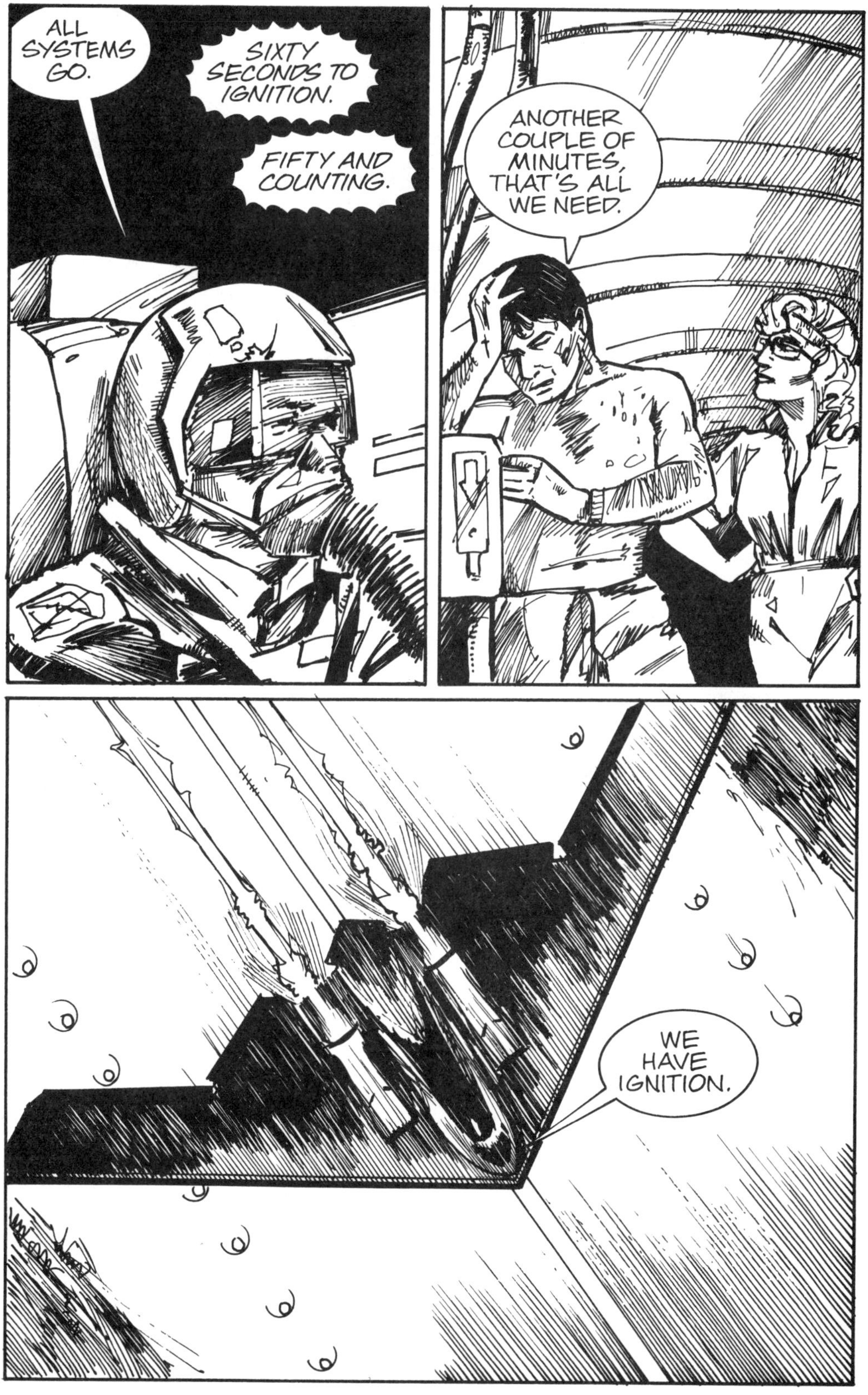
ALL SYSTEMS GO.
SIXTY SECONDS TO IGNITION.
FIFTY AND COUNTING.
ANOTHER COUPLE OF MINUTES, THAT'S ALL WE NEED.
WE HAVE IGNITION.

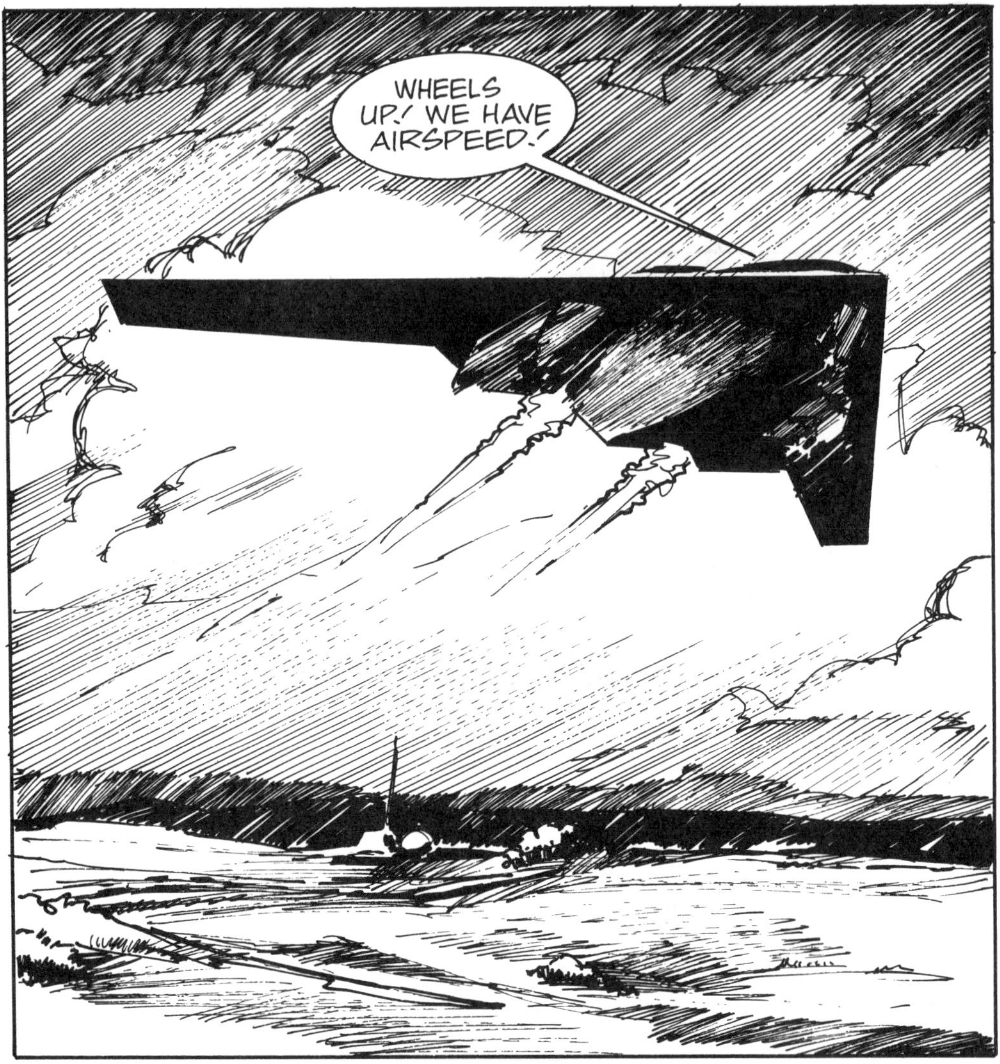
WHEELS UP! WE HAVE AIRSPEED!

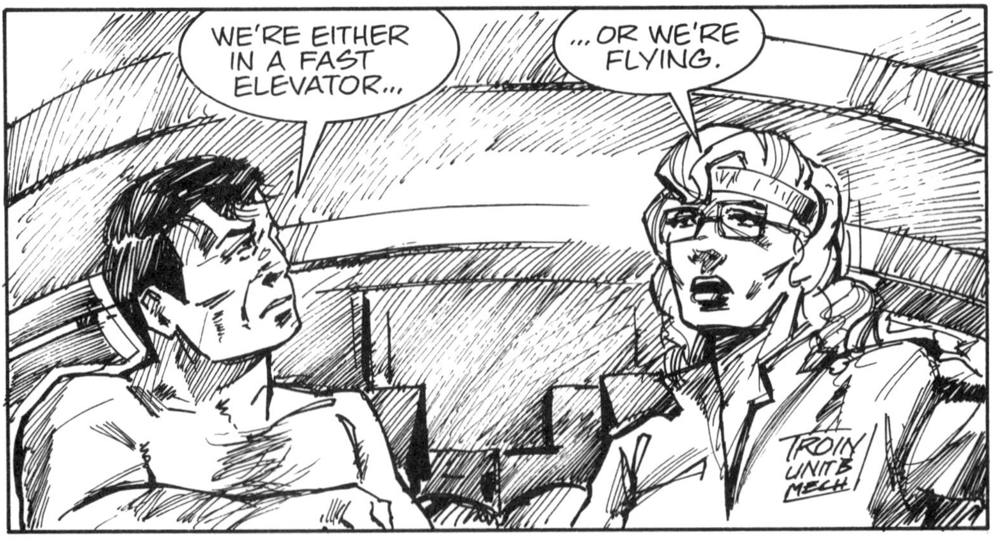
WE'RE EITHER IN A FAST ELEVATOR...
...OR WE'RE FLYING.
TROIN UNIT B MECH

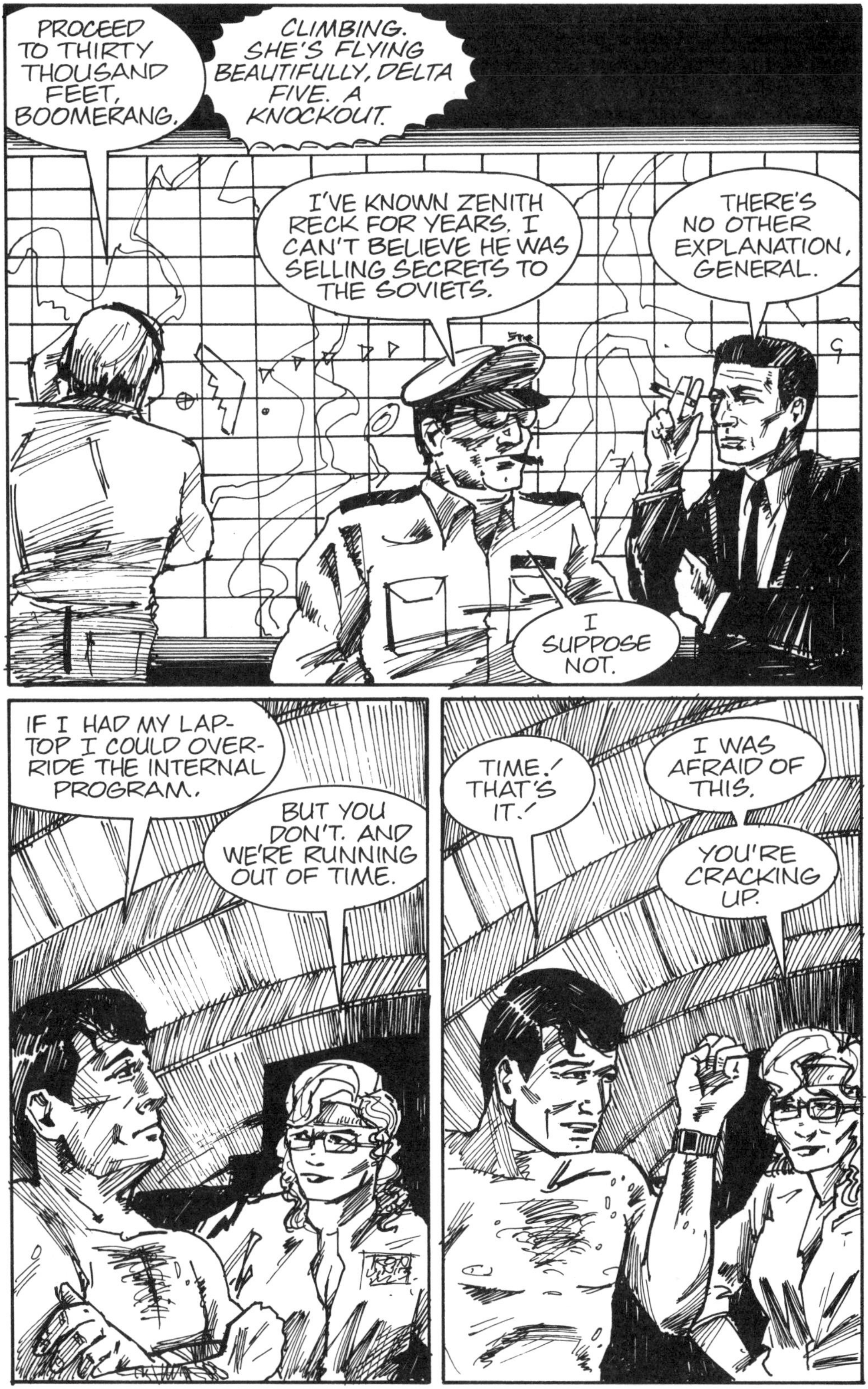
PROCEED TO THIRTY THOUSAND FEET, BOOMERANG.
CLIMBING. SHE'S FLYING BEAUTIFULLY, DELTA FIVE. A KNOCKOUT.
I'VE KNOWN ZENITH RECK FOR YEARS. I CAN'T BELIEVE HE WAS SELLING SECRETS TO THE SOVIETS.
THERE'S NO OTHER EXPLANATION, GENERAL.
I SUPPOSE NOT.
IF I HAD MY LAP-TOP I COULD OVER-RIDE THE INTERNAL PROGRAM.
BUT YOU DON'T. AND WE'RE RUNNING OUT OF TIME.
TIME! THAT'S IT!
I WAS AFRAID OF THIS.
YOU'RE CRACKING UP.

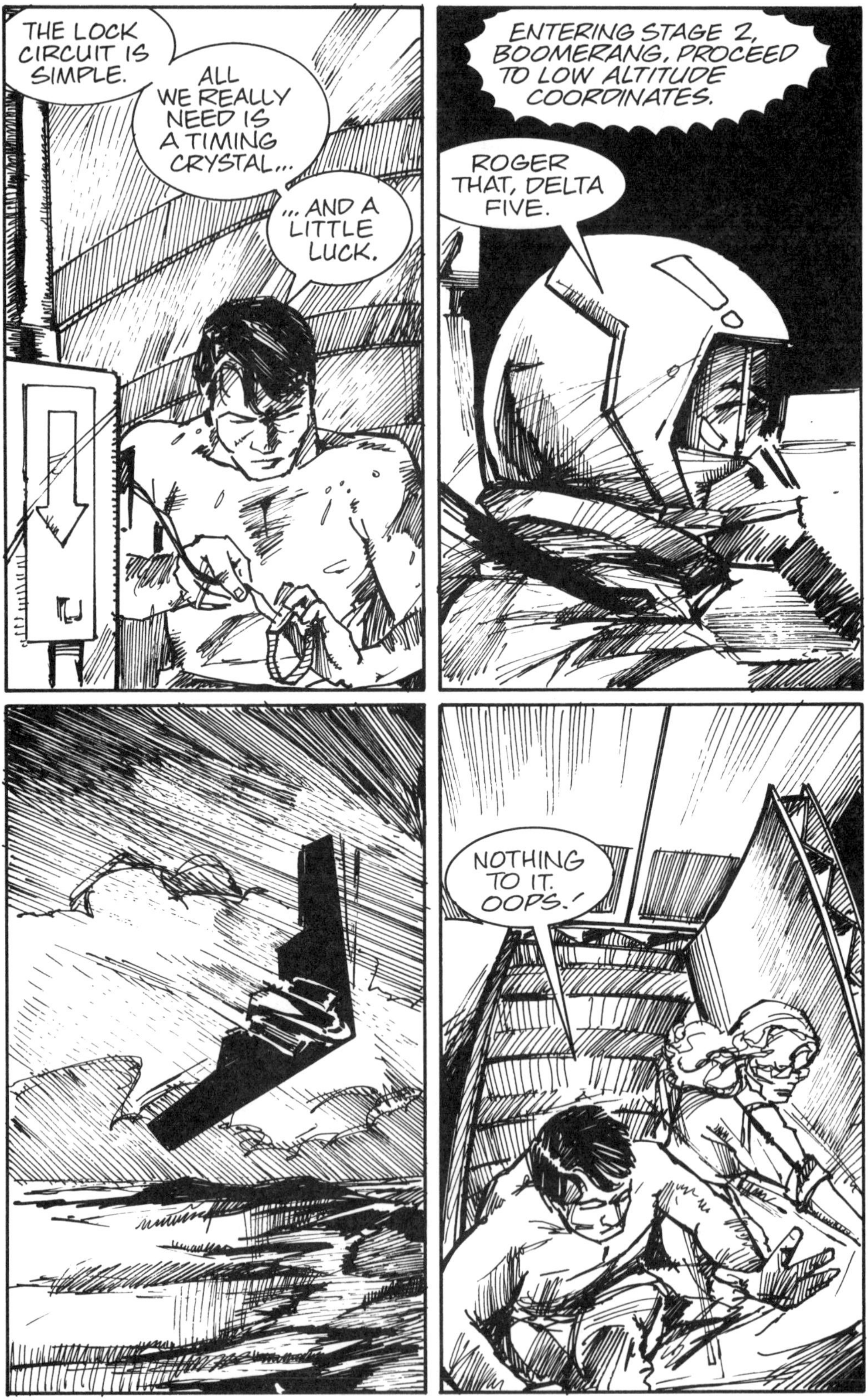
THE LOCK CIRCUIT IS SIMPLE.
ALL WE REALLY NEED IS A TIMING CRYSTAL...
...AND A LITTLE LUCK.
ENTERING STAGE 2, BOOMERANG, PROCEED TO LOW ALTITUDE COORDINATES.
ROGER THAT, DELTA FIVE.
NOTHING TO IT. OOPS.!

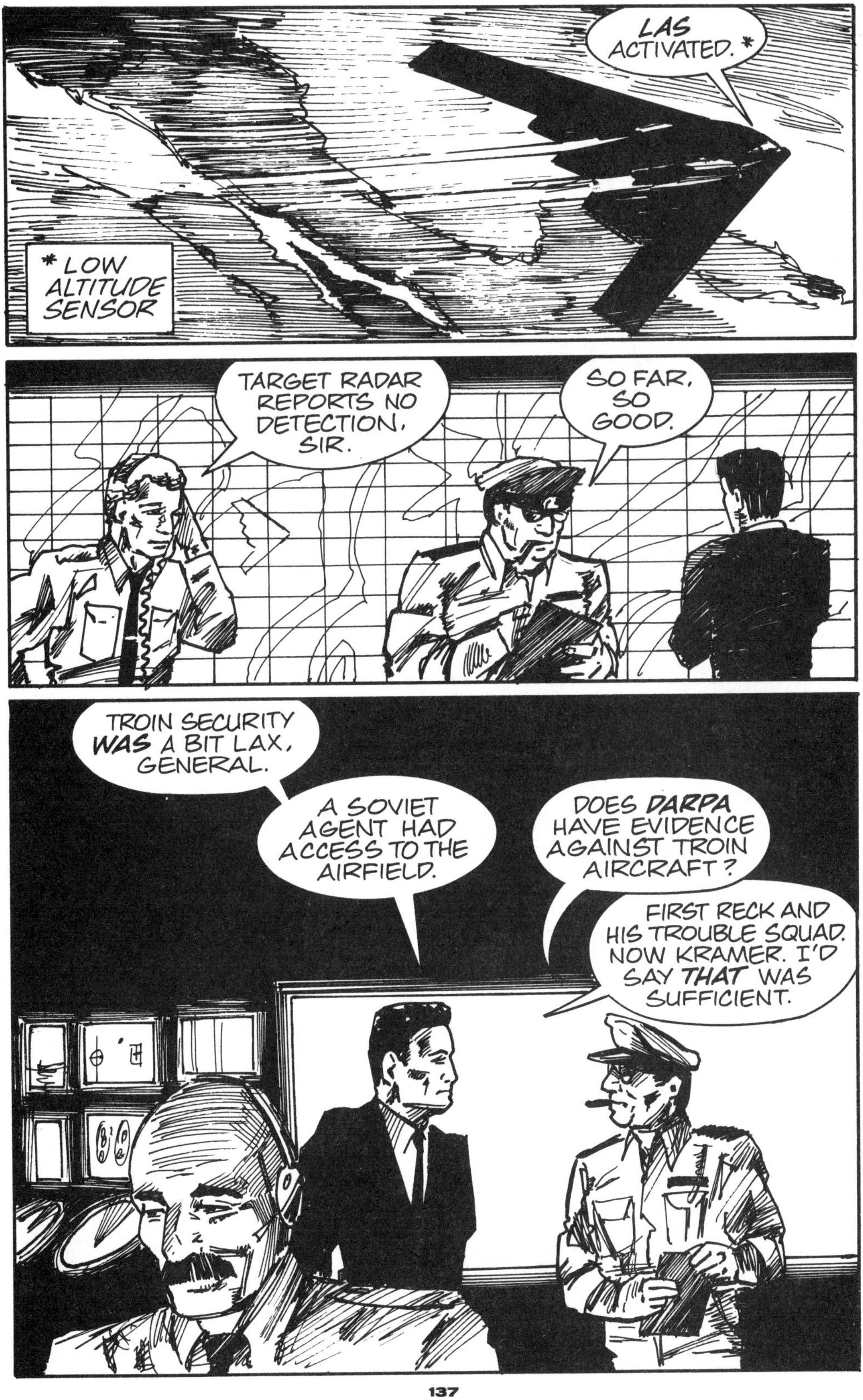
LAS ACTIVATED.*
*LOW ALTITUDE SENSOR
TARGET RADAR REPORTS NO DETECTION, SIR.
SO FAR, SO GOOD.
TROIN SECURITY WAS A BIT LAX, GENERAL.
A SOVIET AGENT HAD ACCESS TO THE AIRFIELD.
DOES DARPA HAVE EVIDENCE AGAINST TROIN AIRCRAFT?
FIRST RECK AND HIS TROUBLE SQUAD. NOW KRAMER. I'D SAY THAT WAS SUFFICIENT.

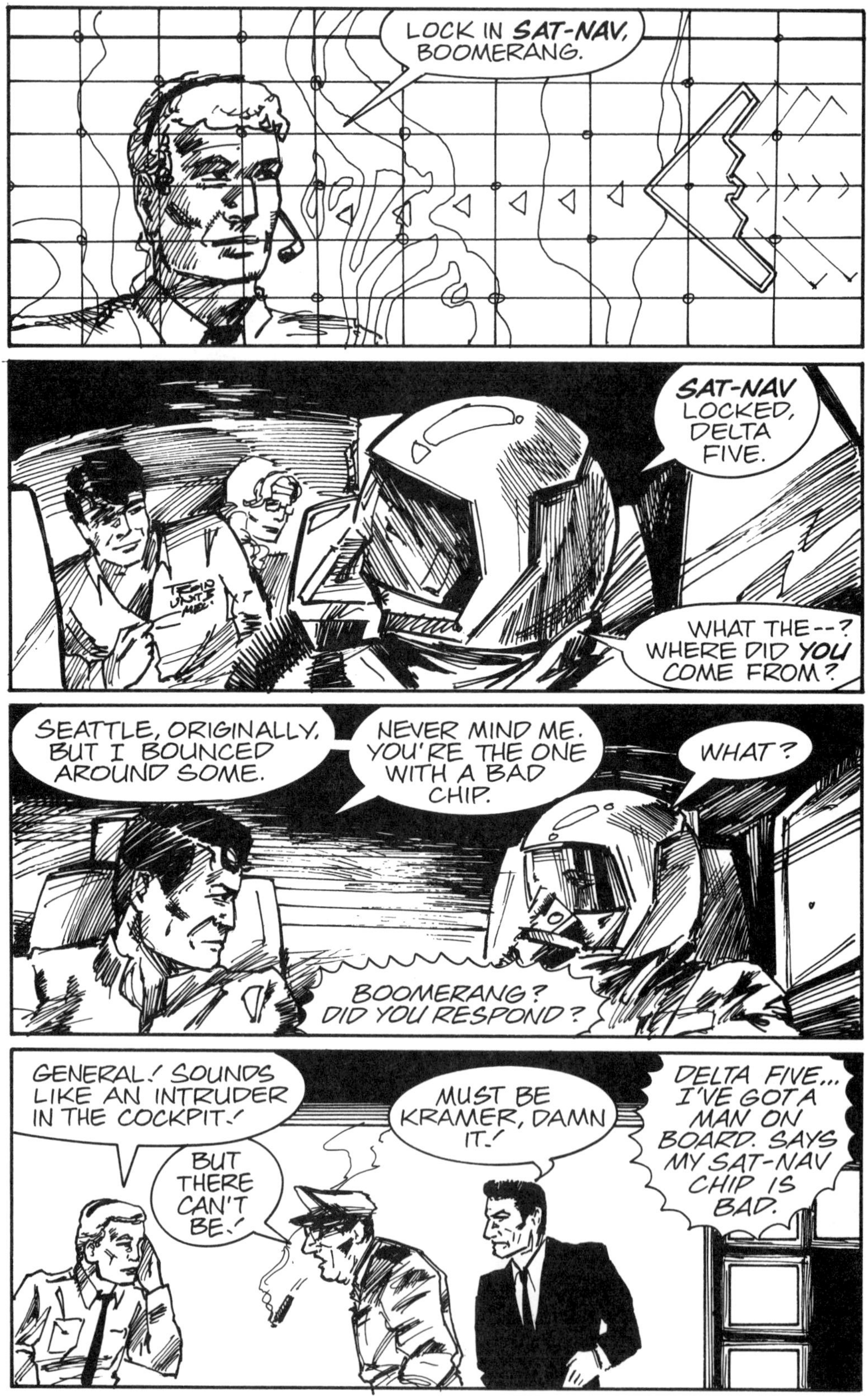
LOCK IN SAT-NAV, BOOMERANG.
SAT-NAV LOCKED, DELTA FIVE.
WHAT THE--? WHERE DID YOU COME FROM?
SEATTLE, ORIGINALLY. BUT I BOUNCED AROUND SOME.
NEVER MIND ME. YOU'RE THE ONE WITH A BAD CHIP.
WHAT?
BOOMERANG? DID YOU RESPOND?
GENERAL! SOUNDS LIKE AN INTRUDER IN THE COCKPIT!
BUT THERE CAN'T BE!
MUST BE KRAMER, DAMN IT!
DELTA FIVE... I'VE GOT A MAN ON BOARD. SAYS MY SAT-NAV CHIP IS BAD.

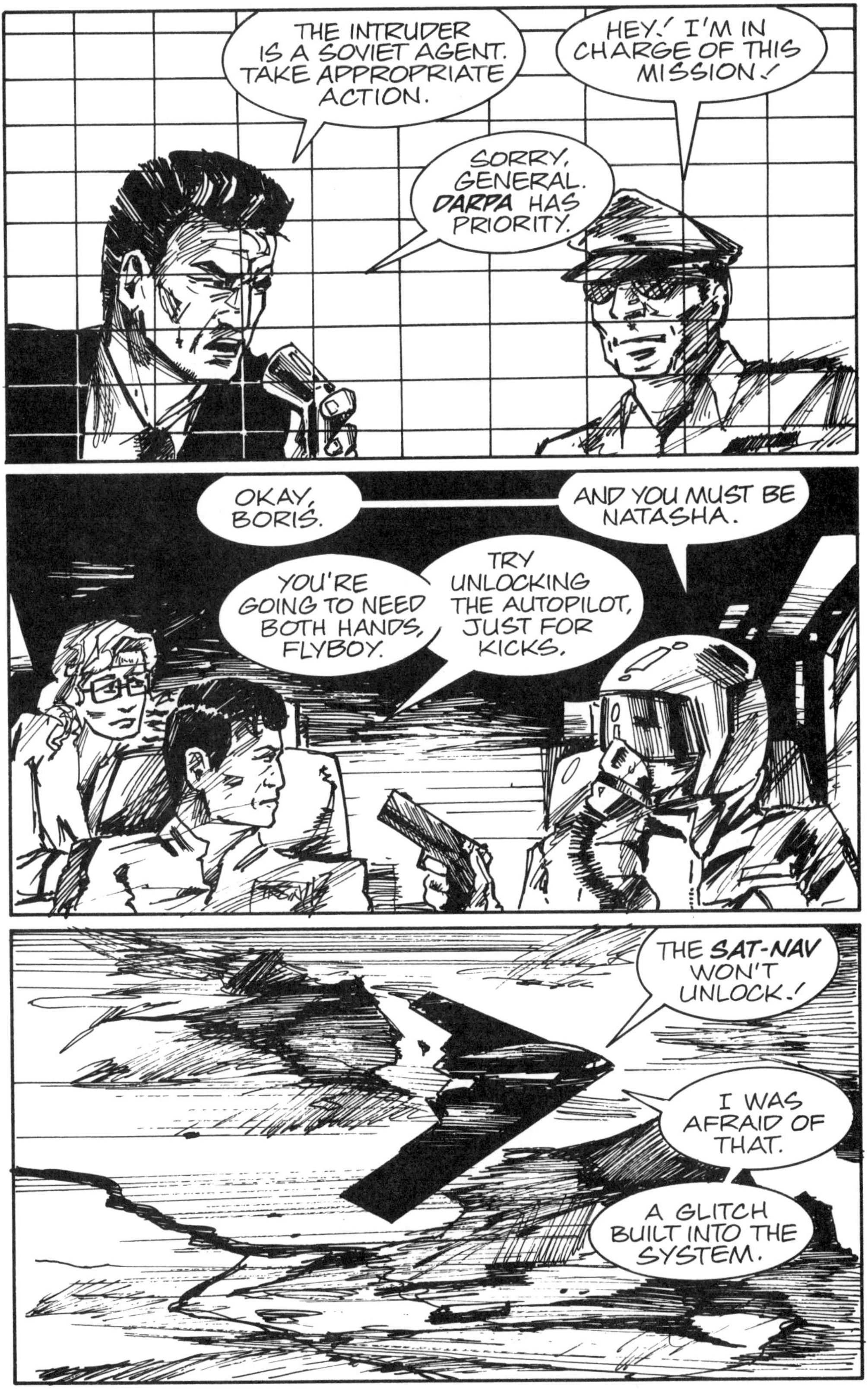
THE INTRUDER IS A SOVIET AGENT. TAKE APPROPRIATE ACTION.
HEY! I'M IN CHARGE OF THIS MISSION!
SORRY, GENERAL. DARPA HAS PRIORITY.
OKAY, BORIS.
AND YOU MUST BE NATASHA.
YOU'RE GOING TO NEED BOTH HANDS, FLYBOY.
TRY UNLOCKING THE AUTOPILOT, JUST FOR KICKS.
THE SAT-NAV WON'T UNLOCK!
I WAS AFRAID OF THAT.
A GLITCH BUILT INTO THE SYSTEM.

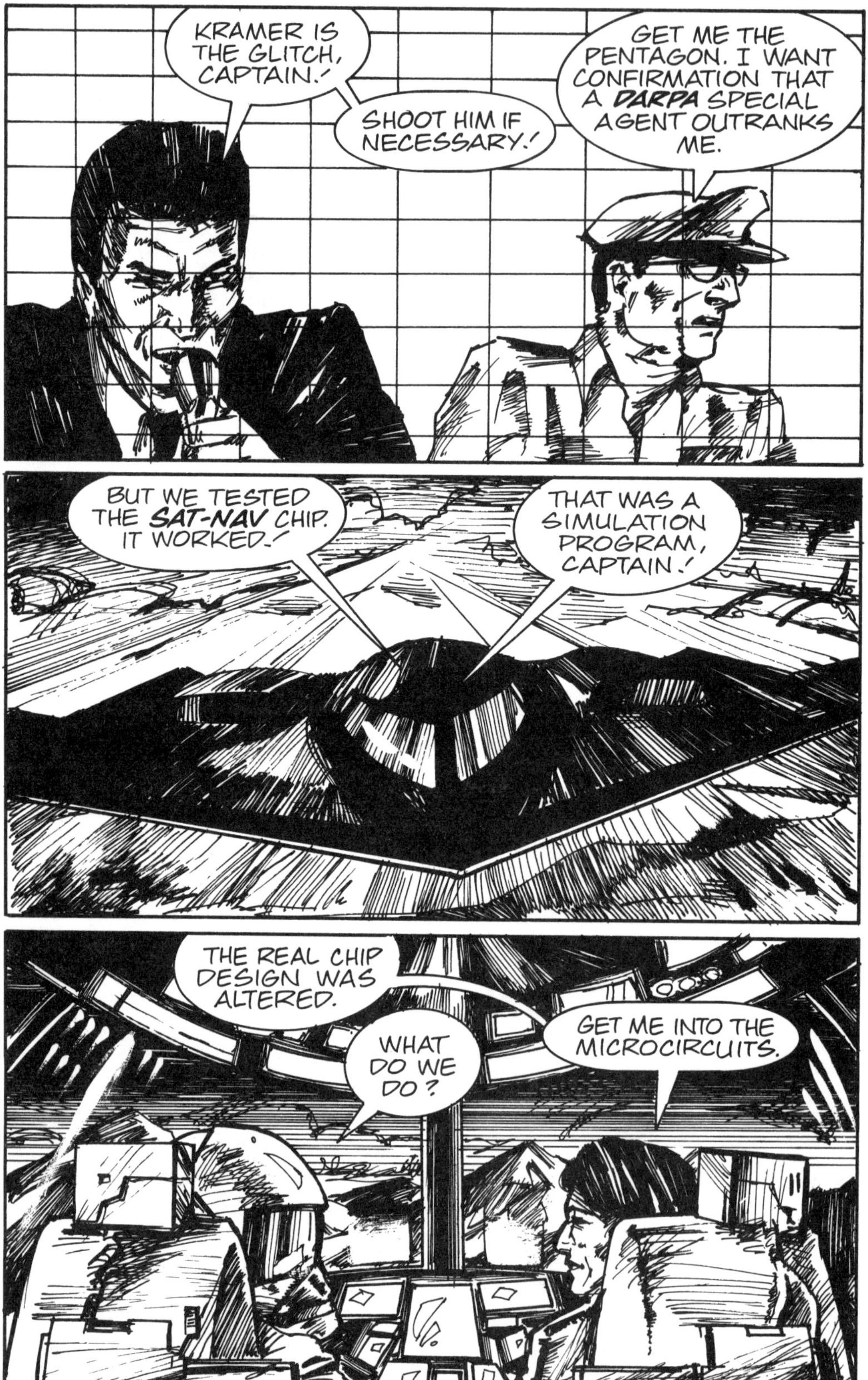
KRAMER IS THE GLITCH, CAPTAIN!
SHOOT HIM IF NECESSARY!
GET ME THE PENTAGON. I WANT CONFIRMATION THAT A DARPA SPECIAL AGENT OUTRANKS ME.
BUT WE TESTED THE SAT-NAV CHIP. IT WORKED!
THAT WAS A SIMULATION PROGRAM, CAPTAIN!
THE REAL CHIP DESIGN WAS ALTERED.
WHAT DO WE DO?
GET ME INTO THE MICROCIRCUITS.

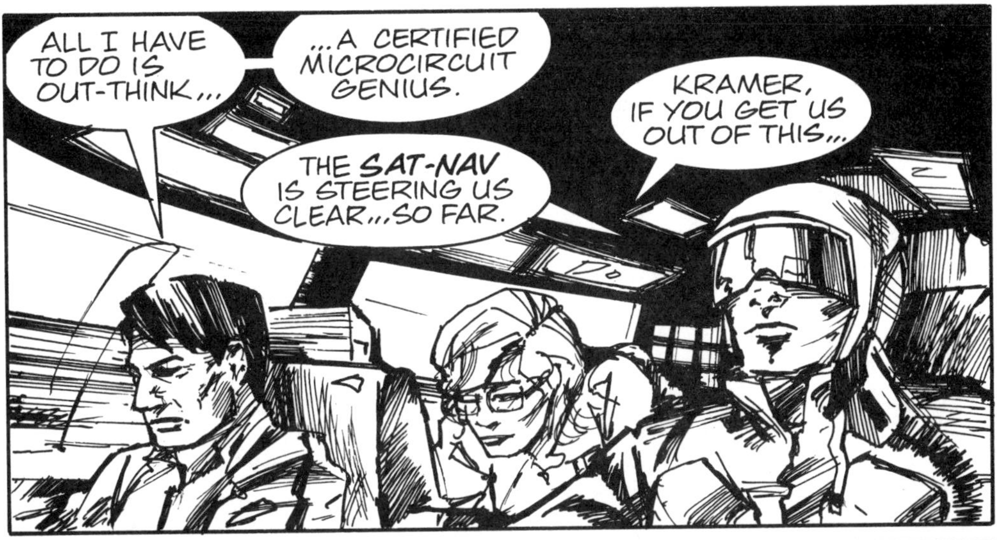
ALL I HAVE TO DO IS OUT-THINK,...
...A CERTIFIED MICROCIRCUIT GENIUS.
THE SAT-NAV IS STEERING US CLEAR...SO FAR.
KRAMER, IF YOU GET US OUT OF THIS...

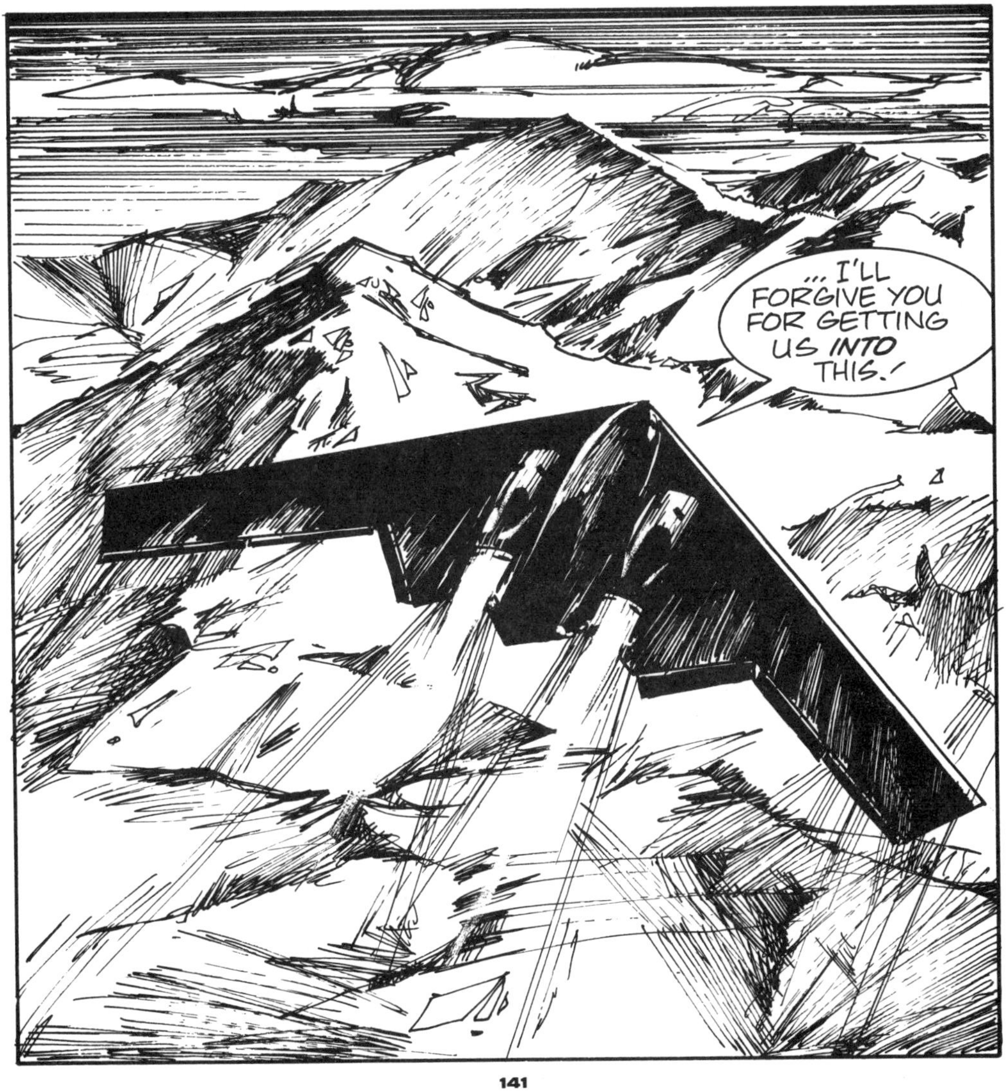
...I'LL FORGIVE YOU FOR GETTING US INTO THIS.!

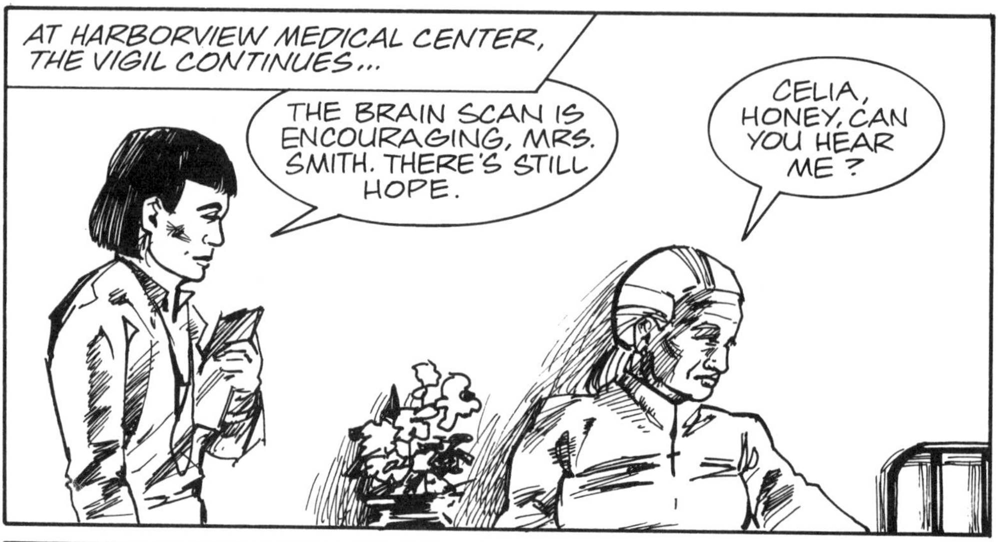
AT HARBORVIEW MEDICAL CENTER, THE VIGIL CONTINUES...
THE BRAIN SCAN IS ENCOURAGING, MRS. SMITH. THERE'S STILL HOPE.
CELIA, HONEY, CAN YOU HEAR ME ?

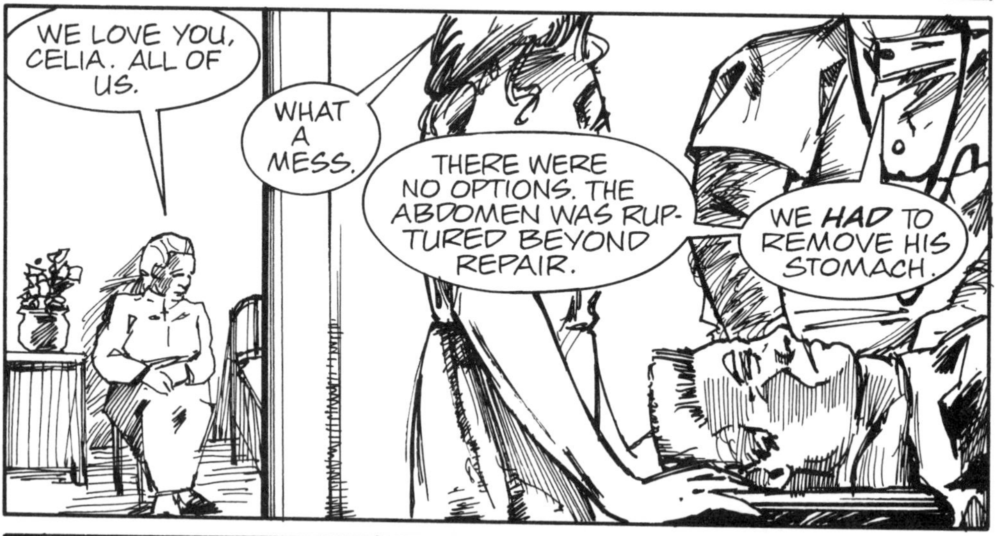
WE LOVE YOU, CELIA. ALL OF US.
WHAT A MESS.
THERE WERE NO OPTIONS. THE ABDOMEN WAS RUP-TURED BEYOND REPAIR.
WE HAD TO REMOVE HIS STOMACH.

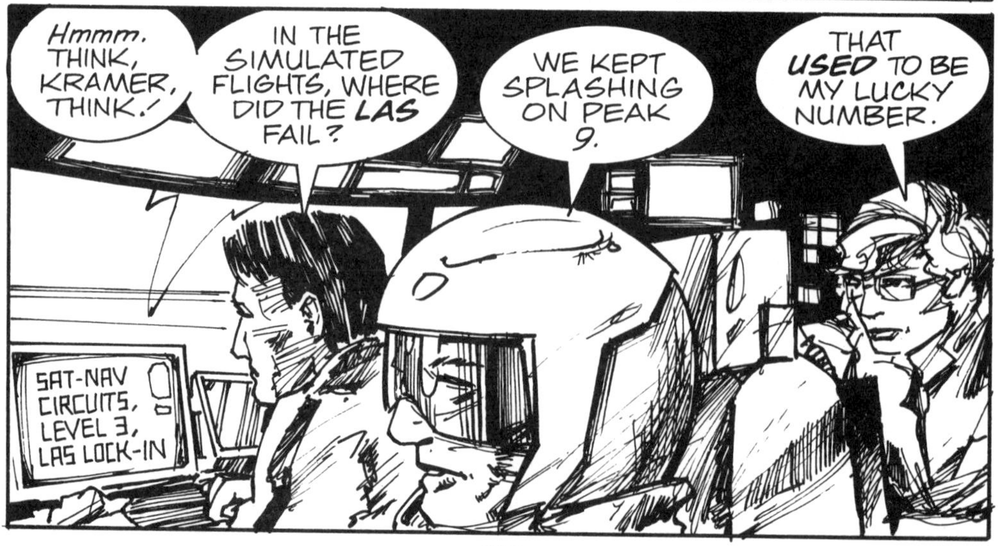
Hmmm. THINK, KRAMER, THINK!
IN THE SIMULATED FLIGHTS, WHERE DID THE LAS FAIL ?
WE KEPT SPLASHING ON PEAK 9.
THAT USED TO BE MY LUCKY NUMBER.
SAT-NAV CIRCUITS, LEVEL 3, LAS LOCK-IN

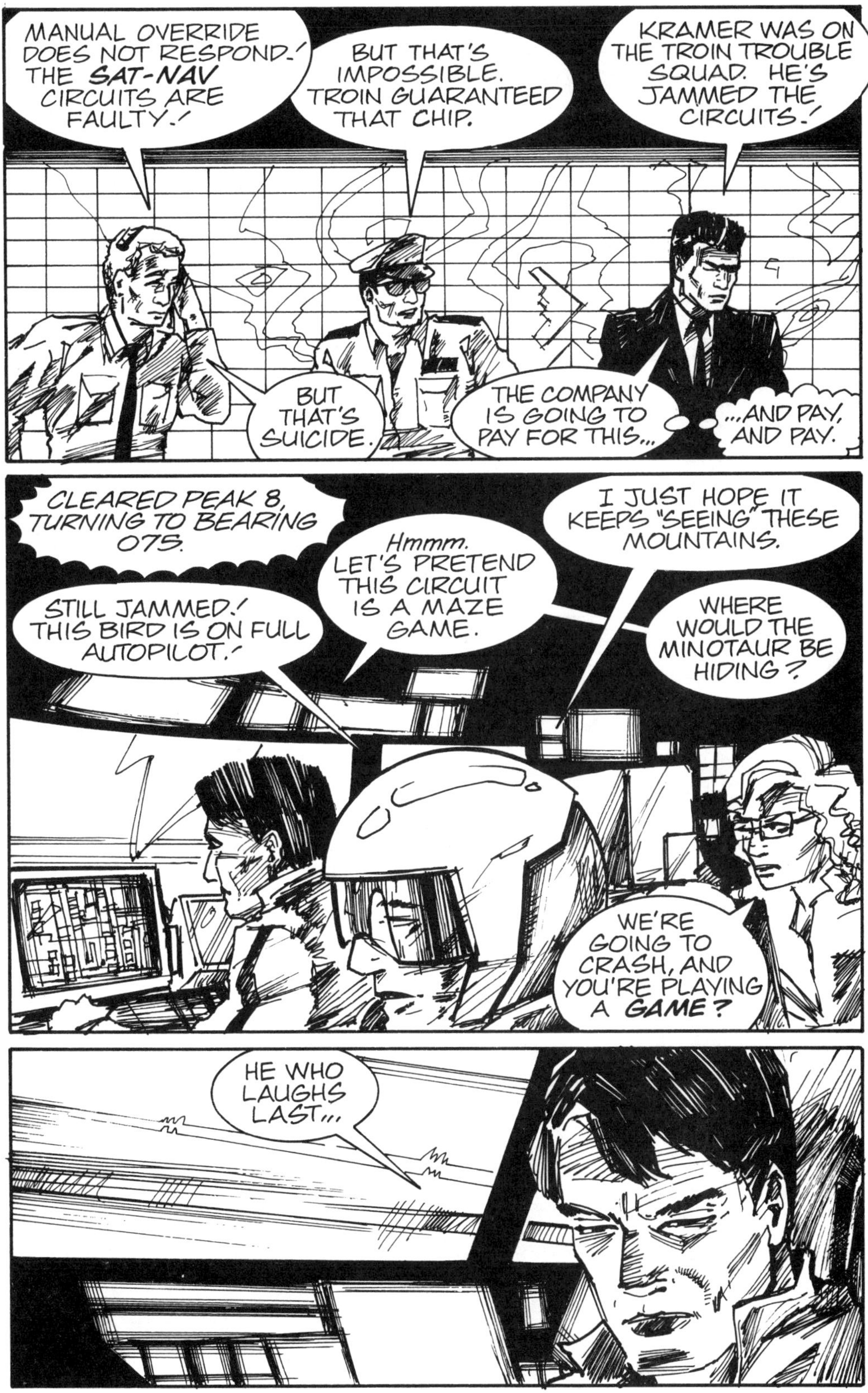
MANUAL OVERRIDE DOES NOT RESPOND! THE **SAT-NAV** CIRCUITS ARE FAULTY!
BUT THAT'S IMPOSSIBLE. TROIN GUARANTEED THAT CHIP.
KRAMER WAS ON THE TROIN TROUBLE SQUAD. HE'S JAMMED THE CIRCUITS!
BUT THAT'S SUICIDE.
THE COMPANY IS GOING TO PAY FOR THIS...
...AND PAY, AND PAY.
CLEARED PEAK 8, TURNING TO BEARING 075.
STILL JAMMED! THIS BIRD IS ON FULL AUTOPILOT!
Hmmm. LET'S PRETEND THIS CIRCUIT IS A MAZE GAME.
I JUST HOPE IT KEEPS "SEEING" THESE MOUNTAINS.
WHERE WOULD THE MINOTAUR BE HIDING?
WE'RE GOING TO CRASH, AND YOU'RE PLAYING A **GAME**?
HE WHO LAUGHS LAST...

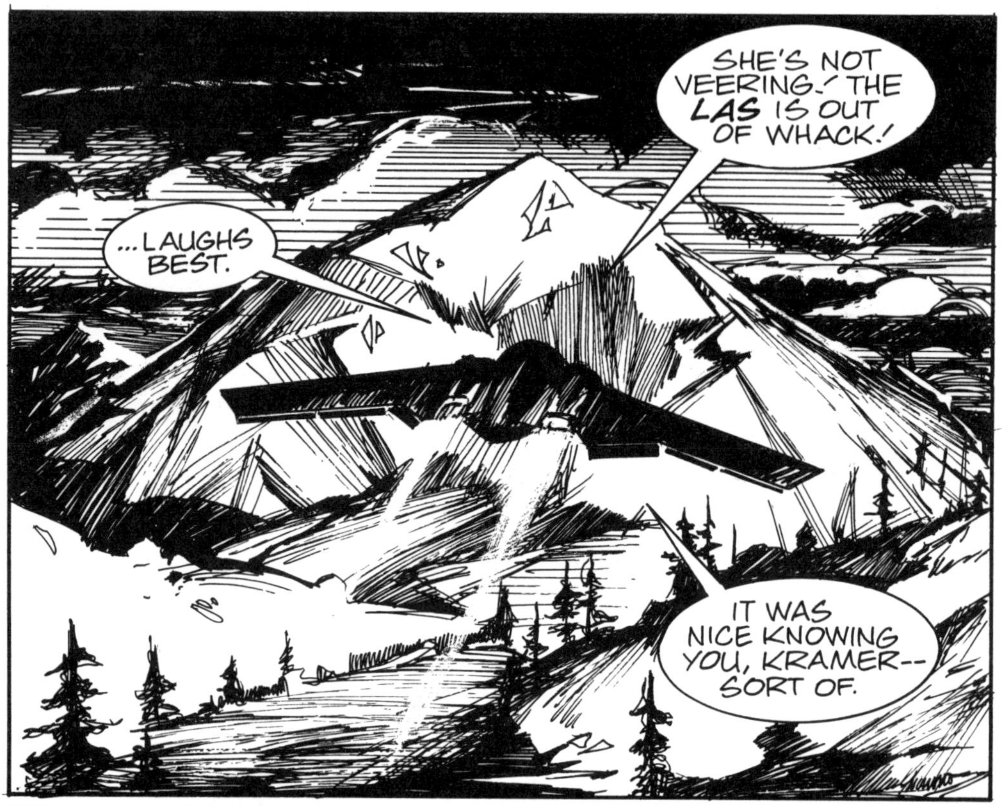
SHE'S NOT VEERING! THE LAS IS OUT OF WHACK!
...LAUGHS BEST.
IT WAS NICE KNOWING YOU, KRAMER-- SORT OF.

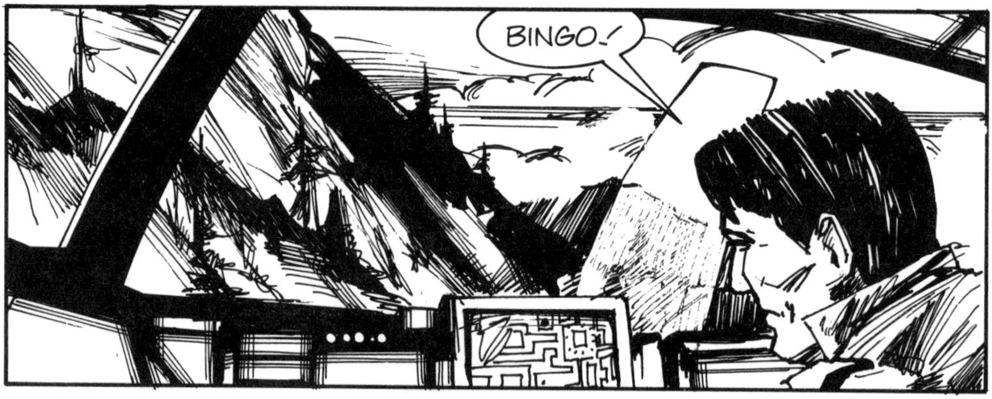
BINGO!

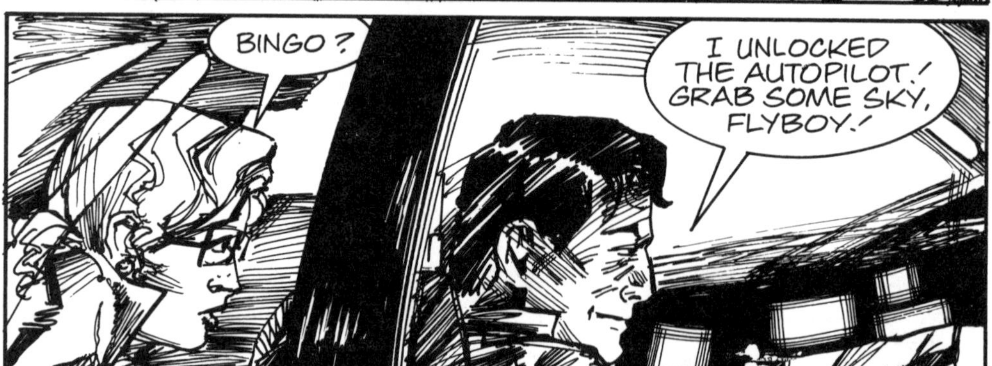
BINGO?
I UNLOCKED THE AUTOPILOT! GRAB SOME SKY, FLYBOY!

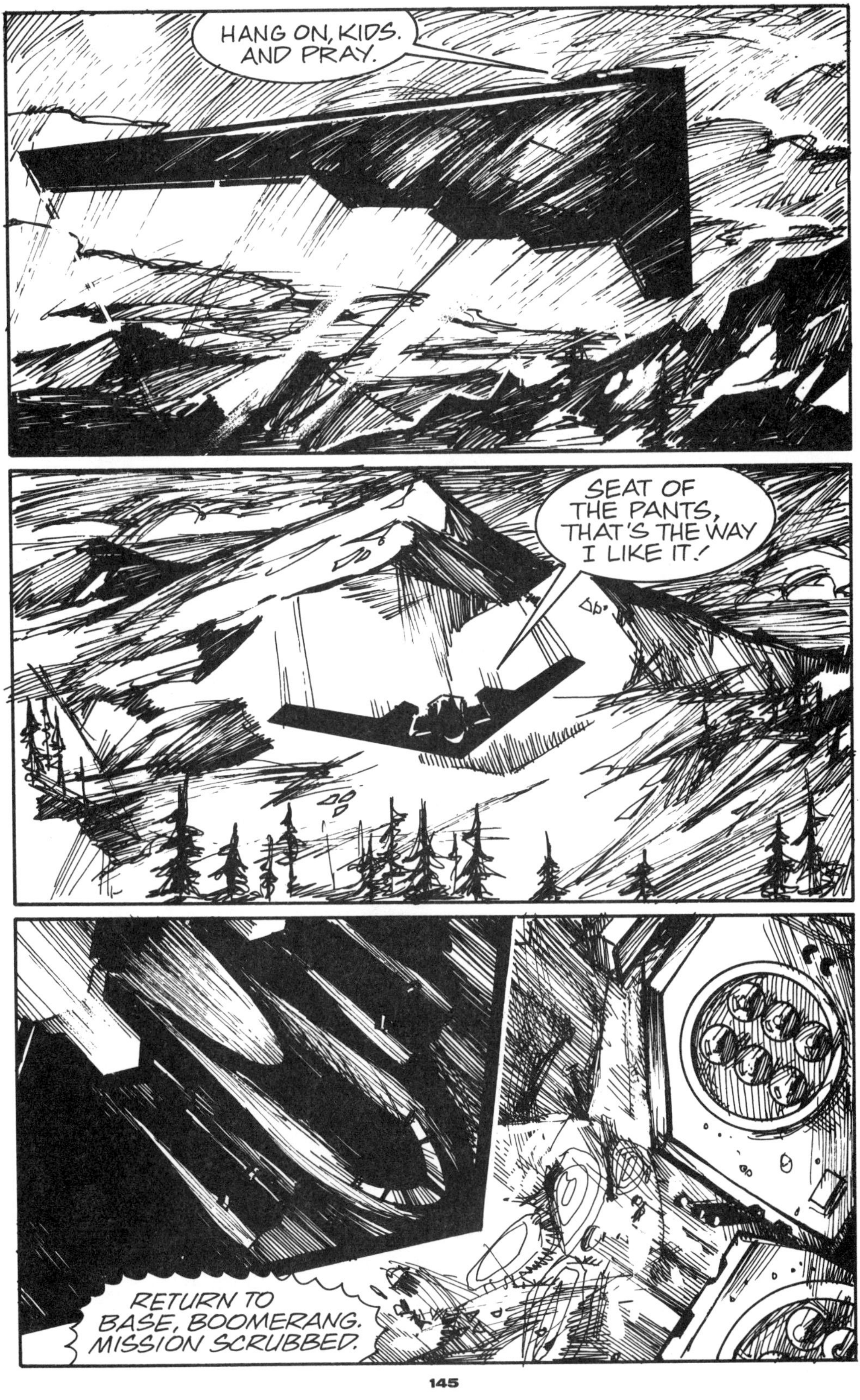
HANG ON, KIDS. AND PRAY.
SEAT OF THE PANTS, THAT'S THE WAY I LIKE IT!
RETURN TO BASE, BOOMERANG. MISSION SCRUBBED.

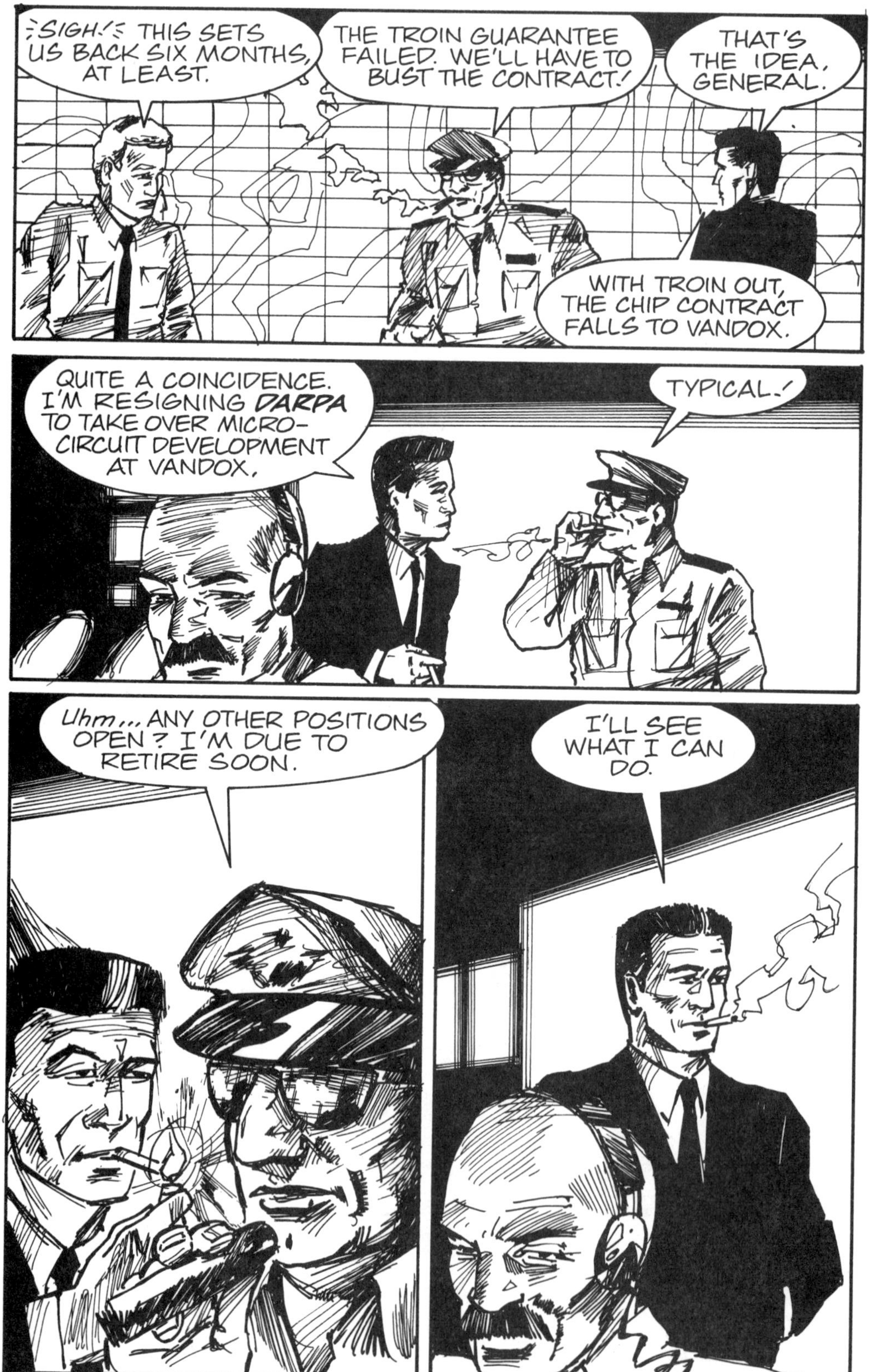
:SIGH:! THIS SETS US BACK SIX MONTHS, AT LEAST.
THE TROIN GUARANTEE FAILED. WE'LL HAVE TO BUST THE CONTRACT!
THAT'S THE IDEA, GENERAL.
WITH TROIN OUT, THE CHIP CONTRACT FALLS TO VANDOX.
QUITE A COINCIDENCE. I'M RESIGNING DARPA TO TAKE OVER MICRO-CIRCUIT DEVELOPMENT AT VANDOX.
TYPICAL!
Uhm... ANY OTHER POSITIONS OPEN? I'M DUE TO RETIRE SOON.
I'LL SEE WHAT I CAN DO.

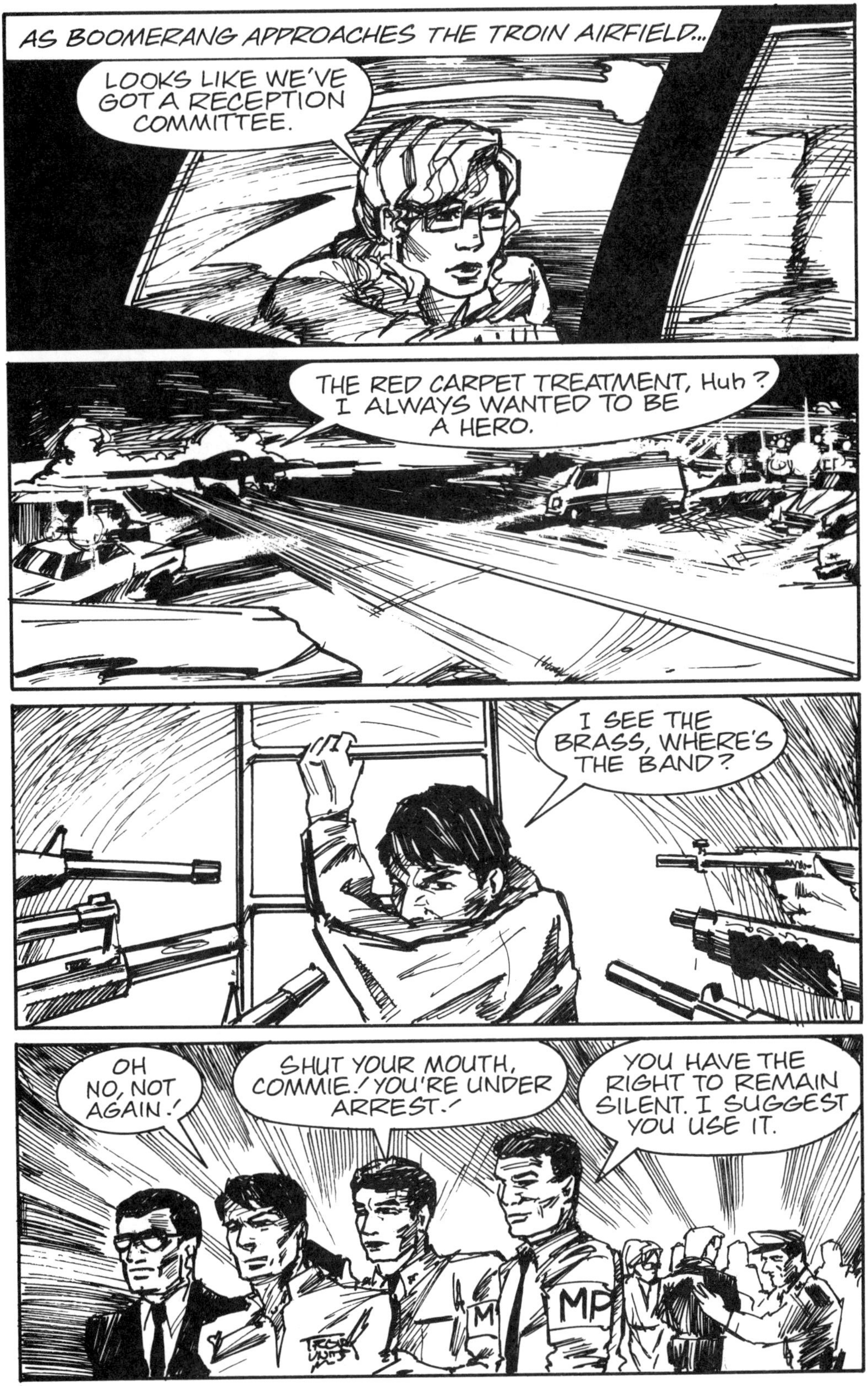
AS BOOMERANG APPROACHES THE TROIN AIRFIELD...
LOOKS LIKE WE'VE GOT A RECEPTION COMMITTEE.
THE RED CARPET TREATMENT, Huh? I ALWAYS WANTED TO BE A HERO.
I SEE THE BRASS, WHERE'S THE BAND?
OH NO, NOT AGAIN!
SHUT YOUR MOUTH, COMMIE! YOU'RE UNDER ARREST!
YOU HAVE THE RIGHT TO REMAIN SILENT. I SUGGEST YOU USE IT.
MP

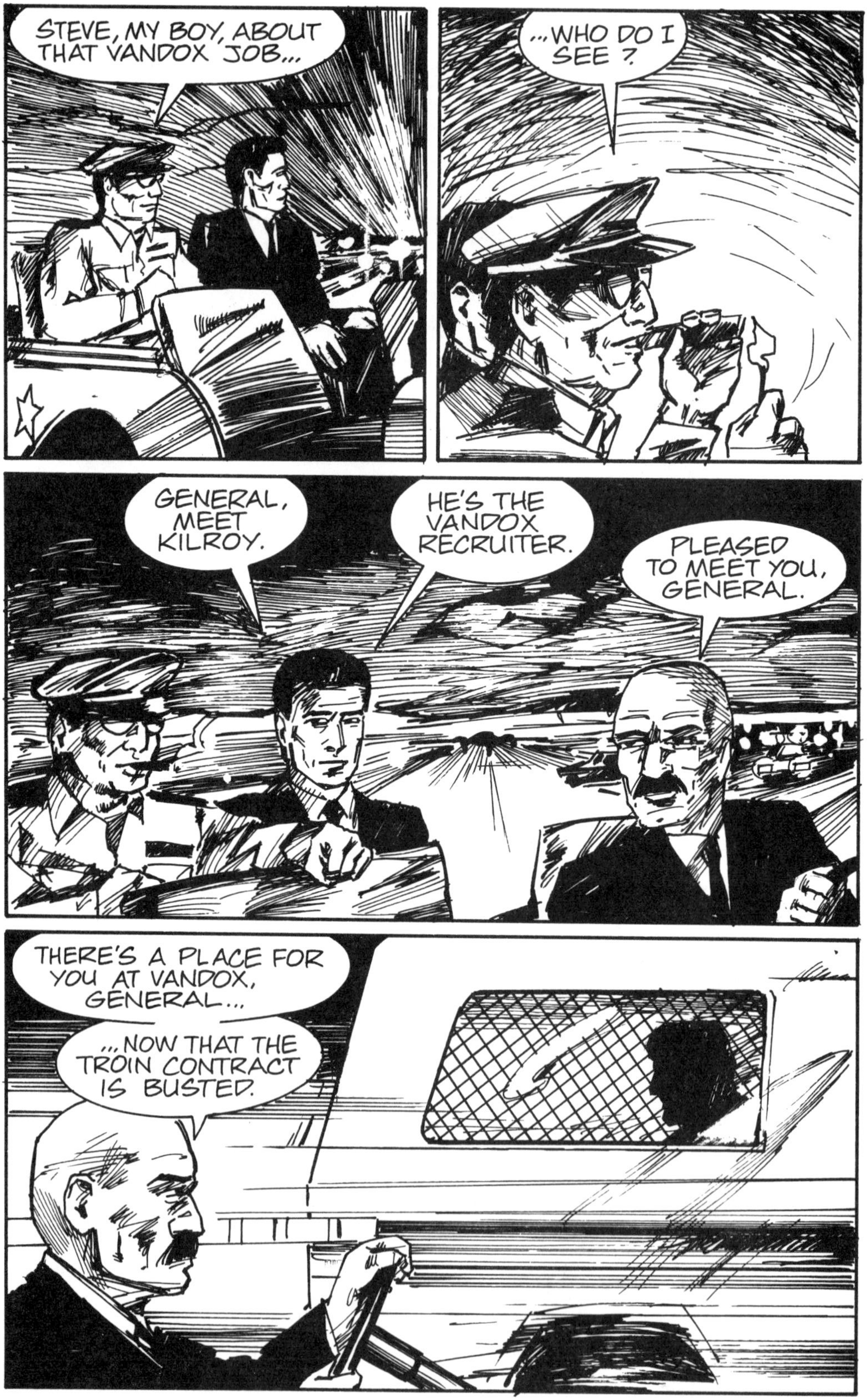
STEVE, MY BOY, ABOUT THAT VANDOX JOB...
...WHO DO I SEE ?
GENERAL, MEET KILROY.
HE'S THE VANDOX RECRUITER.
PLEASED TO MEET YOU, GENERAL.
THERE'S A PLACE FOR YOU AT VANDOX, GENERAL...
...NOW THAT THE TROIN CONTRACT IS BUSTED.

They say it's not over until the fat lady sings. Well, I hadn't seen any fat ladies, only fat cat generals, and nobody was singing yet. Nobody wanted to hear about how I'd been hired by the late Zenith Reck to spy on the Trouble Squad — and incidently serve as fall guy to cover for his stepson. They wanted me to confess, invent a tale about how I'd been working for the Russians, betraying my country.

Me! A guy who never drinks vodka, who roots for the Mariners, no matter how many games they lose! Can you get any more American than *that*?

Okay, so I had an old 45 of 'Midnight in Moscow', a great trumpet riff, but that doesn't make me a Soviet agent. . .

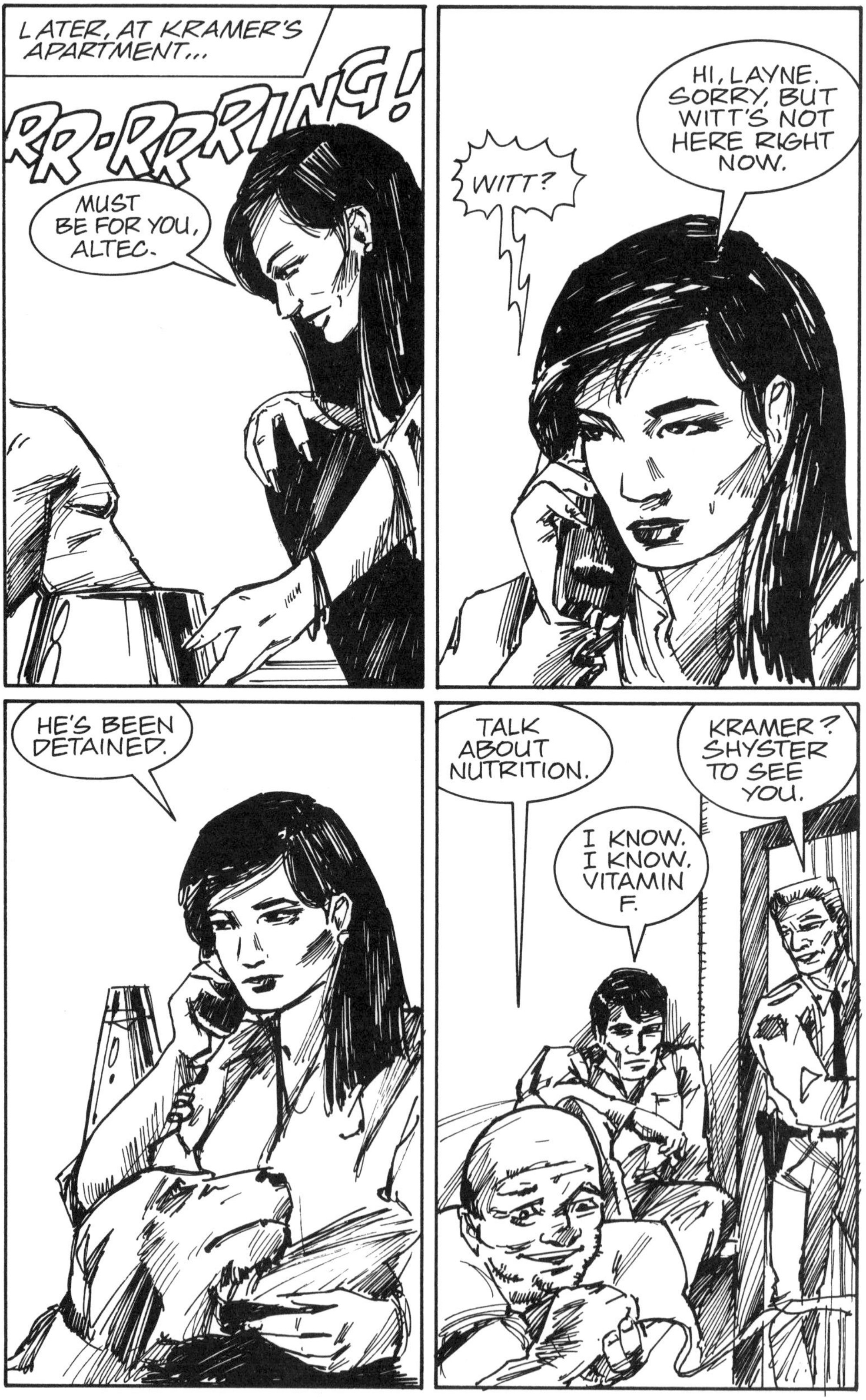
LATER, AT KRAMER'S APARTMENT...
RR-RRRRING!
MUST BE FOR YOU, ALTEC.
WITT?
HI, LAYNE. SORRY, BUT WITT'S NOT HERE RIGHT NOW.
HE'S BEEN DETAINED.
TALK ABOUT NUTRITION.
KRAMER? SHYSTER TO SEE YOU.
I KNOW. I KNOW. VITAMIN F.

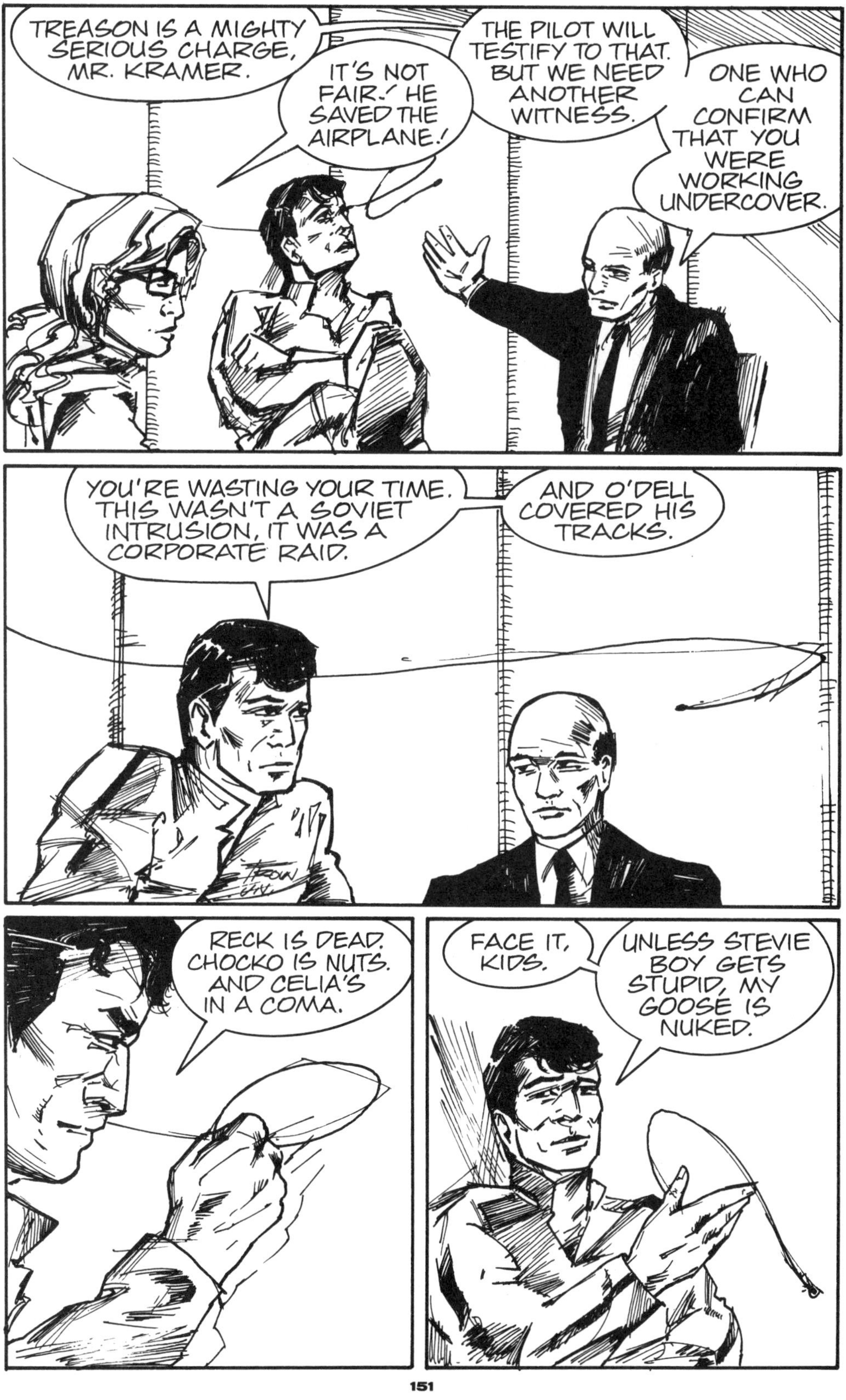
TREASON IS A MIGHTY SERIOUS CHARGE, MR. KRAMER.
IT'S NOT FAIR! HE SAVED THE AIRPLANE!
THE PILOT WILL TESTIFY TO THAT. BUT WE NEED ANOTHER WITNESS.
ONE WHO CAN CONFIRM THAT YOU WERE WORKING UNDERCOVER.
YOU'RE WASTING YOUR TIME. THIS WASN'T A SOVIET INTRUSION, IT WAS A CORPORATE RAID.
AND O'DELL COVERED HIS TRACKS.
RECK IS DEAD. CHOCKO IS NUTS. AND CELIA'S IN A COMA.
FACE IT, KIDS.
UNLESS STEVIE BOY GETS STUPID, MY GOOSE IS NUKED.

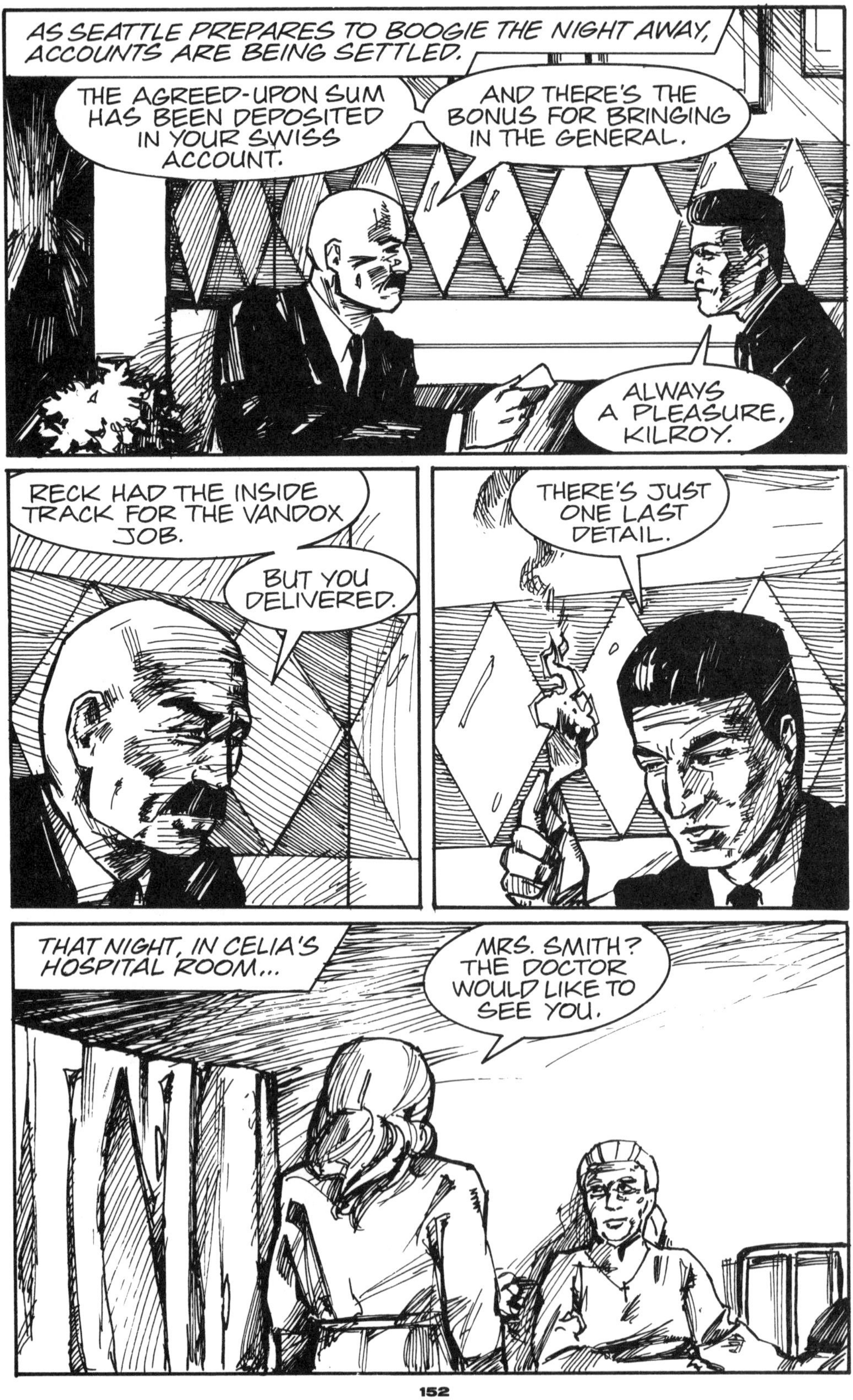
AS SEATTLE PREPARES TO BOOGIE THE NIGHT AWAY, ACCOUNTS ARE BEING SETTLED.
THE AGREED-UPON SUM HAS BEEN DEPOSITED IN YOUR SWISS ACCOUNT.
AND THERE'S THE BONUS FOR BRINGING IN THE GENERAL.
ALWAYS A PLEASURE, KILROY.
RECK HAD THE INSIDE TRACK FOR THE VANDOX JOB.
BUT YOU DELIVERED.
THERE'S JUST ONE LAST DETAIL.
THAT NIGHT, IN CELIA'S HOSPITAL ROOM...
MRS. SMITH? THE DOCTOR WOULD LIKE TO SEE YOU.

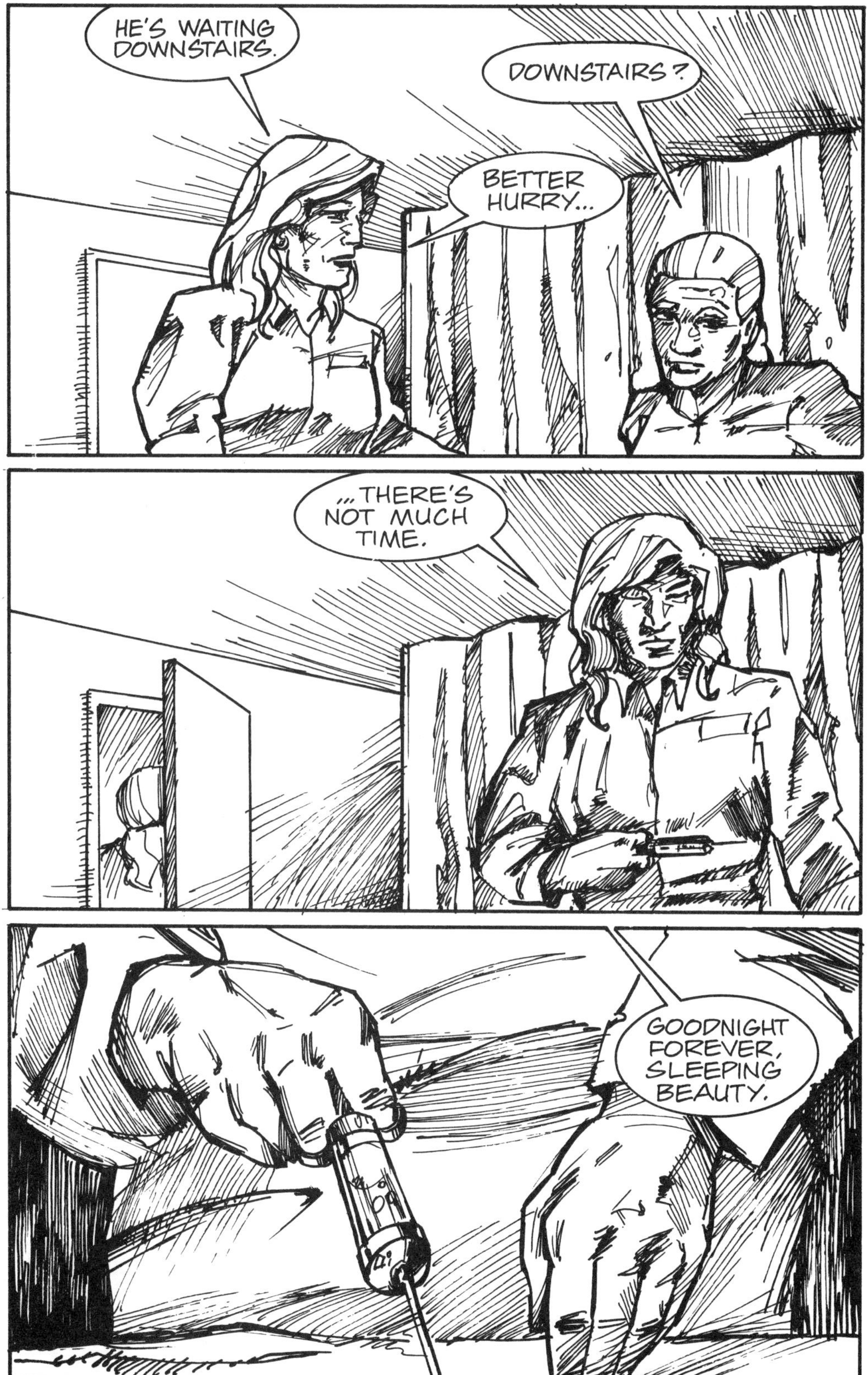
HE'S WAITING DOWNSTAIRS.
DOWNSTAIRS?
BETTER HURRY...
...THERE'S NOT MUCH TIME.
GOODNIGHT FOREVER, SLEEPING BEAUTY.

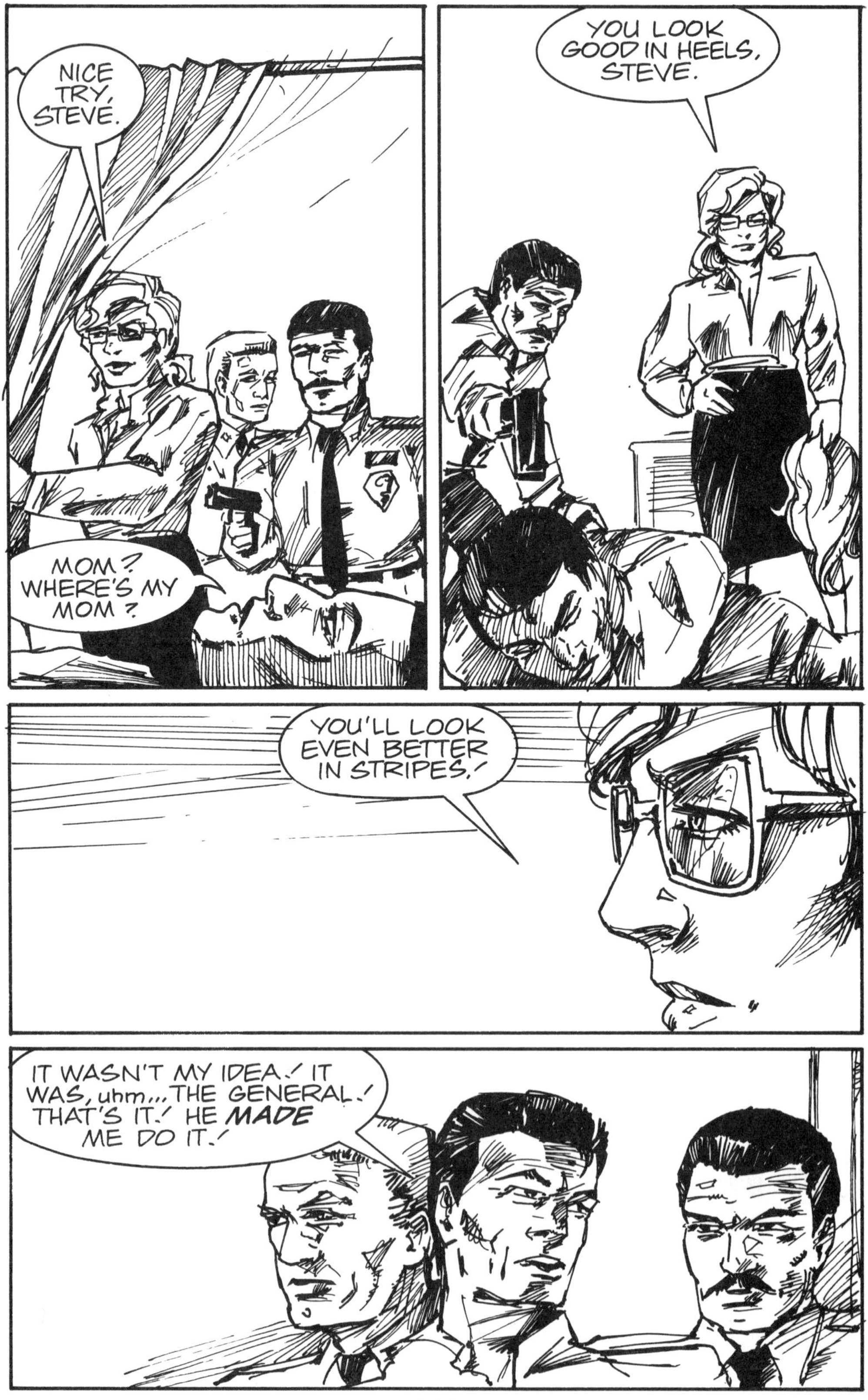
NICE TRY, STEVE.
MOM? WHERE'S MY MOM?
YOU LOOK GOOD IN HEELS, STEVE.
YOU'LL LOOK EVEN BETTER IN STRIPES!
IT WASN'T MY IDEA! IT WAS, uhm... THE GENERAL! THAT'S IT! HE MADE ME DO IT!

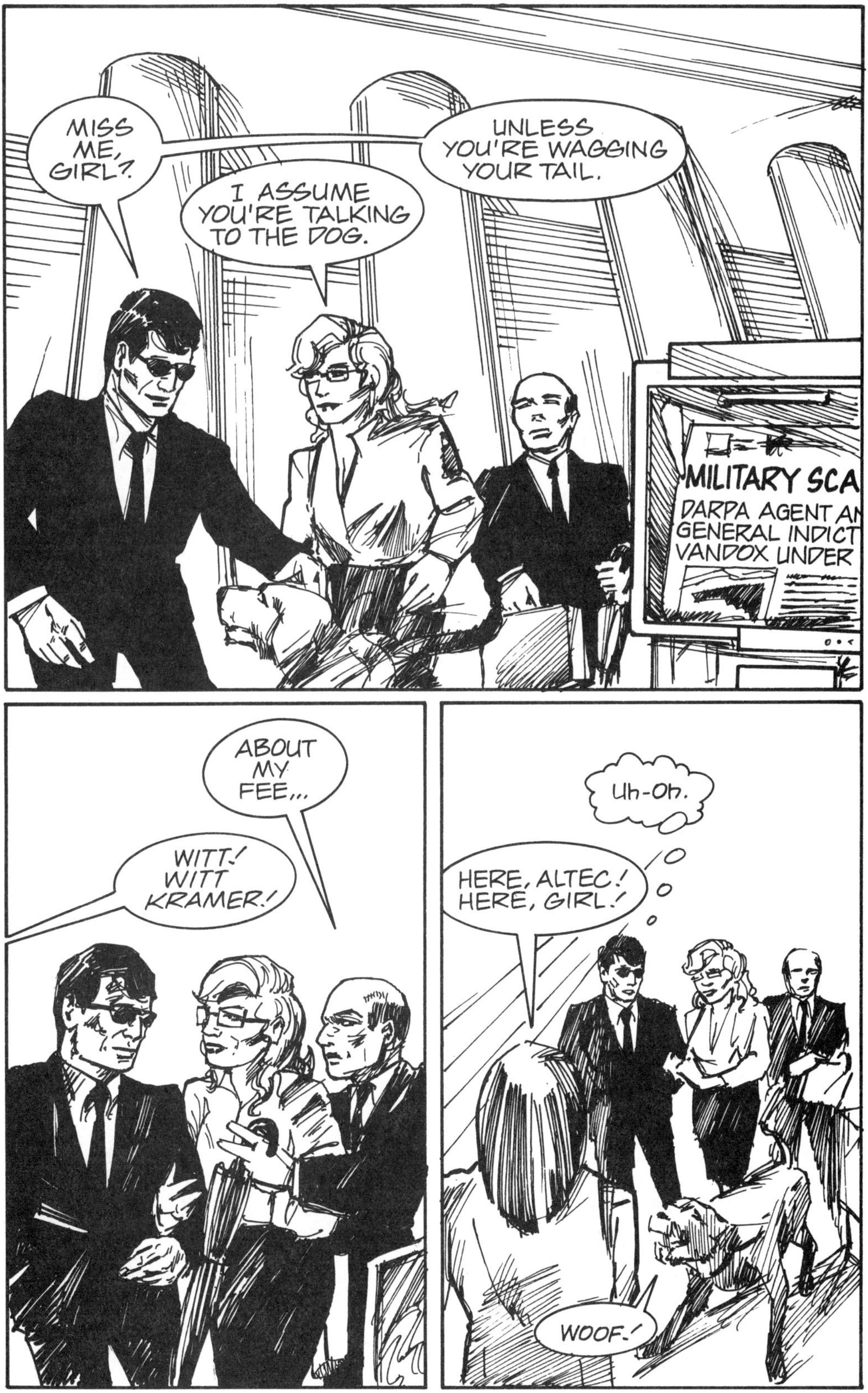
MISS ME, GIRL?
I ASSUME YOU'RE TALKING TO THE DOG.
UNLESS YOU'RE WAGGING YOUR TAIL.
MILITARY SCA
DARPA AGENT AN
GENERAL INDICT
VANDOX UNDER
ABOUT MY FEE...
WITT! WITT KRAMER!
HERE, ALTEC! HERE, GIRL!
Uh-Oh.
WOOF!

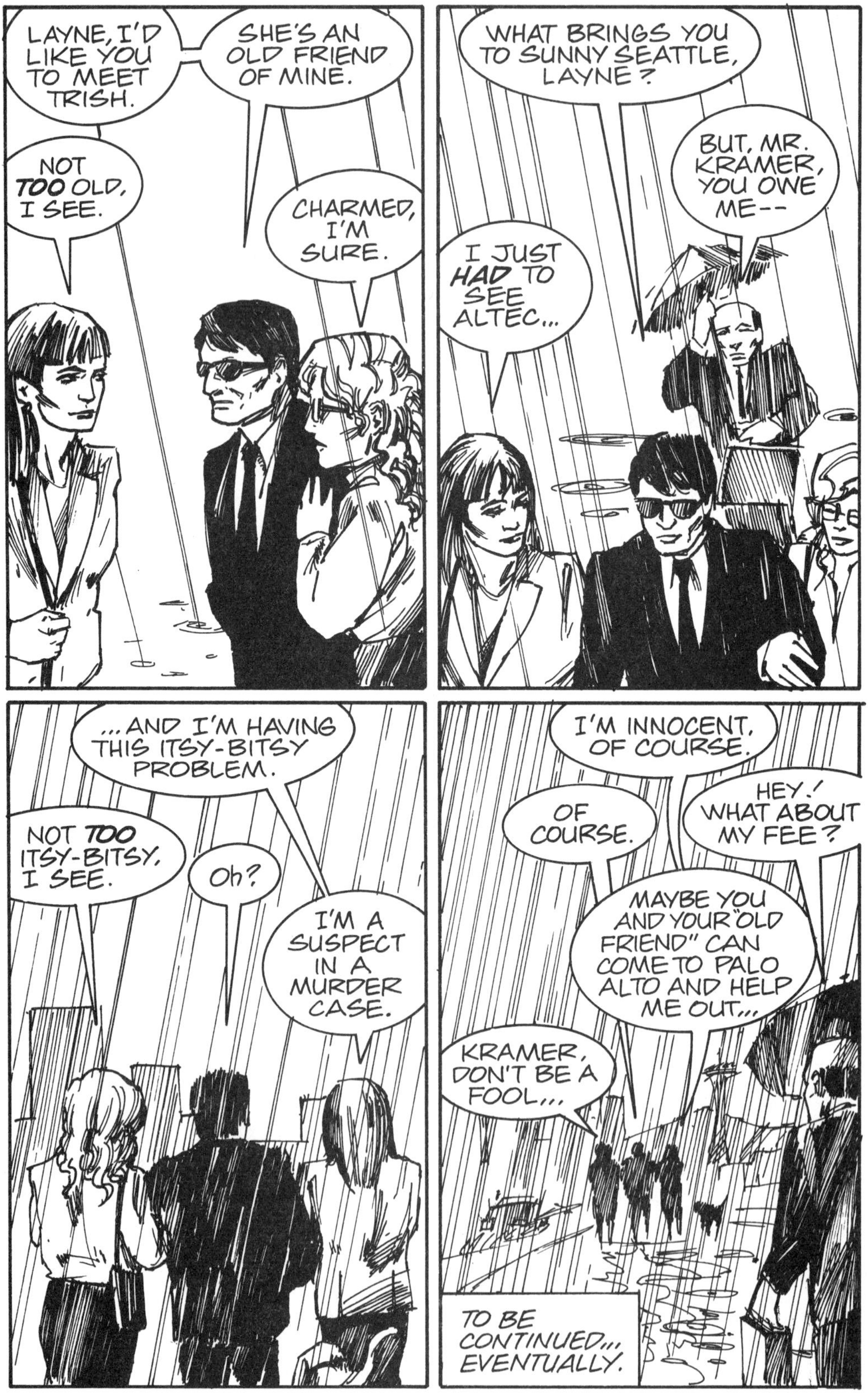
LAYNE, I'D LIKE YOU TO MEET TRISH.
SHE'S AN OLD FRIEND OF MINE.
NOT TOO OLD, I SEE.
CHARMED, I'M SURE.
WHAT BRINGS YOU TO SUNNY SEATTLE, LAYNE?
BUT, MR. KRAMER, YOU OWE ME--
I JUST HAD TO SEE ALTEC...
...AND I'M HAVING THIS ITSY-BITSY PROBLEM.
NOT TOO ITSY-BITSY, I SEE.
Oh?
I'M A SUSPECT IN A MURDER CASE.
I'M INNOCENT, OF COURSE.
OF COURSE.
HEY! WHAT ABOUT MY FEE?
MAYBE YOU AND YOUR "OLD FRIEND" CAN COME TO PALO ALTO AND HELP ME OUT...
KRAMER, DON'T BE A FOOL...
TO BE CONTINUED... EVENTUALLY.